The Testimonies of Indian Soldiers and the Two World Wars

War, Culture and Society

Series Editor: Stephen McVeigh, Associate Professor, Swansea University, UK

Editorial Board:
Paul Preston *LSE, UK*
Joanna Bourke *Birkbeck, University of London, UK*
Debra Kelly *University of Westminster, UK*
Patricia Rae *Queen's University, Ontario, Canada*
James J. Weingartner *Southern Illimois University, USA (Emeritus)*
Kurt Piehler *Florida State University, USA*
Ian Scott *University of Manchester, UK*

War, Culture and Society is a multi- and interdisciplinary series which encourages the parallel and complementary military historical and sociocultural investigation of twentieth- and twenty-first- century war and conflict.

Published:
The British Imperial Army in the Middle East, James Kitchen (2014)

Forthcoming:
South Africa's 'Border War', Gary Baines (2014)
Cultural Responses to Occupation in Japan, Adam Broinowski (2014)
9/11 and the American Western, Stephen McVeigh (2014)
Filming the End of the Holocaust, John Michalczyk (2014)
Jewish Volunteers, the International Brigades and the Spanish Civil War, Gerben Zaagsma (2014)
Military Law, the State, and Citizenship in the Modern Age, Gerard Oram (2014)
The Japanese Comfort Women and Sexual Slavery During the China and Pacific Wars, Caroline Norma (2015)
The Lost Cause of the Confederacy and American Civil War Memory, David J. Anderson (2016)

The Testimonies of Indian Soldiers and the Two World Wars

Between Self and Sepoy

Gajendra Singh

Bloomsbury Academic
An imprint of Bloomsbury Publishing Plc

B L O O M S B U R Y
LONDON • NEW DELHI • NEW YORK • SYDNEY

Bloomsbury Academic
An imprint of Bloomsbury Publishing Plc

50 Bedford Square	1385 Broadway
London	New York
WC1B 3DP	NY 10018
UK	USA

www.bloomsbury.com

BLOOMSBURY and the Diana logo are trademarks of
Bloomsbury Publishing Plc

First published 2014
Paperback edition first published 2015

© Gajendra Singh, 2014

Gajendra Singh has asserted his right under the Copyright, Designs and Patents Act, 1988, to be identified as Author of this work.

All rights reserved. No part of this publication may be reproduced or transmitted in any form or by any means, electronic or mechanical, including photocopying, recording, or any information storage or retrieval system, without prior permission in writing from the publishers.

No responsibility for loss caused to any individual or organization acting on or refraining from action as a result of the material in this publication can be accepted by Bloomsbury or the author.

British Library Cataloguing-in-Publication Data
A catalogue record for this book is available from the British Library.

ISBN: HB: 978-1-7809-3627-7
PB: 978-1-4742-4787-0
ePDF: 978-1-7809-3820-2
ePUB: 978-1-7809-3760-1

Library of Congress Cataloging-in-Publication Data
A catalog record for this book is available from the Library of Congress.

Series: War, Culture and Society

Typeset by Deanta Global Publishing Services, Chennai, India

To my parents, who raised me
and
In memory of the late Colonel Pritam Singh (INA)
Jai Hind!

Contents

Acknowledgements	viii
Abbreviations	x
Introduction	1
1 In Search of Colonial Negatives: Martial Race Theories, Recruiting Handbooks and the Indian Army, c.1890–1945	11
2 'More Like Brothers and Fathers to the Sepoys': Welfare, Discipline and Censorship in the Army	35
3 The Perils of 'Oriental Correspondence': *Sipahis*, Letters and Writing at the Crossroads	65
4 Throwing Snowballs in France: (Re-)Writing a Letter and (Re-)Appraising Islam, 1915–1918	99
5 Mutiny, Fabricating Court Testimony and Hiding in the Latrine: The 5th Light Infantry in Singapore	129
6 'Breaking the Chains with Which We Were Bound': The Interrogation Chamber, the Indian National Army and the Negation of Military Identities, 1941–1947	157
Conclusion: Reading Rebels, Writing Ghosts	181
Notes	193
Appendix I	253
Appendix II	256
Appendix III	259
Glossary	261
Bibliography	266
Index	287

Acknowledgements

No list of acknowledgements can be fully honest. The various lists of people that have to be thanked leave little room for those that should be thanked but aren't because they did not directly impact on this book. I am equally guilty of that here. Those who offered small kindnesses, pieces of advice and companionship have my deep gratitude even if they remain unnamed. Hopefully, you know who you are. Any truly truthful list would have to include a parallel dis-acknowledgements of all those people who you fantasize yourself as writing and being against. Unfortunately, such a list would rapidly dwarf the main text of this book (and there would have to be a whole separate volume devoted to Thatcher). Finally, there are some people who I have never met who have yet had an enormous impact on this work and on my own intellectual and political development. This list of the unnamed and unnameable, however, should not detract from the list of people that are mentioned below. They are those that I have met and who have had a substantive impact on how this book was conceived and written. I remain in their debt.

This book had its gestation in doctoral research undertaken at the University of Edinburgh. I am thankful to the Arts and Humanities Research Council (AHRC) for funding my PhD through a doctoral research award, and for covering the costs of research trips in India. I am (still) hugely appreciative to Crispin Bates for his rigorous and good-humoured supervision, and for the intellectually stimulating advice of Markus Daechsel. The work was subsequently re-written and re-worked during two postdoctoral positions. So thanks are also due to Robert Gerwarth for employing me at University College Dublin (and the European Research Council for paying my salary). And, to Yasmin Khan and Ashley Jackson for making it possible for me to go to Kellogg College, Oxford.

There have been numerous people who have generous in offering their time and advice through the various stages of writing this book. Thanks firstly to Annalisa Urbano, Ben Schiller, Ashok Malhotra, Tom Lloyd, Catriona Ellis, Tim Siddons, Mauritz Baumstark and Shaheed Soherwordi for their friendship, advice, readings bits and pieces of this work, and for plying me with cups of coffee which I am yet to repay. There is an array of people who have pointed me to useful readings, or offered titbits of advice. They include (in no particular order): Owen Dudley Edwards, Paul Nugent, Tom Webster, Ian Duffield, Bob Morris, (the late) Victor Kiernan, Sumit Sarkar, Santanu Das, Ravi Ahuja, Willem Von Schendel, Kaushik Roy, Franziska Roy, Rosalind O'Hanlon, Christian Hogsbjerg, Donny Gluckstein, Gyanendra Pandey, Ben Zachariah, Heike Leibau, Caroline Lewis, Paul Swanapoel, Yasmin Khan, Radhika Singha, Alexis Wearmouth, Ali Raza, Tomas Balkelis, James Kitchen, James Matthews, Matthew Lewis and Mark Jones.

Numerous archivists have offered me help, the names of most of whom I sadly (and somewhat guiltily) cannot remember. I do remember Annamaria Motrescu who helped me sift through the Film Archive at (what was formerly) the Empire and Commonwealth Museum in Bristol; and the staff at the Private Archives section of the National Archives of India. Thanks also to the late Sardar Pritam Singh (Colonel, INA) who was not an archivist but a warm and entertaining host and interviewee.

Stephen McVeigh and Rhodri Mogford – the editors of the series and of the monograph – deserve my gratitude for their efficiency and support. G. Kurt Piehler and Douglas McGetchin offered reviews for Bloomsbury, and I remain appreciative for their detailed and constructive engagement with the work.

Finally, thanks are due to my family. To my parents, Sardar Satinder Singh and Sardarni Jagdish Kaur, who (weirdly) did not mind me entering into the crazy world of academe. And to my brother, Sukhmeet, who listened patiently as I read parts of my thesis to him.

Abbreviations

CIH	Central India Horse
CIM	*Reports of the Censor of Indian Mails in France*
CP	Central Provinces and Berar (now Madhya Pradesh)
CSDIC(I)	Combined Services Detailed Interrogation Centre (India)
DMI	Directorate of Military Intelligence
DSB	District Soldiers' Board
HKSRA	Hong Kong and Singapore Royal Artillery
INA	Indian National Army
PM	Punjabi Musalman/Muslim
MEMC	*Middle East Military Censorship: Fortnightly Summaries Covering Indian Troops*
NWFP	North West Frontier Province (now Khyber Pakhtunkhwa)
RIASC	Royal Indian Army Service Corp
SMR	*Report in Connection with the Mutiny of the 5th Light Infantry at Singapore (1915)*
UP	United Provinces of Agra and Awadh (now Uttar Pradesh)

Introduction

Within the archived film footage of colonial India held at the British Empire and Commonwealth Museum in Bristol[1] are reels filmed by and documenting the lives of Britons in India. In one film, attributed to the wife of the British Resident in Mysore State, amidst scenes of domestic bliss involving the planting of potted plants in a newly created colonial garden and children playing a game of tig, are scenes of the Parachinar Durbar held in the North West Frontier Province (NWFP) in 1929.[2] For the briefest moment before this scene is recorded in full, the viewer catches a glimpse of the Indian *sipahis*[3] involved in the *durbar* before they were called to attention. The soldiers' *pagris* are cast aside, their jackets opened to the waist, some smoke *bidis*, some play cards, and yet more enjoy a joke that neither we nor the civil officer's wife shooting the film are privy to. Then the film flickers, blacks out, and we are returned to what the film-maker intended for us to see: the same soldiers marching in column, with their uniforms neatly pressed and their bayonets sparkling in the sun.

The film footage described above does not appear to be a conscious attempt by the soldiers filmed to subvert the efforts of the officer's wife filming them. On no occasion do any of the soldiers look in the direction of the camera, and when they are later filmed marching in the *durbar*, none of the soldiers appear to be unhappy or uneasy with what they have been asked to do. Instead, the film reveals that a space existed when soldiers were not expected to fight or otherwise be on duty, in which *sipahis* could relax, laugh and discuss among themselves that which concerned them. The purpose of this book is, to put it simply, to investigate that space.

But, it is not quite that simple. Before I can begin to discuss those conversations, two questions and issues have to be resolved: how to define the colonial soldier and how to treat his narrative voice? The word 'soldier' evokes an image of the infantrymen or cavalry trooper, but, in the context of the Indian involvement in the two World Wars, it could refer to artillerymen, clerks, grooms, mule drivers and even labourers placed under military articles. Moreover, even active

Indian Wounded at Brighton, 1915. Q53886. Photograph Courtesy of the Imperial War Museum.

soldiers had moments when they were not soldiering – when they could sit around, smoke and laugh. The narrative voice of the *sipahi* is as problematic. There is no shortage of voices for the historian to listen to, but none can be treated as a simple juridical retelling of facts (even when they claimed to be just that). Each narrative is situated between forms of censorship and the body of the *sipahi* and between testimony proper and rumour. It is these two issues that will be addressed and reconciled in this introduction.

That 'Jungian thing': Defining the colonial soldier

There is a vast literature on the subject of how one should speak to and conceive of the colonial or non-colonial soldier in the ranks. The overwhelming majority of it will not be touched on here. What will be discussed are two works: Samuel Huntington's *The Soldier and the State* and Leon Trotsky's *The History of the Russian Revolution*. These volumes are indicative of the two competing visions of the ordinary soldier that are apparent in the wider literature, and aspects of each approach were present, in part, in the statements made by officers of the

British Raj in India. I will be using both in outlining the direction I have taken in discussing the colonial *sipahis* of the Indian Army, albeit in a way that would have been alien to both the Harvardian and dissident revolutionary alike.

Huntington pioneered a particular approach in studies of the soldier in developing countries. In *The Soldier and the State*, first published in 1957, he attempted to explain the then topical issue of why military coups had so often been attempted in the decolonized world. The result was a set of rules that explained the identity of the soldier in these exotic locales. For Huntington, the very idea of soldiers or a military – *'l'idee militaire'* – was defined by its relation to 'a professional ethic'.[4] This 'professionalization' entailed the training or 'expertness' of the soldier combined with a 'social responsibility' to the ideals of the state and a 'corporate loyalty' within the military institution.[5] If each ingredient was applied in the right quantity, and presumably baked at the appropriate temperature, then one would arrive at the ideal soldier: 'politically sterile or neutral'.[6] Slight changes to Huntington's thesis were applied in following years. Sam Finer in 1962 argued that it was precisely this professionalization or 'esprit de corps' that led to soldiers' involvement in politics because it isolated soldiers from their 'own nationals – the "civvies", "les pekins", "les bourgeois" – and so forth'.[7] In the 1970s, the Israeli diplomat Amos Perlmutter merely substituted the term 'praetorian spirit' for 'professionalization' or 'esprit de corps' when discussing the 'large mercenary armies' of the colonial world.[8] Despite the differences in language and emphases, Finer and Perlmutter echoed Huntington in stating that the colonial soldier is and was ordinarily distanced from civilian life. Resistance, dissent or coups only occurred as a result of either falling short or going beyond this ideal, whether it was an imperfect 'professionalism', a heightened 'esprit de corps' or a 'praetorian spirit'.

Trotsky was, unsurprisingly, in complete disagreement with the idea that civilian and military lives were and are completely separate. During his time as People's Commissar for War, between 1918 and 1925, Trotsky tried to answer the question of why the Russian peasantry had taken up arms to defend the Revolution:

> Herein is the essence of the question. He who understands this will find the correct line for political work in the army. But allegories about a beleaguered fortress will avail little here. It is only a metaphor, an image for a leading editorial or a feuilleton. A Samara moujik on reading this, or hearing someone else read it aloud, will scratch the back of his head and say, "A clever writer is Comrade Kuzmin; he writes fine." But for the sake of this metaphor, I assure you, he will not go to fight.[9]

The question of why he did fight was answered later in *The History of the Russian Revolution* in which he stressed that the soldier did not have a separate identity but was merely the peasant or worker armed:

> An army is always a copy of the society it serves – with this difference, that it gives social relations a concentrated character, carrying both their positive and negative characters to an extreme.[10]

And during the Revolution, the soldier was simply reminded of this fact:

> The worker looked thirstily and commandingly into the eyes of the soldier, and the soldier anxiously and diffidently looked away. This meant that, in a way, the soldier could not answer for himself. The worker approached the soldier more boldly. The soldier sullenly, but without hostility – guiltily rather – refused to answer. Or sometimes – now more and more often – he answered with pretended severity in order to conceal how anxiously his heart was beating in his breast. Thus the change was accomplished. The soldier was clearly throwing off his soldiery. In so doing he could not immediately recognise himself. The authorities said that the revolution intoxicated the soldier. To the soldier it seemed, on the contrary, that he was sobering up from the opium of the barracks.[11]

By the eve of World War I, the colonial Indian Army's understanding of its own *sipahis* operated somewhere between these two poles. On the one hand were attempts to treat *sipahis* as occidental soldiers with similar systems of military law, regulations and bureaucracy (discussed in Chapter 2). On the other were efforts to keep soldiers recognizably Indian. As Bernard Cohn wrote, the desire to rule in a more 'oriental manner' after the Uprisings of 1857 led to the understanding that

> . . . Indians should look more like Indians; those the British most depended on to provide the strength to keep India, the soldiers, should appear as the British idea of what Mughal troopers looked like, with their officers dressed as Mughal grandees. Another characteristic believed to be quintessentially Indian or oriental was a love of show, of pageantry, of occasions to dress up in beautiful or gaudy clothes. Indians, it was believed, were susceptible to show and drama, and hence more occasions were found where rulers and subjects could play their appointed parts and could act their "traditions" through costume.[12]

In other words the *sipahi* was defined by a double vision that was both synchronic and diachronic.[13] There was a static and unchanging component to how colonial *sipahis* were perceived in the legal and bureaucratic processes of the Indian Army. And there was simultaneously a fluctuating and pseudo-historical part to this vision, not just with the introduction of exotic tunics and 'colourful turbans'[14] but with ever-changing constructions of who was and who was not a 'martial race'.

It is this split perception of the soldier that I will discuss throughout this work, albeit with a difference. Every chapter looks, in part, at how colonial authorities tried to manage and condition Indian soldiers in World War I and World War II, through policies that were implemented, half-implemented or forgotten. But, the book's main purpose is to look at how soldiers lived through this double articulation of their own identity. *Sipahis* were at the periphery of British and Indian selves in India – literally so in the case of the 'native lines' in military cantonments, where Indian soldiers were housed between and apart from British barracks and South Asian towns. The present work will therefore explore the role of colonial soldiers as both colonizers and the colonized,[15] or what Private Joker termed, in Kubrick's *Full Metal Jacket*, that 'Jungian thing':

> *Pogue Colonel*: Marine, what is that button on your body armor?
> *Private Joker*: A peace symbol, sir.
> *Pogue Colonel*: Where'd you get it?
> *Private Joker*: I don't remember, sir.
> *Pogue Colonel*: What is that you've got written on your helmet?
> *Private Joker*: "Born to Kill", sir.
> *Pogue Colonel*: You write "Born to Kill" on your helmet and you wear a peace button. What's that supposed to be, some kind of sick joke?
> *Private Joker*: No, sir.
> *Pogue Colonel*: You'd better get your head and your ass wired together, or I will take a giant shit on you.
> *Private Joker*: Yes, sir.
> *Pogue Colonel*: Now answer my question or you'll be standing tall before the man.
> *Private Joker*: I think I was trying to suggest something about the duality of man, sir.
> *Pogue Colonel*: The what?
> *Private Joker*: The duality of man. The Jungian thing, sir.
> *Pogue Colonel*: Whose side are you on, son?[16]

Reading soldiers' testimonies

The question remains of how to treat the testimony of colonial *sipahis*. There is certainly no shortage of soldiers' voices to read or listen to.[17] This work alone contains a medley of narratives culled from collections of censored letters, courtroom depositions, interrogation reports and the odd interview. It is not especially new or controversial, however, to state that each stage of hearing these voices is an exercise in admitting one's own limitations. No one working in the broad spectrum that is 'history' can escape the archive being a place of 'commencement' and 'commandment',[18] that we perform a constant violence against our 'sources' by deciding what is worthy of inclusion in a chapter and cropping even that,[19] and that the knowledge(s) we produce 'suppress difference as well as différance'.[20] But a further complication arises when reading and writing *sipahis*' testimonies (even when reading and writing in a manner that is mindful of these issues). The voice of the *sipahi* is so deeply interwoven with that which conditioned it that I cannot read one without the other. And using these compromised sources becomes an exercise in writing a history of rumour as much as a history of events.

Jacques Derrida wrote, when referring to Heidegger, of the impossibility of effacing the difference between signifier and signified in language:

> . . . he lets the word "being" be read only if it is crossed out (*kruezweise Durchstreichung*). That mark of deletion is not, however, a "merely negative symbol". That deletion is the final writing of an epoch. Under its strokes the presence of a transcendental signified is effaced while still remaining legible. Is effaced while still remaining legible, is destroyed while making visible the very idea of the sign.[21]

I face a similar dilemma in this book. Censoring voices and pauses are everywhere in the sources I have used. Soldiers' letters were cropped, *sipahis* were subject to constant interruption while making their depositions, accounts given during interrogations were often glossed over with ellipses, and the camera could be, and was, switched off. The fact that the sources exist only or largely in English complicates the situation further. It is impossible to know if there were mistranslations in the texts or whether surrogates were found for untranslatable or indecipherable concepts, except for those rare occasions when question marks were pencilled in or troublesome native words were written in full. Any attempt, therefore, to treat these sources as an '*autonomous domain*'[22] in which soldiers alone spoke is doomed to failure. The *sipahi*'s voice, such as it is, finds itself intertwined with that which conditioned and censored it and, even if the two are disentangled, the presence of the latter is made visible by its absence.

There is an additional problem even if the two could be separated. There are two facets to any retelling of a historical moment through testimony. One is a focus upon the particular and individual, 'specifying sites and bodies that carry the marks of particular events, making real in everyday, physical, nameable terms'.²³ The other is rumour:

> Rumour moves in a direction almost contrary to that of testimony: generalizing, exalting to extraordinary (even miraculous) status and employing the sweeping terms of deluge and just deserts (actual or impending). In rumour, language is transformed from a mode of (possible) communication to a particular kind of imperative condition – communicable, infectious, possible (and almost necessary) to pass on.²⁴

The testimonies of *sipahis* have elements of both. Specific events in letters were described through the medium of elaborate (or not so elaborate) ciphers, metaphors or verse. Depositions had an authorship and audience that was both within and outwith the colonial courtroom. And rigorous interrogations could result in soldiers citing works of fiction as much as they could words of fact. To put it simply, I cannot gain a cogent picture of what actually happened by using these sources.

Or can I?

The *sipahis*' voice was conditioned and curtailed by the manner in which it was recorded, and the words that remain accessible to a historian are often ambiguous, but there is, nonetheless, a partial presence of the soldier in these sources. The very process of compiling a report of censored letters, courtroom depositions or interrogations mandated that there be some record of the soldier in them. That presence could be significant even if it amounted to a single sentence or was summarized in a pithy aside. Mikhail Bakhtin, in his essay 'Discourse in the Novel', wrote at great length of heteroglossia – the presence in a single text of multiple meanings and realities. This is as true a description of the vernacular as of the cultured text: of the private as of the public utterance.

> We have before us a typical double-accented, double-styled, *hybrid construction*.
>
> What we are calling a hybrid construction, is an utterance that belongs, by its grammatical [syntactic] and compositional markers, to a single speaker, but that actually contains mixed within it two utterances, two speech manners, two styles, two "languages", two semantic and axiological belief systems. . . . the division of voices and languages takes place within the limits of a single syntactic whole, often within the limits of a simple sentence. It frequently happens that even the same word will belong simultaneously to two languages, two belief systems that intersect in a hybrid construction – and, consequently, the word has two contradictory meanings, two accents.²⁵

With Bakhtin in mind, these sources appear as contested rather than compromised. One can read them to find moments where *sipahis* pushed the boundaries of what was permissible by using those instances of 'rumour' in letters, depositions or interrogations.

It is possible to take it one step further. There was a material reality that informed and was informed by this linguistic double play. If soldiers were able to manipulate their partial presence in the final texts of their testimonies in order to make their voices more pronounced, it could also work in reverse: soldiers could be manipulated by the testimonies they produced. The effort of trying to situate a word or phrase so that it would have an alternate meaning led to many *sipahis* resituating themselves in an alternate space. The letter home metamorphosed into a medium through which soldiers queried their terms of service. The space of the colonial courtroom was reappropriated by *sipahis* in order to thwart the prosecution of their peers. And the interrogation chamber became a forum for many soldiers to demonstrate that they no longer considered themselves subject to the rigours of British military discipline. Hence the importance of viewing 'testimony' as a process, praxis or act and not simply as a word referring to a static text.[26] The act of giving testimony involved an engagement and reappraisal of what it meant to be a soldier at specific moments. Or, to put it in other words, the heteroglot voice of *sipahis* reflected and created their own heteroglossia.

Emplotting the witness

There are two conventional methods of emplotment, the ordering of historical events, when writing a work of history: plotting by time (sequentially moving from one event to the other in the order that they happened) and plotting by space (juxtaposing events in accordance with a methodological or theoretical approach). This book does both. It starts with a broad overview of Imperial attitudes towards colonial *sipahis*, focuses in the middle chapters upon Indian soldiers in World War I, and ends by discussing *sipahis* involved in World War II. At the same time the divisions between chapters broadly correlate with different types of *sipahis'* testimony: censored letters in the third and fourth, courtroom depositions in the fifth and interrogations in the sixth. There are, however, slippages in its writing. It is not quite chronological – World War II makes an appearance in Chapter 3 – nor is it quite divided by the different sources used – the same or similar colonialist voices appear in all the chapters.

There is a reason why these categories are blurred and this work is structured as it is. It is an attempt to reflect the different ways in which *sipahis* could re-shape fractured identities through testimony. Soldiering identities could be pushed in directions that alarmed the institutions that created them, non-soldiering modes of behaviour could be written into *sipahis*' own understanding of their codes of conduct, and there were, at certain moments, refusals to *be* soldiers. The book is shaped to take account of these forms of renegotiation. And if, at times, one chapter references or bleeds into another, it is because these moments were not absolute, and because soldiers could flit from one to the other or to none at all.

The chapters of this study are, broadly speaking, split into two parts. The first looks at how Indian soldiers were seen by the British Raj. Chapter 1 offers a glimpse of the diachronic part of this vision found in discussions of who was and who was not designated as a 'martial race' in India. Within military handbooks there was never one fixed answer but a series of inchoate and fluctuating narratives that operated on more than one exception. So-called martial races were not just exceptions to the majority of unmanly Indians but carefully situated against those that were previously fit for recruitment and those that may become so in the future. Chapter 2 discusses the other side of this vision, through the corpus of Indian military law that was a simulacrum of its British equivalent. Under this legal gaze, Indian *sipahis* were to be indistinguishable from their British peers.

The second and larger part of the work is focused on how *sipahis* lived through this split colonialist vision through the process of giving testimony. The hyperextension of otherwise anodyne words and concepts in soldiers' letters is discussed in Chapter 3. The re-appropriation of sanctioned spaces is the subject of Chapters 4 and 5, through the medium of chain letters and soldiers' depositions in a colonial courtroom in Singapore. Finally, Chapter 6 shows the negation of military identities in the interrogations of captured members of the Indian National Army during and after World War II. In a sense, then, this book is not an attempt to write a history by structuring it either by time or by space. It is an attempt to emplot the witness.

1

In Search of Colonial Negatives: Martial Race Theories, Recruiting Handbooks and the Indian Army, c.1890–1945

Between 1938 and 1939, a retired British Major, Donovan Jackson, penned a series of articles for *The Statesman*, the English-language newspaper published in colonial Calcutta and Delhi.[1] Its written content is not noteworthy. The articles are barely distinguishable from better-known works published at the time that charted the 'glorious' history of Indian regiments and their part in 'the protection and advancement of nations now known as the British Commonwealth'.[2] What make them worthy of comment are the pictures annotating Jackson's words. Each article was accompanied by a 'photograph' detailing the perfect type of recruit to various Indian regiments and battalions. When that regiment happened to have several different 'martial races' in its ranks, a montage of several portraits was effortlessly drawn together.

And yet, the images were not photographs at all, or at least not photographs of actual soldiers. The portraits contained more than one perspective in them (especially in the case of the 'Dogra Rajput'), and Jackson admitted that his pictures were painted when he compiled his articles for publication into a single volume in 1940.[3]

Jackson's sleight of hand was emblematic of others working and writing in his field. There were repeated efforts by colonial military theorists to bridge the gap between idealized images of colonial soldiers in India and the realities they lived. The creation of the Indian Army – from the unification of the three Presidency Armies in 1902 – was presaged by the secondment of British officers from their battalions in order for them to write ethnologies of the soldiers under their command. Various 'Handbooks for the Indian Army' were produced and then revised, abandoned, reworked or forgotten in the last decades of the British Raj. The Handbooks were the pencilled drafts beneath the glossy print

'Types of Men Enlisted into the Frontier Force Regiments – 1938'; Donovan Jackson, *India's Army*, p. 319.

of India's martial races, or they were, to borrow a phrase from Ann Laura Stoler, 'colonial negatives':

> They were colonial negatives in more than one sense: they were cropped and re-cropped and redeveloped. They are absent from colonial histories because they were more often discarded in process and never occurred. As blueprints of distress they underscore what was deemed to have gone awry . . . what might be excised from that picture, and what could not be touched up.[4]

I will attempt in this chapter to shed some light on the negatives contained in the darkroom of the Indian Army. Doing so reveals a panoply of inchoate and half-formed images that related only in part to martial race theories circulated at the colonial metropole. The Handbooks and their associated literature did not just divide 'martial' Indians from the 'non-martial'. They divided those currently fit for recruitment from those who were previously so and hinted at those who would become sufficiently 'martial' in the future. And over time those negatives could be discarded, refound, or reproduced in subtly different ways. This chapter will first deconstruct the mass-produced image of the martial race in India and then analyse the colonial negatives that informed and were informed by it.

Fulfilling colonial fantasies in pursuit of the martial race

In the earliest history-cum-ethnographies of soldiers in India produced for the domestic market, Major George Fletcher MacMunn's *The Armies of India* of 1911, martial races were described simply as men who had 'the physical courage necessary for the warrior'.[5] There was, however, more than one measure of that physical aptitude even in the polished prose of MacMunn's work. It was calculated in accordance with how bracing or enervating the climate was in various parts of the subcontinent: 'a thousand years of malaria, and hook-worm, and other ills of neglected sanitation in a hot climate, and the deteriorating effect of aeons of tropical sun on races that were once white and lived in uplands and cool steppes'.[6] It was deduced later by how willing or not recruits were to adhere to 'unsavoury' Oriental practices of faith and custom; 'of early marriage, premature brides, and juvenile eroticism'.[7] And martial classes were distinguished for their similarity to Europeans with their 'Grecian features', 'aquiline noses' and 'sonsy women'.[8] Various historical works have dissolved the unitary picture of India's martial races invoked by MacMunn and other British Officers into its constituent parts. I will do the same. But only in part. Discussions of climate, Indian custom or how European certain Indians were, were linked by their common invocation of exotica and the bizarre. That element of fantasy, as will be shown below, framed the impulse to distinguish between who were and who were not martial races in India.

Stephen Cohen attributes Frederick Sleigh Roberts as the architect of martial race theory in India.[9] It is not without cause. Roberts, as commander-in-chief of the Madras Army between 1880 and 1885 and then as commander-in-chief for all India [hereafter C-in-C], was noted for the frequency with which he disparaged his 'Madrassi' *sipahis*:

> Each cold season I made long tours in order to acquaint myself with the needs and capabilities of the men in the Madras Army. I tried hard to discover in them those fighting qualities which had distinguished their forefathers during the wars of the last and the beginning of the present [the nineteenth] century. But long years of peace, and the security and prosperity attending it, had evidently had upon them, as they always seem to have on Asiatics, a softening and deteriorating effect; and I was forced to the conclusion that the ancient military spirit had died in them, as it died in the ordinary Hindustanis of Bengal and the Mahratta of Bombay, and that they could no longer be safely pitted against warlike races, or employed outside the limits of southern India.[10]

For Roberts, this was of especial importance given his preoccupation with the Russian threat in Persia and Afghanistan and the supposed fact that no South Indian could match the martial aptitude of the Czar's soldiers:

> It is no use our trying to persuade ourselves that the whole of the Indian Army is capable of meeting an enemy from Central Asia or Europe; they are not, and nothing will ever make them. It is not a question of efficiency, but of courage and physique; in these two essential qualities the sepoys of lower India are wanting. No amount of instruction will make up for these shortcomings, and it would be extremely dangerous for us to calculate upon possessing an army which would most assuredly fail us in the hour of danger.[11]

Roberts' pronouncements had their effect with the abolition of the Presidency Armies in 1895, the creation of several 'class regiments' from northern Indian 'tribes', and the commissioning of official martial ethnologies by British Officers 'who understood Native character'.[12] Roberts also had his ideological protégés. Horatio Kitchener decreed, after wiping away the last vestiges of the Presidency Armies, that his reforms of November 1903, 'The Re-Organisation and Re-Distribution of the Army in India', and January 1904, 'The Preparation of the Army in India for War', would mark the 'complete elimination of units raised from unwarlike races'.[13] And Garrett O'Moore Creagh, after assuming the mantle of C-in-C in 1909, synthesized the reforms of his predecessors into one governing maxim:

> In the hot, flat regions, of which the greater part of India consists . . . are found races, timid both by religion and habit, servile to their superiors, but tyrannical to

their inferiors.... In other parts... where the winter is cold, the warlike minority is to be found.[14]

But, climactic theories of race were only part of the picture. As early as 1812, Sir John Malcolm, at the time a Lieutenant Colonel, compiled a series of sketches of Sikhs in Punjab that made mention of their virtuous 'racial' qualities.[15] Similar material decorated the pages of *The United Service Journal* in the early nineteenth century, with its description of Rajputs as a 'high-minded and brave race', Sikhs as 'slow-witted' but formidable, and Muslims as brave but blinded by 'fanaticism'.[16] There were, therefore, ascriptions of martial characteristics that preceded environmental narratives of race. Douglas Peers and Channa Wickremesekera have characterized these by referring to the first flush of post-colonial histories inspired by Edward Said's *Orientalism*. The martialization of soldiers becomes contiguous to the wholesale objectification and dehumanization of all Indians under colonialism. The only debate is precisely when this occurred. For Peers, the 1830s served as the origin of 'several foundational stereotypes' of who was and who was not fit for recruitment,[17] and for Channa Wickremesekera, it ought to be traced back further into the eighteenth century:

> The essential ingredient for the development of a racist perception about Indian soldiers in the following century ... was well and truly alive in the eighteenth century, and ... the sepoy army was founded partly on that perception. In other words, the racist ideology of the nineteenth century provided a new interpretation for an old perception, giving it a more sinister twist. In the heady atmosphere of empire and scientific progress the inferiority of the Indian soldier came to be treated as a product of an innate weakness and the Indian cultural environment itself came to be seen as the manifestation of that inner weakness, turning simple prejudice into downright contempt and men into specimens.[18]

It is an argument that has some merit. There was a partial ascription of negative feminine characteristics and positive childlike qualities to groups of Indian *sipahis* serving in the Armies of the East India Company, and this became a trope that was used and recycled at a later date. In 1918, for instance, in a parable written for military recruiters to relay to potential recruits in Punjab,[19] a Punjabi Mussalman, Sher Jang, is bedevilled by a salacious *babu* and rescued by a British officer:

> ... an Englishman came up and asked the Babu what was the matter. I explained that I had come to enlist in the Army, but that the Babu did not want to let me go. The Englishman laughed and said to the Babu, "Fikr na kar, Babuji, I'll pay the

amount." . . . I then asked him, "What dalali do I have to give you?" He laughed more than the last time (he always seemed to be laughing) and said, "There is no dalali or dusturi."

There was one other theme to the depiction of India's martial races: the contention that some soldiers were proto-Britons. *Sipahis* were described as either living as Englishmen lived 'in the tenth century'[20] or as being racial offshoots of Anglo-Saxon 'tribes':

> [Maharajah] Dhulip Singh was a Jat. When, after his death, his army insisted a year or so later on rushing onto the bayonets of Lord Gough and the Indo-British Army, and were destroyed for their pains, the British Government endeavoured to restore and maintain the Sikh kingdom. It will be remembered how the Sikh chiefs and the old Sikh Army that survived insisted on trying their fate once more, only to be destroyed in the "crowning mercy" of Goojerat. Then was the Punjab annexed and the boy, Dhulip Singh, eventually sent to be brought up in England with ample revenues. To him his friend, Colonel Sleeman, the famous Indian political officer, wrote, "I see you are going to live in Kent. You will be among your own people there, for you are a Jat and the men of Kent are Jats from Jutland," and no doubt he was speaking ethnological truth.[21]

With the emergence of Indian Commissioned Officers before and during World War II, the language reached its apotheosis. Indian Officers became indistinguishable from the old *Gora Sahibs* in the officers' mess:

> *6. Would I have to serve under Indian Commissioned Officers?*
>
> As Indian Commissioned Officers now serve in all Indian Regiments, it is quite likely that you may find yourself serving under an Indian Commissioned Officer, but this should be no deterrent to service with the Indian Army. Indian Commissioned Officers have proved their worth in the field, both in bravery and powers of leadership. They are trained by the same methods as British Officers and live in the same way in the same Mess. They are finally accepted or rejected by precisely the same standards, so there is no need to fear any loss of prestige in being posted to an Indian Regiment in which Indian Commissioned Officers are already serving.[22]

It also had an effect on the type of patronage given to former soldiers. Pensioned soldiers were sites of social engineering in the canal colonies of Punjab, by being favoured with land allotments, grouped together, and encouraged to build houses on European patterns.[23] In the Chenab Colony, the policy was taken to its extreme. Whole villages were named after 'regimental eponymous heroes': 'Fanepur (19th Lancers, Fane's Horse), Rattrayabad (45th Rattray's Sikhs), Probynabad (11th Prince of Wales' Own Lancers), Hodsonabad (9th Hodson's Horse) and Kot Brosyer (14th Sikhs).'[24]

Thus, there were at least three aspects to martial race discourses propounded by the Indian Army: climactic, the division of Indian on a martial-unmartial axis, and the granting of pseudo-British qualities to *sipahis*. What links them is the common element of colonial fantasy. Climactic theories of race were not new when Roberts chanced upon them, having formed the basis of fictional and then medical works about India in the eighteenth and early nineteenth centuries.[25] Robert Young shows that there was a fantasmatic desire implicit in the characterization of martial or caste communities in India as a *race* apart; their perceived 'chaste abstention from racial sexual transgression, from hybridization and mongrelization'[26] set in stark relief to the majority of Indians:

> It contributes much to these feelings, that Southern Asia is, and has been for thousands of years, the part of the earth most swarming with human life; the great *officina gentium*. Man is a weed in those regions.[27]

And sexual desire was always implicit in comparisons of 'martial' classes to Europeans. It was there in demands that well-muscled soldiers ought to wear no or tight clothing and hold 'the "erect position"' in the *Manual of Physical Training for the Indian Army*,[28] or in the language used to describe the characteristics and appearances of manly soldiers:

> Dogras are by nature tractable and obedient. They have no aspiration after independence, and seem to prefer being under authority. They yield implicit obedience to a ruler whom they admire and respect. . . . In general physiognomy the Dogra are decidedly a good-looking race. Their complexions are generally fair owing to the temperate climate in which they live, and among the higher castes, owing to the purity of their descent. Caste gradations are strongly marked in their aspect, the higher the caste, the purer and more elevated the features.[29]

These elements of fantasy were integral to the reasons why the Handbooks were commissioned. The ethnographies attempted to close the gap between flights of imagination and reality. Officers sought to prove the veracity of colonial fantasies by officially recording the 'characteristics, customs, prejudices, history and religion' of martial classes.[30] And as fantasies changed, and old negatives were found to be inconstant with how groups of soldiers had now to be perceived, new Handbooks were commissioned and the old quietly discarded. That is what occurred in the case studies I will now turn to: of Sikhs, Pathans, and Brahmins.

The dangers of being both 'black' and a 'lion': Sikhs

Perhaps no martial identity has had a longer half-life since Independence than that applied to the Sikhs of Punjab. Half-remembered words and deeds daily creep into the language of Sikhs themselves[31] and even permeated the filming of Star Trek in the guise of the genetically engineered super-villain Khan Noonien Singh:

> *Lt. Marla McGivers*: [He's] From the northern India area, I'd guess. Probably a Sikh. They were the most fantastic warriors.[32]

(Un)Fortunately, the crew of the Enterprise did not always get it right. The martial characteristics ascribed to Sikhs proved mutable even after the advent of the Handbook programme. Quite how far the martialized image of the Sikh changed and fluctuated will be explained below.

Following the annexation of Punjab by the East India Company in 1849, the Board of Administration, established to govern the new province immediately raised five regiments of infantry and cavalry from the former Khalsa Army consisting of 'men, habituated from childhood to war and the chase'.[33] The majority of Sikhs (unsurprisingly) were viewed as being hostile to Company rule and were largely excluded from this category. Their numbers were restricted to no more than 200 in infantry and 100 in cavalry regiments.[34] To some extent this changed with the outbreak of the Uprisings of 1857 and with the recruitment of 23,000 Sikhs to quash it. The language describing Sikhs as a soldierly class came to be used in reports drafted by colonial officials in India and even in the weekly reportage of Friedrich Engels. But, in the hysteria that followed the 'Sepoy Mutiny', the picture engendered of the Sikh – and quite what Sikhs *were* – was still confused and uncertain. Engels concluded his article by asking how long it would be before the 'saucy' Sikh would turn on his colonial master:

> There are now nearly 100,000 Sikhs in the British service, and we have heard how saucy they are; they fight, they say, to-day for the British, but may fight

tomorrow against them, as it may please God. Brave, passionate, fickle, they are even more subject to sudden and unexpected impulses than other Orientals. If mutiny should break out in earnest among them, then would the British indeed have hard work to keep their own. The Sikhs were always the most formidable opponents of the British among the natives of India; they have formed a comparatively powerful empire; they are of a peculiar sect of Brahminism, and hate both Hindus and Mussulmans. They have seen the British "raj" in the utmost peril; they have contributed a great deal to restore it, and they are even convinced that their own share of the work was a decisive one. What is more natural than that they should harbour the idea that the time has come when the British raj should be replaced by a Sikh raj, that a Sikh emperor is to rule India from Delhi[35] or Calcutta?[36]

The systematic ascription of martial qualities to Sikhs by the Army had to wait until Frederick Roberts became C-in-C in 1885. The publication of the first census of Punjab in 1883, and its enumeration and description of various castes and 'tribes', gave a common means of reference and an ethnographic framework to military officers in India. It allowed the *Handbooks for the Indian Army: Sikhs* published in 1899, and written by Captain A. H. Bingley, to ascribe martial qualities to the 'right type of Sikh'. Sikh Brahmans were condemned for their caste prejudice,[37] urban Sikh Khatris for their reluctance to take to the plough,[38] and low-caste Sikh Mazbhis for their supposed criminality.[39] It was rural Sikh Jats who were singled out for praise for being devoid of all these sins and blessed with an impressive stolidity and obedience:

> Hardy, brave and of intelligence too slow to understand when he is beaten, obedient to discipline, devotedly attached to his officers, and careless of the caste prohibitions which render so many Hindu races difficult to control and feed in the field, he is unsurpassed as a soldier. . . .[40]

Consequently, it was Sikh Jats who were favoured for recruitment. During World War I, they formed the majority of the 12–20%[41] of all Indian 'fighting men' that were Sikh.[42]

That was not the end of the matter. While the Sikh Jat was broadly understood to have a soldierly bearing, different and often contradictory soldierly qualities were applied to him from particular locales in Punjab and from different *gols/gotras* or sub-castes. The first of these was the distinction made between Sikh cultivators from the *Majha* and *Malwa* areas of Punjab – the former being roughly contiguous to the districts of Amritsar, Lahore, Sialkot and Gujranwala that were annexed in 1849 and the latter being the area east of the Rivers Sutlej and Beas that the East India Company came to control under treaties of 1809 and 1846. Years of having their own Raj had created, for Bingley, a different cultural and physical specimen of Jat in the *Majha* to what the British had grown accustomed to in the *Malwa*:

> The Manjha [or Majha] Sikh is a rule brighter, smarter, quicker, and more refined than the Malwai, while the latter on the other hand is more stubborn, works quite as conscientiously but less cheerfully, and from his very stolidity and obtuseness is equally staunch, while nowise inferior in either courage or discipline.[43]

Even Sikh Jats within these areas were not all suitable for military service. Innumerable distinctions were made between *gols* of Jats of 'not very good quality'[44] and those sub-castes within both the *Majha* and *Malwa* areas that were seen as being especially suited to the military life. Particular praise was found, for instance, for the Sindhus or Sandhus found in 32 villages of Tarn Taran *tahsil* in Amritsar district[45]:

> [. . . The Sindhus] are the finest of the Amritsar peasantry. In physique they are inferior to no race of peasants in the province, and among them are men who in any country of the world would be deemed fine specimens of the human race. . . . They make admirable soldiers, when well led, inferior to no native troops in India, with more dogged courage than dash, steady in the field, and trustworthy in difficult circumstances, and without the fanaticism which makes the Pathan always dangerous.[46]

Lastly, although 'Sindhu Jats' were 'fine specimens of the human race'[47] when recruited from Tarn Taran *tahsil*, the sons of military pensioners who were settled in the canal colonies of western Punjab evidently were not. Or at least they were not according to settlement officers pressed to explain why so few Sikhs from this area were willing to take up the King's shilling.[48] Bingley's Handbook, therefore, attempted to rank Sikhs in accordance with a racial rather than religious understanding of Sikhism.

However, it did not prove as authoritative as either he or his superiors would have liked. Praise for Sikh Jats was tempered in the aftermath of World War I. Official histories still praised the 'Black Lions' of the Khalsa who died nobly defending the honour of the King-Emperor,[49] but the landscapes in which those lions pranced were decidedly murkier. Following the revolutionary *Ghadar* movement, and the civil disorder that preceded and followed the Jallianwalla Bagh massacre, district gazetteers complained of how poorly Sikhs, and Sikh Jats, were living up to their reputation:

> It is all the more regrettable that the excellent record of the district should have been spoilt to some extent in the aftermath of the war. On 14th and 15th April, 1919, immediately following the outbreak of serious political disorders at Amritsar, there were also disorders in Gujranwala, Wazirabad, Hafizabad and Akalgarh. . . . Communication wires were cut, certain British Officers were interfered with. . . and even the house of Revd. Grahame [sic.] Bailey of the Scotch Mission at Wazirabad was burnt. Also at Gujranwala, the Tahsil, District Court, Post Office, Church, Railway Station and Dâk Bungalow were burnt.[50]

Reports made of areas of Punjab that were largely untouched by violence, or of the later Akali movement for the reform of Gurdwaras, nonetheless contained warnings for individual military recruiters that the 'fine qualities' of Jats 'are often marred by grosser traits, as when their martial spirit and dogged courage exhibit themselves in crimes of violence'.[51] And the figure of the Sikh even began to intrude upon reports previously restricted to the troublesome Bengali:

> With the high-spirited and adventurous Sikhs the interval between thought and action is short. If captured by inflammatory appeals, they are prone to act with all possible celerity and in a fashion dangerous to the whole fabric of order and constitutional rule.[52]

The language used by civil departments of the colonial establishment in India forced a revision of the official military ethnology. Major A. E. Barstow of the 11th Sikhs was chosen for the task, and the tone he adopted was one of alarm. The initial section of *The Sikhs*, published in 1928, replicated the style of Bingley's Handbook and unashamedly plagiarized the early ethnography when charting the 'origin of Sikhism'. But that changed when it came to recount the history of Sikhs under the British Raj. The Sikh community was suddenly split into two: the pure Sikhs in the Army and those who had 'relapsed into Hinduism':

> Throughout the era under review, as is the case at the present time, one of the principal agencies for the preservation of the Sikh religion has been the practice of military officers commanding Sikh Regiments, to send Sikh recruits to receive the "pahul" of baptism, according to the rites prescribed by Guru Govind Singh [sic.]. Sikh soldiers, too, are required to adhere rigidly to Sikh customs and ceremonial

[customs] and every effort has been made to preserve them from the contagion of Hinduism. Sikhs in the Indian Army have been studiously "nationalised", or encouraged to regard themselves as a totally distinct and separate nation; their national pride has been fostered by every available means, and the "Granth Sahib", or Sikh Scriptures are saluted by British Officers of Indian Regiments. The reason for this policy is not far to seek. With his relapse into Hinduism, and re-adoption of its superstitions and vicious social customs, it is notorious [sic.] that the Sikh loses much of his martial instincts, and greatly deteriorates as a fighting machine.[53]

The Indian Army became the one means to inoculate the Sikh from this pernicious disease. And where the Army failed, so the Sikh was found to act in a seditious manner. Summaries were given by Barstow of rural agitation in Punjab in 1907, the formation of the Chief Khalsa Diwan and the 'Tat Khalsa Party', the *Ghadar* Movement, the 'Disorders of 1919', and, finally, the 'Gurdwara Reform Movement' of the 1920s. The 'finger of blame' in each case was firmly pointed towards 'the "advanced Sikh reforming party", which was not merely not orthodox in its religion, but would seem to have been in some danger of falling away from Sikhism altogether'.[54] And in case the reader was not concerned enough by the dangerous activities of these 'Hindu-Sikhs', Barstow concluded, without irony, that they were also secretly Bolsheviks:

> Bolshevism may, rightly or wrongly, be considered to be the coming world peril. Its promoters at Moscow are said to have as their ultimate objective the peoples of the Far East and other Asiatic countries. Be this as it may – but, if India is there objective, then it is well to note that the agricultural conditions of the Punjab much resemble those of the interior of Russia, and as such must attract the attention of their agents.
>
> There is a further point and it is that of religion. In the Punjab if anybody's religion has got anything in common with the basic principles of Bolshevism it is that of the Sikh. To begin with his religion is democratic and preaches equality and nobleness of labour. The dictum of Guru Govind Singh [sic.] was to the effect that everything possessed by an individual Sikh belonged to the whole Panth and that the belongings of the whole Panth were to be equally shared by every individual Sikh. It has seldom been translated into practice. The authority of religion is however thin and the Sikh soil is likely to prove somewhat suitable for the growth of Bolshevism.
>
> The symptoms of the disease are already visible to some extent amongst certain Sikhs although in most cases the would-be victims do not know themselves what disease they are suffering from.[55]

Thus, for Barstow, the manly qualities of Sikhs came to be seen as a double-edged sword. The Sikh was naturally given to sedition unless properly channelled in military service.

During World War II, what was seen as an extra-military problem began to be perceived in the ranks. In January 1941, there were mutinies in the Hong Kong and Singapore Royal Artillery (HKSRA) over refusals to wear steel helmets over, or instead of, their *pagris*. Large numbers of Sikh soldiers joined, and initially commanded, the profoundly anti-British Indian National Army in South-east Asia. And, the Army faced difficulty in dissuading young Sikh men from joining technical units, in which they could avoid battle and gain vocational training, over combat battalions or squadrons. The initial reaction of analysts at the India Office at Whitehall to this problem was to blame recruiters who were seen as enlisting Sikh Jats who did not possess the 'traditional military qualities' of old.[56] It also led to suggestions by Winston Churchill that the Indian Army ought to be reduced in number 'by some 400,000 or 500,000 men' so that it could be staffed once more by those soldiers who had a 'long tradition of military service and loyalty to the crown'.[57] Those within the Indian Army, however, perceived the problem to be more substantive. While the authors of secret memoranda were confident enough to declare in 1941 that 'nationalism' as a creed had no following in the armed forces[58] and that the educated Congressman 'was an object of contempt'[59] for most of those in arms, the attitude of Sikh Jat soldiers was described in drastically different language:

> The Sikhs present a somewhat different problem from other classes. They are a separate, warlike, and politically minded community.[60]

Thus, not only did the proportion of Sikhs in the Indian Army fall, from the 12% it stood at in 1925 to 10% in 1942 and even lower in 1946,[61] but also the naturally seditious Sikh Jat was no longer seen as a fully 'martial' figure in the last days of the British Raj. Even the use of the Sikh salutation, *Sat Sri Akal*,[62] came to be viewed as seditious, at least according to the commanding officer of the 12th Heavy Regiment, HKSRA, pressed to explain how he had allowed his men to mutiny:

> *Presiding Officer*: [I wonder] whether the cry of "Sat Sri Akal" has any insubordinate significance?
> *Lt. Col. J. D. Wray*: It has in fact no insubordinate significance but the way the words were shouted appeared to me to give it that significance.[63]

From noble frontiersman to debauched tribal: The Pathan

It became fashionable in the early nineteenth century to write of peoples at the margins (or beyond) of colonial societies. Walter Scott, in his Highland romances, and James Fenimore Cooper, in his 'Hawkeye' novels, fenced out whole careers writing of the air of nobility, chivalry and 'wildness' that infused frontiersmen:

> Although in a state of perfect repose, and apparently disregarding, with characteristic stoicism, the excitement and bustle around him, there was a sullen fierceness mingled with the quiet of the savage... and yet his appearance was not altogether that of a warrior.... His eye alone, which glistened like a fiery star amid lowering clouds, was to be seen in its state of native wildness. For a single instant his searching and yet wary glance met the wondering look of the other, and then changing its direction, partly in cunning, and partly in disdain, it remained fixed, as if penetrating the distant air.[64]

It is perhaps unsurprising, therefore, to find that the Pathans (or Pushtuns) of the Hindu Kush were described in the same language in military handbooks as the 'Indians' of North America or the inhabitants of Highland Scotland. They became a people naturally given to martial endeavour because they hailed from the frontier. After the NWFP was demarcated, settled and placed under stringent military supervision, however, the same frontier spirit began to be viewed in reverse. Where they were once martial, now Pathans came to embody vices and degenerate practices that were antithetical to military life.

Pathans were first recruited after the annexation of Punjab and the frontier territories in 1849, but they were not initially distinguished as a separate 'military class' from other 'Muhammedans of Punjab' in military and civil reports.[65] On the rare occasions that they were, only fragmentary, and unflattering, descriptions were made of them:

> The true Pathán is perhaps the most barbaric of all the races with which we are brought into contact in the Panjáb [sic]. His life is not so primitive as that of the gipsy tribes. But he is bloodthirsty, cruel, and vindictive in the highest degree....[66]

A distinct and more positive image of Pathans only began to emerge when necessity demanded a closer understanding of them following the creation of the

NWFP as an administrative area separate from Punjab in 1900. *A Dictionary to the Pathan Tribes* was compiled under orders from the Quarter Master General in India in 1899 and was

> ... compiled with a view to providing an index to the numerous ramifications of the Pathan tribes of the North-West Frontier, in such a form that any obscure subdivision may be easily referred to [in] its proper tribal position.[67]

C. M. Enriques, the 'Assistant Recruiting Staff Officer for Pathans', added his own *The Pathan Borderland* in 1910. And finally, Major R.T.I. Ridgway of the 40th Pathans authored the official Handbook in the same year.

The ethnologies all started with the same goal, regardless of the volume or the author: to find a way to distinguish Pathans from Afghans.

> In its streets [Peshawar] India meets Central Asia, and of the crowds which throng its bazaars fully thirty percent are travellers on their way to and from Hindustan, or are stragglers from the neighbouring Pathan mountains. Not the least picturesque [sic.] are the sulky Afghans, who, to judge from their truculent manners, have forgotten that they no longer walk the streets of Cabul. It is the peculiarity of the Afghans that they are always thoroughly at home everywhere, and never seem to realise the necessity of dropping any of their swagger when in foreign lands. In pleasing contrast are the cheery, laughing Pathans, many of whom are "in town" for a holiday, and who, like tripper [sic.] all the world over, are determined to enjoy themselves.[68]

After being distinguished from Afghans, Pathans were compared favourably with their colonial overlords. Their 'tribal code' – the words *Pushtunwali* or *Pakhtunwali* were not used – led to a pseudo-British understanding of 'democracy' and resulted in chivalrous behaviour that no other 'race' in India displayed; apart, of course, from the Briton:

> ... it is beyond question that he appeals strongly to and enlists the sympathies of British officers who have had dealings with him politically or when associated with him in regiments. His manliness is at once apparent, and his proverbial hospitality, courtesy, courage, cheerfulness and loyalty make him an excellent companion, and a valuable soldier, and entitle him to respect and admiration. It is true that he possesses a large amount of pride, and considers himself superior to other races, but this pride has often been of great use, and frequently enabled him to face difficulties which could not have been overcome without the necessary *morale* engendered by it.[69]

At times, those 'debts of honour' compelled Pathans to commit 'crimes of passion' and indulge in banditry. Even that, however, could be excused as demonstrative of an innate British sense of justice and playfulness:

> Nature, too, has cursed him with the countenance, figure and physique of a brigand and *noblesse oblige*. Does not his bold dare-devil, cut-throat appearance saddle him with a terrible responsibility? There is nothing degrading in a barn fowl living the life of poultry, but what would the bird say if the hawk did the same? Why, the very sparrows would point the beak of scorn at him! But what is the Pathan to do? If, being born with a beak and talons of a hawk, he fulfils nature's mandate and goes a-hawking, an unromantic British soldier promptly hangs him; if, on the other hand, he seeks peaceful occupation, say on the railway, he is either scorned as degenerate or mistrusted as a wolf in sheep's clothing. But even here one is more or less dealing with the Pathan of fiction. Yet there does exist the Pathan of sober fact, who, in spite of his clothing, is neither wolf or sheep – the Pathan with whom we rub shoulders daily in our frontier stations – whom we like and to a very great extent admire. It is he who really represents his race. But being the plain matter-of-fact Pathan of every-day life, literature knows him not, and only those are acquainted with him whom duty casts in his midst. To such he is full of interest, and his real picturesqueness lies in the fact that, in spite of his surroundings, he is more like the Briton than any native in India.[70]

In other words, the very primitiveness of Pathans became their redeeming feature. In the years preceding World War I, 12,348 Pathans from both British India and Afghanistan were present in the ranks of the Indian Army,[71] and thousands more were recruited for paramilitary frontier militias.

Because of the equation made between 'tribalness' and martial bearing, different types of Pathans were seen as more 'tribal', and thus more martial, than others. The most pronounced of the distinctions made by military recruiters was between the 'true' Pathan of the hills and the more dubious Pathan of the plains. The latter was seen as the 'possessor of all sort of vices' for dwelling in towns[72] and was accused, more specifically, of diluting his frontier blood by cavorting with 'untouchable' 'Chamar women'.[73] Even those reared in the hills and mothered by Pathan women, however, were not seen in quite the same light. Some groups of frontiersmen were perceived as having 'retained their tribal identity' better than others:

> Those which have retained their tribal identity and been the most powerful . . . are esteemed most highly [by us], while those who have been buffeted about and have a mixed origin . . . are those least popular and lacking in martial qualities.[74]

The Afridis, hailing from the country south and west of Peshawar, were identified as 'wiry and strong' with 'excellent discipline' largely because they all recognized their common kinship from one 'common ancestor'.[75] Khattaks were praised for being 'more civilized and respected than other Pathans' because of their tendency to reside in tight democratic communities that suited them to a soldiering life.[76] While those who weren't identified as sufficiently 'tribal' in nature, such as the quarrelsome Zakha Khel Afridis, were to be condemned as the 'wildest and most turbulent' of all Pathans and so not fit for enlistment under any circumstance.[77]

Just as the very 'tribalness' of Pathans made them useful soldiers before World War I, so it was that very quality that made them objects of suspicion after the start of hostilities. High rates of desertion among Pathan *sipahis* between 1914 and 1918 were part of the reason. Accusations were made that the frontier Pathan was racially incapable of fully realizing that military discipline superseded 'tribal loyalties'.[78] The language hardened further after World War I. The Third Afghan War in 1919 and rebellion in Waziristan between 1919 and 1920 led to Pathan militias being accused of succumbing totally to 'the call of Islam' and defecting to the side of the pan-Islamist 'Mullah' Fazl Din.[79] The main cause, according to the report of the operations, was the racial characteristics of the Pathan that left him open to 'dangerous' religious fervour:

> Their character, organization and instincts have made them independent and strongly democratic, so much so that even their own *maliks* (or elders) have little real control over their unruly spirits. . . . [The] tribesmen carry their lives in their hands and finding that the natural resources of their country do not favour them enough, they eke out their existence by plundering their more peaceful neighbours.[80]

Reports of desertion and perceived fanaticism had its effect on recruitment. New Pathan infantry companies raised during World War I only amounted to 5% of the total,[81] despite the fact that 15% of the Indian infantry companies sent to France in 1914 had once been exclusively Pathan.[82] In other words, there was a transformation of the frontier stereotype into a series of negative qualities made during and immediately after World War I.

In the decades following World War I, the Pathan's tribal peculiarities came to be the subject of an even greater moral condemnation than their predilection for desertion and religious radicalism had previously resulted in; particularly over the issue of homosexuality. The possibility of sexual relations between two soldiers was recognized and legislated against in British Naval and Military law from 1866 when 'Sodomy with Man or Beast' was declared a military offence.[83] Up to and during World War I, it was not a 'crime' that was actually prosecuted in the Indian Army, and that is in spite of possible admissions of same-sex relationships by Pathan soldiers as late as 1917.[84] It was only in the climate of the 1920s and 1930s, when frontiersmen were no longer to be as valourized as they had been before, that homosexuality, which had once been quietly permitted, now came to be openly discussed as the progenitor of all the other unsoldierly vices that afflicted the Pathan. Thus, for instance, in the memoirs of Maurice Willoughby, a British junior officer in India in the 1930s, the soldiering Pathan is first introduced to the reader in a narrative voice mixed with disgust and incredulity:

> On cold nights he would bring along a small boy or even two, sons of nephews, cousins or friends, to share his bed and keep him warm. Nobody even considered it strange.[85]

Later references to Pathans confirm that the only thing worth knowing about 'the fierce tribes along the North-West Frontier' is their 'propensity for boys' and ensuing incest and bestiality:

> When the Royal Welsh Fusiliers, whose Regimental Mascot is a large white goat, arrived at Landi Kotal in the heart of Pathan Afridi country, the locals were puzzled. "What! Only one goat among so many?" Later the Goat-Corporal was the subject of one of the most celebrated court martials in the British Army; that of being charged "Contrary to Good Order and Military Discipline, he did upon certain dates, Prostitute the King's Goat". Apparently he had found himself a nice little earner hiring the animal out to local tribesmen. His defence was that he had only done so for the animal's delectation and pleasure, being sorry for it in its celibate state.[86]

The willingness for the tribal Pathan to contravene the perceived natural order became a symptom of a wider illness: the propensity of the frontiersman to rebel against military authority:

> The levy-man jogs jauntily by, conscious to-day that with his coat turned outside-in he is an irregular trooper of King George, but that with it turned inside-out, why he is . . . as good a raider as those he is out to stop, nay better.[87]

In the early years of World War II, the total number of troops from the NWFP rarely surpassed 6% and little effort was made later to recruit more Pathan *sipahis*.[88] The new image of the Pathan was not the noble frontiersman but the deviant tribal.

Rediscovering the 'oldest of the martial classes': The rural Brahmin

The fidelity that the 'Oudh Brahman' soldier of the East India Company was seen to possess in the early nineteenth century is evident from the fictional narrative of Subedar Sita Ram published in 1873,[89] a figure who appears neither in military pay-books nor in regimental lists but whose life story was conveniently related in full to a British officer, Lieutenant Colonel James Norgate, just before he died:

> Defender of the poor! – obedience, etc., etc., – I have, by the fatherly kindness of the Government, been granted my pension, and according to your desire, I now send your Lordship, by the hands of my son, the papers containing all I can remember of my life during the forty-eight years I have been in the service of the English Nation in which I have suffered seven severe wounds, and received six medals, which I am proud to wear. I trust what I have now written, and what I have before at different times related to your Honour, may prove that there were some who remained faithful, and were not affected by the Wind of Madness [the mutinies of 1857] which lately blew over Hindustan. . . .[90]

Norgate's caricature of the Brahmin soldier, Sita Ram, not only maintains a 'native' deference that is due to all British officers long after his military service is at an end, but this constructed Brahmin is willing to sacrifice both his caste and his first-born son to 'uphold the English rule under which I had served and eaten salt for so many years.'[91] Although the mutinies of 1857 did not affect Norgate's appreciation of the twice-born Hindu soldier, it has become something of a historical orthodoxy to comment on how a later generation of British officers condemned Brahmin *sipahis* for their adherence to caste prejudice, their poor physique and their lax morals.[92] I will show that, while the recruitment of Brahmins from the United Provinces of Agra and Oudh [hereafter UP] was curtailed for a time in the nineteenth and twentieth centuries, the recruitment of soldiers from these communities never ceased entirely, and an understanding that the Brahmin could be the ideal soldier came to be revived as British Imperial power in India began to wane.

In his novel 'Kim', first serialized in 1900 and 1901, Rudyard Kipling makes clear his disgust for the Brahmins of northern India. Even those such as 'Hurree Chunder Mookerjee' who were to be found in the service of the Crown were to be condemned:

> His companion was the whale-like Babu, who, with a fringed shawl wrapped around his head, and his fat open-work-stockinged left leg tucked under him, shivered and grunted in the morning chill.
> "How comes it that this man is one of us?" thought Kim, considering the jelly-back as they jolted down the road. . . .[93]

Much like Kipling, A. H. Bingley and A. Nicholls' *Caste Handbooks for the Indian Army: Brahmans*, published in 1897, also derided the unmanly physiques of Brahmins. If they were not bloated like Hurree, they were emaciated because of the propensity of the Brahmin 'to fill his pocket at the expense of his stomach' and due to the 'wearisome formalities' that high-caste Hindus indulged in when preparing and consuming food.[94] The caste 'exclusiveness' and intricate purification ceremonies practised by Brahmins from northern India were seen 'as inimical to military efficiency',[95] as it was for Kipling,[96] especially when it led to overt 'bigotry' against others.[97] Finally, the famed Brahmin 'love of thrift' was not only seen as leading to cases of Brahmin non-commissioned officers (NCOs) embezzling funds[98] but was also seen as indirectly leading to the 'deep and tricky character'[99] of Brahmins that made regimental discontent more likely.[100] As a result, there was only one regiment bearing the name 'Brahmans' by the time of World War I, and, before the end of the conflict, even a portion of that regiment was disbanded. In 1917, the soldiers of the regiment were condemned for objecting to the 'group system of messing', enforced by its commanding officer, that would have led to ritually impure non-Brahmins preparing their food.[101]

Yet, for Bingley and Nicholls, Brahmins were not to be excluded wholesale. The opening pages of the military manual made clear the authors' intent to show that some Brahmins could once again be placed 'on an equality with the most warlike races of India'.[102] In so doing, they divined two different types of Brahmins in India. One was physically unfit, untrustworthy and bedevilled by arcane caste prejudice and the other was free of those vices:

> There . . . arose [in India] a class of Brahmans who, while retaining the privilege of a Levite class, were in all essentials an agricultural people, of naturally

pacific tendencies, but ready and able to defend themselves whenever occasion required. . . . They were more docile and easily disciplined; they were quicker to learn their drill; and their natural cleanliness, fine physique and soldierly bearing made them more popular with their European officers than the truculent Muhammadans from the north, to whom pipeclay and discipline were abhorrent.[103]

To this end, a distinction was drawn between Brahmins in the rural areas of the United Provinces that exercised a sacerdotal function of being part-time 'priests' who, under no circumstances, were suited for military life,[104] and 'secular' Brahmins who played no religious role in their villages and from whom recruits ought to be obtained.[105] Furthermore, as these 'secular Brahmans' were ranked in order of which 'tribe' or 'sub-tribe' of UP Brahmin would furnish the most soldierly of recruits, it was those communities that would eat animal flesh and who tilled the soil as labourers or landed agriculturalists that were the most highly prized. The reason for this was because they had surpassed their Brahminical heritage by being 'cultivators pure and simple'.[106] Particular praise was reserved for men among the 'Kanoujiya' Brahmins found in the area south-west of Mathura and along the Nepal border. Such was the regard with which the Brahmin agriculturalist was held in by World War II that 37,000 'Brahmans' were recruited in the Artillery, Engineers, Infantry and RIASC; and three-fourths of them were rural *Kanoujiyas*.[107]

Other Brahmins recruited into the Indian Army, as Punjabi Dogras, were so shorn of their Brahmin-ness that they were not described as Brahmins at all by military handbooks. In the 'isolated' pockets of colonial Punjab in which Dogras were to found, primarily in Kangra, Sialkot, Gurdaspur and Hoshiarpur districts and in the princely states nearby, the populace was seen to mirror the practices of pre-Brahminical ancient India rather than the 'priest-ridden' India of the plains. Bingley reasoned that it was because there had been historically no 'Musalman domination' nor loss of Rajput royalty that would have thrown the Hindu population 'wholly into the hands of the Brahmans'.[108] As such, although Brahmins of the region were once again divided by recruiters into the 'ploughman' or the 'priest', 'the former being eligible while the latter is not',[109] care was taken to show that all Dogra Brahmins had benefited from a mixing of their blood 'with the surrounding population, or remnants of the aboriginal aristocracy of the hills'.[110] Further still, the Dogra Brahmin was perceived approvingly as being culturally distinct from the other Brahmins of India, to the extent that they would avoid contact with one another:

> The Dogra Brahmans will not associate with those of the same caste from the plains. Both profess mutual distrust, and neither will eat *roti* cooked by the other; the hill Brahman, moreover, will nearly always eat flesh, which is eschewed by the majority of his down country brethren.[111]

It was another caste entirely, the 'Bhojkis', that were described as assuming the role of Brahmins in the hills by being 'quarrelsome, litigious, and profligate', whereas the Dogra Brahmin was seen to possess the same characteristics as those of the Rajput. Indeed, so un-Brahmin-like was the Dogra Brahmin seen to be that all of the 28,071 Dogras in the Indian Army by the end of 1940 were grouped together in the same companies and sections regardless of caste[112]:

> ... it is among the Dogra ... of our Punjab regiments that we find the best specimens of Hindu character, retaining its individuality while divested of many of its faults. Here we acquire a clearer conception than elsewhere of their high spirit when roused, their enthusiastic courage and generous self-devotion, so singularly combined with gentleness, and an almost boyish simplicity of character.[113]

Thus, the image of Norgate's faithful Brahmin was revived albeit in a different form. Narratives of Brahman martialness in India changed, which helped both to fill the material gap in the numbers of the Indian Army in World War II and to fill the gap in the psyche of the colonial military establishment that was searching for new soldiering classes to replace those that had been lost:

> Brahmans of course are the oldest of the classes to be enlisted in the Indian Army. ... For many years past, however, the enlistment of Madrassis and Brahmans has been very limited, so it may be said that the great increase [in recruitment] which has taken place in the last three years constitutes a welcome innovation.[114]

Conclusion: Following the negative

To write a history of the Handbooks is to write a history of recurring inadequacy: they were never quite good enough for the Indian Army. The Handbooks did succeed in merging fantasy with perceived truth. The Sikh was the archetype of Roberts' perfect soldier: not a religion but a race; not weakened by climate but strengthened by the cool airs of Central Asia. Pathans were how British wished to see themselves: 'chivalric', 'hawk-like' and imbued with an innate sense of 'democracy' and 'fair-play'. The Brahmin was symptomatic of the failings and virtues of all Indians: inscrutable in their fidelity and their treachery. But, the negatives never or rarely outlasted their production. Bingley produced his *Handbooks for the Indian Army: Sikhs* in 1899, but by World War I, it was already outdated. Pathans' frontier nobility was replaced by frontier degeneracy within a matter of years from 1910. Reality always moved too fast, or otherwise eluded, the artfulness of the martial race ethnologists. Brahmins were recruited by the Indian Army in a different guise long before their sudden rediscovery by Claude Auchinleck as 'the oldest of the [martial] classes'.[115]

So, what use are the Handbooks for the historian if they were so easily discarded and so poorly representative of soldiers? For an historian of the Indian Army, their use comes from the fact that they were intellectual justifications of colonialism and the colonial military that at once articulated supreme confidence and unseen fears. Martial Indians were fixed absolutely, down to castes within castes and affiliations within tribes. They were known better than they knew themselves. Even the 'official text-book' for the teaching of Urdu to British Officers warned against actually talking to *sipahis* or Indians and instead drew up a series of fictional dialogues about the 'fighting qualities', 'early history', 'general physique', 'customs' and the nature of Indian 'battalions'.[116] It meant that the Handbooks were never fully forgotten. When new martial classes had to be found, the vacuum was filled by those who were a close approximation for the old: Mazhbi Sikhs or Ramgarias for Sikh Jats. Handbooks could be resurrected in order to prove that new recruits were in no way a deviation from previous policy, as in the case of Brahmins. And, in the case of the mothballed negatives relating to Pathans, of innate *'noblesse oblige'* and 'wildness', they have had a new airing in the twenty-first century in order to excuse/justify wars of occupation/ liberation in Afghanistan.[117]

If the Handbooks are recurring colonial fantasy, so were they recurring colonial nightmare. The soldier only existed in an abstracted form in the Handbooks and its associated literature. Mention was made of him only in parables, jokes, stories, but never summations of what he actually said. Yet, the agency of the soldier permeates through the double exposure of that colonial lens. He appears as a ghostly presence whenever bungalows are set alight, explanations have to be sought for high rates of desertion, and when a military class suddenly proves itself worthy of recruitment. The (re)production or (re)abandonment of Handbooks are a blueprint to where things went awry: where *sipahis* acted in unforeseen ways. And if *sipahis* were not aware of the exact effect their actions had in metamorphosing fantasy to horror, there were, as later chapters will show, more than incidental references in *sipahis*' testimony to how the Army dreamed its colonial Indian soldiery to be.

2

'More Like Brothers and Fathers to the Sepoys': Welfare, Discipline and Censorship in the Army

On the 7 November 2006, Des Browne, the British Secretary of State for Defence, decided to pardon over 300 soldiers executed during World War I.[1] It was a formal exoneration for soldiers of the British Army who were convicted and executed despite the fact that they may have been suffering from combat stress (commonly termed 'shell-shock') in order to remove any lingering 'stain of dishonour' upon their families.[2] For various campaigners and campaign groups in Britain and Ireland, it was a victory,[3] albeit one that denied any descendants or relatives the right to compensation. What was designed to pardon soldiers of the British Army, however, had wider implications. The pardons covered soldiers and labourers of the West India Regiment, Nigerian Regiment, West African Regiment, East African Rifles and the Egyptian, Chinese and 'Cape Coloured' Labour Corps.[4] It also affected Indian *sipahis*, who, unnamed and unnameable,[5] were not included among the 306 British and Imperial soldiers pardoned directly but who were nonetheless referenced in the legislation:

> It is the Government's intention to introduce an amendment to the current Armed Forces Bill during the Lord's Committee Stage to give effect to this. Rather than naming individuals, the amendment will pardon all those executed following conviction by court martial for a range of offences likely to have been strongly influenced by the stresses associated with this terrible war; this will include desertion, cowardice, mutiny and comparable offences committed during the period of hostilities from 4 August 1914 to 11 November 1918. Over 300 individuals from the United Kingdom, her dominions and colonies were executed under the 1881 Army Act. We will also seek pardons for those similarly executed under the provisions of the 1911 Indian Army Act, records of whose identities we have not

been able to locate. We consider that it would not be appropriate to include in the pardon all capital offences and specifically the offences of murder and treason will be excluded.

In each case, the effect of the pardon will be to recognise that execution was not a fate that the individual deserved but resulted from the particular discipline and penalties considered to be necessary at the time for the successful prosecution of the war. We intend that the amendment should so far as possible remove the particular dishonour that execution brought to the individuals and their families.[6]

The inclusion of Indian *sipahis* and reference to Indian military law was clearly an afterthought. No records survive of the number of Indian soldiers executed, no campaigns for their exoneration were ever launched, and World War I does not endure in the public imagination in the subcontinent as it does in Britain. Yet, the colonial Indian military penal code, and the soldiers executed under it, could not be ignored in the legislation because it operated as a simulacrum of its British counterpart. The Indian soldier was conditioned and disciplined by an Act passed by the Viceroy and his Council, the Indian Army Act of 1911, which was a reproduction of the statutes of the (British) Army Act of 1881. Guidance was given in the preface of each Indian military legal manual that the reader should refer to its British parent if anything was unclear.[7] Under this legal gaze, Indian *sipahis* were indistinguishable from their white (or black) counterparts and were to be treated as such long after the Raj had come to an end. It was a synchronic vision of the colonial soldier that acted as a contrasting counterpart to diachronic martial race narratives.

As this *contrasting* counterpart, there were both differences and similarities in how legal scholars realized the colonial soldier when compared to how military ethnologists did so. When Indian military legislation, regulations and legal manuals were to be updated, usually following earlier revisions in their British equivalents, old tracts were not discarded but synthesized with the new. The language in which these tracts were written was one of the subclause and addendum: a slow process of accretion that added another layer of language in the processional search for legal certitude. But, this process of defining the legal body of the *sipahi* was never complete or ever completed. Issues arose ¹ᶠªʳᵉ provisions, military punishments, and military censorship that entiated the Indian from the British soldier. These were only y codifying a literature of the British officer as *ma-bap* – not a parental figure to *sipahis* – into military law and regulations.

Indian military law acted as a simulacrum of its British counterpart: a replica that was still imperfect and which necessitated a smoothing away of those imperfections.

This chapter will analyse the legal gaze that shaped and fixed *sipahis* under imperialism. It will chart the relationship between British and Indian military law that saw the latter echo the form and content of its British equivalent. It will then investigate the differences that were reconciled by appealing to Victorian and Edwardian ideals of parenthood and childhood. Indian *sipahis* were to be nurtured with generous welfare provisions available only to soldiers (and military pensioners), disciplined more harshly than their peers in the British Army, and their voices were to be censored and conditioned in a more rigorous manner. As one piece of military propaganda put it:

> "I have always heard that all Faujdar officers are kind," said old Gulab Khan, "More like brothers and fathers to the sepoys."[8]

The origins and evolution of Indian military law

By the beginning of World War I, there was a plethora of military literature defining, explaining and delimiting the legal space inhabited by Indian *sipahis*. Acts of legislation, military manuals and more provisional 'guides' established everything, from the correct attestation to be made by a soldier upon enlisting[9] to the correct manner of tying a *lungi* ('tied according to the regimental pattern, not stitched or pinned').[10] Despite the abundance of material, however, there was one common source. British military law provided the legal architecture upon which Indian military law was constructed. It provided the framework and ensured that there were only slight, if significant, differences in content by the early twentieth century. This section will chart the evolution of military law in colonial India and the similarities and differences that existed between it and its British equivalent.

Writing a history of Indian military law is deceptively easy. The department of the Judge Advocate General in India produced its own history of the 'origins and extent' of Indian military law when drafting its narrative accompaniment to the Indian Army Act.[11] In what came to be known as the *Manual of Indian Military Law, 1911*, three stages in the evolution of military law in the subcontinent were identified: military law under the East India Company, the legal system under the 'Indian Articles of War' and, finally, the 'Present Code'.[12] In the eighteenth and early nineteenth centuries, there were no formal rules or statutes for the governance of Indian soldiers. Discipline in 'native armies' in the early days of Company Raj was implemented by selectively applying legislation originally passed for the management of European soldiers.[13] After the legal status of these provisions were challenged in the British Parliament in 1813, instructions were given for each Presidency to clarify the status of *sipahis* by creating separate 'Articles of War for the government of all officers and soldiers in their respective services who were "natives of the East Indies or other places within the limits of the Company's Charter."'[14] But, even under this new system, the British Mutiny Act and Articles of War were used as a template:

> Under the statutory section of these two enactments a military code was framed by the government of each presidency and put in force as regards its own troops. These codes still followed to a great extent the Articles of War then applicable to the Company's Europeans, but the only punishments awardable to native officers seemed to have been death, dismissal, suspension and reprimand, and to native soldiers, death and corporal punishment. Transportation and imprisonment were not awardable.[15]

The reliance upon British parent documents enabled the provisions to be combined into a single Indian Articles of War in 1844, until it too was seen as unwieldy, unworkable and in need of replacing:

> As time went on, however, and the Indian Army began to take its share in the imperial responsibilities of the British Army, it was found that an Act originally framed for three separate land forces, each serving as a rule in its own Presidency, failed to provide adequately for the discipline and administration of that army under modern conditions. Owing also to the mass amendments super-imposed on the original articles, these were often difficult to understand, and sometimes even self-contradictory.[16]

The final result was the 'simple and comprehensive enactment' of the Indian Army Act of 1911.[17]

Much like the original Articles of War, the simplicity of the Indian Army Act was owed to its mirroring of British legislation. The British Army Act of 1881 had broken with previous British Articles of War by separating military offences into separate categories and scaling them to accord with forms of military punishment. Rather than having a separate article for each crime punishable by death or 'punishable otherwise than death',[18] crimes were grouped into related categories, such as in the first section of the Act entitled 'Offences in Respect of Military Service':

Offences in Respect of Military Service

4. Every person subject to military law who commits any of the following offences; that is to say,

   1. Shamefully abandons or delivers up any garrison, place, post or guard; or
   2. Shamefully casts away his arms, ammunition or tools in the presence of the enemy; or
   3. Treacherously holds correspondence with or gives intelligence to the enemy; or
   4. Assists the enemy with arms, ammunition, or supplies, or knowingly harbours or protects an enemy no being a prisoner; or
   5. Having been made a prisoner of war, voluntarily serves with or voluntarily aids the enemy; or
   6. Knowingly does, when on active service, any act calculated to imperil the success of Her Majesty's forces or any part thereof; or
   7. Misbehaves or induces others to misbehave before the enemy in such a manner as to show cowardice, shall on conviction by court-martial be liable to suffer death, or such less punishment as is in this Act mentioned.[19]

The formula was replicated in the Indian Army Act of 1911, except that it was the template of the British Act that was used to delineate the boundaries of military discipline in India:

Offences in respect of Military Service

25. Any person subject to this Act who commits any of the following offences, that is to say, -

    (a) shamefully abandons up any garrison, fortress, post or guard committed to his charge, or which it is his duty to defend; or
    (b) in presence of an enemy, shamefully casts away his arms or ammunition, or intentionally uses words or any other means to induce any person subject to military law to abstain from acting against the enemy, or to discourage the person from acting against the enemy, or misbehaves in such manner as to show cowardice; or
    (c) directly or indirectly holds correspondence with, or communicates intelligence to the enemy, or any person in arms against the State, or who, coming to the knowledge of any such correspondence or communication, omits to discover it immediately to his commanding officer; or

(d) treacherously makes known the watchword to any person not entitled to receive it; . . . shall, on conviction by court-martial, be punished with death, or with such less punishment as in this Act mentioned.[20]

The sections within the two Acts were so similar they could have been interchangeable. Or, at least that is the impression given by the authors of the Indian version in the department of the Judge Advocate General in India. The form and format of the 1881 Army Act was so rigidly adhered to in the drafting of the 1911 Indian Army Act that phrases only applicable to British soldiers were accidentally replicated in the Indian version (such as when 'the property of the Crown' was referred to when the proper term in India was 'the property of the Central Government'[21]). These typographical errors were only periodically corrected, because, as the preface to the *Manual of Indian Military Law* indicated, any competent military jurist was expected to refer to the British document whenever anything was unclear in its Indian twin:

> The War Office "Manual of Military Law" has furnished the model on which the present work has been compiled, and the rulings contained in that manual have been largely drawn upon in its preparation. When the works of legal writers, other than the authors of the abovementioned [sic.] manual, have been quoted, the source of the information in the text has been indicated in a footnote.[22]

Despite the similarities in form, however, there were differences in the detail. The Indian Army Act, in its initial guise, lacked the hierarchical division of military jurisprudence that enabled a parallel penal code to exist for officers. The highest penalty a British officer serving in the Indian or British Army could pay for any military crime, except for mutiny and gross insubordination, was imprisonment for up to 3 years or cashiering – the ritual breaking of a sword and dishonourable dismissal from the service.[23] In the Indian Army Act, no such privileges were granted to 'native officers' who had Viceregal rather than King's or Queen's Commissions, and were, therefore, of lower rank than full British officers. Even with the advent of Indian Commissioned Officers in 1934, who did have a full commission, the amended Indian Army Act still mandated a much harsher series of punishments: death, transportation and imprisonment for up to 14 years.[24] Although Indians could, by the 1930s, become officers, they were not quite gentlemen and deserving of the same privileges due to their British equivalents.

There were additional discrepancies in the provisions made for enlisted men. Whereas a separate offence of 'drunkenness' existed for British soldiers, for Indians, the equivalent offence was termed 'intoxication'. The crime of 'intoxication' was phrased as such to cover the greater proclivity of Indian soldiers for cannabis and cannabis derivatives (*charas, bhang* and *ganja*), which, according to the evidence gathered by the *Report of the Indian Hemp Drugs Commission* from 1893 to 1895, resulted in unchecked criminal insanity in the Indian Army:

> Answer 162. The excessive use of these drugs does in my opinion incite to unpremeditated crime. Nearly twenty years ago I knew a man in the regiment to be incited by the use of ganja to a temporary homicidal frenzy.[25]
>
> Answer 200. Have read and heard of instances where sepoys have run amuck or revenged an imaginary grievance after premeditation and the use of bhang.[26]
>
> Answer 209. Yes; it is well known that bhang is thus taken when a man is desirous of running "amuck." A case occurred in this regiment before or about 1870 on parade when a man attacked his European officers and was at once cut down by the other men.[27]
>
> Answer 117. Only one case on record: a sepoy of the regiment ran amuck in 1887 at Yamethinin Upper Burma: he was a known ganja-smoker, though never caught in the act. Ganja, I believe, was found in a parcel sent to him from India, and after he was shot-down a large quantity of majum was found in his kit-bag. This was the only instance I know, and fairly proves that excessive indulgence in hemp incited unpremeditated crime.[28]
>
> Answer 191. No actual case has come within my knowledge: but I know that all the fanatics in Afghanistan were all primed with charas before "running amuck." It is well known that "Ghazis" are well intoxicated by charas before they "run amuck."[29]
>
> Answer 42. Excessive indulgence does lead to crime. Lately a case occurred in the 36th Sikhs: a man known by the name of "Bhangor" – from being addicted to bhang – shot his friend and shot at anyone who approached, and eventually shot himself.[30]

Offences present in the 1881 Army Act were also missing from its Indian equivalent. Indian *sipahis* were not to be prosecuted for offences that would require written evidence of their wrongdoing – including offences in relation to enlistment and of forcing a civilian to provide shelter or 'carriage' (transport).

This was in order to offer protection to the *sipahi* who was presumed to have only a basic level of literacy and was thus open to manipulation by the unscrupulous and lettered Indian *babu*:

> ... an Englishman came up and asked the Babu what was the matter. I explained that I had come to Jhelum to enlist in the Army, but that the Babu did not want to let me go. The Englishman laughed and said to the Babu, "Fikr na kar, Babuji, I'll pay the amount." ... I then asked him, "What dalali do I have to give you?" He laughed more than the last time (he always seemed to be laughing) and said "There is no dalali or dasturi."[31]

The convenience of making the legal existence of the *sipahi* under the Raj indistinct from the British Tommy frayed under the fine print of the Indian Army Act. The soldier in India began to be seen as distinctly Indian and not as any other Imperial soldier.

The creeping Orientalization of the military-legal discourse in the Indian Army Act continued apace after the Act came into force in 1911. The following years and decades saw the addition of new rules, regulations, crimes and punishments in direct amendments to the Act (in 1918, 1920, 1934 and 1937) to clarify and cover new areas of jurisprudence that had not been adequately explained. There was also a build-up of literature beyond the Indian Army Act and the *Manual of Indian Military Law*. Published volumes, pamphlets, guides and memoranda – most notably the *Indian Army Act Rules* and the *Army Regulations, India*[32] – added further to the corpus of military law. More importantly, each amendment and addition took military law in India further from its British prototype. Each additional layer of language added another layer of separation between the Indian and British soldier. The burden of this additional language produced welfare provisions for Indian soldiers that far outstripped anything available in the British Army. *Sipahis* were no longer to be disciplined in accordance with (white) Imperial soldiers elsewhere, because particularly Indian forms of punishment and control that would 'impress them with a deep feeling of terror' were to be created.[33] Elaborate welfare mechanisms were established that took the Indian military penal code beyond a simple list of offences and punishments. And, attempts were made to control and monitor what Indian *sipahis* thought and communicated to one another because of their 'Oriental tendency' towards 'mental disquietude'.[34] It is to a study of welfare, disciplinary and censoring measures that this chapter will now turn.

'These men have defecated in their *dhotis* through sheer fright': Welfare, war trauma and dealing with the Indian insane

In 1979, Pat Mills and Joe Colquhoun created 'Charley's War', a children's comic strip printed in Britain that was periodically censored in the years of its publication and has been widely celebrated since. The fictional story of Charley Bourne, the eponymous hero, portrayed the horror of World War I from a soldier's perspective and was drawn to undermine the jingoistic narratives of war that prevailed in the sub-genre of 'boy's comics' at the time.[35] Deserters and conscientious objectors became noble heroes, British officers were cast as villains, and protest and mutiny against the British Army was justified and celebrated. As a result, 'Charley's War' became the target of shrill criticism by British tabloids and Mary Whitehouse's conservative crusade to protect the innocence of Britain's children. Mills and Colquhoun's intention was to shock and provoke a reaction. What they did not expect was that the most widely objected to portion of the comic strip was the graphic portrayal of the psychological effects of war or 'shell-shock' upon Charley Bourne and his comrades.

The reaction of the British press and self-appointed arbiters of moral probity in the 1980s merely reflected the sensibilities of British military and medical authorities in the 1910s and 1920s. During World War I, the reality of soldiers suffering from 'shell-shock' was first ignored by contemporaries, caused some measure of scandal in the British media and then led to denial by medical professionals that there was such a condition. In the Indian Army, however, the situation was different. Provisions were made that provided treatment for psychologically wounded Indian *sipahis* to a higher standard and far more quickly than for their peers in the British Army. This willingness to diagnose and treat Indian but not British war neuroses will be explained below with reference to the breadth and depth of the welfare system that catered to *sipahis* needs during and after World War I.

Sipahis were never well paid in the Indian Army. The pay of an enlisted soldier was set at Rs. 7 per month in 1860, before being raised to Rs. 9 in 1895 and Rs. 11 in 1911. The wage was fixed to accord with what soldiers had been paid in Mughal India, but, because soldiers had to pay for their own food, clothing and other equipment, the cost of subsistence in the Army was often higher than the wage provided. In 1875, for instance, when a soldier's pay was Rs. 7, the cost of subsistence was estimated at Rs. 7, *anna* 2, *paise* 5.[36]

Charley's War, 1 August 1916 – 17 October 1916.

The low pay of Indian soldiers prompted enquiries in the late nineteenth century and stoked fears that it would dissuade the best 'class' of men from enlisting in future: 'As the bazar prices are increasing, the sepoys pay should be raised, otherwise they would starve and their physique would decline.'[37] It proved difficult, however, for the Indian Army to obtain the funds for a significant increase in wages until 1921 (when the pay of *sipahis* was increased to Rs. 16 per month). So, the military in India took to offering a raft of irregular payments to Indian soldiers over and above their basic wage. These payments ranged from the implementation of good conduct pay and 'hutting' allowances in the nineteenth century to war bonuses and one-off bounties for new recruits in the twentieth. The most systematized form of extraordinary payments was *batt*a, which was initially implemented to cover fluctuations in the price of food grain, but which became a fixed payment worth Rs. 2 *anna* 8 per month in 1887 and Rs. 5 in 1914. Individual British officers were even encouraged to provide gifts to their soldiers as part of the *batta* system and as a way of reinforcing the special bond between the 'native' soldier and his white superior.[38] Although the direct pay of *sipahis* remained low throughout the British Raj, the irregular payments and bonuses attached to being a soldier made it financially worthwhile.

The special privileges that a *sipahi* could accrue continued into retirement and extended to their families. It was regular practice for Indian soldiers who had served in the Army for 20 years or more to be awarded a gratuity in kind or in cash. Pensions were available to former soldiers from the mid-nineteenth century, and if an individual had distinguished himself during his military service by winning a medal or award, the level of pension would be increased further. By the turn of the twentieth century, the reclaimed Canal Colonies in Western Punjab provided a further benefit for Punjabi soldiers near retirement. The Government of Punjab actively sought military pensioners to settle in its model village communities, with a grant of fertile and irrigated land available to each successful applicant:

> . . . on the Jhang and Gugera Branches pensioners have usually been given separate villages to themselves, being grouped together with due references to regiments, as well as tribe, religion and District. Thus there are some particularly homogenous pensioner villages, and in some cases the regimental eponymous hero has given his name to the estate. For instance there are villages named Fanepur (19th Lancers, Fane's Horse), Rattrayabad (45th Rattray's Sikhs), Probynabad (11th Prince of Wales' Own Lancers), Hodsonabad (9th Hodson's Horse), and Kot Brosyer (14th Sikhs).[39]

The bonuses *sipahis* received both during and after their service made soldiering a form of employment through which they could support both families and friends. British officers were instructed to regard their Indian soldiers as wage labourers looking to supplement their agricultural income. According to the guidance given to officers in the second volume of the *Army Regulations, India*, up to 40% of any battalion were to be allowed to head home on furlough or military leave between 15 March and 15 October because there was 'work to be done in the fields'.⁴⁰ If soldiers were on active service and were unable to return home, remittances were commonly used as a substitute and were integrated into the pay structure of *sipahis*. By World War II, soldiers regularly remitted up to half their total pay as a 'Family Allowance'. On the rare cases that soldiers withheld such allowances, military families could still expect free healthcare and education if they were housed in military lines (Dr B. R. Ambedkar being, perhaps, the most famous pupil). And, with the creation of District Soldiers' Boards (DSBs) in Punjab after World War I, these privileges were extended further and beyond the cantonment. The official (British) history of the Indian involvement in World War I, India's Contribution to the Great War, contained a brief summation of the activities of the DSBs by its all-Indian Secretary in 1919.⁴¹ It served to institutionalize what had previously been unwritten forms of relief and patronage, in order to make them available to all soldiers:

> From the demobilization of a large proportion of the Indian Army, no matter how excellently the military arrangements were conceived and how admirably they were carried out, difficulties were bound to ensue that could be dealt with satisfactorily by no existing Department of Government and for the immediate solution of which the establishment of an *ad hoc* transitional board was empathically required. Finding employment for soldiers released from the colours, the grant of rewards to those who had rendered distinguished service, the relief of the dependents of those who had lost their lives in the war, or of those who were incapacitated for future service, the education of the soldiers' children, and safeguarding the general interests of soldiers whether serving or discharged, and of their dependents if deceased, were all matters demanding immediate and close attention.⁴²

Given the extent of privileges and concessions that resulted from service in the Indian Army, it was unsurprising that Sowar Jowan Singh, writing in response to his family asking why he and other Sikhs had enlisted in a letter dated 4 March 1917, stated matter-of-factly that 'people say we enlisted from fear of the police, but we have no regard for Lumbardars or Police or anyone else.... Our object in enlisting was to obtain some benefit from the Sircar'.⁴³

The direct correlation between loyal military service and access to defined and undefined forms of military patronage was absent in the British Army. Even when there was widespread sympathy in Parliament and in wider society for the sacrifices of the British Tommy after World War I, the British Army was reluctant to provide much more than a victory medal. The summer of 1919 was plagued by bands of recently demobilized and angry veterans disrupting peace festivals and remembrance services in protest against the lack of adequate housing, the low level of pensions and gratuities, and the uncooperative attitude of welfare agencies.[44] Disabled British ex-soldiers who did secure pensions and who were selected for state-sponsored retraining still suffered from high levels of joblessness,[45] often by being retrained into skills that were unemployable (such as tailors taught to sew by hand in an age of machinists).[46] The differences in welfare policies were informed by differences in rhetoric and language. Concessions to British soldiers were made on sufferance. The 1920 Report of the Esher Committee, instigated to reorganize the military in India, made several concessions for British troops stationed within the subcontinent. Accommodation was to be improved, free rations were to be made available for soldiers' wives and children, and the overly earnest proselytizing efforts of the Royal Army Temperance Association were to be curtailed. Each recommendation was justified by a reference to the peculiar 'idiosyncrasies' of the modern British soldier and his lack of 'patience' and 'discipline':

> We wish, in conclusion, to point out that the outlook of the present-day [British] soldiers upon life is widely different from that of their predecessors of the old army. They have neither their deep-seated discipline nor their long-suffering patience. They and their wives look for a higher standard of comfort and a somewhat different class of recreation. Their reasonable aspirations must be met, and their idiosyncrasies must be sympathetically studied, if they are to be a contented army while serving in India.[47]

In contrast, additional provisions recommended for Indian *sipahis* were a natural corollary to their improved tastes and knowledge of the world and to ensure that the best class of men still wished to become soldiers of the Raj:

> The Indian soldier has seen the world during the last six years in a way he never has before. His ideas of comfort have risen, and he has acquired certain tastes to which he was previously a stranger. He is well aware of what has been done for the British soldier in the way of amelioration of conditions of life and pay since the war began, and he is now apt to compare his own pay with that of his British comrades.[48]

Even after World War I, enlisted men in the British Army recruited from the urban working classes were agents of moral, spiritual and, at times, racial decay. Indian soldiers, if not quite British, were portrayed as being of the same ilk as their public school-educated British officers: hailing from rural communities with muscular physiques, quiescent before military discipline and aspiring towards the best of European tastes.

World War I and the high incidence of war trauma among British soldiers, officers and colonial troops threatened to destabilize these simple generalizations. From the 1890s, there had been an increasing awareness and commentary upon psychiatric disorders in Europe and North America.[49] Neurology emerged as a science that sought to explain nervous ticks, physical shaking, depression or anxiety as a tangible physical defect of the brain and nervous system. The emergence of literary and political figures diagnosed with 'neurasthenia' – from Oscar Wilde, Virginia Wolfe and Rupert Brooke to Theodore Roosevelt – alarmed medical professionals, sociologists and early eugenicists. Emile Durkheim warned of the rising incidence of suicide in the modern city,[50] and Willhelm Erb, the German nerve specialist, blamed mental illness upon 'the rapid growth of large cities with all its unfortunate consequences: the creation of mighty industrial centres filled with proletarians.'[51] It helped to merge the rhetoric of Samuel Smiles, Robert Baden-Powell and Rudyard Kipling with that of the 'Eugenicists, the conservative politicians, and the ethnologists who conflated race degeneration, lost manhood, and loss of Empire.'[52] And when soldiers in World War I were found to be suffering from 'neurasthenia' as early as November 1914, the military medical establishment in the Royal Army Medical Corps was quick to blame the enlisting of undesirables in the ranks of the British Army. Captain J. I. C Dunn, testifying before the post-war War Office Committee of Enquiry into 'Shell-Shock', for instance, quickly attributed the root cause of war trauma to the high prevalence of Jews, Irish and other 'defectives' in the ranks:

> In peace time high grade defectives were recruited and completed their colour service. Several such cases have come before the Pensions Appeal Tribunal – the war revealed them, in two instances after a long period of testing service (one had a markedly asymmetrical head and face; he had a mild malaria several months before his breakdown). The chances of a breakdown in training these men are great; of an eventual breakdown very great . . . . It must depend on the officer and chance whether he is got rid of before he has been "shocked" or become confused.[53]

By the time of the Enquiry, however, Dunn was in the minority. It was not just the lower orders of the British Army who were and had been suffering from war neuroses. The first six medical centres opened by the British Army to treat war trauma from October 1916 treated officers alone, because they were found to be more susceptible to suffer from psychological disorders than the rank and file. William Halse Rivers Rivers, the pioneering psychiatrist who worked at

Craiglockart War Hospital and was immortalized in Siegfried Sassoon's loving portrait in *Sherston's Progress*,[54] divined there to be two treatable types of war neurosis: 'hysteria' in which the illness manifested itself in a physical form such as 'dumbness or the helplessness of a limb'[55] and 'anxiety-neurosis' in which the illness was more enduring and internalized into 'depression, restlessness, irritability, and enfeeblement of memory.'[56] The first type of illness was to be found exclusively among the enlisted men of the British Army. The symptoms of 'hysteria' were similar to the effects of suggestion under hypnotism, were apparent among ordinary soldiers because they were incapable of thinking too deeply or internalizing their plight, and could be avoided with the cultivation of *esprit de corps* among the ranks.[57] The second and more serious category of 'anxiety-neurosis' could only affect officers burdened with the duties of command:

> Anyone having much to do with those who have taken part in the fighting of the war must have been struck by the extraordinary manner in which an officer, perhaps only just fresh from school, has come to stand in a relation to his men more nearly resembling that of father and son than any other kind of relationship.[58]
>
> ... His conflict differs from that of the private soldier in that it is founded largely upon acquired experience rather than upon instinctive trends. It is more actively conscious than the process which has produced a paralysis or mutism. These disabilities fail altogether to touch the special anxieties which have taken the foremost place in the production of illness [in officers].[59]

Mental illness was the product of a Freudian repression of emotion and of harrowing experiences, and, for Rivers, only an officer was capable of that level of repression:

> Fear and repression and its expression are especially abhorrent to the normal standards of the public schools at which the majority of officers have been educated. The games and contests which make up so large a part of the school curriculum are all directed to meet without manifestation of fear any occasion likely to call forth that emotion. The public school boy enters the army with a long course of training behind him which enables him successfully to repress, not only expressions of fear, but also the emotion itself.[60]

Rivers was not alone in his assumptions and division between different forms of war neurosis. Other Freudian psychiatrists working among soldiers shared his views.[61] And, even Charles Myers, who, as the lone consulting psychologist to the British Army, had coined the phrase 'shell-shock' in reference to what he believed was a single condition, wrote a later retraction admitting that he had underestimated the complexity of the phenomenon.⁶² The official *Report of the War Office Committee of Enquiry into "Shell-Shock"* produced in 1922 adopted the forms of mental illness and methods of diagnosis that Rivers and other psychoanalysts had pioneered. War trauma was to be divided into two preventable and treatable types: 'emotional shock' and 'nervous and mental exhaustion.'⁶³ The former, common among the rank and file, would be avoided by implementing more rigorous requirements for new recruits to weed out individuals guilty of 'previous mental or nervous breakdown, inebriety, the drug habit, sexual excess'.⁶⁴ Sufferers of 'nervous and mental exhaustion', which was the natural 'result of prolonged strain and hardship', were to be treated with greater sympathy. It was defined as an illness of the officer-class alone and, as officers, they were found to be deserving of military-funded care in 'neurological centres' where 'rest of mind and body was essential'.⁶⁵

For Indian soldiers, there was no formal post-war inquiry, because there was a greater openness to the possibility that *sipahis* could suffer from war neuroses. Within 2 months of Indian soldiers being exposed to combat in France, Evelyn Berkeley Howell, the Chief Censor of Indian military correspondence in France, warned of the 'mental disquietude' displayed in soldier's letters:

> The mail to India [from soldiers] which at first was regarded as negligible has now become the most important part of our work. A number of letters from men with their units at the front have been examined. They betray undeniable evidence of depression. . . . The tendency during the month has been for these letters to increase in numbers and in length. At the same time there has been a marked change in tone. Grumbling is still almost entirely absent and there is never a hint of resentment or anti-British feeling. . . . But adverse signs are growing more conspicuous. Many of the men show a tendency to break into poetry which I am inclined to regard as a rather ominous sign of mental disquietude. The number of letters written by men who have obviously given way to despair has also increased both absolutely and relatively. . . . What is more significant still is the proportion of letters which though they show no sign of giving way to despair or of any faltering devotion to duty yet give a melancholy impression of fatalistic resignation to a fate that is regarded as speedy and inevitable. This feeling too appears to be spreading.⁶⁶

It is difficult to say how many soldiers were suffering from war trauma by looking at their letters alone. No attempt was ever made by censors to enumerate or label any particular letters as evidence of shell shock. It did not seem to be that urgent a concern or that much of a surprise to Howell's superiors. But, a quick appraisal of *sipahis*' letters reveals a quiet horror in the language soldiers used to describe their experiences. The mud, cold and exposure to frostbite and trench foot were constantly referred to: 'My feet become like ice in my boots and pain me and this causes me much distress.'[67] The loss of comrades to bullets and shells fired by an enemy that could not even be seen, led to staccato sentences and poetic refrains: 'Teja Singh and Sunder Singh have been killed by bullets. Ladda Singh has been wounded by a bullet in the leg. The corpses lie as thick as weeds in the jungle.'[68] And others wrote simple paeons begging for God's forgiveness for the wrongs Indian soldiers must have committed to be sent to the killing fields of Flanders:

> We are like goats tied to a butcher's stake. We have no idea when he will come, and there is no one who will release us. We have given up all hope of life. It would be a good thing if my soul were to quit my body. How long, how long can we stand all this? If I were to tell you all we have to face it would make a book; but there is no road of escape for this helpless one. Oh God! Turn thine eyes upon us sinners and forgive us![69]

The odd letter went further and discussed the mental breakdown of comrades by talking of individuals who had 'defecated in their dhotis' in terror[70] or of others who had contracted 'fever through fright':

> The next day there was a march and three or four horses dropped their shoes. Lal Khan then thought it was all over with him and got fever through fright and was taken to hospital. He was screaming and crying and the patients were astonished at the sight of this new arrival with his pale face and hair turned white. He said he was dying. The next day the patients all said to the doctor sahib "Either take this man away or remove us from the hospital." He was eventually sent back to India as unfit for service.[71]

A better guide to the precise number of *sipahis* afflicted with war neuroses is the number of Indian military 'mental cases' arriving in Bombay asylums during World War I. Medical authorities in Bombay soon began to conclude that full mental breakdowns were as common among *sipahis* as they were among British soldiers and officers:

> 95 Indian mental cases arrived in Bombay from overseas from 1st January [1918] to date [28th January 1918] and in view of the large number of Labour Corps personnel in Mesopotamia and the increasing strain from climactic and other conditions, there is every reason to anticipate that the number will increase rather than decrease as the hot weather approaches.[72]

The cases that arrived in Bombay were enough to persuade the Indian Army to enact changes in Indian military law and to improve mental health provisions in the subcontinent much quicker than in Britain. The Indian Army Act was amended in 1923 to make allowances for mental illness among *sipahis*. Military courts were instructed to record a finding of 'not guilty on account of unsoundness of mind' in any case where 'the person charged is of unsound mind and consequently incapable of making his defence, or that such person committed the act alleged but was by reason of unsoundness of mind incapable of knowing the nature of the act or that it was wrong and contrary to law'.[73] A *sipahi* offered such clemency could then resume military service if the court martial decreed it, released from the Army into civilian care if there was 'no danger of his doing injury to himself or to any other person', or, in rarer cases, 'transferred to a public lunatic asylum' in India.[74] Asylums to domicile the Indian insane had a fearsome reputation in the nineteenth century as a place of incarceration rather than treatment. But, this changed with the appearance of military psychiatric patients. A pattern for the gradual expansion of psychiatric hospitals and mental health units emerged from 1918 in the Bombay Presidency, because Bombay was the main port of disembarkation for Indian soldiers and shell shock victims were often too mentally ill to be moved. As James Mills has shown, the Indian Army urgently lobbied the Government of Bombay for quicker and more systematic expansion in psychiatric treatment in the latter years of World War I, to the exasperation of civilian colonial officials:

> The Surgeon General is unable to make any suggestion as to how these additional insanes could be accommodated in this Presidency. All available accommodation is already overcrowded and it would be impossible to build accommodation at once for several hundred more insanes even if plans were ready and materials collected. The Assistant Director, Medical Services is being informed accordingly so that he may arrange elsewhere.[75]

By World War II, the Indian Army had succeeded in its aim by having over a thousand beds in psychiatric wards across India especially reserved for Indian sufferers of war neuroses. In addition to more institutions and beds, there is what Mills has identified as an Indianization and professionalization of support staff. Indian medics began to take up senior (if temporary) positions to treat and cure psychiatric cases during World War I, and by the 1930s, psychiatry was well integrated into student syllabuses across Indian medical colleges. There was also a more sympathetic attitude towards asylums expressed by the Indian elite in civilian life, with various institutions attracting large philanthropic donations (half a *lakh* rupees in the case of the Yeravda Hospital in Pune in 1935).[76] Although there was a wider change in civilian attitudes towards mental health in India in the interwar period, the initial impetus behind investment and reform of facilities and training came from the Indian Army.

The speed with which the Indian Army acted to create a support structure for the diagnosis and treatment of military shell shock victims was due to the belief that the Indian psyche was particularly susceptible to war trauma. Indian soldiers were diagnosed with forms of physical hysteria much like the enlisted men in the British Army. But, whereas in Britain the hysterical soldier could be weeded out from the majority of mentally healthy men by better and more rigorous recruiting procedures, in India, all recruits were potential carriers of psychiatric disorders. Montague Eder, an early translator into English of the works of Sigmund Freud and Carl Jung, the author of the first book on the subject of war trauma and later president of the British Psychological Society, wrote unambiguously in his introduction to *War-Shock: The Psycho-Neuroses in War Psychology and Treatment* that:

> A psycho-neurosis occurs in two kinds of persons, those who are inherently below the level of civilization, who may be called degenerates but who are more properly to be regarded as backwards, and those who are ethically in advance of their age. The latter are the harbingers of a new world, of the dawning civilization which may only (or may never) materialize centuries hence. Hence their conscious and unconscious selves are in constant conflict. It is the lot of the neurotic to be in unstable equilibrium by reason of these inner conflicts. Such conflicts seem to be necessitated by the very essence of man.[77]

Eder wrote more forcefully than his fellow psychoanalysts did, but his conclusions were shared by Rivers and by the institution of the Indian Army. British officers were deserving of treatment and rehabilitation because they were 'ethically in advance of their age', and Indians needed to be treated because of the psycho-neurotic degeneracy. The Indian *sipahi* required the nurturing hand of the British Empire because of his primitive psyche. The welfare system constructed by the Indian Army both in the case of shell shock victims and earlier was a system of control as much as it was a system of privilege. To prevent war trauma escalating to cases of 'running amok', and to exorcise the collective colonialist memory of the mutinies of 1857, privileges had to be granted to the Indian soldier:

> "Discipline demands that you should be demobilized. But on the recommendation of Jemadar Khushi Ram, I have allowed a certain latitude. I shall demobilize you

on pension. I think you are lucky to be going back to your village, and I feel sure that you will make a good farmer. . . ."

"Without a farm!" Lalu wanted to say, "without the reward of a square of land that had been promised to each soldier, without the good conduct medal, without. . . ." He wanted to burst out, but the Colonel's apparent kindness, the show of generosity with which he had agreed to give him a pension after his searching inquiries, disarmed him. . . . His whole frame was shaking and sweat poured down his face; his hands were stiff by his side, and he felt a lump rising in his throat.

"Your papers will be ready before twelve o'clock and a free railway pass will be given you if you wait outside," continued the Colonel. And then he got up, shook hands with Lalu and said aloud: "Salaam."

Lalu saluted the elongated red blur before the scalding tears in his eyes and walked out of the Colonel's presence.[78]

'It is by the terror which it inspires that it produces good': Discipline in the Army

Between 1887 and 1894, shortly before the decision was taken to replace the Indian Articles of War with the Indian Army Act, an attempt was made to enumerate and report 'acts of violence' by soldiers in India.[79] It was in response to the wish of Frederick Roberts, the C-in-C, to remove live ammunition from British soldiers in Indian cantonments, in order to prevent,

> A number of cases . . . of British soldiers, who, while under the influence of liquor, and almost irresponsible for their actions, have made use of the ammunition entrusted to them to shoot men against whom they had some fancied grudge.[80]

For Roberts, the best solution was to simply transport the 'system similar to the one in Ireland' whereby only sentries would carry live ammunition.[81] A not altogether surprising conclusion drawn by a man who was born in India but still saw himself as a member of the Anglo-Irish Ascendency. To chart the effectiveness of the solution, cases of suicide and murder were enumerated before and after the policy was put into effect. The collated figures showed that the numbers of suicides and murders among both British and Indian troops were roughly contiguous, and the implementation of the policy led to a slight decline in both sets of figures after 1887 (see Appendix III). But, the process of charting the decline of acts of suicide and murder did not cause satisfaction for 'Bob's Bahadur'[82] and his staff but rather alarm and panic. The colonialist elite in India were haunted by the fear of the armed *sipahi* committing 'acts of violence', no matter what form it took or how small the number. The Government of Bombay warned of the acute 'danger of leaving balled ammunition in charge of any sepoys' in letters to Roberts.[83] And, such crimes, when perpetrated by an Indian, were given a unique appellation – that of 'running amok': 'a case where a sepoy ran amok shooting at 3 or 4 people but wounding none'; 'Also one case of running amok in which [a] sepoy fired several shots but was shot down before he injured anybody'; 'There have thus been 18 cases of running amok in Sind'.[84] To 'run amok' was a term that was and could only be used in relation to *sipahis*. The phrase originated from the Malay *amoq*, defined by William Marsden, the Anglo-Irish author of *A Dictionary of the Malayan Language* in 1812, as,

> Engaging furiously in battle; attacking with desperate resolution; rushing, in a state of frenzy, to the commission of indiscriminate murder; running a-muck. It is applied to any animal in a state of vicious rage.[85]

It was the archetypal Oriental crime. The disavowed and only partially articulable fear of *sipahis* running amok invoked memories of the Indian Mutiny of 1857. And the spectre of 1857 led to a much more severe disciplinary regime within the Indian Army.

There was a draconian punitive system in place in the military in India before 1857, but it tended to discriminate against European soldiers rather than their Indian equivalents. Up to 1850, it was only members of the British Army (serving in regular British regiments as opposed to the East India Company's own European regiments) who were liable to suffer the penalty of transportation to penal colonies in Australia. Flogging was also endemic among European soldiers.[86] The lash (or 'cat'[87]) could be administered easily and to any part of the body, and could be administered as a summary punishment without court martial or any legal process. More importantly still, flogging was seen as particularly important in the company-held territories in India where criminality among the *white* soldiery was 'rampant':

> They slip out of barracks after roll call, steal into the regimental or cantonment bazaar, pawn their accoutrements, get drunk, quarrel with native shopkeepers, are found absent when their names are called over, and then of course are put under arrest.[88]

The image of Indian *sipahis* before 1857, however, was quite different. Transportation was not used to discipline the black body of the 'native' soldier and levels of flogging were much lower (an average of 1.4 soldiers per regiment of the Bengal Army were flogged between 1829 and 1833).[89] In 1835, flogging as a military punishment in India was repealed altogether but only for Indian *sipahis*, and, even when the punishment was reintroduced in 1845, it was rarely used. So quiescent were *sipahis* seen as being, that, as one British respondent to the Commission investigating military punishments in 1836 put it:

> All European troops have native troops to watch them, and to prevent their going out of their cantonments. There are no European corps without natives attached to them.[90]

Indian soldiers suffered a dramatic reversal in roles after 1857. The legacies of the Mutiny in British colonial governance and control in India are numerous and have been well documented.[91] It has been characterized in the military as a clash between the Punjab lobby demanding a new military order (John Lawrence, Brigadier Neville Chamberlain and Lieutenant Colonel Herbert Edwardes) and the 'gradualist' approach of older India hands.[92] The most important changes to the disciplinary management of *sipahis*, however, were inspired by the enactment of Thomas Babington Macaulay's Indian Penal Code in 1860. Its purpose was not to 'digest any existing system of law'[93] but to entirely deconstruct pre-existing legal systems in India and replace it with a legal corpus that would reflect the particular 'native' mentality of colonial subjects. To that purpose, each definition of an offence was accompanied by 'illustrations' to allow readers unfamiliar with the subcontinent a greater glimpse into the unique aspects of Indian criminality:

> *A* intentionally pulls up a woman's veil. Here *A* intentionally uses force to her; and if he does so without her consent, intending or knowing it to be likely that he may thereby injure, frighten or annoy her, he has used criminal force to her.[94]

> *A* threatens to send club-men to plough up *Z*'s field, unless *Z* will sign and deliver certain produce to *B*, and thereby induce *Z* to sign and deliver the bond. *A* has committed extortion.[95]

And, just as there were uniquely Indian crimes, there were also uniquely Indian punishments. In 1858, Port Blair in the Andaman and Nicobar Islands (situated in the Bay of Bengal) was chosen as the site for a penal colony for the settlement of transported Indian convicts. Transportation had been used as a punishment before. British convicts were regularly transported to the American colonies from the seventeenth century and to Australia from 1786. In India, judges in Calcutta were directed to use the punishment from 1773, and, between 1795 and 1817, Brahmans from Varanasi convicted of capital offences were transported out of fear that executing a twice-born Brahman would lead to civil unrest.[96] But, in transporting convicts to the Andamans, there was no ulterior motive of using forced labour to make the colonial frontier habitable or of avoiding controversy. It was solely to move the troublesome Indian body across the *Kala Pani* – the Black Waters of the Indian Ocean and Bay of Bengal – in order to exploit the danger it posed to the *dharm* of caste Hindus. For Macaulay, the psychological effect of transportation on the 'native' mind was the sole justification for its use:

> It will be seen that throughout the code wherever we have made any offence punishable by transportation, we have provided that the transportation shall be for life. The consideration which has chiefly determined us to retain that mode of punishment is our persuasion that it is regarded by the natives of India, particularly by those who live at a distance from the sea, with peculiar fear. The pain which is caused by punishment is unmixed evil. It is by the terror which it inspires that it produces good; and perhaps no punishment inspires so much terror in proportion to the actual pain which it causes as the punishment of transportation in this country. Prolonged imprisonment may be more painful in the actual endurance; but it is not so much dreaded beforehand; nor does a sentence of imprisonment strike either the offender or the bystanders with so much horror as a sentence beyond what they call the Black Water. The feeling, we believe, arises chiefly from the mystery which overhangs the fate of the transported convict. The separation resembles that which takes place at the moment of death. The criminal is taken for ever from the society of all who are acquainted with him, and conveyed by means of which the natives have but an indistinct notion over an element which they regard with extreme awe, to a distant country of which they know nothing, and from which he is never to return. It is natural that his fate should impress them with a deep feeling of terror.[97]

What was initially intended as a civilian penal code began to be applied to *sipahis*. Within the Indian Penal Code, there was a clear separation of civil and military legal systems, and soldiers would only fall subject to the 'provisions of the code' if the offence was not covered under military law.[98] This was being contravened, however, even as the provisions of the Penal Code came into effect. On 24 April 1858, following the Mutiny, special wartime tribunals busily classified 'all persons convicted . . . as rebel convicts for the purpose of removal to the Andamans' regardless of whether they were soldiers or not.[99] After those special provisions had expired, Macaulay's separation of civil and military law was only partly followed. From 1861, any *sipahi* who committed any civil offence would be tried under military court martial and military jurisprudence.

But, the punishment the *sipahi* would receive was to be taken from the Indian Penal Code:

> 41. Every person subject to this Act who at any place beyond British India, or when on active service in British India, commits any civil offence shall be deemed to be guilty of an offence against military law, and, if charged therewith under this section, shall, subject to the provisions of this Act, be liable to be tried under the same by court-martial, and on conviction to be punished as follows; that is to say,
>
> (a) if the offence is one which would be punishable under the law of British India with death or transportation, he shall be liable to suffer any punishment assigned for offence by the law of British India; and
> (b) in other cases, he shall be viable to suffer any such punishment assigned for the offence by the law of British India, or such punishment as might be awarded to him in pursuance of this Act in respect of an act prejudicial to good order and military discipline.[100]

More importantly, the provisions of the Indian Penal Code inspired a new system of military punishments for *sipahis* in the late nineteenth and twentieth centuries. Soldiers became subject to transportation from 1861 for committing offences in breach of military law. Under the Indian Articles of War and the Indian Army Act, over a third of all listed offences (from the use of 'criminal force' to cowardice) would result in death, transportation, or 14 years' imprisonment unless some mitigating circumstances were provided. As a result, military prisoners furnished a high proportion of the 4,700 transported convicts in the Andamans who were not classified as murderers in 1921 (and perhaps some of the 8,000 who were).[101] The death rate in the Andamans – an average of 37.65% of convicts died per year between 1910 and 1919 – made the penal colony a traumatic place of bereavement even for soldiers who did not share Macaulay's brand of psycho-religious horror.[102] That is certainly the case for *sipahis* in World War I, as evidenced by the letters of Lance Dafadar Mahmud Khan:

> Please God, those men who were sent across the Kala Pani will soon be liberated. Do you also pray Government to deliver them from the misfortune into which they have fallen? I am troubled only at the long separation from you, and because of the calamity which has befallen those of my beloved ones who have been sent to the Kala Pani.[103]

There was another aspect to the punishment of *sipahis* in World War I that was absent from their testimonies. Flogging was reintroduced for the disciplining of *sipahis* just as it was being phased out in the British Army. The use of the lash to discipline the white soldier was severely curtailed in 1854 and 1860, before finally being abolished altogether in 1881. Under Indian military law, the process operated in reverse. The punishment was reintroduced in 1845, included in the 1911 Indian Army Act, and implemented throughout World War I. Douglas Peers and Kaushik Roy have argued that the punishment was not used in peacetime[104] and used then to only punish a handful of crimes 'in which the moral fibre of the army was directly threatened'.[105] The reality was quite different. Under both the Indian Articles of War and the 1911 Indian Army Act, a court martial was empowered to sentence an Indian soldier to 'corporal punishment' for every military offence listed under the Act:

> Article 132 – Any court-martial . . . may sentence any person subject to these Articles below the rank of warrant officer to be dismissed [from] the service; or to suffer corporal punishment not exceeding fifty lashes. . . .[106]

This included the catch-all 'devil's clause' – 'is guilty of any act or omission which, though not specified in this Act, is prejudicial to good order and military discipline'[107] – termed as such by British soldiers because of the frequency with which it was used. For officers presiding over a court martial, flogging was a preferable substitute to imprisonment and/or dismissal, allowing a *sipahi* to return to the ranks after punishment. And, under a court martial, soldiers who wanted to remain in the Army and avoid discharge could request to be flogged in lieu of another punishment. In the majority of cases in which corporal punishment was inflicted, however, soldiers had no input or right to appeal. The lash could be arbitrarily applied at any time by any provost-marshal:

> The provost-marshal may punish, corporally, then and there, any person amenable to these Articles below the rank of non-commissioned officer who, in his view or in the view of any of his assistants, commits any breach of good order and military discipline.[108]

There was no equivalent of the military police in the Indian Army until 1942, and so, the title of provost-marshal could be assumed by any officer 'commanding forces in the field.' In peacetime, George Hamilton, the Secretary of State for India between 1895 and 1903, estimated the number of soldiers of the Indian Army being flogged annually at 'one in two thousand' or one every other battalion.[109] This increased in World War I. No official record was kept but at least one case is known of a *sipahi* being flogged in Mesopotamia,[110] and officers, perhaps inspired by the frequency of the practice in the Indian Army, wrongly administered the punishment among other colonial troops.¹¹¹ *Sipahis* rarely discussed it in their letters. A product, perhaps, of the humiliation of being stripped, laid 'on a triangle', and whipped while their friends and comrades watched:

> The Commanding Officer then says, "Go on; and Drum-Major, see that the drummers do their duty." The Drum-Major gives the time to the drummers, by audibly calling, "One," "Two," "Three" &c., in a slow time.
>
> ... The first stroke of the cat occasions an instantaneous discoloration of the skin from effused blood, the back appearing as if it was strictly sprinkled with strong coffee, even before the second stroke. Sometimes the blood flows copiously by the time the first fifty or 100 lashes are inflicted; at other times, little or no blood appears when 200 lashes have been inflicted. During the first 150 or 200 lashes, a man commonly appears to suffer much, considerably more, indeed, than during the subsequent part of a punishment, however large it may be. . . . Left-handed drummers, whose cats are applied to a portion of sound skin, and drummers who have not been sufficiently drilled to flogging, spread the lashes unnecessarily, and excite an unusual degree of pain. Delinquents frequently call out to the drummer to strike higher, then lower, and sometimes alternately.
>
> ... The low sound mentioned by General Napier, which is heard issuing from the ranks during punishment, sometimes resembles what may be called *sniffing*, (drawing the air strongly up the nose,) and which may be occasioned by an increased flow of tears into the nostrils.¹¹²

An amendment to the Indian Army Act in 1920 abolished flogging in the Army, and the punishment of transportation was abolished in March 1921. Yet, the harsh disciplinary framework for *sipahis* was not altogether undone. Transportation returned in 1925, and corporal punishment remained even if flogging did not. 'Field punishments' replaced the utility of the lash as summary punishments for Indian soldiers. 'Field Punishment No. 1', termed 'crucifixion' by the British soldiers who suffered it in World War I, involved tying a soldier's limbs to a fixed position for several hours, days or even weeks:

> He took me over the poles, which were willow stumps, six to eight inches in diameter and twice the height of a man, and placed me against one of them. It was inclined forward out of perpendicular. Almost always afterwards he picked the same one for me. I stood with my back to it and he tied me to it by the ankles, knees and wrists. He was an expert at the job and he knew how to pull and strain the ropes till they cut into the flesh and completely stopped the circulation. When I was taken off my hands were always black with congested blood. My hands were taken around the pole, tied together and pulled well up it, straining and cramping the muscles and forcing them into an unnatural position. Most knots will slacken

after a little time. His never did. The slope of the post brought me into a hanging position, causing a large part of my weight to come on my arms, and I could get no proper grip with my feet on the ground, as it was worn away round the pole and my toes were consequently much lower than my heels. I was strained so tightly up against the post that I was unable to move body or limbs a fraction of an inch. Earlier in the war men undergoing this form of punishment were tied with their arms outstretched. Hence the name of crucifixion. Later they were more often tied to a single upright, probably to avoid the likeness to a cross. But the name stuck... the mental effect was almost as frightful as the physical. I felt I was going mad.[113]

The punishment was abolished in 1928. In the post-war climate in Britain, the fact that over 60000 British soldiers had been 'crucified', and many of them had been restrained within range of enemy weapons, proved an unpalatable truth. But, in the case of *sipahis*, the punishment continued to be used until the end of the Raj. 'Field Punishment No. 1' had emerged in the British Army as a substitute for flogging: 'the essentials in field punishment are the infliction of physical discomfort and the stimulation of the sense of shame.'[114] And, although the British soldier had evolved beyond his need for such a salutary lesson, the Indian, with his Oriental predilection for crime, clearly had not.

Conclusion: The paternal need to regulate sipahis' speech

Sober and synchronic juridical discourses were a contrasting counterpart to mutable and fluctuating martial fantasies. Except that the military legal discourse in India only ever approached synchrony. Legal Acts, manuals and regulations were never quite perfect and required the accumulation of extra phrases and language. And in that accretion of extra language, colonial military jurisprudence adopted its own contrasting twin. Indian military law began as an undifferentiated replica of British jurisprudence but was soon suffused with colonial paranoia: the desire to first bruise and then soothe the body of the *sipahi*. The spectre of the mutinies of 1857, and the fear of their recurrence, provides a partial answer as to why Indian soldiers had to be provided for more generously and disciplined more harshly than their white peers. But, only if that answer takes into account the colonial (ir)rationality informing the response. It is not enough to explain welfare and discipline in the Indian Army as a reaction to 1857 and/or as a reasoned effort to win the loyalty of the Punjabi peasantry as Tan Tai-Yong and Rajit Mazumdar have argued.[115] Policies of inducement and control endured generations after new recruiting grounds had been secured in Punjab. Attitudes towards class and the insane, the evolution of penology, medical discourses and eugenics all informed and fed the legal apparatus of the Indian Army. And the enactment of military law relied as much upon the caprice of an individual officer, empowered with the ability to hand out summary punishments and benefits, as it did upon an ordered military court or bureaucracy. How are we to reconcile the use of flogging in the Indian Army until 1920 with the care provided for Indian sufferers of war trauma? A study of the rhetoric and register in which military-legal tracts were written provides the germ of a more complete answer. Acts, manuals and regulations operated through the process of accretion, where the old was not discarded but added to with a new subclause, addendum or footnote. As Indian military jurists and officers expanded the body of Indian military law, it was taken further from its British prototype and more closely reflected the peculiar norms of British India. *Sipahis* became the epitome of Kipling's half-savage and half-child, in need of a nurturing, civilizing hand *and* back-of-the-hand-discipline. And, of course, only a white British officer could be properly entrusted to administer it:

> In this army is engendered a special relationship between the British Officers and all who serve under them. The relationship between the British Officers and the Indian Ranks is truly unique. I don't think it is any exaggeration to assert that a sepoy places greater trust in the British Officer than he does in many of his own race.[116]

Discourses of colonial paternalism, of the officer as *ma-bap* and the soldier as child, intruded into the language of legal procedure and then came to be enshrined in Indian military law.

It is military paternalism that fed a will to censor the colonial *sipahis*' voice. From the beginning of World War I, the Indian Army encouraged its soldiers to write home to assuage feelings of anxiety, loneliness and despondency. The Army provided green-coloured, self-sealing letter cards in which soldiers were encouraged to scribble their thoughts once per week. Military officials remarked with some amazement at the numbers of *sipahis* who had learnt to write just so they could pen their own letters.[117] Soldiers keenly requested language primers and newspapers and even took to incorporating French phrases in their prose to add to or cover any gaps in their knowledge of their vernacular: 'Of course people would laugh, but "can en fait rien" [sic]'.[118] For those who remained illiterate or unable to write a full letter, there was an intimate, shared literacy that accompanied asking a friend or acquaintance in the platoon to help pen a letter; a collective literacy of shared language, metaphor and sentiment. By the autumn of 1915, there were up to 50000 letters being written by, to and between Indian soldiers in France every week, and, one would expect, tens of thousands more from *sipahis* in East Africa and the Middle East. During World War I, the first attempts were also made to systematically canvass the opinion of *sipahis* in courts collating evidence for military prosecution, instead of merely questioning Viceroy's Commission and senior NCOs. And, by World War II, this morphed into an elaborate interrogation apparatus. From 1914, sanctioned spaces were created in which Indian soldiers were judged able and empowered to speak. Before that time, *sipahis* testimony had been restricted to the pages of colonialist fantasy (or horror) rather than colonial actuality: of officers and officials presuming to voice the supposedly inarticulable thoughts of their Indian soldiery.

> [The rescue] caused the Squadron Commander to mount the banquette, pat his N.C.O. on the back and congratulate him on the smart way he had carried out his little piece of rescue work.
>
> Had Ram Singh been born with a white skin instead of a brown one, he would have flushed with pride at the Squadron Commander's compliments; as it was he merely felt a slight tingle run through his benumbed body.[119]

But, although *sipahis* were allowed to speak, they were never permitted to speak freely. The decision to allow Indian soldiers to voice their fears and concerns was made to further institutionalize and perfect military paternalism. After Indian soldiers arrived in France in the winter of 1914, their letters were no longer to be censored as they were in British battalions – by an orderly reading out aloud a selection of letters to a junior officer who would then withhold any that betrayed operational details. A special Chief Censor of Indian Mails was appointed whose purpose, with the help of his staff, was to read, analyse, translate and record every letter sent by and to a *sipahi* in the field. At first, this was just for *sipahis* serving in the operational theatre of France, but, by World War II, this more stringent censorship covered *sipahis* wherever they served – from North Africa, Italy and the Mediterranean to Burma, Malaya and the Far East. *Sipahis*' court depositions and interrogations were shaped by the hectoring interjections of courtroom judges and colonial officials, and by the fear of self-incrimination. Each space of speech was created as an intelligence exercise: to monitor disillusionment, enhance prosecutions and, in the case of interrogations during World War II, to discover why Indian Prisoners of War (PWS) had rebelled against the King-Emperor (see Chapter 6). And in the written records of *sipahis*' testimonies there was a constant need to translate even poetic verse into English, because 'native' words could not be trusted to convey the correct meaning unless they were placed in soothing parentheses next to their English equivalent. It is the product of this paternal need to record soldiers' speech that will be analysed throughout the rest of this work. It made possible the prospect of mistranslation and misinterpretation; of censors not being linguistically capable of fully transcribing and translating Indian vernaculars and missing the intended sentiment of the author even if they were. The following chapters will explore this grey area between author and censor, product and intention, of *sipahis* manipulating their speech out of an awareness that it was being misconstrued.

3

The Perils of 'Oriental Correspondence': *Sipahis*, Letters and Writing at the Crossroads

In his play *Translations*, Brian Friel portrayed the disruption caused to a fictional Irish village by British efforts to construct an English-language map and guide of the local area in the early nineteenth century. Act Two starts with a long dialogue between an English Officer, enraptured by the mysterious syllables and sounds of Gaelic names, and his Irish interlocutor, frustrated at how poorly the Irish vernacular fitted into a British sense of space and time:

> Owen: Back to the romance again. All right! Fine! Fine! Look where we've got to. (*He drops on his hands and knees and stabs a finger at the map.*) We've come to this crossroads. Come here and look at it, man! Look at it! And we call that crossroads Tobair Vree. And why do we call it Tobair Vree? I'll tell you why. Tobair means a well. But what does Vree mean? It's a corruption of Brian – (*Gaelic pronunciation*) Brian – an erosion of Tobair Bhriain. Because a hundred-and-fifty years ago there used to be a well there, not at the crossroads, mind you – that would be too simple – but in a field close to the crossroads. And an old man called Brian, whose face was disfigured by an enormous growth, got it into his head that the water in the well was blessed; and every day for seven months he went there and bathed his face in it. But the growth didn't go away; and one month Brian was found drowned in that well. And ever since that crossroads is known as Tobair Vree – even though that well has long since dried up. I know the story because my grandfather told it to me. But ask Doalty – or Maire – or Bridget – even my father – even Manus – why it's called Tobair Vree; and do you think they'll know? I know they don't know. So the question I put to you, Lieutenant, is this: what do we do with a name like that? Do we scrap Tobair Vree altogether and call it – what – The Cross? Crossroads? Or do we keep piety with a man long dead, long forgotten, his name "eroded" beyond all recognition, whose trivial little story nobody in the parish remembers?[1]

Owen's speech was a fictional account, part of an imagined dialogue, but his frustration was shared in World War I by the special military censor appointed to analyse the letters of *sipahis* serving in France. Captain Evelyn Berkeley Howell, the first Chief Censor of Indian Mails, was seconded from the 'Political Department of the Indian Civil Service' and charged with subjecting correspondence sent to soldiers to 'systematic examination' and so preserve the integrity of Indian battalions from the wiles of 'Indian agitators'.[2] But, within a matter of weeks, the aim of his operation had changed. Correspondence sent from soldiers was found to be far more dangerous. Letters sent from the trenches to India had rapidly increased in number and in length and were said to collectively emanate a chill of 'fatalistic resignation' or 'mental disquietude' even when any 'hint of resentment or anti-British feeling' was absent.[3] The censor and his staff tailored their operations to try and better comprehend soldiers' letters. They brokered extra funds, tried to find trustworthy translators for any scripts in which *sipahis* were literate,[4] and strived to convince *La Poste* – the French Postal Service – to redirect to his office in Boulogne any mail that may have been posted by Indians using civilian post offices.[5]

It proved a futile task. Howell soon complained that it was 'far beyond' his 'powers' to examine even a small portion of the total letters passing through his office, let alone analyse them 'in detail'.[6] Letters were passed on without any changes because of the reluctance of British censors to excise letters that may have been 'the last will and testament' of the writer[7] and the difficulty in deciphering the inscrutable nature of Oriental turns of phrase:

> The first extract illustrates how almost impossible it is for any censorship of Oriental correspondence to be effective as a barrier. Orientals excel in the art of conveying information without saying anything definite. When they have a meaning to convey in this way, they are apt to use the phrase "Think this over till you understand it", or some equivalent, to the reader. . . . It naturally follows that the news conveyed is extremely vague, and gives rise to wild rumours.[8]

Howell continued his work until he was replaced in 1916 but without his earlier energy and enthusiasm. His reports bitterly remarked that only a work of history or 'some other book' could make sense of the letters his staff had collated.[9] Howell's advice was heeded in part. When Rudyard Kipling was approached to author propaganda pieces for 'neutrals at home' in the United States of America by Brigadier George Cockerill, Director of Special Intelligence to the British General Staff, he was first handed transcriptions of Indian soldiers' letters, proceeded to read through them, and then promptly decided to write his own fictional versions of the letters as they ought to be.[10] By the 1940s and World War II, deep analyses of *sipahis*' letters and their circulation were kept to a minimum. Extracts of correspondence were to be recorded but kept 'under lock and key' and 'destroyed by fire' when they were of use no longer.[11] Much like the attempts to map the village of Baille Beag in *Translations*, attempts to penetrate the collective psyche of Indian soldiers through their letters were abandoned for a few essentialized truths:

> Manus: And they call you Roland! They both call you Roland!
> Owen: Shhhhh. Isn't it ridiculous? They seem to get it wrong from the very beginning – or else they can't pronounce Owen. I was afraid some of you bastards would laugh.
> Manus: Aren't you going to tell them?
> Owen: Yes – yes – soon – soon.
> Manus: But they...
> Owen: Easy, man, easy. Owen – Roland – what the hell. It's only a name. It's the same me, isn't it? Well, isn't it?[12]

Yet, the similarities between Brian Friel's play and *sipahis*' letters go beyond the frustrations of British colonial officials at deciphering alien languages and unfamiliar registers. When Owen/Roland talks of Brian's Well and asks 'what the hell does Vree mean?',[13] it is a question both of language and of memory. 'Tobair Vree' has a shifting etymology of metaphors, allusions and abbreviations that cannot be encapsulated into a single English name no matter how skilled the linguist. The name has its own history of space, time and forgetting. It exists upon a half-recalled local memory and the imperfect transmission of that memory such that the place retains the name Brian's Well even though the 'well has long since dried up' and few have any idea who Brian was.[14] *Sipahis*' letters also contained their own references to unknown spaces and shared memories. Shared truths and knowledges were often elided over or only tangentially mentioned: 'you will understand what I mean', 'think over what I say'.[15] Each invocation of collective memories and spaces allowed for specific meanings and ideas to be relayed that were only partially decipherable by the censor and partly understandable to the historian. The fact that military letters were conditioned and regulated by the Army, but rarely interrupted and excised, provided a greater incentive for *sipahis* to use only partially interpretable language and concepts. Indian soldiers were aware that their military letters constrained the possibilities of ordinary speech. The length of letters was regulated by the thick blue borders of 'letter cards' or pieces of paper upon which *sipahis*' letters had to be scribbled. Letters were read out and translated by an NCO to an officer, often in front of other men or the letter-writer as a form of regimental censorship. After that, any letters would have to pass through the office of the 'Chief Censor' and were then marked with a censor's stamp. At each stage, the language of *sipahis*' letters was deeply conditioned, but it was precisely those conditions in which letters were written that fostered polysemy. Regimental and supra-regimental censorship forbade the explicit relaying of information and encouraged soldiers to use metaphors, allusions and abbreviations. *Sipahis*' letters, much like Brian's Well, were situated at the crossroads: static yet mutable, censored but indecipherable.

By being at the crossroads, *sipahis*' letters were shaped by the competing colonialist visions of the soldier but were never fully fixed under them. Loyalty, discipline and other aspects of military life were internalized and could be explained by invoking *izzat, dharm* and *shaheed/shahadat*; as part of a duty to one's sex, kin, religion, or to traditions of martyrdom.[16] But, they could also be reasoned as part of a simple economic exchange of labour and contingent on how much material benefit a soldier had accrued: 'First of all you do your duty towards your Emperor of India whose salt you eat, and then you will be a loyal subject when you return to your country, after that you can get your own back. What is the use of firing blank cartridges from France?'[17] Both could occur, as it were, in the same breath. A single soldier could argue in a single letter that loyal service was the result of an innate sense of honour and dependent on how much he had been paid or recompensed. And, although *izzat, dharm, shaheedi* and the salt metaphor approached a colonialist understanding of *sipahis* as martialized body and/or mercenary soldier, it was never fully captured by either half of the colonialist gaze. In that in-between space, letters became instruments that merged imagined wrongs with real grievances, created expectations that the Indian Army was unable or unwilling to fulfill, and mobilized soldiers to realize partly imagined demands.

This chapter will reappraise the censored letters that so disillusioned Howell, were later set aside and re-written, and, in World War II, were marked for destruction: '[They] should be kept under lock and key in suitable custody or destroyed by fire if not required for record.'[18] I will not read the letters as 'hidden transcripts' as James C. Scott once suggested – a readable 'critique of power that was spoken behind the[ir] back'[19] and which had the potential to evolve into overt forms of 'resistance'.[20] In *sipahis*' letters, authorial intent, reception and meaning are uncertain. I am forced to discuss patterns of sentiment, metaphor and tone as much as cold, establishable fact. And, any form of 'resistance' was rarely overt and involved an intimate connection with colonial military discourses. The chapter will begin with an analysis of the register used in soldiers' letters and how its language could act to both affirm and re-interpret the twin identities of colonial *sipahis* established by martial and juridical discourses. Unrealized (and unrealizable) demands and expectations merged into discourses of honour and loyalty. The chapter will end with a discussion of the articulation of three specific demands – of sex, military contracts and support for military families – and the measures taken to realize those unfulfilled expectations during both World Wars.

Re-envisaging the colonial gaze through Asian eyes

Rudyard Kipling wrote his own version of *sipahis*' letters from France that were published in the *The Saturday Evening Post*, an American weekly, between May and June 1917 and then republished in *The Morning Post* in London. The narratives did not carry Kipling's name or any admission as to their provenance until after World War I when the letters were collated and published as works of fiction under the title *The Eyes of Asia*. Kipling even wrote in the occasional Indian word, included phrases in pigeon English and French, and imagined his own bracketed translator's comments next to imperfect translations in order to deepen the mystique. It is only Kipling's private diary and correspondence that reveals the reason why he created his own fictionalized letters. It emerges that he was tasked with writing a propaganda piece by British Military Intelligence as part of an effort to combat any 'seditious' or pro-Indian nationalist sentiment in the United States of America, and was provided with extracts from *sipahis*' real letters as a guide to what soldiers were thinking.[21] Kipling quickly concluded that the letters were a 'complete revelation' and decided to write a propaganda piece that would adopt its form but which would replace its content with his own.[22] The first narrative, 'A Retired Gentleman', begins by exoticizing the manner in which *sipahis* conveyed names and a sense of time and space:

> *From Bishen Singh Saktawat, Subedar Major, 215th Indurgurh (Todd's) Rajputs, now at Lyndhurst, Hampshire, England, this letter is sent to Madhu Singh, Sawant, Risaldar Major (retired) 146th (Dublana) Horse, on his fief which he holds under the Takore Sahib of Pech at Bukani by the River, near Chiturkaira, Kotah, Rajputana, written in the fifth month of the year 1916, English count.*[23]

Racial essentializations and differences were affirmed through Bishen Singh's admiration for British masculinity and wonder at the Britishers' stoic resolve even in grief:

> The nature of the young men of high caste is as the nature of Rajputs. They do not use opium, but they delight in horses, and sport and women, and are perpetually in debt to the moneylender. They shoot partridge and they are forced to ride foxes because there are no wild pigs here. They no nothing of hawking or quail-fighting, but they gamble up to the hilt on all occasions and bear horses laughing. They card-play is called Baraich (Bridge?). They belittle their own and the achievements of their friends, so long as that friend faces them. In his absence they extol his deeds. They are of cheerful countenance. When they jest, they respect honour. It is so also with their women. . . . None of these women lament their dead openly. The eldest son of my Baharanee (Baroness) at the English Hospital where I am made welcome, was slain in battle. The next morning after the news my Baharanee let loose the plate-pianos (turned on the gramophones) for the delectation of the wounded.[24]

Symbols of modernity and 'progress' in Britain cowed Kipling's soldier into wonder and awe, and reflect upon how kindly the British had treated *sipahis* when 'we are not even children beside them'[25]:

> We have been deceived by the nature of the English. They have not at any time shown us anything of their possessions or their performances. We are not even children beside them. They have dealt with us as though they were themselves children talking *chotee boli* (little talk). In this manner the ill-informed have been misled. Nothing is known in India of the great strength of this people. Make that perfectly clear to all fools. . . . There is no reason except the nature of the English that anything in their dominions should stand up which has been ordered to lie down. It is only their soft nature which saves evil from destruction. As the saying is, "We thought it was only an armed horseman. Behold, it is an elephant bearing a tower!"[26]

Until finally Kipling's letter comes to a close with his soldier pliantly accepting his fate as a loyal soldier of the Raj: 'My youth and old age have been given to the service of the Government, and if the Government can be served with the dust of my bones it is theirs.'[27] Kipling's account may be problematic, but it was not wholly wrong. *Sipahis*' actual letters could and did affirm ideals of duty, honour, sacrifice, and British paternalism. What Kipling missed, due to his treatment of *sipahis*' letters as pieces of 'entertainment'[28] or indicative of 'the unaltered India of the present,'[29] was that every utterance affirming a British ideal was coupled with re-interpretations or additions to the corpus of knowledge established by martial and military-legal discourses. These ranged from how soldiers employed the standard genuflection of 'God Save the King' to how soldiers justified their enlistment and continued service as military personnel, to what *sipahis* expected of the officers commanding them. Soldiers' letters in both the World Wars operated at the intersection between a split colonialist gaze, mirroring elements of its form but not all its content.

After Howell had recovered from his initial shock at the obfuscatory nature of 'Oriental correspondence',[30] he tried to anticipate what his superiors wished to read by highlighting letters that 'either express sentiments of loyalty' or were written in such a manner that 'these sentiments may fairly be inferred'.[31] He had a surfeit of letters to choose from. But, many had a double (or even more) meaning(s). This was particularly so when stock phrases such as 'God Bless the King' were used or acts of deference or friendship towards British soldiers were described. An example is contained in a letter written in September 1916 by Jemadar Hasan Shah that recounted a fictional meeting with a dying British soldier in a battlefield in France. The censor concluded that the story Hasan Shah told was indicative of the affection for 'Tommys' that all *sipahis* possessed. The main purpose of the letter, however, seems to have been to use the voice of the British Private to express the fatigue and homesickness that the *sipahi* felt but could not openly admit:

> I was on the battlefield accompanied by a sowar, and came upon a wounded British soldier. "Well friend," I said to him. "How are things with you?" "Quite all right," he replied. "I am proud I was of service in the fight, but I am thirsty." I gave him water to drink and asked if he wanted anything else. "I regret nothing," he said, "except that I shall not meet my sweetheart. She would have nothing to say to me at first but 4 months ago she wrote and said that in the whole world she loved only me and begged me to come to her soon." "My friend," I said to him. "May the All Merciful God satisfy the desire of your heart, and unite you with your beloved." "I am finished," he said. "And when my end comes, my one regret will be that when my love called to me I was unable to go to her." "My friend," I said, weeping with pity. "My own condition is the same as yours."[32]

On another occasion, Sepoy Gurdit Singh transcribed a song in Gurumukhi that he claimed to be a popular soldier's ditty sung at the time. But, the boastful veneration for the King-Emperor articulated at the beginning of the piece became the means to excuse the hint that all was not well with the Indian soldiery at the end:

> The King of England wired to us "You must go tonight
> Valiant men of India, you must know how to fight
> Take the Eepree [Ypres] trenches, take Hill Sixty-two,
> Let Lahore Division show what it can do!"
> Off we march as quickly as our feet can go!
> See us in the morning opposite the foe!
> Fix up our machine gun! But we may run away!
> All alone it can eat up a regiment a day![33]

Finally, in a letter intercepted from Amir Khan, a *sipahi* of the 129th Baluchis on 15 March 1915, two pieces of paper were found. One contained the words: 'I am not wounded and hope that all will be well. There is no other hardship. . . . I speak with certainty, our King – God Bless Him – is going to win and will win soon'.[34] Another piece of paper that was concealed in the folds of the one on top contained a dramatically different narrative:

> God knows whether the land of France is stained with sin or whether the Day of Judgement has begun in France. For guns and of rifles there is now a deluge, bodies upon bodies, and blood flowing. God preserve us, [from] what has come to pass. From dawn to dark and from dark to dawn it goes on like the hail that fell at Swarra Camp. . . . God grant us grace, for grace is needed. Oh God, we repent, oh God, we repent.[35]

Ideals of *izzat, dharm, shaheedi* were widely invoked and widely expressed in *sipahis*' letters from both World War I and World War II. Military honour, links between caste and military service, and military/religious martyrdom existed in various forms and in various communities and were well established before colonialism. Each was, however, heightened under imperial rule and the colonial fascination with the fully martialized soldier. For example, in 1897, during low-intensity fighting with Afghan and Pathan peoples in Malakand (the northern part of present-day Khyber-Pakhtunkhwa in Pakistan), what was initially described as a 'very gallant' if futile 'resistance' of 23 Sikh *sipahis* against 'wild-spirited' Afridi and Orakzai Pathans[36] was carefully cultivated into an elaborate myth. The soldiers, who had all died, were said to have faced odds of 10000 Afghans and had slain at least 180 of them, posthumous medals were awarded, each Sikh regiment was ordered to honour 12th September as 'Saragarhi Day', and a plaque was erected at the holiest of Sikh shrines inside the walls of the Golden Temple complex in Amritsar:

> The Government of India have caused this tablet to be erected to the memory of the twenty one non-commissioned officers and men of the 36 Sikh Regiment of the Bengal Infantry whose names are engraved below as a perpetual record of the heroism shown by these gallant soldiers who died at their posts in the defence of the fort of Saragarhi, on the 12 September 1897, fighting against overwhelming numbers, thus proving their loyalty and devotion to their sovereign, the Queen Empress of India, and gloriously maintaining the reputation of the Sikhs for unflinching courage on the field of battle.[37]

But, the nature of warfare in World War I and World War II dispelled cherished colonial fantasies; or at least it did for Indian soldiers. The reality of modern warfare, consisting of the trenches of France or British reverses in North Africa, differed dramatically from how soldiers had been trained or instructed to envisage fighting. An Indian soldier in Egypt in October 1942 expressed his surprise that a war could last for over 2 years and that every day he had to 'work, work, and [do] more work',[38] and a Sikh soldier writing from Flanders in October 1915 lamented his fate for being in a war where he could die without even seeing his enemy:

> What you say in your letter about not being disloyal to the Emperor, and it being the religion of Sikhs to die facing the foe – all that you say is true. But if only you yourself could be here and see for yourself! Any shriveled charas-sodden fellow can fire at us and kill a score of us at our food in our kitchen. . . . There is no fighting face to face. Guns massacre regiments ten miles off. Put swords or pikes or staves in our hands, and the enemy against us with like arms, then indeed we shall show you how to fight! But if no one faces us what can we do? No one stands up to fight us. Everyone sits in a burrow underground. They fight in the sky, on the sea in battleships, under the earth in mines. My friend, a man who fights upon the ground can barely escape. You tell us to fight face to face to the foe. Die we must – but alas not facing the foe![39]

The fact that *sipahis* were never safe from harm, in spite of how brave or cautious they were, led to many soldiers questioning their continued service in the Army, as in the case of Khilullah, a *sowar* attached to the 2nd Lancers:

> I am sick to death of this Military life, and I wish to ask your advice. If I return alive from this war I shall certainly take my discharge and I want your advice as to what sort of work I should take up. My wish is to enter the Forest Department. Do

not speak of the matter to my father or to any one among my relatives. My father is not conversant with the times. He thinks service in the Army to be the best and most honourable; but those times are gone when honour was shown in the Army. Nowadays the Army is without honour. Perhaps in 40 or 50 years such a time will return when the Army will enjoy honour; now it has none.[40]

Ideals of *izzat, dharm* and *shaheedi* became mediums through which soldiers expressed grievances, rather than satisfaction, with military life. It is not surprising that this was so, particularly during World War I, given the nightmarish, steampunk nature of fighting during the conflict: of cavalry troopers armed with a lance and side-arm being pushed into combat next to a trundling tank and of infantrymen having to fix bayonets while being machine-gunned.

A similar inhabitation and twisting of military rhetoric occurred when soldiers discussed pay, promotion and the slew of additional benefits that were made available through Indian military law and regulations. The Indian Army created an appetite for irregular payments and less measurable forms of patronage (see Chapter 2) but did not legislate for perceptions of military service as a temporary phase in *sipahis* lives; that it was conduit for social advancement and enduring patronage that would lead to other forms of employment. Most *sipahis* did not intend to see out their lives as soldiers. The monetary reward of loyal military service was always an attraction for new recruits through World War I and World War II. On 8 November 1917, Nur Zaman Khan of 36th Jacob's Horse wrote home to his five unemployed brothers demanding that they should all enlist to secure the 'precious prize' of 'a bonus of Rs. 50'.[41] Soldiers throughout the two World Wars echoed Nur Zaman's call. War bonuses, bounties and the relaxing of physical fitness requirements made military service attractive for individuals who had previously been disbarred or had not thought about it as a career.[42] But, even when soldiers were acting in pursuit of monetary gain, the greater attraction to military service was that it was seen as a stepping stone between one form of employment and a better opportunity in the future:

> I am at present doing honorary [unpaid] work in one of the local camps for the orphans but the moment I find a fit young man from the locality to take my place in the camp, I would leave the orphans for a time and follow you into the army. My aim in joining the army is to ensure a steady monthly income back to camp. Many of the locality are of the same mind as I am.[43]

Once in the Army, soldiers sought and wrote voluminously about securing promotion. *Sipahis* assumed that promotion was their due after a few years of loyal service, even though the space for extra NCOs in an Indian battalion was more limited than that in the British Army (due to the existence of Viceroy's Commissions (VCOs)). *Sipahis* viewed promotion as having advantages for social networks beyond the Army. In the cases of Atta Mohamed of Patiala State and Fakir Mohamed of Shankargarh in NWFP, it would result in higher status brides and presumably bigger dowries for themselves and their families.[44] For others, promotion was a vehicle for securing government pensions and land grants. This applied even if they did not hail from a region where such grants were on offer, such as in the case of Rahman, a Pathan of 57th Afridis (Wilde's Rifles):

> You should tell the Doctor you got ill through carrying ammunition boxes from the support trenches to the firing line. That will probably get you a [higher] pension, and if so it will be an excellent thing. . . . Say that it was lifting the support boxes to the firing line that made you ill – that should certainly get you a higher pension. . . .[45]

It was also a means of ensuring that the apparatus of the Indian Army would care for their families. Obtaining a promotion allowed for a higher amount of a soldier's wage to be transferred in family remittances and was perceived as offering a guarantee that extra provisions over and above this would be made in emergencies:

> You have written to state that brother's family allotment has been stopped. I will approach the higher authorities to try to find out if the family allotments of all the prisoners of war have been stopped, and if so why. Is this the reward for services rendered to the Government by men who have joined the Army to sacrifice their lives? Is this the way to recognize their services, that, if at some time they unfortunately fall into the hands of the enemy, they are deprived of the little support their relatives have in the shape of family allotments? What will happen to their families? How will their wives and children feed themselves if in utter disregard of their services their family allotments are stopped? When a prisoner who is in the hands of the enemy comes to know that whatever little his wife and children are getting has been stopped, hatred and dislike will naturally arise in his heart against his Government. I am at a loss to understand how the families of soldiers manage to feed themselves when the rate of wheat in India is Rs. 15/- per maund and especially when these few rupees of a/c [sic] of family allotment are also stopped. . . . Must they fill their stomachs with bricks and stones? May God spare even the enemy from experiencing such a state! . . . By such deeds neither the Government nor the country or Nation are benefited![46]

Finally, with the opening of the Indian Military Academy at Dehradun in 1932 and the 'Indianization' of the Officer Corps of the Indian Army, promotion at a young age to the rank of an NCO or VCO opened the possibility of being selected for officer training. It was an attractive prospect even if it could lead to social ostracization from the men you had previously been comrades with, as in the case of Gurbaksh Singh Dhillon who was first a *sipahi* in the 14th Punjabis, rose to become a Lieutenant in the 14th Punjabis, and then became a Colonel in the Indian National Army:

> At that time my father received a letter from his friend and previous superior officer Captain J. F. L. Taylor. At the moment I could little guess how momentous that letter was going to be in my life. Taylor proposed that I should join the Indian Army as a combatant in the lowest rank of a sepoy. I was advised to improve my educational standard and general knowledge. I should work hard and strive to be selected for the I.M.A. (Indian Military Academy), Dehra Dun. If successful, I would become an I.C.O. (Indian Commissioned Officer) starting in the rank of 2nd Lieutenant in His Majesty's Indian Land Forces.[47]
>
> ... After seeing my father off as I entered the barrack, Mohan Singh shouted, "Yesterday you asked me where your 'seat' was. How dare you use an English word: Couldn't you say *charpoy*? Don't be proud of your education. My *ustad* used to be very strict with me, and I am going to see that I am with you stricter than he was with me. I understand that you have come here to go to Dehra Dun?" I had just uttered, "Yes Naik" that [sic.] Mohan Singh cried out, "Say Havildar Sahib, this is how a Naik is addressed by a junior. You are just a recruit. Don't forget I am your Platoon Havildar. You shall have to obey all my orders. As you are the only recruit in the Platoon I will see that you keep the barrack clean other-wise I may have to derail your train leading to Dehra Dun!" (*Tumhari Dehra Dun wali gari ulta doonga!*)[48]

And, when promotion was not to be had, first complaints were issued[49] and then soldiers advised one another to leave military service and look for another form of employment:

> If for any reason you are passed over [for promotion], first make a representation and then make endeavours to return.[50]

Sipahis' discussions and writing about the purpose and conduct of their officers, whether British or Indian, went further than the simple habitation and distension of colonial military rhetoric. Soldierly adjuncts were made that went over and above army regulations or discourses of paternalism. Part of the reason was that a code for the correct conduct of officers was only vaguely defined in the corpus of military law and regulations. According to the *Army Regulations, India*, the duties of a British 'unit commander' of the rank of Second Lieutenant or above was defined as

> the training, administration, health, maintenance of discipline, efficiency, and the state of the accounts in the unit under his command. . . . he will supervise and control all duties performed by those under his command. He is responsible for the security of buildings, armaments, equipment or other stores in the[ir] charge, and that they are complete, serviceable, and in accordance with the latest pattern. . . . It is the duty of every unit commander to see that no officer, soldier, follower or civilian employee who is unfit to perform his duties is retained in the service. He is responsible that all orders published by superior authority are communicated to those under his command whom they may concern. He is responsible that the rules for the handling of explosives . . . are strictly adhered to.[51]

In addition to this purely mechanical role was the cultivation of the idea that the British Sahib would act trusted confident, parental figure and teacher to the Indian soldiery under his command. This notion, however, was never fully defined and could vary widely from British officers seeing it as their duty to provide extra clothing and equipment,[52] to more stilted 'pep talks':

> At that moment, wonder of all wonders, Captain Owen came up to their compartment like a fashionable young yokel jumping to the footboard of a train.
> "*Acha hai* sepoy *log*? Not far now – the destination!"
> "God may sweeten your mouth for saying so, *Huzoor*," said Kirpu. "Come in and grace us with your company."
> Captain Owen smiled his gracious, shy smile, but did not enter.
> All the sepoys turned to him with respect, arranging themselves the while.
> "Don't move, as you were," said Owen Sahib.
> "This is like going to war on the frontier, *Huzoor*," said Havildar Lachman Singh, referring to the comradeship that was reflected in the Sahib's visit, for he recalled how the British officers of the 69th had once shared the same lorries with the sepoys in Waziristan.
> The Adjutant moved his head, then flushed and, shading his mouth shouted:
> "Yes. *Jung!*" And he made a gesture of despair.
> But his words were being smothered by the shrieking of the brakes, and, for a moment, he closed his eyes, and contracted his face. Then he said: "Too much traffic near the front."
> "Come inside, *Huzoor*," Kirpu said.
> "*Sab acha?*" said the Sahib and, jumping down, walked towards his compartment.[53]

Little emphasis was placed on ensuring that officers behaved in a fair and impartial manner to their men; the expectation that Britishers would live up to the fabled public school/cricketing ethos of fair play,[54] even though that was exactly what *sipahis* came to expect of their British officers. In the 98th Goods and Provisions Transport Company of the RIASC, for example, a British Major and a Captain were furiously arraigned in soldiers' letters. They were criticized for bringing up men on charges 'without sufficient cause' after demanding that they show 'undue servility'[55]; for repeatedly placing the same men on charges even after they had been cleared by a military tribunal[56] and for promoting others without regard for their seniority in the Company.[57] Soldiers viewed their British officers as more than just military personnel but as physical embodiments of the colonial government of India. They were expected to hear and offer redress to soldiers' petitions and pass on to higher authorities those to which they could not directly respond. These petitions ranged from simple demands for higher pay and extra food allowances for wounded men[58] to simple requests for leave:

> We have all of us given a Memorial, that is a petition to the honoured and exalted Viceroy of India, that, "Whereas we have been separated so long from our homes and children and our relatives and have been compelled to adapt ourselves to new methods of life, to which we were altogether unaccustomed, to save the exalted government in a cold country without any leave etc., and whereas we Indians are so circumstanced and conditioned that we cannot remain abroad for very long, etc., etc., therefore, as an act of grace, let other men be quickly brought in our place, so that we may be able to remove those misfortunes which have sprung up in our absence and may be expected to increase so long as we remain away."[59]

'Native' Indian officers holding a VCO and those Indians who were permitted to serve as fully commissioned officers after 1920 (KCIOs or ICOs)[60] had demands made of them that differed in type from those made of their British counterparts. The regulations of the Indian Army viewed the task of the Indian officer as the confidant of the (British) commander: 'responsible for keeping him acquainted with every occurrence, circumstance, or condition among the native ranks'.[61] *Sipahis*, on the other hand, expected the ideal Indian superior to be the confidant of the men and to be in full sympathy with all their hardships. Soldiers would write long eulogies of Indian officers who had been killed if, as in the case of Subedar Gul Mohamed Khan of the 69th Punjabis, they had become renowned for the kindness they had shown towards young soldiers:

> The Subedar has been killed. We are all very sorry, but his day had come. . . . He had been known in the regiment as "Khan Bahadur" and the Subedar Gul Mohamed Khan showed himself [to be] a pattern of valour. . . . He was ever on the look-out for the fainthearted, and if he heard anywhere of a young man who was troubled in mind he went to him and talked to him in such a way that all his discomforts of exile and homesickness faded away.⁶²

On occasions where Indian officers were found to have sided with the British *Sahibs* against their men, the language used to describe them transformed dramatically. Behari Lal wrote of the 'Indian Lieutenants' that were in his section as being akin to the '*dhobi's* dog "belonging neither to the home nor the washing place"' (*dhobi ka kutta; na ghar ka na ghat ka*) for deigning it beneath themselves to eat alongside their fellow Indians.⁶³ And Signaller Sher Khan wrote with undisguised glee of the social ostracization to which he had subjected a Risaldar:

> He [the Risaldar] is such an evilly disposed man that even here in the place of death, he practices his evil designs. I expect to return soon, and I expect too that the Risaldar Sahib will remember me till his dying day. The rest of the regiment are with me and he wanders alone like a mad dog. Lal Khan tells me that the Risaldar Sahib now asks for pardon saying "it is a mistake, it is proper that you excuse [me]" but I will never utter words of pardon. . . . Everything from A to Z has been reported to the [British] *Sahibs* and everything has been proved. . . . I showed him up properly.⁶⁴

What was common to both Indian and British officers was that they were expected to lead by example and be as hardy and brave as the men they commanded. It was with undisguised disdain that men such as Rifleman Gokul Singh Rawat wrote of his VCOs who had 'defecated in their *dhotis* through sheer fright', 'melted' their 'livers' through drink, and had consequently given 'their men a bad name'.⁶⁵ This was the case even though, as was likely, the individual was suffering from forms of war neuroses that Indian soldiers had previously witnessed among their own comrades (see Chapter 2). In other words, Indian officers were expected to be more resolute. Nur Mohamed Khan, of a Signal Company in France in October 1916, not only wrote disparagingly of his Jemadar but also wrote approvingly of the efforts his comrades had taken to remove him from command:

> The next day there was a march and three or four horses dropped their shoes. [Jemadar] Lal Khan then thought it was all over with him and got fever through fright and was taken to hospital. He was screaming and crying and the patients were astonished at the sight of this new arrival with his pale face and hair turned white. He said he was dying. The next day the patients all said to the doctor sahib "Either take this man away or remove us from the hospital." He was eventually sent back to India as unfit for service.[66]

A similar series of disparaging remarks were made of British officers who were condemned for refusing to put themselves in harm's way in a battlefield or for 'running away' to England whenever their 'attraction to home' grew 'too great'[67]: 'The brave English have evolved such a rule as is advantageous to them. The red pepper is little used while the black pepper is used daily to the extent of at least a thousand *maunds*. From this there is a great advantage to the [English] troops. I can't write any more.'[68] These could evolve into a grander critiques of all *Angrezis* or 'whites' if, as in the case of Yusuf Khan in October 1915, soldiers had an opportunity to visit the colonial metropole and saw that many British men displayed a reluctance to enlist or fight (the Derby Scheme was announced on 21 October, which encouraged men to register their name under the promise that they would only be called up if necessary)[69]:

> The news is that the white men here have refused to enlist, declaring that the German Emperor is their King no less than is the King of England. An Indian black man went off to preach to them. He asked them if they were not ashamed to see us come from India to help the King while they, who were of the same race, were refusing to fight for him. But really the way these whites are behaving is a scandal. Those who have already enlisted have mutinied.[70]

There was a difference between the roles delineated for soldiers and how soldiers reasoned their own service through their letters. This is evident from the language *sipahis* used, the perceived benefits they expected to accrue as enlisted men, and the expectations they had of the officers commanding them. Yet, soldierly views of service did not amount to rejections of the views put forth by officials in the Indian Army, but rather as *habitations* of them and *adjuncts* to them – occupying a discursive space, taking it outwith its initial context and applying it in ways in which they were not supposed to be applied. This was as true in the understanding of *izzat*, *dharm* or *shaheedi* as it was with colonial patronage and in expectations *sipahis* had for those in command. Rudyard Kipling, in drafting his own versions of *sipahis'* letters, was correct in labelling them as *The Eyes of Asia. Sipahis'* letters did involve a re-imagining of colonial discourses, even if their subtleties were poorly reflected in Kipling's volume. But, letters could do more than just re-envisage a colonial gaze. When soldiers' expectations were not realized, the letter became an agent of discord and protest within the military. It is to those instances that I will now turn.

'Eating sweetmeats' in Brighton: Traversing sexual frontiers and the Kitchener Indian Hospital

A month after an Indian military hospital was established in the former Workhouse in Brighton in January 1915, the largest of several in the area,[71] Colonel Sir Bruce Seton was appointed as its commander.[72] Seton immediately set about rectifying what he deemed to be vices prevalent among the Indian soldiers under his care:

> It was evident from the very first that drink and the sex problem were factors which would have to be reckoned with. A large proportion of the followers, the sweepings of Bombay City, were to be found to be habitual drunkards; and the ill-advised conduct of the women in the town, though partly innocent in intention, was bound to result in the gravest scandals. To deal with these problems it was necessary to draw up absolutely inflexible rules governing the granting of permission for passes outside the precincts.[73]

Seton prefigured the fear that Ann Laura Stoler has characterized as *'métissage'*: the 'threat to white prestige', 'European degeneracy and moral decay' implicit in the sexual mixing of the colonizer's body with that of the colonized.[74] Unsurprisingly, the measures Seton took to prevent sexual liaisons between Indian men and British women at the Kitchener Indian Hospital, as the establishment came to be known, were met with disapproval and anger by the *sipahis* concerned. In the letters written by Indian wounded and hospital staff, concerns were expressed that their officers were overstepping the bounds of legitimate authority; parallels were drawn with the maltreatment of Indian soldiers elsewhere; and forms of protest were enacted to force Seton into a rethink.

The colonial body in Britain during both World Wars became a troubling mixture of desire, envy and revulsion. As Richard Smith has argued, the broadening of recruiting practices beyond regular soldiers and reservists in Britain brought about a crisis of white masculinity. It arose in the context of the sudden prevalence of psychiatric disorders among soldiers (see Chapter 2), the constant necessity to relax requirements for military service because of the poor health and stature of British men,[75] and a well-established Eugenics movement warning of the fear of racial degeneration:

> The average physique was good enough, but the total included an astonishing number of men whose narrow and misshapen chests, and other deformities or defects, unfitted them to stay the more exacting requirements of service in the field. . . . Route marching, not routine tours of trench duty, made recurring casualties of these men.[76]

The colonial soldier offered a striking contrast, whether it was the 'magnificently proportioned' Caribbean soldiers,[77] Black GIs in Britain during World War II – 'Honey you should see how the "old women" like to go around with negroes here. Perhaps they like to go around with them because they have immense Penises'[78] – or the 'beautiful' men of India:

> Friday, October 30th, Boulogne. – While we were at Nieppe, after passing Bailleul, a German aeroplane dropped a bomb on Bailleul. After filling up at Nieppe we went back to Bailleul and took up 238 Indians, mostly with smashed left arms from a machine gun that caught them in the act of firing over a trench. They are nearly all 47th Sikhs, perfect lambs: they hold up their wounded hands and arms like babies for you to see, and insist on having them dressed whether they've been done or not. They behave like gentlemen, and salaam after you've done them. They have masses of long, fine, dark hair under their turbans done up with yellow combs, glorious teeth, and melting dark eyes. One died. The younger boys have beautiful, classic Italian faces, and the rest have fierce black beards curling over their ears.[79]

The colonized body became the site of sexual fantasy and consensual sex. But, in both conflicts, this was not without its consequences. Prosecutions and less formalized violence against Black American soldiers was the subject of Graham Smith's seminal work *When Jim Crow Met John Bull*, Richard Smith has documented some of the racist attacks of interracial couples that occurred in London and elsewhere from 1917 to 1919,[80] and the BBC created a recent television series examining the official horror in Britain at the presence of the 'half-caste' child in its port cities.[81] Indian *sipahis* also shared in this tale of sexual success and official frustration.

In the case of Indian soldiers, British military authorities took pre-emptive action to try and segregate Indian men from white women. British nurses were barred from attending to wounded Indian military personnel, with the exceptions being Lady Hardinge Hospital at Brockenhurst in Hampshire, which was the only hospital funded by a private charity (the Indian Soldiers' Fund under the auspices of the Order of St John of Jerusalem), and a handful of female nurses who served in hospitals in France. Commanding officers of Indian battalions and hospitals in Europe forbade any interracial marriages, even without official prompting, and resisted French attempts to relax the restriction until the autumn of 1916. But, in spite of these efforts to limit contact, encounters with European women and Indian men were common. A large number of soldiers' letters referred to European *mems* of all backgrounds. Wealthy French spinsters and widowers were portrayed as desperate to secure the 'carnal pleasure' of *sipahis* – Sikhs and men of the Service Corps apparently earned as much as '6, 7 or 8 francs' a time[82] – or as matronly figures showing platonic concern:

> My mother, like you this French mother does all she can for my comfort and thinks much of me. I cannot write sufficiently in praise of what she does for me. If on any day, by reason of the press of work, I do not return till evening, the people of the house come in search of me and complain about me being absent for so long. At the time when I was away and could not find time to write either to you or her she came close to the place where I was and where no one is permitted to come, and asked to see her boy, and brought with her a hamper of things to eat. What more can I say about the concern she has for my welfare?[83]

Sex workers were written about voluminously. Jai Singh relayed at length his intention to journey into the 'fairylands' of Paris and his plan to spend 'Rs. 250 in four days',[84] and others commented on the easy sexual gratification available outside their hospital grounds or on the streets of English towns:

> English girls are very free in their nature and they love Indians very much. . . . Lovemaking and breathing in Europe is nothing but a matter of choice, friends are plenty when purse is full.[85]

And more 'virtuous' girls of marriageable age made their way into soldiers' narratives. Many *sipahis* indicated that they were in consensual relationships with one or, in the case of Abdul Jaffar Khan, two Frenchwomen by 1915.[86] Others commented on their desire to wed the English '*mems*' that they had met:

> I am sick, but there is nothing the matter with me, nor am I wounded. . . . Tell [censored] not to be anxious about me, for when I come back I will bring him a

lovely girl to marry such as he could not find among all the Mahsuds. If the war comes to an end I will bring you a "mem" from England. So do not be distressed, but pray always, for safety is difficult.[87]

Thus, not only did soldiers partake in sexual relationships with European women but also the issue of these trans-colonial liaisons formed a large part of their correspondence. Europe was reimagined as orgiastic phantasmagoria for the colonized soldier.

For some *sipahis*, the sexual contact spurred deeper thoughts. It became a conduit through which they could question what it was that made them, as Indians, different from their white counterparts. One hospital worker began his letter in wonder of European sexual liberation and pleasure in extramartial affairs – '[she said] it does not matter how poor you may be I am quite ready to lie openly with you'.[88] This prompted him to ponder why it was that these consensual relationships involving Indian *sipahis* were condemned and frowned upon by their officers when similar liaisons involving British soldiers did not receive the same treatment.[89] Mithan Lal, a storekeeper at the Kitchener Indian Hospital, wrote of the contrast between the freedoms given to the English populace of Brighton to the freedoms denied Indians at the hospital. Mithan went on to compare the life of *sipahis* in hospital to that of the political prisoners and convicts in the penal colonies of the Andaman Islands: 'Convicts in India are sent to the Andaman Islands; but we have found our convict station here in England. Tell me, how are they treated?'[90] Finally, Ram Jawan Singh, a wounded soldier at Brighton, unfavourably compared the treatment of Indian soldiers in Britain to how the French treated their 'Algerian subjects':

I believe that you must have got my previous letter to this. When you send a reply to that, please note that you should inform me about the treatment of the French Republic towards its Algerian subjects or fellow-citizens [or] whatever you like to call them. . . . First, how are they kept? Whether they are allowed to go out to the town when off duty without any guard to look after them, which means a sort of generous trust placed in their characters and good conduct [. . . and] which also means a liberal treatment of the matter and not snatching away the rights and privileges of good ones for the faults of the bad [and] where a cool judgement is needed to draw a wise line [sic]. Second, what pay do they get under the French Republic? Is it what the French soldiers receive or with some differences and why? What uniform are they given? I think that in the matter of uniform there will be some distinction . . . which too in my humble opinion [there] should not be when fighting under the same French flag.[91]

It may not quite have amounted to a *Fanoniste* moment – the claiming of a 'white whiteness through the caressing of a white breast'[92] – but there was a tentative questioning of colonial truths that accompanied the more carnal side of *métissage* at Brighton.

It was the ideas and assumptions engendered by trans-colonial liaisons that were seen to be the most dangerous aspects of interracial relationships: it was 'detrimental to the prestige and spirit of European rule'.[93] Seton did not just stop at barring Indian personnel from leaving the hospital grounds[94] – with the exception of VCOs and hospital staff who could leave if granted a pass. He ordered 'barbed wire palings' to be erected on the walls surrounding the hospital. (British) Military Police guards were stationed around the perimeter of the hospital in order to prevent 'cases of "breaking out"'[95] and ordered to punish soldiers breaking the rules with a 'dozen lashes'.[96] Measures were introduced to prevent visits to and from neighbouring military hospitals,[97] and rations for patients were cut, to the extent that one soldier claimed that he only received '2 *chataks* of *ata* [flour]' per day and 'those who eat sugar do not get milk, or ghee'.[98] Finally, limits were imposed on how many of the seriously wounded at the hospital would be invalided back to India or transferred elsewhere out of suspicion that soldiers would feign illness to escape Seton's measures.[99] *Métissage* in all its forms – from sexual encounters to the exchanging of ideas – had to be prevented at the Kitchener Indian Hospital, and stringent measures were taken in order to suppress it.

It resulted in an almost immediate response from soldiers unwilling to accept this new draconian regime. These ranged from attempts to sneak past the guards posted at the hospital grounds in the dead of night to *sipahis* endeavouring to arrange their transfer to other hospitals.[100] One particular instance of dissent is noteworthy, involving Sub-Assistant Surgeon Jagu Godbole, both because it is referred to in several soldiers' letters[101] and because, after his arrest and conviction, the man in question was unafraid to outline his reasons for committing the crime. Jagu wrote a series of letters to his father on the 14, 16 and 19 December 1915. They all began with the hospital worker questioning the view aired by his parents and teachers in Bombay that 'our morality is higher than the morality of the English'[102] because, for Jagu, it led to the denial of bodily desires:

> It is natural that our minds should lean towards those we love, and the English song ["It's a long way to Tipperary"] brings out this feeling. Among us we would immediately say, "What a fool you are, to thus take the name of women when

going to war, instead of naming God. Owing to this fear, in place of saying the words 'sweetest girl' we should say the name of Pandurang or some other god. Thus, while actually thinking of our women we will make pretence and put into our song the name of a god. How can this be looked on as moral?[103]

While Jagu expressed his admiration for the greater sexual freedoms found in England in his letters, however, he went on to describe how the permissive atmosphere of Brighton had changed for the worse:

The same forces are, however, in operation, notwithstanding what I have said, in England, which is following in the footsteps of India. I meet many people here, and old men and women say to me "Do whatever you like, but do not approach any girls". They must be doing the same thing to their own people. . . .[104]

It is this perceived change that Jagu used to justify his crime – the attempted murder of Colonel Seton – for which he received 'seven years' rigorous imprisonment'[105]:

Now, please listen to what I have to say carefully. I have committed a great crime. Notwithstanding the fact that *lakhs* of Hindus are dying for the sake of England, they have not been allowed to go about here freely. This very ungratefulness I have been unable to bear. So one day taking a pistol I went to kill the Colonel and was caught, and have been in imprisonment for the last month. . . . If I get off well and good; if not, I will live the life of an ascetic. Do not be anxious and do not look for any letters, and do not write to me.[106]

Jagu's example inspired others. Although the majority of those at the Kitchener hospital did not attempt anything as dramatic as the assassination of Seton, a series of collective but anonymous petitions appeared to the King-Emperor and the Viceroy of India. They were embedded in *sipahis*' correspondence and written in order to inform 'the public of England' that 'the military authorities in charge of our hospital are not treating us as they ought to have done'.[107] As time went on, these petitions appeared to grow in size and number as they captured the mood of wounded soldiers treated elsewhere and motivated them to create joint petitions with their fellow *sipahis* in Brighton, such as that of April 1915:

From [the] Indian Sick in Hospital "Barton" [in Milford-on-Sea]
 To the Emperor of India, England, from the sick of whose Petition this is that no British Officer nor Indian Doctor cares for us. They deal hardly with the sick.

The British Doctor beats the sick. . . . Let the King, God bless him, understand more than a little of what is written. Your Majesty's order was that a man who had been wounded once should be allowed to return to India or that if he is recovered he should not be made to serve again. The heart of India is broken because they inflict suffering on the sick. Blessed King what can I say? There is nothing worth describing. We do not get new clothes. In the morning only . . . tea, at ten o'clock a *chapatti* and a spoonful of *dal*. In 24 hours 5 cigarettes. In the evening the *chapattis* are half-baked and there is no meat. No sick man gets well fed. The Indians have given their lives for 11 rupees. Any man who comes here wounded is returned thrice and four times to the trenches. Only that man goes to India who has lost an arm or a leg or an eye.

Indian School Hospital. Sections A, B, C, D, E.[108]

Some of the men who admitted drafting 'applications' or 'memorials' in their correspondence, such as Ram Jawan Singh, regarded this activity as only the first stage in their protests. He and others were prepared to 'move on further if we do not find any satisfactory reply.'[109] While there is no evidence that the *sipahis* at Brighton did 'move on further' before the hospital was closed some months later in December 1915, what did occur at the Kitchener does nonetheless show how differing attitudes towards *métissage* in the military created discontent both for individuals such as Jagu Godbole and for Indian patients as a whole.

'What you've all got to go through for the Emperor': 'Contracts', self-mutilation and malingering during World War I

Shortly after World War I, Jaroslav Hašek began to recount his own experiences as a Czech soldier in the Austro-Hungarian Army during the conflict through the prism of the 'good soldier' Švejk. He devoted a lengthy passage in his work to Švejk's experiences in a military prison after he was accused of malingering:

On reaching the military prison, Schweik was placed in the hut used as an infirmary which contained several of the faint-hearted malingerers.

On the bed by the door a consumptive was dying, wrapped up in a sheet soaked with cold water.

"That's the third this week," remarked Schweik's right-hand neighbour. "And what's wrong with you?"

"I've got rheumatism," replied Schweik, whereupon there was hearty laughter from all those around about him. Even the dying consumptive, who was pretending to have tuberculosis laughed.

"It's no good coming here with rheumatism," said a stout man to Schweik in solemn tones, "rheumatism here stands about as much chance as corns."

"The best thing to do," said one of the malingerers, "is to sham madness."

... "That's nothing," said another man. "Down our way there's a midwife who for twenty crowns can dislocate your foot so nicely that you're crippled for the rest of your life."

... "My illness has run me into more than two hundred crowns already," announced his neighbour, a man as thin as a rake. "I bet there's no poison you can mention that I haven't taken. I'm simply full of poison. I've choked arsenic, I've smoked opium, I've swallowed strychnine, I've drunk vitriol mixed with phosphorous. I've ruined my liver, my lungs, my kidneys, my heart – in fact all my inside outfit. Nobody knows what disease I've got.

... "Well," said Schweik, "you see what you've all got to go through for the Emperor."[110]

In writing of acts of self-mutilation and malingering in the Austro-Hungarian military, Hašek avoided asking the question of why his soldiers were acting in the way they were. It may have been to avoid censorship or because the answer was self-evident. It is, however, worth asking that question about Indian soldiers in World War I. In their letters, many *sipahis* admitted that they were malingering or intended to do so. They also, simultaneously, justified their actions. The widespread belief that by 1917 soldiers had already exceeded the maximum length of their 'contracts' led to the conclusion that they were entitled to feign illness to avoid duty.

The belief that soldiers' war-time service was restricted under a 'contract' was partly a legacy of the attestation Indian soldiers had to make upon enlistment. *Sipahis* did not, unlike their British counterparts from 1870, swear to serve for a minimum term in either their oaths of attestation or in a separate declaration. The precise duration of service in the Indian Army was left vague and unclear. In the years before World War I, however, the active service in the NWFP had been restricted to a set period of time after which an individual *sipahi* could expect to be moved to a more peaceable location. The huge expansion in new military 'classes' suitable for recruitment during World War I, especially in Punjab from 1917, contributed to a lack of clarity or understanding about the ordinary durations of military service and active military service in India. Finally, interactions with men of the Indian Labour

Corps in France, who arrived in February 1917 and who did have their length of service prescribed to a single year, led to the assumption by *sipahis* that they too must be subject to similar contracts. By the middle of 1917, *sipahis* began to assert in their letters that their 'contracts' had now expired and they were being forced to fight illegally. Sipahi Senchi Khan recounted on 4 May 1917 that an officer had personally told him to '"Cheer up! . . . the men can't be long now as the three years agreement is nearly up. There is every hope that at the end of the three years the Force in France will go back."'[111] By 29 June, this rumour had become a fact, at least for Azizuddin of the 6th Cavalry, who instructed his family to thank Allah that 'the three years are nearly up'.[112] And a month later, on 30 July 1917, Kaka Singh of the 38th Central India Horse was confident enough to add more details still:

> We have very strong hopes of one of three things happening. The first hope is that we shall all be sent back this winter. The second is that if we don't all return, those who have been here for three years will be sent back. The third is that failing all else, leave to India will be opened.[113]

Any sense of hope turned to bitter disillusionment when neither leave to India nor repatriation was permitted. For Kallu Khan of the Jodhpur Lancers, it clearly meant that the *Sarkar* could no longer be trusted. Soon, he anticipated, even the sick and wounded would be forced back into the trenches unless they were 'likely to die on the voyage out [to India], or a few days after their arrival.'[114] Abdul Wahab Khan penned furious letters that *sipahis* were being kept in France in contravention of their terms of service:

> Put away from you every thought about my coming on leave. In this matter our Master's made sport of us . . . but we in our stupidity thought that they were in earnest, and communicated the prospect of [our] coming to you, thus bringing on you our subsequent disappointment.[115]

The response by soldiers in the fighting units of the Indian Army differed from their compatriots in the Indian Labour Corps. Among Indian labourers, various strikes and work stoppages were attempted in 1918 when they were not repatriated after their initial contracts had expired.[116] In the Indian Army proper, the punishments meted out to *sipahis* were far too severe to risk such protests. Soldiers constantly relayed apocryphal warnings to one another of the severity of punishments in France. Sowar Man Singh of the 6th Cavalry, for instance, wrote of the despondency that had swept across his troop upon learning that two of his compatriots were to be shot for the 'minor crime' of 'not relieving each other on sentry duty and leaving the place without any sentry'.[117] Another Afridi *sipahi* relayed how close a friend of his had come to being accused of malingering by officers watchful for the slightest indiscretion:

> Sikander Shah has come here too. I have made thorough enquiry from him. He told me that a man of the 57th came and our people asked how Inzar Gul was. He replied that Inzar Gul himself had hit his own hand. Then the Doctor caused him to be arrested, saying "You have caused your own injury." [But] There was another sepoy with him who said "I saw him hit," ie. he gave evidence in his favour. Then the Doctor let him go. The man is not known to me who said this but [by] God will be known to you. If you know his name send it to me. When I rejoin I will make enquiry before the Colonel to find out about that sepoy and discover who it was that delivered him from the Doctor.[118]

Part of the reason for the heavy punishments for *sipahis* was the high prevalence of wounds to the left hand in the winter and spring of 1914 and 1915. Over half of all Indian soldiers admitted to hospital by 3 November 1914 had some sort of injury to the hand (1049 out of a total of 1848).[119] Not all were necessarily self-inflicted. Gordon Corrigan has argued that it was the natural result of soldiers exposing their left hands over trench walls as they were bracing their rifles to fire.[120] But, there was a far higher incidence of this type of wound among Indian *sipahis*, and those soldiers who were wounded in such a manner could barely contain their relief at escaping from the intensity of the fighting: 'I have been wounded by a bullet in the hand. A little bit of bone was broken above [sic], but I am glad because my life is safe.'[121] More pertinently, coded instructions were also sent between *sipahis* in 1914 and 1915 instructing the uninitiated of the correct method of using a gun or bayonet to inflict self-harm:

> Eat the fat, but preserve the bone carefully"[122]

> You can draw your own conclusion from what I wrote to Nanak. It is with reason that the greybeards call the winning wrestle "Bacha" [escape]. If you are wrestling with your friends, wrestle carefully and save your legs and arms.[123]

Preventing these acts of self-mutilation proved to be one of the successes of Howell's censorship operation. By the summer of 1915, Indian military medics took an active stance in prosecuting men suspected of self-mutilation, leading to *sipahis* documenting the horror of having the witness the execution of their friends or family:

> My brother Johan Singh was hit on the hand on the first night. He died on the 27th of Kalik [sic.?]. The Doctor declared he had shot himself, and the Doctor had him killed.[124]

And, by the middle of 1916, no more illustrations or allusions to wounds to the hand were made in soldiers' letters.

Official action to prevent self-mutilation among *sipahis* in 1914 and 1915 did not prevent later and more subtle forms of self-harm. Towards the end of 1916 and in the early months of 1917, soldiers began to write home and enquire whether contacts in India knew of anything that would 'produce sores on the legs or on the neck or on the chest' that would not 'be found out as being self-inflicted'.[125] These enquiries were stated frankly in some letters and far more obliquely in others. Talib Mohamed Khan penned a short note congratulating a *sipahi* for successfully returning to India – 'I am very glad to hear that you have arrived safely in your native country. May God grant us all to get there soon!' – before writing in brackets at the margins of the letter:

> (I wish you would be good enough to send me something which will make the doctors declare me unfit for Service and at the same time will not be dangerous to life).[126]

Whole lists of dark and grisly ways in which military medics could be deceived were sent in response, usually involving the application of toxic substances to the groin and testes (thus tapping into fears at the time of venereal disease).[127] But, by far the most common 'remedy' that was prescribed involved the use of seeds of the *bhailawa* plant.[128] They were ordinarily used by *dhobis* or washermen to mark the clothes that they had washed, and so, no one could question their presence in a *sipahis'* kit. They had the added advantage of causing a serious but temporary inflammation of the skin that would last 'three days'[129] and could be applied by *sipahis* in more than one way depending on the resources available to them:

> ... the smoke of the Bhulawan plant is used for this purpose. The plant is ground down and then thrown on burning coals. The smoke is allowed to play upon that part of the body on which is desired to cause an inflammation.[130]

> And what I wrote to you about Bhilawan, if you have got them, you should mash them up, and then smear them on the body, afterwards heat the places on the

body where you have out the Bhilawan. Then put some of the smearing mixture on the lower part of your stomach and in your mouth, and fumigate yourself also with it.[131]

Soldiers from the 40th Pathans,[132] 20th Deccan Horse, and 9th Hodson's Horse,[133] all somehow circumvented the postal censor, secured the seeds and used them to good effect.

To the Punjab will come having saved their lives those men who have been wounded and are not fit for the service of Government, and those who have bodily sickness which is not likely to get better soon. But here, at present, this is the state of affairs. Men feigning and pretending all kinds of sickness, and being brought before all sorts of committees, get sent [back] to the Punjab. Since [the fighting grew fierce] many men who can hear, pretend to be deaf and those who can speak to be dumb, some complain of pains in the loins, knees, or body, others say they have giddiness in the head, or something the matter with their lungs. Each one gets before some committee and is sent back to the Punjab, thus saving his life by some way or another. Because the Doctors are a set of blind people, there are many diseases they cannot diagnose, [so] some men, feigning all kinds of illness, save their lives and get back to India. Otherwise it would be difficult, for there is no sign of the war stopping, or of peace being made, and the whole world is being destroyed.[134]

Thus, the *bhailawa* seed restored what *sipahis* in France believed was their due: the right to return.

I dreamed and dreamed of getting back to India . . . but the dream ended in nothing more than a dream: Famine and falling houses during World War II

On 28 December 1943, Lieutenant Colonel M. G. M. Mair, deputed to censor Indian correspondence in the Middle East, North Africa and the Mediterranean, penned a warning to his superiors that,

There remains no length to which writers will not go to obtain a return [to India]. Commanding Officers, Deputy Commissioners of every degree, even the Commander-in-Chief himself, continue to regularly receive a large number of plaints. Parents and wives continue to write on their "death-beds" apparently without respite, since their number is now swollen beyond all reasonable proportions. Another amazing aspect is the speed with which so called "critical" conditions transpire after the posting overseas of the soldiers.[135]

Nothing more was said on the matter. It appears that neither Mair nor the men he was reporting to wanted an explanation. Soldiers relayed graphic accounts of famine and starvation in India between 1943 and 1944 that contrasted absolutely with the newspapers and broadcasts the Indian Army prepared for soldiers' edification. Fear that such horrors were about to afflict their own homes compelled *sipahis* to explore illicit means through which they could travel back to their families. While Mair's reports, throughout this period, remained steadfast in asserting that there was no famine and, aside from some hysteria, soldiers were unperturbed by any news received from home.

Throughout World War II, the Indian Army provided publications to its soldiers serving overseas that would 'remove the men's apprehensions' about the state of affairs in India. The weekly newspaper *Fauji Akhbar* acted as a running commentary on the rural economy of India[136] and the *Digest of Indian News* was filled with a series of lurid headlines carefully designed to avoid reporting on anything of substance: 'A Freak Child', 'Punjab War Songs Competition', 'Ex-Convict Arrested', 'Man Burnt to Death in Saving Child'.[137] *Sipahis*' letters were, however, a parallel means of exchanging news. Between 1943 and 1944, there was only one story of note in those letters: famine in Bengal. Snatches of radio broadcasts or newspaper articles would be heard or found and *sipahis* would ask what was 'really' going on. It was by radio that a Bengali *sipahi* in January 1943 came 'to know of the condition of Calcutta and Chittagong'[138] and led to another requesting more information:

> The radio program relayed from home gives us a vivid idea of the miserable state of affairs prevailing there as we listen to it regularly, and how the poor are hard up [. . . and] depressing and overwhelming feelings are growing in my mind.[139]

The letters that trickled through did not present a positive picture. The huge increases in the price of rice in Bengal were charted from the already inflated 'Rs. 7 or 8 per *maund*' in December 1942,[140] to 'Rs. 35/36 per *maund*' in June 1943,[141] to Rs. 40 per *maund* by August 1943[142]:

> The food situation is tragic in this country. Do not be startled to learn that rice is selling at Rs. 40/- a md. [It is] Strange to say, [but] sometimes money can't purchase it. Death caused through starvation seems to be the order of the day. Famine and epidemics are prevailing everywhere and as a result of it a large number of people

are dying daily. . . . If no immediate help is possible from your end in this dire crisis, I am sure that we are doomed and the end is lurking outside our door. . . . Many people are dying of starvation daily. The prices are as follows:-

Rice. . . Rs. 40 a *maund*.
Atta. . . Rs. 35 to 38 a *maund*.
Coal. . . Rs. 2½ a *maund*.[143]

More graphic descriptions of what life was like in eastern parts of India were provided by *sipahis* passing through famine-struck areas:

> I see many people returning with great disappointment from Government Ration Stalls, because there is no rice left to ration. . . . Anyone can live without food for one or two weeks if there is hope of getting it in the end, but when there is no hope, then on what ground will he live? Moreover, wealthy people have the hope that they can get food at any cost; but what about the middle and poor classes who have no money and who are depending on daily or monthly wages? India has never suffered so much before. . . . The same India which was not in need of anything and was helping other countries in their distress, has now become a beggar and is begging others for food, and can't get it. . . . All its beauty has vanished and those young boys and girls, men and women who were full of fresh and vigorous blood, the signs of which could be seen on their cheeks, are now as withered trees. There is no flesh on their bones, no sign of their youth, but only signs of worries and miseries, and people of all ages, youths, or young ones can be seen lying as dead on the foot paths or on the pavements in the burning sun without food. . . . Who is going to feed them or satisfy them, and who is responsible for it? . . . India was a golden bird in olden times but now this war and its selfish powers has made it a beggar country.[144]

The effects of this commentary on the Bengal famine were just as significant, if not more so, for the majority of *sipahis* that were not Bengali. Reports of high prices for basic necessities outside Bengal stoked fears that mass-starvation would soon occur throughout India. A Garhwali *havildar* wrote a letter about the 'Indian food problem' in June 1943 in which he imagined that the conditions in Bengal were being replicated in his own village:

> From my personal experience I can tell you that the food we get here is much better than that we soldiers get in India. But whenever I sit for my meals, a dreadful picture of the appalling Indian food problem passes through my mind leaving a cloudy sediment on the walls of my heart which makes me nauseous, and often I leave my food untouched.[145]

A Tamil *sipahi* in Italy wrote to a friend in India in November 1943 and warned of the calamities that were to come:

> All the letters from home are pathetic and touching and I am now in an ocean of sorrow. What is the use of such a life? I do not know when I am going to start a happy life. I received a letter from my wife that my house is washed away by floods in the Adyar Cooum River and they are now sheltering in a *choultry* in Madras. It often drives me mad. What is to be done? In such a condition how can man be happy when his family is in such a dangerous plight?[146]

Finally, a Punjabi soldier from Sargodha district wrote unequivocally of what he foresaw for his friends and family in Punjab in February 1944:

> Everyone in India knows well how people suffered in Bengal and millions died of starvation and now they want that you should die in the same way. . . . How funny the army and its rules and orders are, and how miserable those poor dependents are, whose supporters are in the army. How happily you were living before, but now you are the worst sufferers in all respects. May God end this war soon and make us free from the blessed army life, and its rules, regulations and orders.[147]

It became commonplace, therefore, to transplant the images evoked by the news from Bengal to the villages and provinces from which non-Bengali soldiers hailed.

It did not lead to a single response. For some *sipahis* – their names excised by Mair – it was enough to seek reassurances that their monthly remittances were reaching their families[148] and hope for this amount to be increased:

> Dear mother, I am fed up reading all your letters which often drive me mad. You should know very well by now that I am here in the rank of a sepoy. My total pay, plus overseas allowance, is Rs. 30/- only, and out of it I have allotted Rs. 15/- to you. A sepoy in the army is allowed to allot that much only, that is why I am sending Rs. 6/- to 7/- to you in addition to the F.A. [Family Allowance]. . . . Pray to God for [a] general increase in the pay of other ranks of the Indian Army.[149]

Others petitioned local DSBs to make domestic necessities available to their families at a subsidized rate (if they were from Punjab),[150] or to appeal to their Officers and District Commissioners that such institutions should be established outside Punjab.[151] Yet, more *sipahis* made a number of petitions to their officers in which soldiers laid forth 'genuine requests' 'under very pressing circumstances' for compassionate leave.[152] What united all these demands and requests made by the rank and file was that they proved unsuccessful, because monthly allotments were not increased, Soldiers' Boards did not operate with any degree of cohesion outwith Punjab, and leave proved extremely difficult to obtain.

> I dreamed and dreamed of getting back to India and also believed it would come true. But the dream ended in nothing more than a dream. My hopes are shattered to pieces and I feel extremely disappointed.[153]

When legitimate means had been frustrated, soldiers turned to the surreptitious. In August 1942, several soldiers of the 4th Battalion, 11th Sikhs were able to obtain extraordinary dispensation to return home from Egypt because 'our house has fallen in', 'one of my [father's] legs is fractured' and 'mother has turned blind'.[154] What seemed to be remarkable coincidence revealed itself to be the work of soldiers' ingenuity, when the same formula for securing leave came to be used by other *sipahis* throughout 1943. At the beginning of the year, one soldier recounted how he had been told of 'a really good excuse' that originated 'from one of my friends' in another regiment.[155] Quite what that 'excuse' was remained unclear until April, when another *sipahi* sheepishly informed his father that he had been portrayed in an 'excuse' as 'a blind old man' who was 'unable to pay his land revenue of fifty *bighas*'.[156] At the end of 1943, so common had this deception become, that men of 5th Battalion, 5th Maratha Light Infantry had each submitted '10/12 applications' of this type.[157] And with its popularity came subtle amendments and alterations to the formula; some soldiers adding that they were also recently married[158] or that their brother was a prisoner of war,[159] others that they had documentary proof of their parents' illness,[160] and some combined all these elements as they enjoined their supposedly ill relatives to petition on their behalf:

> I reported the illness of my father to my Coy. Commander. I also added that I was poor, while all my older brothers were well-off and wanted to confiscate all my heritage after my father's death and that I had a wife . . . You will please get an application sent by father to our C.O. saying that he is an old man, dead nearly and requests the C.O. to send me back very soon.[161]

Such activity proved difficult for British military subalterns or more senior officers to turn down because of the fear of what may occur if all these applications were summarily dismissed:

> I have sent off a bunch of lads on leave again lately [but] none of the former lot I sent off have come back. [. . . Yet if I refuse] it breeds discontent, [and] one gets very tired of making excuses and holding out false promises.[162]

Thus, incidents of falling houses increased as news of calamity in India reached soldiers. And they were informed by the belief that the Indian Army had failed in its duty to protect their families.

Conclusion: Casting a shadow (imperfectly) over Lalu

Some two decades after the Armistice, Mulk Raj Anand wrote his novel *Across the Black Waters*. The novel was the second part of a trilogy narrating the experiences of Lal Singh from adolescent rebellion, to military service in World War I, to his return home and involvement in revolutionary activity.[163] For Anand, it was at once a memorial to a soldiering father from whom he was estranged, and frustration at his father's social conservatism. Anand's *sipahis* were sexually liberal,[164] horrified by the brutality of battlefield justice,[165] and constantly questioned their officers' worth:

> Listen, boys, listen: First Battalion Connaught Rangers, Ferozepur Brigade, will go by military transport at once to Wulvergham to join Cavalry Corps under General Allenby. On the return of the motors, the 69th Rifles under the command of Karnel Green Sahib will move up to Wulvergham and join the 2nd Cavalry Division under General Gough Sahib Bahadur.
>
> "But what about the rest of the Brigade?" asked tubby Dhayan Singh.
>
> "Aren't we all going into action together since we have come together?" queries Rikhi Ram.
>
> "Shall we be separated even from our own Brigade?" asked Kharku.
>
> The sepoys seemed to be panic-stricken at the announcement.
>
> "Our regiment will be together," said Havildar Lachman Singh to console them. "So we will be all right."
>
> But the sepoys edged away, their faces tinged with the regret that from now on there would be partings after which each man will probably have to go by himself. From the congregational life of their past and, more particularly, through the long journeys with thousands of sepoys, they had come to accept their togetherness as a law of nature and they had naively expected that they would all be put to fight side by side with each other.
>
> "Where is Wulvaga?" a sepoy was asking.
>
> "Where is the place, *Holdara*?" another repeated the inquiry. "When are we going?"
>
> "Why is it that only the *Gora* regiment and our regiment are going, Uncle?" Kharku turned to Kirpu. "What is the meaning of all this?"

"'The Sarkar is like a bitch, son,' said Kirpu. 'It barks its orders and does not explain. What I am concerned about is where are we going to stay. Can't stay in the cold out here . . . I hardly slept a wink last night: These Sahibs are. . .'

'Illegally begotten!' added Kharku.[166]

The fragmentary and episodic picture of *sipahis* gleaned from their letters lived up to Anand's vision, and, in parts, surpassed it. Details of sexual encounters were exchanged that recounted brief sojourns in brothels and more consensual relationships. Acts of malingering were described and enacted that deftly avoided firing squads or summary executions. *Sipahis* offered more substantive critiques and expectations of their officers than mumbling *madarchod* or 'mother fucker' under their breaths.[167] At the same time, the letter could be used strategically to spur illicit activity. Petitions, *bhailawa* seeds, and news of falling houses were all relayed through oblique metaphors, using stock phrases in new contexts, or by (literally) writing at the margins.

There was one aspect, however, in which letters were not in accord with Anand's novel. The activity described did not automatically lead to disenchantment with the Army and British colonial rule. Anand's Lalu returns to India with the words of *Ghadari* agents[168] circulating as a mantra in his mind: '"Brothers-in-law, you like your fathers, the English! . . . You like to lick their testicles! . . . You. . ."'.[169] There were a handful of letters that were sent to soldiers from the *Ghadar* Party, but the only response by *sipahis* was to distance themselves from their revolutionary programme.[170] Soldiers, even those malingering, did not describe themselves as fundamentally disloyal or their actions as challenging the legitimacy of military authority. Instead, letters were the flip side of military regulations: adding adjuncts to the roles delineated for *sipahis* and working to obtain lost privileges or means of escape. As one *sipahi* wrote, when commenting on the high rates of malingering and self-harm, *sipahis* were merely 'showing loyalty' for the amount of 'salt that they had eaten'.[171]

4

Throwing Snowballs in France: (Re-)Writing a Letter and (Re-)Appraising Islam, 1915–1918

On 11 July 1916, Captain G. Tweedy, the newly appointed Chief Censor of Indian military correspondence in France, alerted his superiors to a slip of paper he had found hidden in an otherwise anodyne letter by a Punjabi Musalman *sipahi*. It was the nature of the concealed missive, as much as the fact that it was hidden, that alarmed Tweedy. It took the form of a message that had been relayed from the Prophet Mohamed, and the injunctions contained therein directed the Muslim soldiery of British India to put their loyalty to their faith before any loyalty to their *Sahibs*:

786. Order of Mustapha

Order of the Highness the Prophet Mahomet to Sheikh Ahmad, Khadin [sic. "Khadim" or Custodian] of the auspicious Mauseleum at Medina.

I Sheikh Ahmad of Medina saw in a dream the Prophet reading the Koran. He said to me "Sheikh Ahmad I am weary beyond all measure of their sins. Between two Fridays 9 lakhs of people died, of whom only 70,000 were in the true faith and all the rest were Kafirs. God Almighty sent the angels to me with the following message 'Mahomet, look at the condition of your followers. I can bear it no longer and I shall have to change the state of things because your devotees are full of sin. They have given up their prayers and do not give the Zakat to the poor. They devote themselves to theft and backbiting, fornication, false evidence, eating swine's flesh, and misappropriation of others property. They do not keep their caste and do not give alms to the poor and disobey my orders. They are too much devoted to the world and in fact all Mahomedans are guilty of these sins. Therefore I think it necessary to change them into the original type of Mahomedans.' His Highness the Prophet prayed God to bear with His people and promised to issue further instructions to Islam and said "If they do not hear this last injunction then Thou are the Master do as Thou pleasest." Then the Prophet said to me "Instruct all the followers of Islam that the Day of Judgement is at hand and the sun will soon rise in the West and the mountains will begin to burn. These are the signs of the end of the world." Once more [in the past] I gave this warning to the faithful but no one attended to it and [they] grew even more absorbed in sinful pleasures. Now I issue clear orders to the faithful to avoid the sins I have mentioned and that they should call to mind the manifold pains and anxieties the Prophet has undergone for their salvation. Do Musalmans want the Prophet to spend all his time in begging God's forgiveness for their sins? The Prophet has clearly said that if you do not obey this last call he will have nothing more to do with you and will implore the Almighty no more for you. Whoever will copy this message and circulate it from city to city and read it out to others the Prophet will stand by him in the Last Day, and who does not do this will be his enemy and he will do nothing to save him however regular and abstinent his life may be. Sheikh Ahmad takes a solemn oath that this dream is true, and that if it is not true he prays God to smite him dead as an unbeliever. This news has come from Medina the Holy. Impress on every Mahomedan to obey the instruction if he wishes to escape from Hell fire.[1]

The missive from Medina came to be termed the 'Snowball' letter[2] because it helped to frame a debate that Muslim soldiers conducted over their religion, and the frequency with which it was referred to increased as the War raged on. At the time, Tweedy busied himself with trying to find where the letter had originated from in (what proved to be a vain) hope that it could be stopped at the source. For the purposes of this chapter, however, the precise origins of the missive are unimportant. As it was read, received and transmitted by soldiers it was internalized and altered to reflect their own reality. Vernacular words and concepts such as *lakhs* and caste infiltrated the religious prose; the words and metaphors of the missive changed each time a soldier transcribed or quoted from it; and the actions it inspired resulted in everything from increased numbers fasting during Ramzan to outright mutiny. Furthermore, the letter came to be used as a response to, and operated in a space created by, earlier attempts to interfere with the religious practices of Muslim *sipahis* that were sanctioned by British and German military authorities. So, rather than seeking to locate who first threw the 'Snowball', I will attempt to follow the path it took as it journeyed and grew in size.

The chapter will begin with a brief account of German propaganda and the *Ahmadiyya* Movement before and during World War I. It will recount their attempts to influence religious discourses among Muslim soldiers and the unintended consequences this activity had of spurring Muslim *sipahis* into questioning the compatibility of faith and military service. This will be followed by an analysis of the part the Snowball letter played in this re-appraisal of how soldiers understood their religion. Finally, the chapter will conclude by showing how this occurred with reference to two particular issues: interracial sex and the Turkish entry into World War I.

Circulating the words of the Prophet(s): Chain letters, German propaganda and Ahmadi missionaries

The 'Snowball' letter was not the first of its type. In the *Bibliothèque Nationale de France*, Jonathan G. Katz has discovered a series of eighteenth- and nineteenth century-accounts written in different scripts and locales, all of which invoked Sheikh Ahmad's dream:

> Praise be to God, He alone. In the name of God the Merciful the Munificent, May God bless our lord and prophet and master Muhammad and his family and companions, and may He grant continued peace unto the Day of Judgment. It is told of Shaykh Ahmad, trustee (*wakil*) of the precinct of the Prophet (God bless him and grant him salvation!) that he said, "I was stationed in the Prophet's *mihrab* on the right side of his noble tomb Friday night reciting the word of God (May He be honored and glorified) when a man approached me. Light issued from his eyes in the middle of the night. I did not know what to think. Then I understood that this beauty belonged to our intercessor, our lord Muhammad (God bless him and grant him salvation!).
>
> He said to me, 'O Shaykh Ahmad, you know the condition of my community as to its good and its bad and what issues forth from my community.'
>
> And when I saw this beauty I stopped and clasped my hands.
>
> Then he said (God bless him and grant him salvation!), 'You are sinners. Indeed, I have seen at this time 70,000 of whom 700 are in accordance with the faith and the remainder not in accordance with the faith. We take refuge in God from this evil, O Shaykh Ahmad.'
>
> Then he said (God bless him and grant him salvation!), 'I am ashamed before God Almighty and the angels because the people of my community disobey their mothers and fathers, and they do not recognize the condition of the poor and the unfortunate. Indeed, they study worldly desire. Do not the "*ulama*" have goodness that no one listens to their speech or honors them? [sic.] The wine session and the distraction of slander is preferable in their opinion to the session devoted to knowledge, *hadith* and *dhikr*. We have already sent to them prior to this two messages, and they did not pay attention to the matter, and not one among them saw it. I, God's servant, am ashamed before God Almighty and before the angels,

while they neither have shame before God nor before us nor before the angels. While their faces bear the marks of faith, they have reviled the faithful.'

He said, 'The *khatib* approached me and said to me, "Your community fears neither sins nor disobedience. They recite the book of God the Great. O Muhammad, your community commits these sins and they turn their faces. It is your nature, O my beloved, O Muhammad, (to show) mercy upon the believers."'

Then the Prophet (God bless him and grant him salvation!) said to me: 'Supply them this paper, O Shaykh Ahmad, God's deposition with you. Propagate this message to my people lest they abandon the faith: Obey God and the Prophet. Perhaps you will be granted mercy. Only (note that) the thing is near. Remorse has no benefit after death. Only (note that) the Resurrection is near. On account of the door of repentance being open, repent unto God of (your) sins. You and your faces are the faces of believers but your actions are the actions of Christians and Jews, and you will die not according to the faith. We seek God's protection from this evil. Only (note that) the accounting is near. The deed came to pass upon your heads before (the years) 1220 and 1230 [1805–1824 C.E.]. In the year forty the corruption will be great and death will be great in the year fifty. Cities will be destroyed in their entirety and signs will appear. In the year sixty stones will be hurled from the sky on the heads of sinners. In the year seventy the sun will rise in the west, and in the year eighty the word of God the Great will ring out and afterwards the Antichrist [*al- Dajjal*] will set forth.'"[3]

The letters, posters and telegrams are, for Katz, proof that 'a pious Muslim of the eighteenth or nineteenth century' could 'express concern over the moral and spiritual health of the Islamic community for its own sake and without any explicit reference to the existence of the "Other"' or the 'West'.[4] What may be true of the eighteenth or nineteenth century was not true of the twentieth. The later version of the missive was conditioned by the site of its production and shaped by the circulation of German and Ahmadiyya propaganda among Muslim *sipahis*.

Shortly after the start of hostilities and the appearance of Indian soldiers in France, the *Nachrichtenstelle für den Orient* (Information Centre for the Orient) was established in Germany. Its goal, as outlined by Max Freiherr von Opponheim, was to sow propaganda among colonial soldiers of the French, Russian and British armies. Special newspapers were produced, provisions for religious worship were met, and leaflets written in 'Oriental' languages were prepared[5]:

> . . . You have been deceived. You are meant to fight here, on foreign soil for the British who hold your home country in bondage. But you do not know that at this moment the people of your country have risen against the English to win their freedom. This is confirmed by reliable news and telegrams from your native

country. The English hide this information from you. . . . But, men of India! The Germans do not want to kill you with their terrible weapons. They love your country and are well-disposed towards you. . . . Although you cannot participate in the freedom fight of your brothers being as you are in a foreign country, you can help them by not fighting for their enemies here. Throw down your weapons and give yourselves up to the Germans![6]

At least some of this material originated from diasporic networks of revolutionary Indian nationalists in Europe and North America. Pamphlets and newspapers were being exchanged between the headquarters of *Ghadar* in San Francisco – an organization that was largely Punjabi and contained a significant number of pensioned *sipahis* in its ranks – and the German Consulate in the city from the end of 1914 to the beginning of 1915.[7] It is difficult to assess how successful this propaganda was among soldiers at the Front. No soldiers wrote of having seen such leaflets, and nor would they since it was a crime to secret away and read enemy propaganda. It was also extremely difficult for British censors to intercept material thrown from one trench to another or dropped by aircraft. One letter from an Indian Prisoner of War held in Germany in August 1915 was found and censored, but it was only discovered because it was posted to India by mistake.[8]

Although it is hard to discern quite how much German propaganda made its way through to *sipahis*, its effect is not. It could spark off rumours, speculation, flights of fancy that had an effect greater than the number of soldiers reading it. The case of Jemadar Mir Dast of 58th Vaughan's Rifles is a prime example. Mir Dast defected to the Germans in February 1915 with 12 other *sipahis*. The fact that his brother had won the Victoria Cross[9] led some *sipahis*, particularly fellow Afridi Pathans, to speculate that Dast had been awarded the Iron Cross by Kaiser Wilhelm II.[10] That in turn led to the belief that the German Kaiser had subsequently converted to Islam:

> A letter has come from those of our men whom the Germans took prisoner, from the men of our regiment, saying, "We are now under the German king. You can please yourselves. We are well and happy, because here there is a Muslim King." About 200 of our regiment were taken prisoner.[11]

And it led to suggestions, by October 1915, that the Germans were preparing to liberate Muslims in India by invading through Afghanistan:

> I have heard that an army of the Sultan Badshah and of the Germans has come to Kabul and I have heard that it numbers 11 *lakhs* of men and with it Jemadar Mir Dast too has come. . . .[12]

This rumour at least was not completely without foundation. By the end of 1915, Kabul had become a significant hub for South Asian anti-colonial and pan-Islamist activity. The group in Kabul included a number of overlapping and competing interests: students who had emigrated to Afghanistan in the hope of taking up arms under the Turkish Khilafa, representatives of the radical *ulama* at Deoband, and an official German-Turkish mission led by the former-*Ghadari* Maulana Barkatullah and Raja Mahendra Pratap.[13]

It was while these conversations were ongoing that the first *Ahmadiyya* literature appeared and was passed on to soldiers without any censure or much comment. The *Ahmadiyya* Movement and its adherents were a small minority among South Asian Muslims but had an influence greater than their size. It was founded in 1889 by Mirza Ghulam Ahmad as part of an explosion of public religious discourse in late nineteenth-century Punjab; of pamphlet wars and verbal jousting between Hindu, Sikh and Muslim revivalist groups. Ghulam Ahmad's English-language journal *The Review of Religions* published from 1902 until his death in 1908 was full of articles issued in direct response to *Arya Samaji* critics of Islam (the issue of March/April 1903, for example),[14] critiquing Sikh religious reformers of the Lahore Singh Sabha and the Chief Khalsa Diwan ('The Discovery of the Chola of Nanak'),[15] or as part of ongoing debates with more orthodox Islamic scholars. Iqbal Singh Sevea has described Ghulam Ahmad's activity as 'a print jihad'; of an extension into print of the public religious debates (*munazara*) in the streets of Punjab and northern India[16]:

> ... ours is the age of publicity and propaganda and now Islam will come to its own not through military conquest but by conquering the hearts and minds of men, with its beautiful teaching. . . . Islam's greatest need and opportunity lies in the diffusion and dissemination of its message which possesses a far greater striking power than any sword, gun or bomb.[17]

Following Ghulam Ahmad's death in 1908 and a dispute over his legacy (the largest group, the Qadian faction or *Jamaat-i-Ahmadiyya*, claimed that Ghulam Ahmad was a continuation in the line of the prophets and not just a *mujtahid* or renewer of Islam), the *Ahmadiyya* Movement spread beyond the geographical contours of Punjab. By 1916, the Qadian faction had established missions in Britain – at Woking, Surrey and at Great Russell Street in London – and from there sought to propagandise among the Muslim soldiery of the Indian Army in France. *Ahmadiyya* propaganda among soldiers was probably not the result of formal and open collusion with colonial military authorities. The movement had always adopted an uncontroversial position over the nature of British rule. Ghulam Ahmad made repeated pronouncements that the British Government had been a boon to the Muslims of India and had acted to preserve Islam.[18] As a consequence, *Ahmadiyya* had come to be widely celebrated in the pro-British Indian press during the early months of World War I as 'a sort of Protestant Muhammadanism'[19] and in evangelical literature for their 'absence of political controversy'.[20] It is likely that the reason why *Ahmadiyya* propaganda was allowed to pass uncensored to Muslim *sipahis* is it was counted as one of many loyalist voices that the Indian Army wanted its soldiers to hear (alongside regular visits by former officers, colonial officials and Indian royalty).[21]

The form that *Ahmadiyya* propaganda took in the trenches was not through the circulation of printed texts, as was the method of transmission of *Ahmadiyya* teachings in the post-war period. Large packages were difficult to send to *sipahis* on active service, and the types of trench literacy that permitted the writing of letters through the use of shared metaphor and imagery would have made the formalized prose of the English-language *Muslim India* and *Islamic Review* difficult to comprehend. The form that *Ahmadiyya* propaganda took among soldiers were either handwritten digests of printed material or convoluted arguments and instructions to individuals deemed to be receptive to the *Ahmadiyya* message in order that they could then pass it on by word of mouth. This allowed for the *Ahmadiyya* message to be tailored to reflect major happenings in the War or act as rebuttals to certain rumours engendered by German propaganda. It also made the letters a running series of proofs that Ghulam Ahmad's prophecies were coming true and that the British Raj would endure. After the February Revolution in Russia in 1917, for instance, a summary of a pamphlet was sent to Sub-Assistant Surgeon Raffi-ud-din Khan that contained 'proof' that Ghulam Ahmad had predicted the event, before using the sudden fall in grace of the Czar as a sign that British rule over India had been ordained by God:

> He [Maulvi Mahomed Ali Khan – a prominent Ahmadi] remarks that before the war the Tzar of Russia was the most powerful King on Earth, since his word was law over 16 million people, and yet today, he asks what is the position of the Tzar? And he answers his question by saying that he has not only lost his crown and is a prisoner in the hands of people who before were as nothing in his estimation, but he is separated from his wife and family and his last state is one of utter ruin.
>
> He observes that it is due to the blessing of God, that though the Tzar has been deprived of his "Crown" no harm has come to our Government, which [is] prosecuting the war successfully.[22]

This desire to demonstrate to *sipahis* that it was their religious duty to show fealty to the British Crown was put in more frank language to the few soldiers who were *Ahmadis* and who had been spreading the word to their peers:

> Subscriptions are being sent regularly to Kadiani Sharif. Mufta Mohamed Sadiq and Kazi Abdulla and Abdul Hali, Arab [sic.], are having a good propaganda in London and English people, men and women, are becoming their disciples. We are being very successful. The prophecies of the Messiah are being fulfilled daily. The Mohamedans who are ignorant of our religion remain unsatisfied and suffer in pain. His Highness and the Prophet laid down that non-Musalmans who were our friends should be helped and supported and . . . [we should fight] against their enemies. The English Government is our supporter and protector and this Government is for us Indian Mohamedans, a blessing and a benefit. This is the Government under which we can follow our religion, and this Kingdom of England, especially London the capital, has a favourable atmosphere for Islam. There is no hindrance to our propaganda. It is our duty to fight for such a power and combat its enemies.[23]

The reception the *Ahmadi* message received among soldiers, however, was decidedly lukewarm. In the 18th Lancers, open scorn was shown for the *Ahmadiyya* Movement and the specific pamphlets and letters that were circulated within the regiment. Abusive correspondence was directed to *Ahmadi* missionaries from regimental lines which accused them of being 'false Musalmans' for eating meat killed by non-Muslim butchers.[24] On other occasions *Ahmadis* were accused of secretly being Christians[25] and gleeful tales were relayed of *Ahmadi* literature being burnt in the trenches.[26] Such was the vituperative response within the 18th Lancers that the one *Ahmadi* within the troop, Dafadar Haq Nawaz, who had been the conduit through which *Ahmadi* propaganda was passed to others, suffered a change of heart. The reason, as he explained, was that he had been influenced by men within the regiment who were issuing counter-arguments to those put forward by the *Ahmadis*;

> . . . I have seen, that the condition of all the Mohamedans is precisely what you have described on reference to this text. I do not contend with them; but when I listen to their talk, I am moved to utter a prayer "May God put them on the right way." On the surface they are faithful but in their hearts there is emptiness. . . . I get full of burning wrath when I hear the complaint of my companions that our death has become unlawful.
>
> PS. There is a matter on which I desire to consult you. Kindly give me your advice. The meaning of the text is "To obey God, to obey His Prophet and to obey

the Authority placed over you." Now God is holy and the Prophet also is holy, should not the Authority placed over us also be holy? That is to say, one must follow in the footstep of the Prophet, and act in accordance with the example he has set, [but] must one also walk in the footsteps and act in accordance with the example placed over us? Must one in fact conform to the religion of our present King? These are the questions which a Shiah Moulvi in the regiment has raised after reading your tract, saying "We cannot accept [it] as the Authority mentioned in the text, [is] an Authority which eats swine's flesh, drinks spirits and commits fornication." They [Muslim soldiers] admit that they are greatly in error saying "We do not serve the Authority from our hearts; but on the surface we show more than obedience. So without doubt we greatly err." For myself, since this discussion was started, I find myself unable literally to follow in the footsteps of the Authority . . . If the precepts of the Prophet are the precepts of God and the precepts of the Authority are to be regarded in the same way as the precepts of the Prophet, then they say the precepts of the Authority should be pure.[27]

For other soldiers, it was not enough to merely counter the *Ahmadiyya* message, but necessary to find genuine alternatives to what the *Ahmadis* preached. This took the form of personal letters to *pirs* or *maulvis* in India asking their advice or religious instruction – 'is it lawful for Mohamedans to take milk from the cow by the hands of Christians?'[28]; have 'we sinned for not keeping the Ramzan fast?'[29]; 'has God abandoned us for fighting in this War?'[30] Another approach was to take an interest in prominent Muslims involved in the nascent nationalist movement in India. Lance Dafadar Sher Mohamed of 38th Central India Horse wrote to the Editor of *Khabit* – a Muslim newspaper published in Delhi at the time – demanding that he send his regiment all the news he had on Maulana Abul Kalam Azad because 'I know his writing and as I am a devout Mohamedan I have a great affection for him.'[31] *Sipahi* Mohamed Yousuf wished to see the proceedings of the All-India Muslim League after they agreed to share a joint platform with Congress in 1916,[32] and his peers discussed avidly Edwin Montague's tour of India in the following year.[33] Thus, while German propaganda and Ahmadiyya missionary activity certainly did had an effect among Muslim soldiers of the Indian Army in World War I, it did not have the intended effect. Rumours circulated of the German veneration for Islam and that the Kaiser was preparing to invade India, but it never resulted in anything resembling Sir Roger Casement's German-backed 'Irish Brigade' despite the best efforts of the *Nachrichtenstelle für den Orient*.[34] Ahmadiyya literature and sermons won few adherents and spurred soldiers to investigate other competing religious and politicized voices within Islam. But, both German and Ahmadiyya propaganda contributed to a climate that allowed for Shaikh Ahmad's dream to be revived and reinvested with contemporary meaning for Muslim South Asian soldiers.

Shaping Snowballs in France: (Re)reading and (re)writing the Snowball letter

The Snowball letter emerged as part of the conversation that Muslim *sipahis* were engaged in about their religion. It was a document shaped and informed by pre-existing discourses, cultures and traditions of the soldiering Muslim in South Asia; the 'religious world of the sepoy' as Nile Green has put it in his study of *faqirs* in the cantonments of colonial Hyderabad.[35] The religious practices of Muslim *sipahis* were the sites of sustained, if not systemic, attempts to rationalize Islam by both Protestant Evangelicals disturbed by the presence of perverted rituals and *ganja*-consuming holy men[36] and the only slightly less forgiving attitudes of Muslim religious reformers in South Asia. They were to be a conduit through which rationalizing, reforming visions were to be projected into the closed space of Indian home and hearth. At the same time, however, they became the conduit through which the rural world of miracles, saints and dreams from the Prophet could re-enter the cantonment and trench. The army could act as a catalyst for the trans-regional and transnational expansion of cults around particular Sufi saints[37]; of stories being transmitted as one battalion moved from one cantonment to another, or as soldiers congregated in the 'back areas' in France during reprieves from active service. The Snowball letter reflected and furthered the ability of Muslim *sipahis* to act as religious conduits and catalysts.

It was no accident that the version of the Snowball letter that was first intercepted and recorded in full was sent by *Sipahi* Gasthip Khan, a Punjabi Muslim soldier serving in France. Punjabi Muslims were both the largest represented of the 'martial races' in the Indian Army in the years before World War I and formed the highest proportion of Indian Army combatants recruited during the conflict (136,126 out of a total of 657,739).[38] Aspects of the Snowball letter took on a textual counterpart to *munazara* – public religious debates within Islam and between Muslims and other religious figures which were initially linked to Mughal Courts at Fatehpur Sikri and Lahore, and which received a new, more popular, impetus from the early nineteenth century in response to Christian missionaries and religious reform movements.[39] By the late nineteenth century, printed pamphlets and tracts became a new means for the dissemination of these verbal debates by Deobandis and Arya Samajis, Singh Sabhites and Ahmadiyya. Each publication was a means of advancing a particular name and cause, demonstrating the extent of one's religious and cultural learning and deriving authority and status from that fact. Mughal decline and British imperial rule necessitated the broadening of the social, cultural and intellectual space of *munazara* for North Indian Muslims, but, as Justin Jones has shown in his study of Amroha, it still remained a forum for a learnt religious elite and the reified reliving of a lost Mughal past.[40] The Snowball letter was a subtextual counterpart to soldiers' own *munazara*, dependent on metaphor, myth and devotional Islam. The version transcribed by Gasthip Khan contained obvious allusions to the *Ahmadiyya* message and the letter was used to offer a retort to *Ahmadi* Muslims by Gasthip or one of his predecessors in the chain of the letter's transmission. The Snowball contained an inbuilt authority through its dream symbology of the Prophet's message, the imminent Day of Judgement and the eponymous figure of Sheikh Ahmad. It was influenced by a Sufi and pre-Islamic Arab tradition of revelation coming through the form of a dream sequence; of the dream acting as a conduit between direct human experience and the spiritual world (*alam al-Jabarut*) that would reveal truth and meaning without the need for formalized tuition. The letter shared the register in which the Ahmadiyya message was packaged to soldiers – 'Those who were wont to sleep in linen white as the jessamine flower will in the morning find themselves sprinkled with blood like the plane tree'[41] – along with the prognosis that most Muslims would be found wanting by God during the imminent Day of Judgement.[42] But, in the Snowball letter, or at least Gasthip's version of it, the reason why Muslims had angered Allah and the Prophet was that the former had deviated from the 'original type of Mahomedans' and had dared to listen to supposed heretical beliefs.[43] It warned that the 'followers of Mohamet' have become 'Kafirs', and the kind of apostates they had become was made clear when the vices of these 'false Muslims' were listed.[44] The sins of eating 'swine's flesh', 'backbiting' by attacking fellow Muslims, and misappropriating 'other's property' were vices that soldiers had already levelled at *Ahmadi* Muslims and in language that was only slightly more intemperate than in the *munazaras* of Punjab.[45]

Yet, the Snowball letter was never just a document by Punjabis or responding to religious reformers from Punjab. *Sipahis* in the Indian Army were transregional and transnational itinerants. Before World War I, individual *sipahis* could expect to experience service on the Afghan frontier, in Malaya and the

Far East, and circulate between several dozen large cantonments in India. The Imperial reach of World War I allowed the soldiering bodies of the Indian Army to be transnationalized further. *Sipahis* based in Malaya at the advent of World War I were shipped to Marseilles through the Suez Canal, diverted to fight in Mesopotamia and Palestine or sent to Zanzibar for expeditions into German East Africa. Muslims in the Indian Army experienced the pan-Indian and global reach of Islam during World War I and, due to exigencies of the conflict, shared an intimate physicality on board ship or in a trench with other Muslim 'martial classes'. Punjabi Muslims were the largest of the martial races recruited into the Indian Army during World War I, but the definitions of martialness in India were malleable enough to extend to Pathans on the Frontier, rural Muslim communities deemed to be descended from Pathans or Rajputs in the Indo-Gangetic plain, Rajputana and Central India and 'Dekhani Mussalmans' recruited from Hyderabad. Thirteen percent of all the combatants recruited into the Indian Army during World War I were non-Punjabi Muslims (86,552 out of 657,739),[46] and an even larger proportion were recruited into technical and ancillary units. Furthermore, although Gasthip Khan's version of Snowball of 4 July 1916 was the first version that was transcribed by the Censor, the letter was known about and was being discussed by soldiers in non-Punjabi units at least a year earlier. On 23 August 1915, Havildar Umr-al-Din Khan, an Orakzai Pathan, forwarded on a version of Snowball that had been handed to him by 'those of the Faith' working at 'the telegraph offices', but the Censor, deeming the telegram to have little importance, failed to record its contents.[47] In May 1916, Abdul Alim, a Hindustani Musalman Signaller, confided that he heard the message read out aloud by members of his Signal Troop and proceeded to offer his own interpretation of what it meant:

> Habibullah then told Battye Sahib this parcel of lies. . . [that] Ahmed Yar Khan (helped by Fazlali and Yar Khan of Troop No.2 and Yasim Khan and Abdushakim [sic.]) read out an address in which he said that for a Mohamedan to fight against a Turk would be the mark of an infidel, and that all those killed in fighting against the Turks would not go to Paradise. This was all false for his lecture was really to the effect that the Mohamedans who drank wine and committed fornication and did other things forbidden by Islam would die the death of an unbeliever. He said that all who died after living such lives were lost and that it was therefore incumbent on all to go back to their good old-fashioned habits. Anyone who doubted this was a Kafir pure and simple. This was all contained in the letter which I saw and which had come from Mecca.[48]

And, shortly after Gasthip's letter, Fyazuddin, a printer from Agra, shared the same version of Snowball in October 1916 with a Muslim Rajput soldier serving in the 38th Central India Horse in France that Gasthip Khan had communicated back to India.[49] The Snowball letter circulated between intimate contacts in the army and disparate spaces and communities at home and then back again. The significance of the Snowball letter came from its existence as a chain letter and from the myriads of interlocutors it passed through. The demand made at the end of the letter that it was mandatory for any literate Muslim to 'copy the message', 'circulate it from city to city' and 'read it out to others' led to it being shaped to accord with the beliefs and understanding of the individual receiving and sharing the message. At the same time and in the same space it allowed for an individual in the 38th Central India Horse to feel connected to a Punjabi Muslim soldier in another regiment, and together remark on the global reach of Islam: 'It went to India, to the City of Delhi, and then in this fashion, moving from strength to strength among the people, and especially amongst those of the Faith by means of the Telegraph offices it has come here.'[50]

The Snowball's simultaneous existence as authoritative dreamscape and malleable chain letter allowed for it to be re-written and re-packaged each time it was read, written and passed on but still retain the register of Sheikh Ahmad's dream. The pliability of the letter is evident from the accounts soldiers gave of how they first heard the message and how they then proceeded to share its contents. Havildar Umr-al-Din Khan wrote of how the message had reached his unit by telegraph, presumably from another source within the Indian Army, but his excitement stemmed from the fact that 'the paper' had travelled from 'Holy Medina … to India, to the City of Delhi, and then in this fashion, moving from strength to strength among the people, and especially among those of the Faith by means of the Telegraph offices it has come here.'[51] Sowar Rahmat Khan, in December 1915, confessed that he had providentially stumbled upon a version of the letter lying on the floor of his hospital and was immediately going to send 'three copies to Jandiala, one for the mosque and two for the brotherhood'.[52] It is unclear whether either Rahmat or Umr-al-Din Khan shared versions of Sheikh Ahmad's dream that were similar to the Snowball of July 1916. But, their soldiering peers certainly did begin to appropriate the content and form of the message and invest it with different meanings. Dil Khan of the 129th Baluchis labelled himself a *pir* upon hearing of one version of the letter and merged half-correct quotes from the Snowball into the sermons that he gave to friends and family in France and in India. He was unsure precisely where the letter had originated from and misquoted the figures of those who had been saved and those who had been condemned, but the basic message of Snowball remained:

> Perhaps this world is not for our people and the end is not for our people. You are a religious and prayerful man. . . so know that a letter has come from Mecca or Medina in which it says that all Musalmans have turned infidels through lust of this world, and the times are evil. They eat through the fast and do not pray and in two weeks 70000 thousand, you know, received forgiveness and 19 lakhs went to Hell. The moon rises in the West. [At] First it rose from the East. . . . It is the beginning of death. The end is at hand. Since I was born I never heard the like of this letter that comes from Holy Mecca.[53]

Abdul Ghani, a *sipahi* who had been wounded and had returned to Punjab, wrote to a soldier in France and quoted a fragment of the Snowball missive, in proto-Rushdean vein. He claimed that the words had not come from a letter at all but from the mouth of a woman in a nearby village who had been born from the womb of a cow and had been found sucking at its teat:

> I have also heard that at Nambal a man's cow brought forth and gave birth to a woman. . . . he gave her clothing and in fear went to Maulvi Faqir-Ullah, and asked him what was this miracle. The Maulvi replied "If the woman can speak, go and ask her." So he came back and asked her and found her drinking the cow's milk. She said "I am born to make trial of you, for the Day of Judgement is at hand. The people do not say their prayers, nor [do they] keep the fast. They eat that which is unlawful and drink wine. They do evil deeds. Refrain from these things."[54]

Even when the Snowball letters were not being directly quoted from at all, the sentiments contained therein informed the everyday correspondence of *sipahis*. It was referenced when soldiers wrote to their homes and asked their families to distribute *zakat* or alms on their behalf 'for this is the last time'.[55] It was hinted at in letters written in the latter parts of the War in which *sipahis* discussed how and why they had been keeping the *Ramzan* fast in the trenches:

> We are keeping a fast since 2nd July, and we have now completed 25 days. May God look kindly on our effort, Amen. I have had much discussion with Abdul Khalik Khan about the keeping of the fast. He said "Your people gain no credit by keeping the fast, since God has dispensed with us all, whereas you continue to fast." I replied "The life which we are now leading is one which God would not inflict even on a dog, as it is a time of unspeakable hardship with death always at

hand, and perhaps by the grace of God we may gain heaven by reason of our self-denial in having kept the fast. Amen! If God in his mercy takes us safely home again, it will be time for us to enjoy ourselves . . . ." Tell me when you write whether our self-denial has obtained us credit with God or not.[56]

Finally, the Snowball letters intruded upon pieces of prose lamenting the fallen state of the contemporary Muslim, whether in India or in France:

> Khan Sahib the fact of the matter is that we have given up God's law which he gave to us and we have thus been disgraced. The people of Europe have not followed this law in its entirety but have gone some way in that direction and hence the blessings which have been bestowed on them. How true is the saying of Syed Ahmad
> "The table of laws which we broke
> The people of the west have joined."
> I have now seen this with my own eyes in Europe and understand why God is pleased with the Europeans. There are no doubt shameful things here among individuals, but if there were no blemishes of any kind they would all be angels, and they would have escaped the punishment which has fallen upon Europe. What can I say more, Khan Sahib? If God takes pity on us we may pull through but without his help I see no prospect of our becoming men at all! God has given us many things which Europe does not possess and if we only follow God's law, Europe will be as nothing beside us.[57]

Thus, the process of transliteration and interlocution of the Snowball letters allowed for parts to be emphasized over others, parts to be re-written, and others to be ignored. It had a semantic legacy on subsequent correspondence even when it was not being referred to directly or consciously. But, the Snowball letters did not just shape the language and sentiments of subsequent correspondence. As will be shown in the rest of the paper, they helped to alter existing attitudes towards sex and the legitimacy of the War.

'Could a man be so perverted to lose his religion for the sake of a woman?': Sex, intercourse and religion in France

In the winter of 1916 and 1917, the Indian Army in France decided to sanction marriages between Muslim *sipahis* and French women. It was, officially, a favour to the French Government which had requested that bars on interracial marriage, in this particular case, be relaxed,[58] and partly to appease the supposedly lascivious tendencies of young Indian men that had already been witnessed in Brighton.[59] French women suddenly became acceptable repositories for Indian (Muslim) sexual desire. The reaction from the *sipahis* concerned, however, was mixed. *Sipahis'* correspondence charts the descent from initial glee, to concerns that it was all a ruse to detain soldiers in the killing fields of France or convert them to Christianity, to an eventual push for sexual abstinence. *Sipahis'* began to mirror their superiors' horror at what the racial mixing of bodies would mean for their own religious identities.

Much like the soldiers of any other army at any other time, and as described in Chapter 3, both Muslim and non-Muslim Indian soldiers wrote of their sexual adventures in France in quite graphic and earthy language. Novel European sexual positions were discussed – 'contrary to the custom in our country they do not put their legs over the shoulders when they go with a man!'[60] Soldiers exchanged boasts that they had bedded more than one woman at a time or that they were so popular with French women that they themselves were being paid to have intercourse with them:

> The state of affairs here is this. Ten annas are equal to one franc. So by paying 6, 7 or 8 francs the [French] women get men to have carnal intercourse with them. So that for little money sexual pleasure is sold, especially by Drabis [men of the Transport Corps] and Sikhs [who] have got a lot of money from this.[61]

And more than one *sipahi* talked of settling down with a French partner or two:

> Just tell me, if I were to bring them out what would be the difficulties in the way? Do you think that I should bring them with me? Would there be any harm? Of course people would laugh, but "can en fait rien" [sic. "ca ne fait rien" or "that doesn't change anything"]. Your mouth will water when you see them but you won't be able to see. You will do your best no doubt to peep around the corner! Well write me at length what the drawbacks may be, as compared with the advantages. Both of them are quite willing to come![62]

There was, of course, the odd letter, or two, at this time in which the writer asserted that he was appalled or disgusted at the prospect of sleeping with European women, but they were more to appease concerned parents or loved ones in India than any indication of genuine sentiments.[63]

When the first marriages were sanctioned between Muslim Indian *sipahis* and French women in October 1916, the initial reaction was also largely positive.

Men such as Nazir Ullah were motivated enough to leave the army and go in search for work that would offer better remuneration because of the feelings that he had towards his 'Mademoiselle':

> I have arrived in India. I have given up the idea I had of going to Mesopotamia. I am in search of some means of livelihood which will enable me to satisfy my longing to marry my "Mademoiselle". At present she remains in Marseilles.[64]

Those that were engaged to marry, such as Inayat Ali Khan, wrote long letters that unequivocally defended the women who had captured their hearts from claims that they were sex workers or were otherwise 'morally impure':

> Whatever you have written about Bernadette is entirely false. She is an unmarried girl and surrounded by modesty and moreover, I rely on her, and she has given me her youthful promise that she will never look at another man. Further my actual seal remains imprinted upon her.[65]

Finally, some non-Muslim *sipahis* appeared to have actively considered converting to Islam or Christianity so that they could marry in France, in spite of the unease it provoked among their parents:

> Consider, how could I possibly consent to your becoming a Musalman and marrying a Moslem wife, or embracing Christianity and marrying a Christian wife? Have you no shame? Do you think I brought you up so that you might marry a Christian wife? Could a man be so perverted to lose his religion for the sake of a woman? You were one who had a promising future before you in the world, and yet you proceed to wreck your life by being a traitor to your faith! . . . It is the greatest disgrace for a Hindu to become a Mohamedan or a Christian, do not therefore blacken your face before the whole world. . . . Now I give you my last advice, viz. to put away this unprofitable idea from your mind, and never to allude to it in future. And if you reject my advice, take care how you bring such a woman to my house, for she will be beaten on the head with a shovel a thousand times. . . .[66]

Thus, both Muslim and non-Muslim soldiers were fairly open to interracial sex, sexual experimentation and even marriage – at least in the first few years of their time in France.

All this changed as the Snowball letter passed through squadrons and regiments containing Muslim *sipahis*. Suddenly and unexpectedly the issue of interracial sex leading to interracial marriage became an issue of faith. In August

1916, the supposedly lax sexual mores of Muslims began to be seen as a reason for God turning his back on the followers of Islam:

> The holy festival of Ed was celebrated here by the Egyptians in a very strange way.... The festival lasted from 1st to 3rd August [sic].... During these 3 days we did not meet a single Egyptian who was not the reverse of virtuous and well conducted. Each man encountered was more or less the worse for drink, and having at least one "nightingale" sitting beside him in his carriage indulged in all kinds of lewd and obscure songs. It was all very wrong.... The part of the town occupied by Courtesans was worth seeing. On one side a "nightingale" in the possession of an Arab sang loudly. On the other a "nightingale" embraced an Egyptian, while some poor Hindustani looked on and wondered when his turn would come.... Great Kazis [Judges] and Muftis [Law-givers] and Devotees, who had rigorously kept the fast for a month, merely awaited their opportunity at the approach of evening to carry away their "nightingales" and despoil them in the dark. It was a strange sight watching the flittings in and out, here and there, of the "rose-faced" ones. Shame! Shame! The very ground cried out for protection, and praying to God said "for a day like this make a new earth for I am no longer able to endure the suggestive gait and the thrust of the painted heels of these creatures."[67]

In November 1916, coded letters emerged which were sent to individuals who were known to have had relationships with French women and which accused them of adopting the garb and customs of European men in an attempt to become 'Misters' or 'Gentlemen'.[68]

> Alongside me a Bulbul is lying. I had intended putting her in this envelope and sending her to you. But I realise that you have no desire for an Indian Bulbul. Tell me, have you a Bulbul [in France] or not? You surely must have one "Mister"! Do you understand what I mean?[69]

In case these warnings were too oblique, in 1917 these letters metamorphosed into threats of harsh repercussions for any individuals found to be taking 'cups of tea in hotels' (visiting brothels) or who were engaged to French women; both were seen as the first steps to an individual abandoning his faith and 'becoming a Christian'.[70] The nature of these repercussions became apparent in the 38th Central India Horse where Ajab Khan wrote in October 1917 of the social ostracization that met soldiers who were found to have venereal disease:

> If I had not done my best to advise and restrain Wazir Zada Khan his condition would have been disastrous. As soon as he reached Marseilles he contracted venereal disease. The same thing happened when he went to Rouen. In the Sircar's

house if anyone commits murder he gets punished and the matter is finished; but if a man gets venereal disease each and everyone perpetually looks askance at him.[71]

The result of Muslim soldiers 'looking askance' at other *sipahis* who had pursued relationships with French women can be seen in the 6th Cavalry. Several *sowars* in that squadron appeared to have married Frenchwomen and a significant number of those had had children with their partners. By the end of 1917, however, not one of those *sowars* claimed to be content with married life. Lance Dafadar Mohamed Khan began his first letters after his wedding by defending his decision to marry a Frenchwomen and refuting allegations that he intended to stay on in Europe and convert to Christianity:

> You seem to have made up your mind that Mohamed Khan will never return to India. This is an absolute error. Do you suppose that because a man has married he cannot come back? . . . I made the girl a Mohamedan before I married her. Why are you so displeased? If my wife likes to go to India well and good. If not she can stay in France. I will not stay here and nor did I ever promise to do so. . . . Do not imagine that because I married a European I have become a Christian, never![72]

After he was stripped of his 'stripe' due to the insistence of the men under his command in June 1917, he wrote letters claiming that he had been forced into the wedding through no fault of his own:

> I want to tell you of my misfortunes. I was stationed in a village and was in a house where they were very kind to me. There was a young woman in the house and the parents were very pleased with me. She wrote to the King in London and asked permission for me to marry her and the petition came back with the King's signature on it granting leave. But she did all this without my knowledge. The Colonel sent for me and asked whether it was true. I said it was and asked his leave to marry but said I must make the girl a Mohamedan. The Colonel and the men then got very angry and took away my rank of Lance Dafadar and said they would not give me leave to get married. When this came to the girl's ears she sent another petition to the King and the Colonel gave leave and said that directly [after] the marriage was celebrated he should be informed. According to His Majesty's order the wedding came off on the 2nd April. . . . But I swear to God I did not want to marry but after the King's order I should have got into grave trouble if I had refused.[73]

Finally, after being flooded with letters from as far afield as Calcutta that accused him of being an apostate, Sowar Mohamed Khan begged forgiveness for the 'sin' he had committed and cursed his own child for being the daughter of a 'Kafir':

> I have wept much since Kariz Fatima's illness. What you have written that Margaret is my daughter now and that I don't care about Kariz Fatima at all, is wholly false. Kariz is part of my heart and Margaret is the daughter of a Kafir from whose hands it is unlawful even to drink water.[74]

It is impossible to know exactly how many troopers in the 6th Cavalry had had contact with Sheikh Ahmed's dream. There is no direct evidence that the Snowball letter was sent to any member of the troop. The search for bodily purity was certainly influenced by individual experiences of the horrors of trench warfare and an internalization of institutional concern for what sexual contact might mean for white prestige. And yet, interracial sex only became a problem for Muslim *sipahis* of the Indian Army. Sikhs and the various caste Hindu soldiers recruited as Rajputs, Dogras and Jats were still writing voluminously of the 'fairylands' of Paris, even as soldiers in the 6th Cavalry were being socially ostracized for not abandoning their French partners. Sex in France became an issue for Islam just as the Snowball letter was being read and passed on in larger and larger numbers. And, although there is no direct evidence of its presence among *sipahis* who were suddenly concerned by the issue of interracial sex from 1916, it shared signs and manners of speech with those who took up the cause: 'Shame! Shame! The very ground cried out for protection, and praying to God said "for a day like this make a new earth for I am no longer able to endure the suggestive gait and the thrust of the painted heels of these creatures."'[75]

'Show the frenzy of Islam in the fight, Oh Musalmans!': Jazirat-al-Arab, 15th Lancers and mutiny in Mesopotamia

On 29 October 1914, the Ottoman Empire entered into hostilities against the Allied powers by shelling the Imperial Russian fleet at Odessa.[76] The timing of the act could not have been worse for the commanders of Indian divisions overseas and the India Office in Whitehall. Fears were raised that Indian Muslim *sipahis* would sympathize with their co-religionists, and instructions were given to the Chief Censor of Indian military correspondence in France to report any such instances that he came across. Remarkably little was found. Muslim *sipahis* began to discuss the Turkish[77] entry into the war in the early months of 1915, but the Censor discovered only a handful of letters that appeared to display any dismay. Yet, when units containing Muslim *sipahis* were sent from France to fight against the Ottomans in Mesopotamia (Iraq), the 15th Lancers (or Cureton's Multanis) mutinied as soon as they disembarked. The mutiny, and the wider change in attitudes displayed by Muslim *sipahis* towards Turkey, was due to the Snowball letter.

While in France as part of the 3rd Lahore Division,[78] and before the advent of World War I, the 15th Lancers had an exemplary service record. The regiment was formed during the Uprisings of 1857 from six *risallahs* of 'Multani Pathans' by a Captain Cureton and continued to be an exclusively Punjabi Muslim cavalry unit recruited from the Multan area. After being sent to France, the regiment fought at the battles of Neuve Chapelle, Aubers, Festubert, Loos, La Bassee, Messines, Givenchy and St Julien in 1914 and 1915, and did so, by all accounts, with some distinction. More importantly, the men in the regiment appeared to show scant regard for Turkey or for its entry into the War:

> What better occasion can I find than this to prove the loyalty of my family to the British Government? Turkey, it is true, is a Muhammedan power, but what has that got to do with us? Turkey is nothing at all to us.[79]

In other words, the 15th Lancers had little history of dissent even when hunkered within the trenches of the Western Front.

Despite these expressions and signs of loyal service, there was a simmering in attitudes towards the *Sarkar*. By the summer of 1915, soldiers had begun to discuss the progress of Turkey in the War by using language that the Censor only partially deciphered.[80] One means of doing so, identified by the Censor, was to cast belligerents as fictional villagers or as animals and place them within poetic parables. Risaldar Zabida Khan used this method in 1915 to convey his dismay that the Sultan and Khalifa of Turkey had become involved in the conflict, before taking some small comfort at the fact that no confrontation had yet happened with Britain:

> I am sorry about Talmand Khan [Turkey] but it is the will of God. God is gracious and you are praying. We will see what happen[s]. He has staked his head and his body but life is the thing most precious to everyone and he is sitting down and biding his time.[81]

When the forces of the British Empire were cast into battle against the Turks at Gallipoli and in Mesopotamia, Abbas Ali Khan of the 38th Central India Horse used the same metaphor to express his secret desire that 'Sultan Khan' would emerge victorious:

> You are continually writing and saying that there is a conflict between Fateh Khan [Britain] and Sultan Khan [Turkey], and you ask me to pray that Fateh Khan may obtain the victory. I however am very concerned about Sultan Khan because he is an honest person whereas Fateh Khan is a great rascal, and dishonest. I pray for Sultan Khan, that he may obtain his rights.[82]

And when in March 1917 the British captured Baghdad and routed the Turkish army, Sowar Gul Mohamed Khan used another parable to express his state of mind:

> You asked me how the groves of the pomegranates and medlars [Arabia] are getting on. My reply is that the nightingales have looted the fruits of both groves and when they were plundered you were not there. It is a great pity.[83]

Amidst these letters that conveyed specific information about the progress of Turkey in the War were others that sought to link the decline of the Ottoman Empire with the perceived decline of Islam. Each took the form of dream sequences or poems that mirrored elements of the Snowball letter, and each came back time and time again to the threats facing the *Jazirat-al-Arab* – the 'island of the Arabs' and the cradle of Islam. In one letter, the author of which is uncertain, the dream took the form of a *Hajji* entering a Hindu temple for 'a sweet offering', but when 'he had received [it] once, he drew his hand back and put forward the other. A dog carried off the sweetmeats which were in his hand and from the other the vessel was turned aside'.[84] In another, Sowar Ajab Gul wrote of a Kafkaesque vision he had had of his father being killed by his brother after he had taken the form of a harmless insect:

> I have had a dream and must tell you about [it]. My father appeared in the shape of a dried up insect and brother Hazara Gul drove him away and he fell on the ground. My mother said "you tyrant that was your father and you have killed him". . . . I then prayed that God would give me a glimpse of my father and I went to sleep again and had another dream and saw my father washing his teeth seated on a charpoy. I then woke up and prayed to God that if he were dead I might see him as he was and then fell asleep and saw my father in his grave in our own house. Then his hands and feet appeared and he came out of his tomb. I was delighted and said "Father are you all right?". He replied, "No

I am not". Then I saw a Mullah appear and my father and he began to read the Koran together. Then I put my father back in his tomb and directly afterwards the grave was illuminated and I woke up. I am disturbed in mind. What does it all mean?[85]

Finally, constant inferences were made to the plight of Muslims across the world in poetic verse[86];

> The ship of our country is in distress far from home
> The day of resurrection has commenced behind the curtain of tyranny.
> Confidents and sympathizers of your country
> The wind that reaches you is laden with grief.
> It says to you "We are far from home – keep us in remembrance."
> Those who are dying for their country, this is their cry,
> "Our blood proclaims our fidelity."
> The civilized world acknowledges their worth,
> If their necks be bent at all it is a passing stage.
> Alas, that in our hearts the flame of love has not been kindled!
> The caravan of our country is grieving in a foreign land,
> Tyrants are not shamed by their tyranny,
> They ravage the plot, which one time bloomed with flowers.
> Where formerly sweet melody reigned supreme
> Is now heard the clinking of handcuffs.
> To them, as travellers, all roads have been closed,
> Fetters are bound on the innocent ones.
> If in your heart there is not yet the spirit of modesty,
> Read the funeral service of the honour of your race and faith.
> . . .
> Consider the love of Islam,
> It gave to its deadly enemy the cup of death.
> Now is the opportunity of your brother's honour!
> The duty is a real one, not the price of generosity.
> If now the heart of Islam turns to water,
> A thousand pagan jeers will fall on Mohammedanism.
> Show the frenzy of Islam in the fight, Oh Musalmans!
> Otherwise the honour of your race will depart, Oh guardians of that honour!
> Remember the race from which you sprang, show the might of your country!
> Your country is oppressed with troubles, [so] recollect the obligations of your duty.
> The Prophet has bequeathed to you his humanity and generosity
> You are the living monuments of the sense of honour of the Arabs.[87]

Thus, the impact of Turkey's entry into World War I can be measured through *sipahis*' correspondence, but not in the manner that the Censor thought. There was little direct reference to the Ottoman Empire or to its military defeats. But, the 'dogs' that troubled pious Muslims in the dreams that soldiers relayed, the 'fathers' who were accidentally killed by fellow soldiers, and the 'tyranny' that was troubling 'our country' are constant reminders of the sentiments engendered within many Muslim *sipahis* at the prospect of fighting their co-religionists.

In the 15th Lancers, these feelings reached their acme. The 3rd Indian Division, of which the 15th Lancers were part, was ordered to Mesopotamia in December 1915 after the first British campaign against Turkish forces in Arabia ended in failure. Dada Amir Haider Khan, then a *lascar* serving on board a troop transport ship, wrote in his memoirs of the voyage to Basra from France. He recalled that there 'were nearly fifty men who had come from the area of my home' of Rawalpindi on board, and they regularly relayed 'the day-to-day information' of the unease within the 15th Lancers:

> As Muslims they believed it was a sin to fight against their co-religionists and an Indian officer, a non-commissioned Jemadar, took up the lead in inducing them to refuse orders to go to the front. For true Muslims, he said, it is better to disobey and even fight here and die for one's faith than to go to the front and fight against one's Islamic brothers and die as *Kaffirs*. . . . they must resist if the authorities tried to disarm them and fight to the end as an example to all Muslims stationed there. It would be more worthy than to die as *Kaffirs*.[88]

It was an echo of the rhetoric of Snowball. 'Maulvi' Ghulam Sarvar, a trooper within the 15th Lancers, wrote a first-hand account of what occurred upon landing at Mesopotamia in January 1916. Every man within the regiment took an oath with 'the Koran in his hand'[89] to make 'some representation' as they disembarked because Basra and Arabia were 'held most sacred by Mussalmans.'[90] But, the Indian officers betrayed their oaths and co-religionists by informing their British superiors:

> The account of my misfortunes is a long one and I now proceed to relate it. We left France and voyaged for one month to Basrah. [sic.] As soon as we arrived at Basrah the Sirdars held a meeting, and after a discussion came to the conclusion that some representation should be made because the place is held most sacred by Mussalmans. Each one took the Koran in his hand. But a few of the Sirdars commenced to act treacherously in spite of having taken up the Koran, and reported the most trifling matter to the Colonel Sahib from time to time, notwithstanding

the fact that they themselves were the very ones who started the plea that it was not proper for us to fight in this area of the war. . . . The Colonel Sahib reported the matter to the General Sahib, and immediately a battery of artillery and 3 or 4 British Regiments surrounded our camp. None of our men realised what was being done, and when they were told to parade without arms they forthwith did so. [. . . But] the Sirdars sitting in their tents had written out nominal rolls of the men who had refused service. The British troops collected our arms, and looted our private property, taking the money of some, the shaving implements and watches of others. In the evening we were placed on board ship again, and for 3 days a Court Martial was held.[91]

During the Courts Martial, Ghulam was one of 429 who were punished for their role in planning to mutiny. Three 'Kot-Dafadars' were sentenced to 'penal servitude for life', the other NCOs were to be transported 'for 15 years', the 'senior privates' received '7 years transportation', and the eighty draftees to the regiment were dispatched to Bombay for 3 years' imprisonment[92]:

Our ship then left for sea and reached Bombay after a voyage of 5 or 6 days. There the recruits were disembarked, and our ship continued the voyage to the Andamans. When we arrived there, we were placed on a separate island, [and] a Colonel of the 4th British Infantry Regiment and 2 doctors were sent with us. Our uniforms were collected and sold for auction and the proceeds sent to our homes, and we were given convicts' dress. Four Sirdars had been sent with us to the Andamans, three of whom were from our district, and they returned as soon as we had landed. . . . The work we did was this. We built houses. We made a road, we felled trees and we made bridges of stones and the officials who came to inspect our work were astonished at what we had done, and left excellent written reports about us. . . . The Commissioner of the Andamans wrote to the Viceroy on our behalf saying "These men are entirely blameless." The doctor sahib also used much influence on our behalf, and after 12 or 14 months the Viceroy, having pity on our lot, set us free.[93]

Perhaps because of the experiences that he had been through, Ghulam styled himself as a 'Maulvi' even while offering to serve as a soldier again. Yet, there was no contrition on his part, for as he and other *sipahis* in the 15th Lancers stated: 'We were blameless.'[94]

Muslim soldiers in France and India seemed to agree. Within months of the mutiny, dozens of letters were exchanged recounting the 'story' of the 15th Lancers and expressing their outrage over the punishments they had received. On 24 March 1916, Ashrafali Khan, a regimental instructor in the 6th Cavalry in India, wrote of how he had overheard the former Colonel of the 15th Lancers talk to 'his Sahib' and proceeded to give an exhaustive account of all that he had learnt before concluding that 'the deeds of the regiment' were now 'written in letters of gold'.[95] Fateh Khan, some months later, wrote in awe of how the men had 'declined to take up arms against their brother Musalmans' and asserted that this in no way constituted a crime:

> ... it has been reported in the newspapers that the new Viceroy [Viscount Chelmsford] has ordered that these men should be sent to some other theatre of war, since they did not in reality decline to fight for the Sircar, and should not be called upon to fight against the Turks against their wish. I do not know why action has not been taken on this order. It is very sad that fate should have dealt thus [and so] cruelly with the regiment in the end, after they have done such good service and gained so much renown elsewhere.[96]

For others, their letters took the form of prayers pleading for the release of those *sipahis* who had been to the penal camps of the Andaman Islands:

> Please God, those men who were sent across the Kala Pani will soon be liberated. Do you also pray Government to deliver them from the misfortune into which they have fallen? I am troubled only at the long separation from you, and because of the calamity which has befallen those of my beloved ones who have been sent to the Kala Pani.[97]

The soldiers involved began to petition for their release;[98] in at least one district in Punjab, *lambadars* from Niazi villages[99] refused to allow access to recruiters from the 15th Lancers,[100] and rumours persisted of other *sipahis* in Mesopotamia engineering conditions of 'friendly fire' against British soldiers.[101] It is this enduring legacy of the mutiny in January 1916 that explains the decision taken at the end of World War I to disband the regiment. Ordinary Muslim *sipahis* had demonstrated the depth of their feelings towards their 'brother Musalmans' and had presaged the programme of the nascent Khilafat movement in India.

Conclusion: (Re-)writing a letter and (re-)appraising Islam

World War I was not the last time Sheikh Ahmad had a dream or Snowballs were thrown. Nearly a full century after the letters discussed in this chapter, chain emails continue to reprise Sheikh Ahmad's message for the South Asians at home and abroad:

> GIVE FIVE MINUTES OF TIME TO ATLEST [sic.] READ IT TO THE END INSHAALLAH
>
> Subject: DONT DELETE! IF YOUR [sic.] A MUSLIM! PLEASE READ THIS!
>
> This is true. From Madina Sheikh Ahmed has sent this news. On a Friday Sheikh Ahmed fell asleep reading the Quraan. Then he dreamt the Prophet Muhammed (saw) standing in front of him and saying that in one week seven thousand people died but not even one was a true Muslim. None did what ALLAH wanted. He also said now is a bad time. These days Wives dont [sic.] look after their Husbands, Girls go round without being covered they do not respect parents or others, Rich do not look after the poor, they do not give gifts or money or do not give fulfil zakaat.he also said to Sheikh Ahmed make people understand to give zakaat, To do prayer and to keep fast [sic.]. The day of judgement is near. When There is a single star in the sky, straight away the path of forgiveness will close. The writing in The Quraan will disappear (vanish). The Sun will lower itself with Earth. The Prophet said whoever reads this news to someone else,
>
> "I WILL ON THE DAY OF JUDGEMENT MAKE HIM A PLACE IN PARADISE, AND IF SOMEONE DOES NOT BELIEVE THIS NEWS TO BE TRUE THEY WILL BE BANISHED FROM PARADISE"
>
> If a poor person gives out this news to other people his/her good wish will come true. Sheikh Ahmed said if this is not true then my death will be off a Non-Muslim. The Prophet said
>
> "KEEP FAST, DO PRAYERS, GIVE ZAKAAT AND GIVE KINDNESS TO THE POOR"
>
> Whoever Forwards this will get his/her reward in three days. One Person forward[ed] it to 40 people he had 8,000 thousand, take prophet in his Business. [sic.] One Person did not believe this news and his son died. One kept Saying he will forward it today, tomorrow but never forward[ed] this News he died as well.
>
> PLEASE DO NOT THINK THIS IS NOT TRUE.
>
> PLEASE FORWARD THIS TO AS MANY PEOPLE AS POSSIBLE![102]

The email transcribed above was subsequently forwarded (at least) 19 times. Pictures displaying the Mosque of the Prophet at Medina were added, and then, just as easily, omitted. Parts of the message were written in bold or red type or inflated to such a size that the recipient has to scroll down with his or her mouse in order to read his or her sentence. And preambles were added, drawing attention to particular parts of the text, or to just songs from Bollywood movies: *'Mohabbat To Ik Javeda Zindagi He . . . Mohabbat Jisse Bakhash De*

Zindgaani . . . Nahin Maut Par Khatam Uski Kahaani . . .'.[103] Sheikh Ahmad's dream was repackaged, transmitted through a new medium and then reworked as it was cut, pasted and forwarded on.

The emailed Snowball of 2009 mirrored that of 1916, not just in its form but in its reception. The continued circulation of the email frustrated at least one of the recipients in its chain, unhappy with its unsophisticated and patriarchal take on Islam; depths of frustration that were even greater for the Chief Censor unable to stop or regulate its transmission during World War I. Both email and letter also fostered authorial and textual polysemy. Both were manifestations of a particular eschatological dream that had been circulating in the wider Islamic world from the late eighteenth century, and infused with contemporary, South Asian relevance. But, whereas this was achieved in the email by adding prefaces and references to Bollywood songs, in its 1916 guise, its form and tone was shaped by the street debates of Muslim reform movements in colonial India as well as by German and *Ahmadiyya* propaganda in the trenches in France. And, as the letter of 1916 was transcribed and re-transcribed and then passed on, the language of the letter slipped into the everyday prose and concerns of soldiers. The borrowed prose became a way of conveying the horrors of trench warfare; its apocalyptic tone and prospect of redemption given new relevance amidst the broken bodies and unburied corpses of France – 'The life which we are now leading is one which God would not inflict even on a dog, as it is a time of unspeakable hardship with death always at hand, and perhaps by the grace of God we may gain heaven by reason of our self-denial . . . . Amen!'.[104]

The Snowball letter was also marked by its impermanency. As the letter was read, re-written and re-transmitted, it evolved into forms that are tangentially connected to the original. The version of Snowball that was finally transcribed by the Censor in July 1916 hints at earlier versions – 'Once more [in the past] I gave this warning to the faithful but no one attended to it . . . '[105] – and it is possible that Sheikh Ahmad's dream was re-packaged into another quite different version later in World War I. It is impossible to know for certain. Only a fragment of soldiers' correspondence was ever intercepted, transcribed and censored. It becomes difficult to ascertain quite how far its message reached and to what extent attitudes towards interracial sex and Turkey shifted solely in response to the Snowball letter. But, even though the Snowball letter was only part of a wider and now largely imperceptible conversation that Muslim soldiers were engaged in over their religion, it remains significant. It exposes how colonial soldiers lived between ideals of colonizer and colonized, home and periphery. *Sipahis* lived at the interstices of Empire, shifting colonized and colonizing bodies that engaged in long conversations over the nature of French imperialism in Algeria,[106] the possibilities of future constitutional settlements in India,[107] and, more prosaically, how women in Europe 'contrary to the custom in our country . . . do not put their legs over the shoulders when they go with a man.'[108] The Snowball letter reveals a sub- or semi-textual counterpart to the printed tracts of the Muslim reform movements of the time; more dependent on dreams, metaphor and constant re-interpretation rather than force of argument. Finally, it demonstrates that Muslim *sipahis* could continue to act as conduits for the return of miracles, saints and prophetic dreams into the rational colonial projects of cantonments and the Army into the twentieth century. The letters of *sipahis* were originally to be censored because of concerns that Indian political agitators abroad – *Ghadar* and the Indian Independence Committee in Berlin – may make attempts to suborn serving soldiers. The transmission of Sheikh Ahmad's dream reveals that the militarized Islam of the Indian Army was quite able to politicize itself without the need for any agents provocateurs:

> I suppose I am young and young men are rather foolish. Else why did I leave my father and mother and come away from my country to lose my life in the service of the infidel? . . . Corpses lie unburied on the ground, just as stones lie in our country. They are in a dreadful state, and the shots from the big guns life up the men from the ground as in our country the whirlwinds lift up little things in the air.[109]

5

Mutiny, Fabricating Court Testimony and Hiding in the Latrine: The 5th Light Infantry in Singapore

In 1915, in the early summer heat of colonial Singapore, a mutiny occurred. For several days in February, the Muslim Rajput soldiers[1] of the 5th Light Infantry killed their officers and other Europeans in positions of authority,[2] took control of large swathes of the city, and co-opted other Indian *sipahis* stationed nearby into their revolt. The reaction of the colonial government was just as dramatic. A total of 47 *sipahis* and NCOs were executed[3] and 64 were given the sentence of 'transportation for life' (often no better than a death sentence).[4] In spite of the severity of the revolt and the reaction to it, R. W. E. Harper and H. Miller's *Singapore Mutiny*, one of only three published histories of the event,[5] has no space for the mutineers as the subjects of the revolt. It begins with an exhaustive 'Dramatis Personae' of 80 names, mentioning everyone from the Governor of the Straits Settlement to Mrs Marjorie Binnie and her aunt. But, only one Indian *sipahi* is included, and even he only makes the list with the soothing parenthesis next to his name: 'killed by defence forces'.[6]

Despite what Harper and Miller may have concluded, there was more than one soldier who was an actor in the Mutiny and more than one who survived. Before and during the courts martial of the men of the 5th Light Infantry, a parallel Court of Inquiry was established in Singapore in order to collect 'evidence for presentation to Summary General Court Martial' for the trial of mutineers and to 'report upon the causes (direct and indirect) of the Mutiny'.[7] Few *sipahis*, however, gave evidence in the manner that their *sahibs* wished after being herded into the dock. Lance Naik Feroze Khan answered his summons by maintaining that he had been buying a tin of milk when the Mutiny had occurred and then, when confronted with evidence to the contrary, began to justify his role in the revolt.[8] Fazal Azim surprised the Court by voluntarily appearing before it and promising to identify 'all the thieves'.⁹ Sazawar Khan was able to convince the Court that he had been a target of the mutineers and should be treated as a victim and not as one of the accused.¹⁰ And, Dost Mohamed effectively asserted that he knew nothing of the mutineers because he had been an officer's batman and was not known or trusted by most of the men of his company.¹¹ Each of the roles that the four *sipahis* played in the courtroom – of the unrepentant mutineer, the turncoat, the victim and the outsider – were all, to varying degrees, constructed fictions. The slippages in their own testimony and those of their peers reveal that all four men were involved in taking up arms against their officers. Further, and perhaps more importantly, the purpose behind the testimony which these *sipahis* gave was to defend their friends, relatives and messmates from prosecution and to implicate the dead, the unpopular and those of a different caste.

This chapter will try to rehabilitate the soldiers of the 5th Light Infantry who have been either ignored or scantily treated by historians. Four soldiers – Feroze Khan, Fazal Azim, Sazawar Khan and Dost Mohamed – will be the subjects of this work, and what will be analysed in particular is how they re-appropriated the physical and linguistic space of the colonial courtroom. The suggestion will also be made that the testimonies given by these *sipahis* were dependent upon a further re-appropriation of ethnic, geographic and operational military identities. In so doing, there is no intention to imply that these depositions are of greater worth than the dozens of others that are not analysed in detail. The reason for focusing upon four rather than all of the narratives that soldiers gave in 1915 is, to echo Certeau, to 'refer to a reality which once had a living unity, and which *no longer is*'¹² instead of distilling that unity in a fragmented analysis. Before embarking on a study of the four soldiers' testimony, however, I will begin with a summary of what the members of the Court of Inquiry wished to hear from the *sipahis* who gave evidence and how their own priorities conditioned that which Indian soldiers relayed to them.

'L'audace toujours L'audace': The objectives of the Court of Inquiry

Brigadier-General Frederick Aubrey Hoghton, the man who came to preside over the Court of Inquiry, and who later wrote a report summarizing his findings, concluded that the size and scale of the Mutiny was always preventable:

> The time honoured maxim of *L'audace toujours L'audace* when dealing with Orientals was apparently lost sight of. We believe that resolute action by a formed body of Europeans would . . . have exercised a marked effect upon the course of the mutiny.[13]

This statement by Hoghton was not only the product of a specific Singaporean colonialist mentality that 'raised more racial barriers' than elsewhere in the British Empire,[14] but also reflected the type of evidence that Hoghton and his peers wished to gather. There was a desire to ascribe the actions of the majority of the mutineers as due to an ever-present, and profoundly irrational, fanaticism that was fanned by poor officership and by the malefic influences of a handful of malcontents. Apportioning equal amounts of blame on poor officers and insidious ringleaders would avoid any systemic critique of the Indian Army or of the colonial governance of Singapore.

The Court of Inquiry began by seeking to find the single 'opening event' of the Mutiny, and this was quickly located in a parade address given by Brigadier-General Dudley Ridout, the General Officer Commanding, Singapore, to the assembled men of the 5th Light Infantry at Alexandra Barracks on 15 February 1915. The substance of the speech, the manner in which it was given, and even the time it was delivered was disputed by the various officers called upon to give evidence. For Ridout, the speech was a simple message to congratulate the *sipahis* for their smart attire and to inform them that they would soon be departing Singapore for Hong Kong.[15] Statements by junior officers of the 5th Light Infantry, in contrast, asserted that the speech was so lengthy that it necessitated a translation into Hindustani by the commanding officer of the battalion, Lieutenant Colonel Martin, whose own lack of preparation and faltering grasp of the language resulted in a garbled address.[16] Finally, Subedar-Major Khan Mohamed Khan, when asked about this, stated matter-of-factly that neither he nor his fellow Viceroy's Commission (VCOs) had any idea of what had been said and that after the parade had been dismissed:

> I heard the men saying "We are going on service [to Europe]," but I said, "As we are going to Hong Kong, nothing is yet certain about service." They all said, "No, we are going on service; the general has said it." I said, "No, you don't understand." After breakfast I went to the office and my double company writer (Allah Baksh) said, "Is the regiment going on service?" I said "No, why?" He said, "Well, all the regiment says we are going on service."[17]

The Court, keen perhaps to avoid criticizing Ridout directly, concluded that a general lack of 'dash' and daring among officers cultivated a detrimental 'impression in the minds of some of the men'[18] and a reduction in the deference due a British *Sahib*.

According to Hoghton, the creation of a detrimental 'impression' in the minds of *sipahis* in the 5th Light continued apace after 'A' and 'B' Companies attacked and looted the regimental armoury at, or shortly after, 2 pm on 15 February. When Lieutenant Colonel Martin had been awoken from his mid-afternoon nap with the news that men of the right wing of the battalion had 'run amok', he promptly barred the doors and windows of his bungalow and returned to his study deciding (wisely) that discretion was the better part of valour.[19] The more junior British officers of the battalion – Major Cotton, Captain Bell and Captain Boyce – did attempt to rush to their Double Companies so that they could be mobilized to quell any disorder, but, as Hoghton recounts, they were accosted by the Indian officers and prevented from continuing further 'on the grounds that their lives would be endangered' and that they would be 'helpless to restrain the men'.[20] Those VCOs and senior NCOs who were in the 'sepoys' lines' when the first shots were fired were either accused of assisting the mutineers or, in the case of Colour Havildar Jamaluddin, found that they had pressing business to attend to on the lavatory.[21] As a consequence, over half of the proceedings of the Court of Inquiry were devoted solely to collecting the testimony of officers and analysing their perceived failures.

The other priority of the President and Members of the Court was to identify the supposed ringleaders of the Mutiny. As the Court of Inquiry made it clear, the inadequate performance of the 'leaders' of the '[military] community' allowed certain 'native' soldiers to gain undue prominence among the rank and file and create 'states of unrest' within the regiment.[22] Of the *sipahis* in question, certain VCOs were accused of being particularly troublesome, with the Muslim Rajput Indian officers of the right wing of the battalion accused of bickering endlessly with those who were not of the same caste or religion:

> We have indisputable evidence of the existence of serious dissension amongst the Mussulman Rajput Indian Officers of the right wing. We know that for reasons going back for some years, of which we can obtain no clear definition, there had been disagreements between the Subedar-Major Khan Mohamed Khan and Subedar Wahid Ali on the one hand, and Subedar Dunde Khan, Jemadar Chiste Khan and Abdul Ali on the other. As is the invariable custom amongst Indians, each of the separable cliques had its own particular followers among the rank and

file. . . . We are told how the fact of these officers being at variance frequently militated against the maintenance of discipline, and how the fact of one side favouring any particular policy or measure in the regiment was at once the signal for its rejection by the others.[23]

Subedar Dunde Khan and Jemadar Chiste Khan, in particular, came to be apportioned much of the blame for the Mutiny, and the two VCOs were shot in a botched public execution even before the Court of Inquiry had been convened.[24] The Court endeavoured to find *post facto* justifications for the executions that ranged from the suspicious manner in which they smoked cigarettes to claiming that the two Indian Officers were present at certain events during the Mutiny even when they were not.[25] A significant portion of the Court's efforts, therefore, was spent proving that supposed malcontents among the 5th Light Infantry did indeed have a malefic influence.

The search for ringleaders also went beyond the Army. The Court quickly began to search for seditious Indian civilians who may have had contact with *sipahis*. Hoghton admitted that he had 'no direct proof' that any Indian residents of Singapore had 'promoted fanatical unrest and general disaffection' among Indian *sipahis* of the 5th Light Infantry,[26] but, nevertheless, two civilians, Kasim Ismail Mansur and Pir Nur Alam Shah, were arrested and hanged. These executions were clearly an attempt by Hoghton, Ridout and others to link what had occurred in Singapore with the pan-national and transnational *Ghadar* Conspiracy. The Court of Inquiry submitted its report a month after the first trial of *Ghadaris* had begun in Lahore on 26 April 1915 (the Report of the Court of Inquiry was submitted on 20 May) and just as sensational news stories of the plot were beginning to circulate in Britain and abroad.[27] As a consequence, the copy of the *Singapore Mutiny Report* sent to General Sir Beauchamp Duff, Commander-in-Chief of the Indian Army, contained an addendum by Ridout in which he attributed his success in quelling the Mutiny to his hand-picked spies who had infiltrated the ranks of Indian soldiers in Singapore[28] – a similar tactic to that used by Lahore Police to foil the Ghadar insurrection of February 1915.[29] The fact that Ridout's spy network amounted to a single agent, and that he had been prevented from working with the 5th Light Infantry, was conveniently ignored. In truth, there was very little evidence to connect the Singapore Mutiny to the *Ghadar* Party, or *Ghadar* to Mansur or Alam Shah. Members of the *Ghadar* Party did seek to take credit for the Mutiny after the event. But, a cursory study of *Ghadar* sources in the United States of America reveals that Mansur and Alam Shah were not *Ghadari* agents and that no individuals were connected to

Ghadar in Singapore at the time. The first news *Ghadaris* received of the Mutiny was transmitted after it had been suppressed, via a telegram of 2 March 1915 from the Philippines.[30] The *Ghadar* Party Headquarters in San Francisco had so little contact with the accused in the ensuing trials that its publications were still reporting that the 'Indians of Singapore were still executing the English' and that 'some portion of the town is under the possession of the Ghadar party' as late as April 1915.[31]

In addition to Indian civilian agitators, the Court also investigated the possibility of German collusion. It found very little evidence of German involvement, but subsequent accounts, originally in German, claimed that the Mutiny was a German plot. All of these originated from a single narrative by Julius Lauterbach, a German Prisoner of War held in Singapore in 1915, whose story was published as a piece of war-time propaganda under his own name as *1000Pf Sterling Kopfpreis – Tot Oder Lebendig* in 1917, reworked by Reinhard Roehle in the same year as *Als Fluechtling um den halben Erdball*, translated and reworked again in 1930 by Lowell Thomas for the German-American market as *Lauterbach of the China Sea* (which was subsequently retranslated back into German), and finally reworked for the fourth time into a historical novel by Nigel Barley entitled *Rogue Raider*. In all of these versions of the narrative, Lauterbach claimed sole credit for instigating the Mutiny:

> At first the idea of fomenting a mutiny among our guards never occurred to me, but suddenly on a day early in February the idea came to me like a flash. At first I did whatever I could to spread propaganda among the Indian regiments that might give my friend the enemy a little trouble. But the scheme rapidly grew into a definite plot with mutiny as the objective.[32]
>
> Step by step I planned every detail with them – taking the English prisoners and putting them in our barracks, seizing the wireless station, the destruction of all government works. It would all be quite easy. At any rate, I made them think so.[33]

In the early months of World War I, men from the 5th Light Infantry had acted as guards for a camp at Pasir Panjang in Singapore at which German sailors,[34] and any civilians in the city accused of being German, were imprisoned. So, it is possible that there was some interaction with those who were held in captivity. Furthermore, during the Mutiny, some Muslim Rajput soldiers did break open the gate of the camp and were seen throwing rifles and ammunition at the men and women who were interned there in the expectation that they would join them. But none did. Lauterbach explains that this was due to the realization that the Mutiny was doomed and that they were reluctant to take part in the 'rape and ravishment of white virgins, [and] the dashing out of the brains of innocent children'.[35] It is more likely that the interned Germans had no knowledge of the *sipahis*' revolt. The German prisoners not only refused to participate in the Mutiny but also many subsequently assisted their British captors with identifying and capturing mutineers.[36]

As Sho Kuwajima has argued, it is difficult to identify any one single cause for the Singapore Mutiny.[37] If a single, large cause is to be attributed to the Mutiny, it was one that the Court was not willing to admit existed: a desire to avoid the horrors of war in Europe. The Court received translated copies of official military correspondence originally sent by *sipahis* in France to their brothers and relatives in the 5th Light Infantry in Singapore. Its language and content is an echo of the letters discussed earlier in this work:

> Those who have gone to war have all been destroyed. And your brothers live in civility [sic.]. And about the recruiting which is open, don't get any man enlisted as all are being taken to the war. All will be caused to be killed [sic.]. Don't enlist.[38]

> A prayer carpet is being sent by parcel. When it is received donate it to the mosque. Pray for us, it is a very bad hour. Fighting is going on all four sides. May God be merciful. And tell the people in the village that no one should enlist, enlisting is not good.[39]

But, these letters were not referred to in the Proceedings of the Court of Inquiry and were merely filed away in an appendix to its report. It did not fit with what the Court wished to know.

The result of the Court of Inquiry having preconceived ideas as to what caused the Mutiny in Singapore is evident by a mere glance at the transcribed narratives of the *sipahis* who gave evidence. Amid long passages in which *sipahis* described their caste, when they had enlisted and their experiences in the 5th Light Infantry, the voice of 'The President' intruded to force the witnesses to adhere to his own priorities. Men giving evidence would be interrupted with sudden questions that indicated the impatience of the governing voice: 'But what is the cause of this outbreak?'[40]; 'Who were the blackguards in the regiment?'[41]; 'Have you ever been to a mosque outside the lines?'[42] Yet, this intrusion of the President into the testimony of soldiers both restricted and enhanced the agency of *sipahis* speaking before the Court. By offering the Court of Inquiry the half-truths that they wished to hear, the soldiers of the 5th Light Infantry could conceal other, more substantial information, as in the cases of Feroze Khan, Fazal Azim, Sazawar Khan and Dost Mohamed.

Silences, ciphers and buying tins of milk: The testimony of Feroze Khan

In the public testimony given by Vietnam War Veterans in February 1971 – in what was known as the Winter Soldier Investigation – one of the GIs, when asked about 'shamming' in the military and his whole experience in the 'Nam', simply replied 'Man I can't talk, I can't tell you people the instances or whatever you want to hear'.[43] The words of the American soldier could just as easily have come from the mouth of Lance Naik Feroze Khan of 'C' Company of the 5th Light Infantry. The only difference is that, when Feroze was called upon to give evidence before the Court of Inquiry, he knew that he had been identified as a mutineer in the preliminary evidence given by British Officers and some *sipahis*, and he chose to convey a fabricated account of what he did during the Mutiny rather than remain silent.

In the proceedings of the Court of Inquiry, it was accepted practice for *sipahis* to begin their evidence by declaring their caste, the place of their enlistment and how long they had served in the 5th Light Infantry. Feroze Khan, however, did away with this convention and began his evidence in a more confrontational manner by declaring forthrightly that he was not present when the first shots of the Mutiny were fired:

> About 2.30 or 3 P.M. on the 15th February, I went down to Pasir Panjang to buy a tin of milk. It is more expensive at Pasir Panjang but better quality. Before I got to Alexandra Road I heard the "Alarm" sounded so I returned.[44]

He further talked of the confusion that reigned in his own mind after he had made his way back to the cantonment, and that this was the reason why he subsequently dispensed with his uniform, picked up some discarded ammunition and hid his rifle:

> When I got back I saw everybody rushing about. I went into the lines and put on my uniform and went towards the *Kote* [Armoury] to get my rifle. There was nobody there. I looked towards the quarterguard and thought what I should do. I had my rifle, and I heard firing from behind me. A shot struck near me and I fled. As I passed between the barracks I saw a broken ammunition box with one unbroken and one broken package of ammunition in it, which I took and went into the jungle. I sat there alone for some time hearing firing. At dark I rose and moved towards the town. I was afraid and charged the magazine and chamber of my rifle. I remained till morning near Alexandra Road when I thought the best

thing for me to do would be to give myself up. I was going along the road when I heard firing on my right so I again went into the jungle towards Mount Faber. I was afraid I might be shot by either mutineers or [British] soldiers so I hid my rifle near a Chinese Temple so that I might find it again. I found other rifles there. I took off my uniform.[45]

Feroze also criticized the extrajudicial punishments that were meted out to Indians in uniform after the Mutiny for preventing him, a *sipahi* who wished to aid the British, from surrendering to the police or to European soldiers:

I met a Malay policeman. I asked him where the police *thana* was and he said "Pergi". I next met a Sikh who said that if any of us went near a *thana* we would be killed. I went to a mosque near Kampong Jawa where I bought some food and prayed. There were two more of our men, one Sepoy Jaher Mohamed and Sepoy Mohamed Hussain. I slept in the mosque. In the morning Sepoy Abdul Ghanni joined us. He said he had come in the day before (16th). While there the police came at 11 A.M. [on the] 17th, and they arrested all of us.[46]

Feroze's initial account conformed to that which he thought the Court would wish to hear. He claimed that he was unable to surrender because the lack of strong leadership and good officerial conduct during the Mutiny left him confused and fearful of what would happen if he turned himself in.

The terms and tone of Feroze's narrative changed when the governing voice of the President intruded upon it. Rather than denying any knowledge of events that were seen to have led to the Mutiny or absenting himself from them, the Lance Naik began to admit certain realities that the Court already knew and even offered a tentative justification for the actions of the mutineers. When asked by the President how he came by a cap of the Malay States Volunteers – a primarily European force used to quell the Mutiny – that he was brazenly wearing in the presence of the Court of Inquiry, he quickly quipped, 'I found the Malay cap I am wearing in the mosque'.[47] After Feroze was confronted by evidence that he had asked for his discharge from the 5th Light Infantry on the morning before the Mutiny, he excused his actions by stating:

I had some time before this, for family reasons, asked to be sent to the depot and just before the General's parade, I heard the men saying that there was a number of men asking for their discharge or for transfer to the Depot. I left the hospital and saw the Colonel who said, "Wait till we get to Hong Kong, I will make it right."[48]

Finally, when Feroze was questioned over why he had been accused of malingering by officers in command of the 5th Light Infantry, he abandoned his earlier evasiveness and accused his officers of being in breach of military regulations because of their practice of imposing irregular fatigues on men who should have been in hospital:

> On the morning of the General's parade I was one of those who fell out. I was taken to the doctor. I was given medicine. The doctor did not say that there was nothing the matter with me. The doctor said that those not fit for duty would remain in hospital. I did not remain [i.e. he was forced into a fatigue]. I was taken before the Colonel in connection with this and in connection with the matter of a fatigue party of which I was in charge on the same day [which refused to do the work asked of it].[49]

These were partial and incomplete admissions of a far more intimate knowledge of what had caused the Mutiny among the men of the 5th Light Infantry.

But, even these admissions did not broach what he actually did before and during the Mutiny. In the days and weeks preceding the revolt on the 15 February, he had come under the notice of some of the British officers of the battalion for his 'insubordinate' tendency to make complaints against his immediate superiors.[50] One *sipahi* recounted that, after Sepoy Ismail of 'C' Company had fired the first shot of the Mutiny, Feroze had applauded and welcomed the act: 'Lance Naik Feroze Khan came into the guard room and asked where this lion Ismail was . . . "Where is the lion? He has done very well."'[51] According to the testimony of two other soldiers who were patients in the isolation ward of the cantonment hospital, at 'about 2.30 P.M.' Feroze led or was part of (there is some confusion over the issue) a large group of *sipahis* that had fired upon the hospital staff.[52] Finally, after the Mutiny had been underway for several hours, Sepoy Fateh Mohamed Khan witnessed him 'firing at least two shots' at 'two or three white men' at Tanglin barracks, although he did not know 'whether he hit them or not.'[53] Other *sipahis* did defend Feroze Khan from the accusation that he was a mutineer,[54] and some of those who gave evidence against him did so to satiate personal vendettas,[55] but if only a handful of the complaints made against Feroze Khan were true, then the testimony he gave before the Court was false.

So, the question remains: why did Feroze give a fabricated testimony?

Certainly, part of the motivation was a personal desire to avoid the executions that he would have been able to hear from the gaol in which he was held. The whole of the battalion was interned in the months following the Mutiny, many aboard a prison hulk docked in one of Singapore's harbours. At the time *sipahis* were giving evidence, however, they were moved to within earshot of firing squads executing the men who had already been convicted:

> [the crowd seemed] to utter some kind of gasp. From within the prison, however, came an anguished wail, the voices of comrades of the dead men. . . . Such, with one exception, was the pattern of each group of executions that I witnessed.[56]

But, even if Feroze was shocked into amending his testimony by the swiftness of colonial justice, it cannot have been the sole reason. The adjuncts that he made to his original deposition do not read as an appeal for clemency.

The possibilities of other motives emerge when an analysis is made of his choice of words and what Feroze chose to omit from his account. Throughout Feroze Khan's testimony, the *sipahi* studiously avoided naming any of his fellow soldiers. The names of the soldiers he was arrested with made a brief appearance, but aside from that, every other Indian protagonist in his narrative was hidden behind a cipher, be it the 'Sikh who said that if any of us went near a [police] than we would be killed'[57] or the 'the Orderly Havildar – I don't know who it was – [who] gave out [the order] that nobody was to talk about service' in France.[58] Other *sipahis* appeared at the edges of Feroze's depositions, but their numbers, names or precise activities were never disclosed. Thus, the Court was informed that 'When I got back I saw everybody rushing about'[59] but, as Feroze quickly returned to where *he* went and what *he* did, no indication is given of who was in that crowd nor where they were rushing to and from. Similarly, when Feroze Khan admitted that 'I hid my rifle near a Chinese Temple' and also added that 'I found other rifles there',[60] the precise number of rifles that was present and whom those rifles belonged to was quickly glossed over. What is revealed, therefore, when an analysis is made of the words and silences within Feroze's testimony was his desire not to mention any *sipahi* other than those the Court of Inquiry knew he had been with. Consequently, one can conclude that the reason that Feroze constructed a fabricated account of his actions during the Mutiny rather than remain silent was to ensure that no other soldier would be impugned for knowing him.

Naming 'all the thieves' as the Court's approver: Fazal Azim's testimony

As soon as Lance Naik Fazal Azim, of "D" Company, approached the dock in March 1915 to give his account of the Mutiny, the soldier was informed in no uncertain terms by the President of the Court of Inquiry 'that they had evidence that he went to Tanglin' barracks in the company of mutineers 'and wanted to give him the opportunity of telling us anything he may know with regard to anything that happened'.[61] The response by Fazal Azim appeared to be one of complete compliance. In his testimony, he gave a full account of the moment he learnt of the Mutiny and recounted at length what he and those around him subsequently did, all under the rubric of being the Court's approver:

> I knew all about it and can put you on[to] all the thieves and I am prepared to prove it.[62]

In spite of what the Court came to believe, however, Fazal did not completely disclose everything he witnessed and there was an ambivalence to each revelation he made.

The Members of the Court of Inquiry came to apportion a greater value to Fazal Azim's deposition than those of other approvers.[63] It was because the *sipahi* was careful to extricate himself from what the Court of Inquiry deemed to be the worst offences of the mutineers and because he was willing to offer a list of names of those involved. Throughout his testimony, Fazal emphasized his continued shock and alarm at the actions of men who were willing to take up arms against their officers, such as when the *sipahi* first learnt that a mutiny was underway:

> I was sitting in my section "D" Company, No.26, playing cards with three or four men. . . . A shot was fired from the quarterguard. Immediately afterwards or very shortly afterwards, Abdul Ghani, my section commander came out of the barrack[s] room towards me with his apron full of ammunition and his rifle in his hand. Then I saw Sepoy Ismail and Sepoy Hoshiar Ali of "D" Company carrying an ammunition box between them. Sepoy Hoshiar Ali on the right, and Sepoy Ismail on the left. Then Subedar Wahid Ali, the Company Commander, and Naik Nur Mohamed came towards the right half company from the left half company.
>
> I went up to Subedar Wahid Ali, who was a relation of mine by marriage – he has twice been married into my family – and thinking he might be in danger, I followed him. When he got close to the centre of "L" block, which is to the right company of "D" [sic], I saw that ammunition box had been put down on the ground by the west end of the block, and that Naik Ruk Nurdin was standing on the ground immediately below the block to the south. He slapped his hands on his thigh, and said to Subedar Wahid Ali "Go away, Subedar Sahib, or you will be shot". Then Havildar Murad Ali Khan said the same thing.[64]

To emphasize how unwilling a mutineer he was, the Lance Naik maintained that it was only his desire to protect his commanding officer from harm that led to him unwittingly being thrust into the midst of the conspiracy:

> Subedar Wahid Ali then went through "L" block northwards towards the native officers' lines. He came between the two blocks of "D" and "E", and moved south. While he was passing through the blocks two sepoy, namely, Maizar and Fulkhan of "D" Company, clicked their bolts [i.e. prepared to fire]. They were inside the barrack room. I was very much afraid for the safety of Subedar Wahid Ali, and took ten rounds of ammunition from the box I have mentioned. I charged the magazine with five rounds; I don't know what I did with the other five. I put them down somewhere. I remained near "L" block with the intention of protecting Subedar Wahid Ali if I could. Meanwhile he had gone away, but I don't know where. I remained there for a long time. I then went to a little rising ground close to the cookhouse of "N" and "O" blocks. The Colour Havildar Imtiaz Ali, with four or five other men, were standing between the blocks "A" and "B" and with Imtiaz Ali were Sepoy Nur Mohamed of "A" Company, and Sepoy Raffi Mohamed of "A" Company. I had my rifle with me. Colour Havildar Imtiaz Ali said to me "Where are you wandering about [to]?" I said "I have come from my Company." Colour Havildar Imtiaz Ali then said "I have sent Havildar Ibrahim, Naik Munshi, and Naik Zafir Ali and a lot of men to Tanglin." He said "Why are you not doing something?" I gave no reply as I was afraid. The motor lorry was then standing in the front of the Quartermaster's stores, and I went round by the motor lorry, past the mosque, back to the cookhouse of my Company blocks "L" and "M". By the cookhouse came Lance [Naik] Feroze Khan of "C" Company, who was identified at the same time as myself. He came from the direction of "E" Company, blocks "D" and "E". He said to me "Come with me; we will go and see something."65

Finally, after being compelled to join the Mutiny, Fazal claimed that he managed to slip away before he committed a serious offence and fired his rifle:

> I went with him [Feroze Khan] and in front of us were walking five or six Sepoys. They were going towards Alexandra Road in the direction of the cross roads between Alexandra Road and the path to the Indian officer's quarters. I recognized Basharat of "A" Company, Inayat of "A" Company, Sepoy Bahar Ali of "B" Company, and Sepoy Rahimdad of "B" Company. I cannot remember the rest. They had rifles and ammunition. When we came to these five or six sepoys, Lance Naik Feroze spoke to them and said "Where are you going?" They replied "We are going along." [sic] He said "Is it for you to give me orders or for me to give you orders?" and he began to talk to one of the sepoys, but I don't know what

he said. We then all joined up together. We went along in a northerly direction towards the hospital. I went with this party as far as the little hill beyond the Isolation ward of the hospital and got into the jungle and there I got frightened as to what they were going to do and separated from them and went towards the Green Hill. I sat close to a Chinese hut at the foot of Green Hill. About dusk, Dost Mohamed of "B" Company came to me. He had a rifle and his haversack was full of rounds, I asked him if he had turned against the Government and he replied "No." I took his rifle and examined it. It had been fired. I then removed the magazine of his rifle and my own and I hid them at a spot I can point out. He [sic, We] then went over Green Hill. It was then getting dark and we placed both rifles in a spot I can point out and we slept close to a Chinese hut. The reason I hid our rifles was that I was afraid of being shot on sight for having a rifle on me, and I took particular note of the places where we hid them and the magazines to prove that we did not hide them for any ulterior purpose. About 6 or 6.30 next morning we came to a police station somewhere close to town . . . and we were brought to the Central Police Office.[66]

Throughout the narrative, Fazal Azim combined his attempts to exonerate himself from blame with what seems to be a full and frank list of names. The soldier mentioned those whom the Court had already identified as prominent mutineers – Lance Naik Feroze Khan, Colour Havildar Imtiaz Ali and Sipahi Ismail – a list of their cohorts with whom the Court was less familiar – Naik Ruk Nurdin, Havildar Murad Ali Khan and Sepoys Maizar and Fulkhan – and a handful of others who, Fazal claimed, were compelled or coerced to join the revolt – Basharat, Inayat, Sipahi Bahar Ali and Sipahi Rahimdad.

Fazal Azim embellished his narrative further in response to the questions the Court posed to him. When the Lance Naik was asked what he thought were the causes of the Mutiny, he initially replied that he did not know the causes before defaming coyly, and then not-so-coyly, Jemadar Chiste Khan and the men associated with him:

God knows [what was the cause]. A shot was fired and everybody seemed to go mad. The firing was at the instigation of Colour Havildar Imtiaz Ali.

All I can tell you is this: that Chiste Khan used to talk to my section in "D" Company and tell them all the news regarding the war that was unfavourable to the Sirkar. We used to hear news of the successes of the British, at which we were very pleased. Chiste Khan used to say exactly the opposite; that the British had been defeated, etc. I heard him say these things with my own ears. I have no doubt that he used to tell the sepoys other news, but he was very suspicious of me, being a relative of Subedar Wahid Ali, who was his enemy and he never would talk much when I was there. In fact, he would not let me sit in his Mess. He used to talk to the men in the afternoons and very frequently at night, and sometimes used to sit till 11 or 12 o'clock at night talking to the men. With him used to be Abdul Ghani, Abdul Rahmat, Havildar Murad Ali, Naik Ruknuddin and Nur Mohamed. Sepoys both of my Company and of other Companies used to sit there listening. At night, sepoys of other Companies did not come as a rule, but by day they used to, lots of them. The day that the General Officer Commanding made his speech saying what fine fellows we were, after parade Chiste Khan, Havildar Murad Ali, Naik Nur Mohamed and Naik Karim Khan told the section that we were not going to Hong Kong and that we were going to the war, and that we were being deceived about this ... when the officers and non-commissioned officers began to spread these stories, who was to believe anything? When Subedar Wahid Ali came into the lines as I have described on the 15th, after the "Alarm", if these non-commissioned officers whom I have mentioned – Murad Ali, Abdul Ghani, Nur Mohamed, and Ruknuddin – if they had lifted a finger to help them and had given a single order to the men to remain loyal to him (Subedar Wahid Ali) no one would have done anything. They were the real authors of the mischief led by Chiste Khan.[67]

After he was asked if he had anything to add to his statement, Fazal claimed that he had recently overheard conversations between *sipahis* in which the soldiers had incriminated themselves.[68] This precipitated the apparently spontaneous declaration that he would hereafter act as an agent for the Court within the gaols and prison-ships in which the soldiers of the regiment were interned:

> If I am sent to the prison ship and allowed to live there I will get any amount of information.[69]

Thus, Fazal differentiated himself from other *sipahis* who turned Court's approver both by offering a more complete account of the Mutiny and a list of those involved, and by making the open-ended promise to supply 'any amount of information' in the future. It is clear then from both the content and the sentiments of Fazal Azim's deposition that he not only gave king's evidence but also that he desired to be seen and remembered as the perfect approver.

Part of the reason that Fazal was so eager to adopt the guise of the perfect collaborator was to deflect attention from what he actually did on 15 and 16 February 1915. Two *sipahis* who were malaria patients in the isolation ward of the cantonment hospital both disputed Fazal Azim's claim that he played a minor role in the Mutiny. Sepoy Maksud, a 'Pathan of the Rohtak District', stipulated that after the hospital came under fire from mutineers and he fled from it, he ran into another group of rebellious soldiers that were led by Fazal Azim.[70] The other patient, Gulam Mohamed, went further by claiming that there were 20 or 30 *sipahis* with Fazal, that they were being led in a double or quick march, and that they all had their 'accoutrements' with them:

> I saw Lance Naik Fazal Azim. I don't know his number or Company, but I know him well. He was in the signallers. He had 20 or 30 men with him. He was conducting this party along the road. They were all armed with rifles. I cannot say if they had bayonets. If they had [bayonets] they were not fixed. They had all their accoutrements. They were going towards Tanglin in extended order. I could not say if they had ammunition. They passed me at 30 yards distance. They were in no formation, but going in a clump along the road. They were going at the "quick, stepping out [pace]." The party had gone on ahead of me, but Lance Naik Fazal Azim passed me when I was near and I could recognize him.[71]

Even Subedar Wahid Ali, who one would expect to have supported Fazal given that the Lance Naik claimed he had followed and protected the man from harm, stated:

> On the 15th of February when the outbreak occurred and I went to my company, I did not see Lance Naik Fazil Azim [No.] 2523. He belongs to the right wing. He is a relative of mine, and [I] know him well. He may have been there. There was a crowd of people [there], but I did not see him.[72]

It seems likely that part of Fazal Azim's enthusiasm for becoming an approver was to avoid his own court martial, especially given the fact that, before and after Fazal's testimony, witnesses inferred that he led a party to Tanglin barracks, at which 11 Europeans were killed.

The Court of Inquiry was happy to oblige Fazal Azim. Its reluctance to dismiss the evidence of one its few approvers led to it dismissing all evidence that contradicted the Lance Naik's account. The testimonies of both Maksud and Gulam Mohamed were treated as the product of a grudge the men held against Fazal for some wrong he had committed against them in the past. Consequently, both *sipahis* were re-examined, forced to pick out Fazal from an identification parade, and, after one of them failed in identifying him successfully, their testimony was ignored.[73] Subedar Wahid Ali was not accused of bearing the Lance Naik any ill will. The Court was, however, disposed to viewing all Indian Officers as incompetent and Wahid Ali's failure to notice a man, who was after all his relative, was seen as symptomatic of wider failings.[74] If there were other soldiers who could have highlighted the inconsistencies within Fazal Azim's deposition, such as the man with whom he surrendered, they were either never called to give evidence or the Court failed to ask them about the matter.[75]

But, Fazal was not just interested in saving his own skin. There was another reason why Fazal chose to give evidence. Throughout his account he only impugned the dead or soon-to-be dead. Fazal Azim identified several prominent mutineers or ringleaders in his evidence, but, of these, Jemadar Chiste Khan had already been executed, Lance Naik Feroze Khan was in the process of being court-martialled and Colour Havildar Imtiaz Ali had died during the revolt. All of the other men the *sipahi* had accused of acting in a seditious manner were already lying in their graves. These included those whom he had witnessed 'clicking the bolts' of their 'rifles' and hoarding ammunition[76] and those NCOs he had accused of failing to give a 'single order to the men to remain loyal'.[77] The few soldiers Fazal Azim named who were still alive were each defended or had their actions excused to some degree.[78] It was claimed that Sepoys Basharat, Inayat, Bahar Ali and Rahimdad had all been forced to join the group of mutineers that headed towards Tanglin and that Fazal could not 'remember the rest' of those that accompanied them.[79] It is difficult to ascertain whether military authorities ever charged the soldiers that Fazal Azim defended, but since they were never called upon to give evidence, one can assume that Fazal succeeded in convincing the Court of their innocence. Thus, what is significant about Fazal Azim's testimony is the ambivalent nature of each revelation he made. Those soldiers who featured as mutineers in his narrative were already dead and those who may have been mutineers and who were alive were barely mentioned at all.

'If you wish to save your life, run!': The deposition of Sazawar Khan and embracing victimhood

Naik Sazawar Khan, of "C" Company, was among the first Indian soldiers whom the Court summoned to give evidence. This was because Sazawar claimed he was (and was treated as) a victim of the Mutiny. The Naik was detailed in a fatigue that was fired upon in the initial stages of the revolt, and the colonial authorities did not possess any preliminary evidence to suggest that he had supported the mutineers. It was believed that the *sipahi* would reveal and disclose more than other *sipahis*, and at first it appeared as if he might well do so when Sazawar promised that 'I have no reason for concealing the truth. I have no fear of being punished'.[80] The Members of the Court of Inquiry proved to be mistaken, however, in their belief that Sazawar Khan's evidence would prove useful for later prosecutions. They were also mistaken to think that the *sipahi* was completely disassociated from those who took part in the revolt.

Naik Sazawar Khan was present in a group of *sipahis* and *khalasis* (labourers)[81] that were detailed to load ammunition and 'drums of oil' from the regimental armoury and onto a lorry on the afternoon of 15 February 1915. Owing to the fact that the half-loaded vehicle and the cantonment armoury were the first targets of the mutineers, he was well placed to describe the first stages of the revolt:

> Naik Sadiq was standing on the lorry and Mahbub, the Khallassi was handing him empty drums of oil. There were about three or four drums still to load. I am unable to say whether Ismail was sentry on the quarterguard,[82] [but] Ismail, who fired on the motor lorry, did so from the position of the quarterguard sentry. He shouted something, but I am unable to say what, but after firing he came on towards the lorry with his bayonet fixed at the "charge". All the whole fatigue ran away, including myself. I stopped on the road opposite the quarterguard. Ismail then reloaded and said to me, "If you wish to save your life, run", presenting his rifle at me I backed across the road towards a small footpath near the Chinese shop. I got under cover and distinctly heard Imtiaz Ali shout to the men "Fall in".[83]

The Naik did not dwell over what occurred in those initial moments, however, and spent the rest of his time in the dock describing how his fear of the mutineers and his subsequent flight from them did not leave him in a position to add anything more:

> There was a tremendous noise going on, but I saw very little of what was the cause as I was hiding under cover. While I was standing on the road just previously described I looked towards the quarterguard, but I could see no one except Ismail who fired the shot and was standing by the lorry in the road. I ran [a]round the dhobi lines in the band barrack, which is "C" block and I could hear firing going on in the lines, but I am unable to say where. There were a confused lot of men running about. A lot of men were running about with rifles in their hands and I could hear firing in the distance. I went into cover to the south of the band barrack. I remained under cover in this spot till about five o'clock. Then I crept along under cover in the direction of the range. I heard firing going on. I remained in the cover

near the range for the whole night. I had intended to go to the Mess, but I was frightened.

. . .

I am absolutely unable to describe any reason for the disturbance. If I knew of any I would tell you at once, but I don't. All I know is that when the outbreak occurred the ringleader appeared to be Imtiaz Ali who was shouting to the men.[84]

The Court of Inquiry did use Sazawar's deposition as further proof that the men of the 5th Light Infantry were worried at the prospect of being shipped to France, in spite of the brevity of his evidence. But, Sazawar Khan neither confirmed nor denied this hypothesis.

There is a break in the stenographer's transcription of Sazawar's testimony before the *sipahi* appears once more on the page, indicating that he was either recalled or there was an adjournment in the proceedings of the Court. Whatever the cause of the lacuna, the testimony of the *sipahi* afterwards differed from what had been recounted before. Lance Naik Feroze Khan was suddenly mentioned in Sazawar's deposition and, in particular, his suspicious and 'sulky' behaviour before the Mutiny:

There was a Lance Naik in my company named Feroze. About the 13th or 14th of February the Subedar Major commanding my company sent for all non-commissioned officers of my company to his quarters. Jemadar Hoshiar Ali was there, and the Subedar Major told us the regiment was not going on service, but [that] it was the desire of the Commanding Officer to know if it was a general wish and the Subedar Major wanted to know if we would volunteer for service. The Lance Naik said to me "Why don't you volunteer?" Feroze Khan said this in a very insubordinate way. He belongs to the same village as the Subedar Major. The Subedar Major said "All right, I will give my name. Will you give yours?" A few days before the outbreak Feroze came back from Tanglin and I heard him say to the company "I am not going either to Hong Kong or on service." I remonstrated with him and told him he was not to make such remarks to the sepoys. Feroze Khan has always been a very active man and has been a scout, and was always running about. When he fell out from the General's inspection parade I began to think there must be something wrong with him and that he was sulky.[85]

Sazawar also added that at Christmas the NCOs of the regiment failed to offer their regards to their British Officers as they had done the year before and implied that this could have been due to some simmering unease and disquiet:

. . . I recollect that last Christmas I said to Lance Havildar Taj Mohammed: "Let us go and make our salaams to the British Officers according to our custom."

Taj Mohammed said: "No, I am not going." He gave no reason, but just said he was not going. It has been the custom for the majority of the Non-Commissioned Officers to go to see their British Officers on Christmas day to make their salaams, but last Christmas I went and saw the Havildar Major there and Babu Atta Mohammed [a clerk], but I saw no one else. I am unable to say what happened.[86]

But, the Court of Inquiry never utilized these adjuncts that Sazawar made to his testimony. It consisted of equivocation and not the 'facts' that the Members wished to hear.

Approver Sazawar's frequent equivocation can be attributed to his desire to protect himself from prosecution. The accounts of civilian and military witnesses to what occurred to the fatigue, of which Sazawar Khan was part, offered a narrative that differed from what the Naik had recounted. Sazawar was unable to tell from where Sepoy Ismail had fired upon him, but, as far as Havildar Mohamed Yar Khan was concerned, the *sipahi* was only standing 20 yards away from the fatigue when he opened fire.[87] Khalasi Mahbub Khan seconded this and added that because the mutineer was standing upon the elevated veranda of the building housing the Quarter Guard, Sepoy Ismail could be clearly seen by everyone present.[88] Even an individual like Sambhudutt – a Singapore Indian who was running a grocery shop nearby – who did not see the shot being fired but only heard it knew that the shot had to have come from the Quarter Guard because only those men had access to live rounds in the cantonment.[89] Furthermore, the men of the Quarter Guard clearly saw Sazawar Khan even if he did not see them. *Sipahi* Mahbub Khan recounted that some hours after the Mutiny began:

> I saw Naik Sazawar Khan come to the Company kote, which is on the east side of "P" block and burst open the door with an axe and take out three or four rifles which he gave to the Malay States Guides, who came running from the direction of "B" Company barracks. I am not able to recognize these men [Malay States Guides]. I am prepared to swear to this. In the presence of Naik Sazawar [sic. I was in the presence?] that Subedar Dunde Khan who was standing up by his own Company shouted out to Naik Sazawar Khan to give rifles to the Malay States Guides. Naik Sazawar said "All right Subedar Sahib, I will."[90]

The only moment in his testimony where Sazawar did not prevaricate was when he mentioned the names of Lance Naik Feroze Khan and the Subedar Major. Yet, the referencing of those names did not amount to a full disclosure of those whom Sazawar genuinely thought were at fault. The Naik's explanation of the insubordinate behaviour of Feroze Khan before the Mutiny, and Subedar

Major Khan Mohamed Khan's strange tolerance of it, was that Feroze belonged 'to the same village as the Subedar Major'.[91] He did not dwell over the matter, but the regional loyalties that Sazawar condemned among some of the men helped to still his tongue when it came to condemning others. This is particularly the case with Acting Colour Havildar Jamaluddin Khan,[92] the man who was in command of the Quarter Guard at the time when the first shot was fired and a man who was both of the same caste and came from the same village as Sazawar. Jamaluddin was seen on the veranda alongside Sepoy Ismail by some men,[93] and was seen helping the mutineers by others,[94] but was completely absent in Sazawar's account.[95] One can only speculate over the precise relationship Jamaluddin and Sazawar had. Jamaluddin and Sazawar may have been related in some way, they may have been friends before entering the military, or perhaps the Naik wished to avoid difficulties from the soldier's family if and when he returned to his village. Regardless of the reason, it is clear that Sazawar sought to deceive the Court of Inquiry to protect Jamaluddin while casually impugning men who belonged to a different locality. Claiming to be a victim of the Mutiny allowed him to achieve this end.

Occupying the margins and 'being' the outsider: The testimony of Dost Mohamed

The evidence of Sepoy Dost Mohamed, of 'B' Company, was not as full or as lengthy as that of other *sipahis*. The transcribed version of his testimony amounted to a single paragraph containing several succinct sentences. The reason for this is two-fold. Dost claimed that, as a newly recruited officer orderly or batman, he had barely spoken to other men in the regiment and so had little to tell:

> I don't know who they were. I have only been two and a half months in this battalion.[96]

Further, given that the Court of Inquiry was unlikely to include extraneous information in their reports, it is probable that the *sipahi's* statement was edited to appear shorter on the page than it actually was. Dost both claimed to be an outsider, and his testimony was treated as being marginal and incidental. But, as will be shown below, it is likely that Dost Mohamed wished to be seen as an individual who had nothing important to convey in order to avoid having to give a full account of the Mutiny.

Dost's evidence, according to the transcription of it, began with the *sipahi* describing his lowly position in the battalion and how he was taken by complete surprise when the first shots of the Mutiny were fired:

> I have done about a year's service. On the 15th February I was orderly at the adjutant's office. Between 2 and 3 P.M. I was told to go and get my food. I was in the latrine when a shot was fired. I cannot say where it was [fired]. I washed my hands and came straight up to my Company lines. I found the Company Barrack absolutely empty. I got frightened, and I wrapped a blanket round myself and lay underneath a bed cot. . . .[97]

Hiding under a blanket only proved to be a temporary respite, for Dost was soon discovered by Colour Havildar Imtiaz Ali and was told in no uncertain terms that he would be killed if he did not join the mutineers:

> . . . whilst I was there Colour Havildar Imtiaz Ali came in with two or three men and shouted out "Is there anybody in this barrack room?" and told his men to shoot anybody they could find. I got frightened and I flung off the blanket and ran up to Imtiaz Ali with folded hands. I said to him "Don't shoot me. I am an office orderly and have just come back from duty". He said "I don't care a blow who you are. If you don't go and get a rifle and ammunition at once I will shoot you." Imtiaz Ali took me to the Company bell of arms [sic] and gave me a rifle, one of two or three which were there, and he gave me with his own hands two complete packets of ammunition and three chargers full. Imtiaz Ali had three other men with him, and he ordered me to go take up my position in an entrenchment which is near the other side of the Indian quarters.[98]

After taking the rifle and ammunition from the Colour Havildar, Dost recounted that he fled into the jungle at the first available opportunity, stumbled upon Lance Naik Fazal Azim and buried the arms that he had been given:

> I immediately ran away in the direction of the shops opposite the quarterguard and was shot at by all four. I got away into the jungle. I went straight over to Alexandra road into the jungle and then came to another road. On my way I met Lance Naik Fazal Azim of "D" Company who asked me where I was going. I said to him "I am going to Singapore." He said "Why? Are you not disaffected." I said "No, I am not." He said "Nor am I. Come along with me." Lance Naik Fazal Azim and I hid our rifles with the ammunition in a pineapple field. I am prepared to identify the place where they were hidden. I never went to Tanglin [Barracks]. I stayed out all night and fed on fruit. The next morning we were going along the

road to Singapore when we met two Europeans in a motor car. They stopped and took us in front of the motor to some Major. I cannot tell you his name, and we were arrested. I know no more. Three men who were with Imtiaz Ali fired at me when I ran.[99]

Thus, in his short stay in the dock, Dost Mohamed did not tell the Members of the Court anything they had not already heard. Imtiaz Ali and Fazal Azim, the only two *sipahis* who were mentioned by name in his account, were either already known to the Court as prominent mutineers or had already given evidence as Court's approvers.

Dost was recalled by the President of the Court of Inquiry, Frederick Aubrey Hoghton, sometime after he had first given evidence. The reason for this was that Dost had been ordered to lead a deputation from the Court to the location where he had hidden his rifle, so that it could be recovered, only for him to assert that he no longer remembered where he had dispensed with his arms: 'On a former occasion he said he could find the place . . . now he says he is not certain.'[100] Dost Mohamed's explanation was unconvincing. The *sipahi* claimed that he had lost all sense of his bearings after fleeing from Imtiaz Ali and he had had to rely on Lance Naik Fazal Azim's judgement to tell him where he was when he was hiding his weapon:

> I ran into the jungle close to the bunya [sic] bazaar, which is near the crossroads. When I got into the jungle I met close to a footpath, which goes in the direction of Mt. Faber, Fazal Azim. This was about 5 o'clock. Fazal Azim told me it was Green Hill.[101]

Although the Court of Inquiry accepted that Dost was genuinely disorientated, it led its Members to re-examine other elements of the *sipahi's* original testimony. Hoghton, in particular, barked at Dost Mohamed, 'If they [the men that shot at Dost and who were accompanying Imtiaz Ali] belong to your Double Company you should be able to recognize them.'[102] The *sipahi's* answer was not one that instilled fulfil the Court with any degree of confidence, but it did serve to allay any further questions they may have had: 'he said he could not tell me'.[103]

Dost's final statement that 'he could not tell' the President anything more had a double meaning. Dost Mohamed was both unable and unwilling to elaborate on his deposition, and there were parts of the *sipahi's* evidence that contained inconsistencies beyond those the Court recognized. One such instance was when Dost claimed that Imtiaz Ali gave him a rifle and ammunition from the Company Armoury. While it was possible that he could have obtained a rifle from that place, Dost could only have been given ammunition from the regimental armoury – where all the mutineers were gathered. Another occasion was when the *sipahi* recounted that he had fired none of the rounds that he had been given. Fazal Azim claimed in his testimony that Dost Mohamed's rifle had been fired before the *sipahi* buried it, something he discovered by examining the weapon.[104] Finally, Dost changed his initial declaration that he had served for 'about a year'[105] in the battalion to 'two and a half months'[106] in order to emphasize his point that he knew few people in the regiment. In all these cases, Dost told half-truths in order to avoid being put into a position where he would have to name other soldiers – be it the *sipahis* who were at the regimental armoury, those with him when he had fired his rifle, or those he had known in his time serving in the battalion.

It would be mere conjecture on my part if I were to suggest that Dost Mohamed was a mutineer. There are hints and suggestions that he was involved in the Mutiny but nothing more, and it is not clear if he was found guilty for any offence by court martial. Yet, it was to make his name absent from later records and other accounts of the Mutiny that was the purpose of Dost's testimony. Dost Mohamed may or may not have occupied a marginal role in the 5th Light Infantry – he was a lowly peon and he may genuinely have had few friends – but he also used the time given to him in the colonial courtroom to situate himself further on the margins than he might otherwise have been. The fact that the Court of Inquiry omitted the *sipahi's* name from later reports and that the transcribed version of his testimony was truncated shows that he was successful in his endeavour.

Conclusion: Remembering to act like what we are

In the 1957 motion picture *Paths of Glory*, Stanley Kubrick portrays the heroism of a French battalion during World War I and the injustice of the men of that unit being accused of cowardice after a failed attack upon the German lines. After three men, representing each company within the battalion, are remanded and accused of 'cowardice in the face of the enemy',[107] Colonel Dax, played by Kirk Douglas, enters the burnt-out building in which the men are imprisoned, looks directly into the camera and states:

> Dax: You've all got to understand that the reason why you were picked [for the court martial] is immaterial. Whatever the reason you're on trial for your lives.

Stick to your stories, and don't let the prosecutor shake you out of them. Now remember, you'll be soldiers in the presence of superior officers ... so act like what you are.
Soldiers.
And brave ones at that.[108]

The accused proceed to act like soldiers, but not as Douglas' character would have them act. During the trial, Private Arnaud lets slip the fact that he has only been accused because he was unlucky enough to draw a slip of paper marked 'X' from a hat. Corporal Paris states that the heavy bulk of an officer falling on top of him prevented him from advancing towards the German lines. And, Private Ferol responds to the accusation that he was a coward with an ironic smile, a shake of his head and the statement "You're kidding, sir."[109] By behaving in the manner that they did, Kubrick's soldiers exposed the futility and impossibility of living as their officers wanted them to live: whether it be in tune with Dax's kindly paternalism or the brutish military justice of the courtroom.

The soldiers who appeared in the dock in Singapore suffered as swift and as uncompromising a fate as Arnaud, Paris and Ferol did. By the time Hoghton had made his final report into the causes of the Mutiny, on 20 May 1915, 214 men had been punished for their involvement in the revolt. In addition to the 47 *sipahis* and NCOs who were executed and the 64 who were given the sentence of 'transportation for life,' a further 73 were sentenced for transportation of up to 20 years and 28 were imprisoned.[110] But, also like Kubrick's soldiers, the Singapore Mutineers frustrated their officers' expectations and manipulated the contours of the punitive, disciplinary space of the colonial courtroom. The *sipahis* of the 5th Light Infantry were not quiescent victims of colonial justice, as the testimonies of Feroze Khan, Fazal Azim, Sazawar Khan and Dost Mohamed show. Instead, the soldiers re-appropriated the punitive, disciplinary space of the dock. Feroze Khan fashioned an identity for himself as an intransigent mutineer so that the Court of Inquiry would be forced to question the reliability of the evidence he had given. Fazal Azim took on the guise of the Court's approver and used it to weave his own narrative of events for the Court's edification. Finally, when giving their evidence, Sazawar Khan and Dost Mohamed both utilized and played upon colonialist assumptions of who and what they were: as a victim of the mutineers or as a lowly, marginal figure.

Alongside the re-appropriation of the physical and linguistic space of the courtroom came the re-appropriation of what it meant to be a soldier in the

Executions of men of the 5th Light Infantry. Q82505 and Q82506. Photographs Courtesy of the Imperial War Museum.

5th Light Infantry. Feroze Khan prompted the Court to dismiss his deposition as unreliable so that he would avoid naming men who had been involved in the Mutiny by his side. Fazal Azim became an approver in order to construct an alibi for himself and other *sipahis* in his Company. Sazawar Khan clung to a partially invented sense of victimhood in order to defend a man from his own village. Lastly, Dost Mohamed claimed ignorance and a marginal position in the regiment so that he could avoid all questions about the identity of the mutineers. Intra-*sipahi* loyalty – whether ethnic, geographical, or regimental – was an ideal that the Indian Army encouraged in the belief that it would make its troops better than they might otherwise be. In the early summer heat of colonial Singapore, it was these same ideals that were used to try and thwart the desire to discipline rebellious colonial soldiers.

6

'Breaking the Chains with Which We Were Bound': The Interrogation Chamber, the Indian National Army and the Negation of Military Identities, 1941–1947

The British Raj was bracketed at its beginning and end by the two largest rebellions in British military history. The first, involving the mutinous *sipahis* of 1857, is so well known that popular representations of 1857 still obscure the varied origins and motivations of its actors under the cypher of the seditious soldier (whether real or imagined).[1] The other is not so well known or documented. It took place in the context of the British military debacle in Malaya that culminated in the fall of Singapore on 15 February 1942 and the surrender of 120,000 military personnel (85,000 of whom surrendered at Singapore and 50,000 of whom were soldiers of the Indian Army). The dramatic collapse of British Imperialism in South-east Asia was obscured amidst the ebbs and flows of World War II and has been better recounted in works of literature than of history (ranging from J. G. Farrell's *The Singapore Grip* to Amitav Ghosh's *The Glass Palace*). The periphery of each of these literary texts is haunted by the presence of the Indian soldiers,[2] and, more specifically, soldiers of the Indian National Army (INA),[3] because the dramatic fall of British forces in Singapore was followed by an equally dramatic event 2 days later. On 17 February 1942, PWs were marched into Farrer Park in the northern part of Singapore and informed that a new 'National Army' was being created to fight for the liberation of India:

> At the close of my speech, I declared that about ten thousand soldiers of the Indian Army had already joined the Indian National Army and that I was determined to go ahead with the expansion of this force until India was liberated. I then asked the soldiers to raise [their] hands if any one from amongst them would like to join this force and fight for the liberation of his country. There was a spontaneous

response from all of the soldiers. Along with the raising of hands, thousands of turbans and caps were hurled up in the air in a frenzied fit of ecstasy. Almost all the soldiers jumped to their feet and filled the air with prolonged shouts of "Inquilab Zindabad" (Long Live Revolution). It looked as if, overwhelmed with enthusiasm, the whole crowd had gone mad. It took me quite some time to calm them down....[4]

The gleeful throwing of caps and turbans in the air by tens of thousands of Indian PWs[5] was, for Mohan Singh, Acting Major of the 1/14th Punjabis and later General of the INA, the moment where *sipahis* returned to the national stage as soldiers for India's freedom. Mohan Singh's account was an exaggeration both of his own influence and of the attitude of the men in Farrer Park. But, this did not result in the INA being militarily ineffective, as suggested most recently in Christopher Bayly and Tim Harper's *Forgotten Armies: The Fall of British Asia, 1941–1945*.[6] The INA failed to achieve its goal of liberating mainland India, aside from the brief hoisting of the tricolour in Moirang in contemporary Manipur in April 1944, but its 1st and 2nd Divisions did inflict heavy British casualties during the Japanese retreat through Burma in 1945. The *Azad Hind Fauj* also had a history and identity distinct from the politics, goals and machinations of its leadership: a reality ignored in studies that collapse the history of the INA into the personal struggles of Subhas Chandra Bose,[7] the motives of Japanese Intelligence,[8] or the plight of a handful of INA officers prosecuted for treason in Delhi.[9]

The purpose of this chapter is not to simply redress this balance by offering a reappraisal or counter-narrative of the rise and fall of the INA. Peter Ward Fay's *The Forgotten Army: India's Armed Struggle for Independence, 1942–1945* (a title inconveniently appropriated by Bayly and Harper) has already offered a detailed argument as to why historians ought to treat the 'war the Indian National Army undertook' as 'the real thing, a true war of independence, entitled as such wars are to our attention and respect.'[10] My own narrative will instead start after the war was already lost, at the end of the INA's life in the summer of 1945, when a small group of its (re)captured personnel were kept in the depths of the *Lal Qila*/Red Fort in Delhi. Each man was taken away, one after another, by a bespectacled 'Mr. Bannerjee',[11] interrogated over their defections from the British Indian Army and accused of 'Waging War Against the King' in the tropical forests of Burma and Malaya.[12] The interrogations did not go well. Major General Arcot Doraisamy Loganathan, the highest ranking member of the group, refused to accept that he and his men had committed a crime and began to use the space of the interrogation room to interrogate the interrogators:

> He has originated at CSDIC(I) the new term "BIFF" [British Influenced Indian Forces], which he has used objectionably on more than one occasion as an opprobrious designation of Indian officers working here. He has at the same time attempted to cross-examine such officers on *their* motives in remaining loyal and has given *them* subversive advice. On these occasions he has demonstrated an attitude to Indian members of the (British) Indian Army even more hostile than his attitude to the British.[13]

Loganathan and his fellow officers were not alone in their expressions of hostility. Of the 23,266 military personnel of the INA who were captured and then grilled by British Military Intelligence up to 28 January 1947,[14] only 3,880 men were deemed to be unconditionally loyal to the Crown.[15] But, this was not because the majority of soldiers had suddenly become '"Nationalistically" minded,' as British Officers sifting through their interrogations assumed.[16] In the interrogation room, *sipahis* occupied a space in which they could reason, conceive and speak of the INA and of the British Indian Army. And in that space, more often than not, they simultaneously negated the conventions of the interrogation room and rejected the whole concept that a soldier ought to show fealty towards his officers – whether they led an Army formed for the freedom of India or for the defence of the Empire.

The other side of this rejection of military deference was the creation and relaying of histories of the INA in which ordinary *sipahis* were at the forefront. Individual soldiers, recounting the reasons and methods by which they had defected to the *Azad Hind Fauj*, spoke of vast conspiratorial networks or of them having been the personal envoys of nationalist leaders under the noses of their officers. Others explained what life was like within the ranks of the INA by referring to the plays that *sipahis* wrote and performed about their experiences. And, yet more *sipahis* spoke of the mutinies and protests they had engaged to force the nascent rebel army into changing its policies when it was perceived to be failing its soldiers. In each type of testimony, there was an elision between truth and fiction, but what remained constant was the paramount place the ordinary soldier had in these narratives.

This chapter will begin with an account of how and why the machinery for the interrogation of INA personnel was created. The first accounts of an anti-British army having been formed among PWs paralysed detailed analyses of why the defections had occurred and led to premature conclusions that the

Army could recover and rehabilitate its soldiers if proper programmes were established. The chapter will then discuss how *sipahis* subverted the whole process of the interrogation, by refusing to respect the ordinary relationship between interrogator/interrogated or officer/soldier, and investigate the *sipahi*-led histories that they created. In particular, the men of three units of the Imperial Indian Army and its Nationalist counterpart will be discussed: the 1/15th Punjabis, the 'Dramatic Party' and HKSRA. Each of the men of the battalions, regiments and units had different experiences in, and of, the INA. Their testimonies further benefit from being more complete and from being summarized in a less disjointed and fragmentary manner than those of their peers.[17]

Segregating 'White' from 'Black': The need to interrogate

Publishers in Britain have rarely presided over works devoted wholly to the subject of the INA.[18] When the men of the INA or 'Jiffs' ['Japanese Indian Forces'] are mentioned, they haunt the periphery and are referred to in hushed whispers as in Paul Scott's *The Day of the Scorpion*:

> He paused, opened his eyes, glanced at her. "You know about the Jiffs?"
> "Jiffs?"
> "They're what we call Indian soldiers who were once prisoners of the Japanese in Burma and Malaya, chaps who turned coat and formed themselves into army formations to help the enemy. There were a lot of them in that attempt the Japanese made to invade India through Imphal."
> "Yes, I've heard of them. Were they really a lot?"
> "I'm afraid so. And officers like Teddie took it to heart. They couldn't believe Indian soldiers who'd eaten the king's salt and been proud to serve in the army generation after generation could be suborned like that, buy their way out of prison camp by turning coat, come armed hand in hand with the Japs to fight their own countrymen, fight the very officers who had trained them, cared for them and earned their respect. Well, you know. The regimental mystique. It goes deep. Teddie was always afraid of finding there were old Muzzy Guides among them. And of course that's what he did find. If Teddie had been the crying kind, I think he'd have cried. That would have been better, if he'd accepted the fact...."[19]

The failure to mention the INA after World War II is in part a reflection of reticence within the Indian Army to discuss the matter during the conflict.

And the figure of Teddie unintentionally – or perhaps not, given that Scott served in the Intelligence Corps in India in the early 1940s – correlated with the belief in the higher echelons of the Indian Army that the INA soldier could be recovered for the Raj. It is how this article of faith came to be the official policy of the Indian Army, and how it resulted in the creation of interrogation centres, that will be discussed below.

The existence of the INA was publicly pronounced at Farrer Park in Singapore on 17 February 1942, but it took several months for British forces in India to admit its existence to the War Office in London. There seemed to be a particular reluctance to openly discuss the matter to avoid embarrassing the British Empire in the eyes of its American allies.[20] In a report finally written by the Directorate of Military Intelligence in India (DMI) on 12 November 1942, proposals were made for the future treatment of men who had joined the INA, but the language was riddled with late colonialist angst. Those Indian personnel who were adjudged to have 'flirted' with the INA without showing any commitment to the cause were to be treated as 'White' and were to be allowed to return to their regimental centres or sent on military leave after the War.[21] Those who were subjected to 'some propaganda' and 'have been affected thereby, but are not considered to be fundamentally disloyal' were 'Greys' and they were to be quickly whisked off to 'reconditioning camps' upon recapture.[22] And then there were the 'Blacks' (and occasionally the 'Blackest of the Blacks') who were as far removed from the 'Whites' as they could be, for their 'loyalty is definitely in question' and they 'are regarded as dangerous from a security point of view'.[23] Yet, although various categories were delineated by DMI, their report ended with the admission that it was impossible to tell who, if anyone, still felt 'loyalty to the Sirkar' with any degree of certainty[24]:

> Indian military personnel are recruited from beaten armies, who have seen white troops on many occasions at their worst, being swept away by an Asiatic army. Upon these men incessant propaganda is played, not only by the Japanese but by their own countrymen. A study of Japanese broadcasts shows the most innocuous of the type of "news" regarding the war and India which is being incessantly dinned into their ears. In Major Dhillon's [an escapee from Singapore who provided detailed information] opinion, since the arrest of Gandhi [following the "Quit India" resolution], such propaganda has raised the percentage of the INA who are genuinely anti-British from 10% to 50%. We cannot afford to disregard the possibility that there is genuine belief that adherence to the INA is a service to the motherland.[25]

The concerns of the DMI were echoed even more starkly by the Combined Services Detailed Interrogation Centre (India) (CSDIC(I)). The organization was initially established after the start of hostilities in Europe to interrogate detainees, defectors and PWs suspected of harbouring detailed information about Nazi Germany. Its Indian branch was deemed initially to be of little import and it rarely compiled reports during the first weeks and months after its inception.[26] That changed in November 1942 when officers who had escaped from Japanese custody volunteered information about the INA and when the Quit India movement created fears that INA agents were already working within India.[27] In the appendices that followed this initial report, the INA metamorphosed from an exploding shell to a monster and then to a disease that the British could not counter:

> No one knew anything about the INA before the fall of Singapore. It came like a bomb-shell after the capitulation. . . . [But] The idea of a National Army has a great attraction for the rank-and-file. If one thinks "From where do our recruits come?" it will be found that they are [of] the same material and come from the same places where the Congress made frantic efforts to win over "the rural population of India." These seemingly inarticulate millions have in fact been made politically conscious to an appreciable degree by Congress propaganda. The modern recruit of the Indian Army is very different to his predecessor of 1914–1918. Hence this lurking danger, this already prepared foundation for [the] INA, is always there. A little real or imaginary grouse, a little subversive propaganda, and a reverse to the Allies have their hidden possibilities [sic.]. This monster will not dare show its face till the last minute when prevention or cure may be impossible.[28]

Thus, the early conclusion reached by British Intelligence in India was that the *sipahis* who had joined the INA were all 'black' and were merely reflecting the dark thoughts that simmered in the hearts of all Indians.

The pervading melancholia seen in reports into the INA was dispelled in the months preceding Archibald Wavell's ascension to Viceroy from Commander-in-Chief of the Indian Army in June 1943. On 18 March 1943, Wavell's office circulated a memorandum into the origins of the INA that contradicted the early assessments of Intelligence officers. INA soldiers were no longer to be treated as dangerous radicals but as bewildered and confused soldiers who had been bullied into rebellion:

> [The INA was created by the] Changes in the classes from which men and particularly Indian commissioned officers are drawn, [the] shortage of experienced

British Officers with knowledge of the country and [who are] able to command personal respect and affection, combined with consistent "nationalist" propaganda which is sapping the foundation on which the morale and loyalty of the old Indian Army was based. At the same time the concept of "loyalty to India" which in theory should be developed by "nationalistic" propaganda is unable to replace the other loyalties referred to above in the case of newly introduced elements or the older elements (i.e. the martial classes). The latter are so bewildered and confused by political developments which they do not understand but which they instinctively feel will react [sic.] to their disadvantage in the long run, that these older loyalties are rapidly losing their potency.[29]

Wavell's assessment of the INA was repeated a month later in a communiqué that was sent directly to the DMI:

The Indian Army, as today constituted, contains two main elements – one represented by the older VCOs and men of the "martial races", hitherto credited with a conservative attitude on political matters, and the other, newly enlisted classes and ICOs with "forward" political views. The latter probably now predominate at least in potential influence and at the same time, are, in theory, the most fruitful ground for enemy propaganda. Yet the bulk of the active INA personnel are representatives of the classes (Sikhs and PMs in particular) which formed the backbone of the prewar Indian Army. These are facts, which it would be wise to bear in mind. . . .[30]

The favoured solution of Wavell, therefore, echoed that of 'Teddie' in Scott's novel – the stoic British officer winning back control of the errant 'martial races' by looking them in the eye and shaming them once more into taking up the King's shilling. The only difference between Wavell and Teddie was that the former had the authority to create and change military policy.

On 3 May 1943, Wavell announced that there would be active attempts to counter the propaganda and message of the INA:

. . . it was ruled [previously] that the dissemination of information about the INA and kindred activities should be confined [to British Officers] . . . . It has now been decided that we should put the situation plainly to all Indian ranks and prepare them to meet a method of attack which they are at present largely unconscious.[31]

It took a year for this policy to be fleshed out further, by which time Wavell was firmly ensconced as Viceroy of India. Even with all his added responsibilities, he took a decisive role in what was finally proposed. Every commanding officer of every unit of the Indian Army was instructed to create '"Josh" Groups'. Each of these was to parallel the activities of 'Jif' columns by 'immunising' soldiers before the latter was able to suborn them:

> Josh is the strongest and most effective counter-propaganda method yet involved to combat the Japanese "I" [Intelligence] offensive against the morale of Indian troops. "Jif" means Japanese inspired fifth column . . . . "Josh" means "pep", and it is the morale counter-offensive weapon against these dangerous activities.[32]

The precise means by which this was to be done was explained further. Any antipathy *sipahis* may have towards 'Britishers' would pale in comparison to the hatred that would be fanned for the Japanese:

> Josh Groups are intended to: (a) build in every Indian soldier the knowledge and firm faith that the Japanese and everyone who represents the Japanese are his own personal enemies; (b) introduce stories of our victories against the Japanese and so turn the conversation around to the topic of why the Japanese are India's enemies and why and how they will be defeated; (c) introduce stories of the bravery of Indian soldiers in action and his comradeship-in-arms with his Allies; (d) utilize entertainment, radios, dramas, information rooms, picture layouts etc., to bring home to the sepoy, through every medium that strikes his imagination, the existence of his chief enemy – the Japanese; (e) inoculate the Indian soldier with a sound factual basis of true knowledge so that false rumours and brazen lies spread by Japanese, Jifs and Japanese agents can be easily shown as such.[33]

In addition to the creation of these instruments of inoculation within each military unit came the expansion of the CSDIC(I) and attempts to diagnose and treat those men who had already caught the contagion. All captured INA personnel, regardless of their rank, were to be interrogated by the organization. The expectation was that they would be assessed somewhere between 'White' and 'Black', reconditioned, and then returned to their old military units. But, as will be shown in the remainder of the chapter, *sipahis* commonly refused to accept any of the medication that was on offer.

Being in the employ of *hamare Neta*: The defection of 'X' Battalion

On 27 February 1943, 23 Sikh *sipahis* of 8 Platoon, 'A' Company, 1/15th Punjab were sent on a fighting patrol near Buthidaung in western Burma. Their task was to search a village 'suspected of harbouring enemy troops'[34] but instead the men of the Platoon used the opportunity to defect to the INA. As a result, the 1/15th Punjabis became the first military unit to be the sole subject of British intelligence reports relating to the INA. The men of the battalion were cited as an example of how low Indian soldiers had fallen. They were described as radical religious zealots and dangerous communist conspirators all in the space of two reports in March 1943. And they were such pariahs that even the name of the unit could not be mentioned but was effaced by a large 'X'. The reason for this was the means by which the men of the unit joined the INA and the subsequent interrogation reports of the soldiers involved.

It was not the incident of the desertion itself that caused specific attention to be drawn to the *sipahis* of 1/15th Punjab. Similar stories had already been circulated of Indian soldiers crossing over to 'F' Kikan and the Indian Independence League throughout the Japanese advance into Malaya and Burma in 1941 and 1942.[35] It was the fact that the men who defected were of the 'older "martial races"' and that they did so without any 'newly enlisted classes' or Indian Commissioned Officers being present that caused reports to be drafted about the matter in March 1943. In the first report, there was an attempt to explain the defection of the Sikh soldiers as being due to their shared faith and in the light of mutinies that had occurred among Sikh soldiers who had been ordered to wear steel helmets over, and instead of, their *pagris* (turbans):

> The Sikh Company first came to security notice . . . when a reservist, backed by three others, tried to make the wearing of steel helmets a religious question (September 1940). One of these reservists had already been noted corresponding with a Sikh NCO who had been imprisoned for playing a leading part in mass desertions of Sikhs from another unit on the eve of its departure overseas.[36]

When, on 11 March, 14 Hindu Jat *sipahis* of 'B' Company, 1/15th Punjabis also defected to the INA, this initial analysis was quickly revised. The blame was instead laid at the door of Communist *agents provocateurs* without much reason and less thought:

> Following a police report by a man on leave that secret meetings were held in the unit by subversive elements, security investigations resulted in seven subjects being removed. While the investigations were in progress the Sikhs (reservists) deserted under suspicious circumstances. There is little doubt that this trouble was linked with the Kirti Communist plot, which formed the background to the 3/1st Punjab desertions, the RIASC [Royal Indian Army Service Corps] mutiny in Egypt, and the CIH [38 Central India Horse] mutiny.[37]

What marks these first reports into the defection of 8 Platoon, therefore, was this desperate desire to find some cause for *sipahis*' disloyalty that was external to their own body or consciousness.

It was as part of this attempt to find an external cause for the desertion and defection of men of the 1/15th Punjabis that Sepoy Fakir Singh was interrogated in depth in April 1944. The soldier gave an account in which the men of 'A' Company were duped into crossing over to the Japanese. According to Fakir Singh, after the platoon had come under fire during their patrol, Havildar Surat Singh, the platoon commander, conferred in secret with Havildar Major Massa Singh, Naik Jaggat Singh, Naik Kabul Singh, Havildar Mela Singh and Sepoys Gurdial and Dalip Singh. When the men dispersed,

> The NCOs then returned to their sections and it was explained that the Platoon was to advance in the following order:
>
> Nk. Kabul Singh's Section
> Nk. Jaggat Singh's Section
> Hav. Mela Singh's Section.
>
> With the two sepoys mentioned above, as connecting files back to the Company. In this order the Platoon advanced, led by the Hav. Major and the Pl. Commander for about one mile, when suddenly B312 [Fakir Singh] found that they had walked into the Japanese and that Hav. Surat Singh was carrying a white flag. The Pl. then laid down its arms and was marched off.[38]

Fakir then recounted that the 16 soldiers outwith Surat Singh's clique were not best pleased at being led over to the Japanese:

> The next day Hav. Maj. Massa Singh and Havs. Surat Singh and Mela Singh were taken away and the men of the platoon began to argue about the desertion, those who were unwillingly captured blaming the NCOs already mentioned in the list above and also
>
> L/Nk Hazara Singh
> Sep. Dalip Singh
> Sep. Gurdial Singh.[39]

Fakir Singh's testimony confirmed part of what his interrogators had theorized. In his narrative, the *sipahis* were tricked into rebellion by their NCOs and rued their fate after the event. And, although Fakir Singh was only treated as a 'Grey' – largely because he claimed falsely that he later deserted from the INA – his account was treated, for a time, as fact.

It was treated as largely truthful until the interrogation of Havildar Surat Singh, the Commander of 8 Platoon, 2 years later.[40] When Surat was detained and interrogated in January 1946, it is clear that his interrogators hoped he would confess to having duped his men into defecting to the Japanese and the INA. The *sipahi*, however, refused to cooperate beyond relaying some basic details of his military service – that he had passed his matriculation exam, he had enlisted in 1/15th Punjab on 10 August 1932, and that he had become the Commander of 8 Platoon, 'A' Company in July 1942.[41] Sometime later, Surat was confronted with the captured diary of an Indian civilian working for the INA that made mention of him communicating and conferring with INA contact parties before his platoon crossed over. The only reply from Surat was that his captors had obviously fabricated the document:

27 Feb. '43.

Gobindara returned this morning. It is said that my letters have proven successful and that 23 men have come over who will be brought to us tomorrow morning.

28 Feb.'43.

After the morning tea, [I] saw the Indian soldiers who had come over on reading my letters. They were 23 Sikhs of A Coy of 1/15 Punjab Regt. They brought with them Bren guns, tommy guns, and many other weapons. Their commander's name is Surat Singh. They told us everything. Surat Singh is an honest and sincere man. The Japanese had a suspicion that these men had been sent as spies by the British, but after having [heard] their statements I assured the Japanese that these men were not sent by the British and that they had come over on reading my letters.[42]

In the end, Surat's silence so infuriated his interrogators that the only judgement made of him was that he was 'an inveterate and bare-faced liar.'[43]

But, there was no truth to be discovered about what occurred in 1/15th Punjab. Even the most comprehensive of accounts from captured personnel contained elements of wilful fancy that their interrogators could not accept. Company Quarter Master Havildar Hardial Singh, for instance, mentioned that men in the battalion began to talk about the INA after several INA personnel 'in civilian dress' were captured in December 1942 and January 1943.[44] Hardial also recounted that on 20 February 1943 every Platoon Commander of 'A' Company was summoned before the Company Commander and told of 2 leaflets 'which were recovered by No.7 Pl. in the front area on a bamboo pole in a paddy field'.[45] The Company Commander proceeded to read the contents of the leaflets aloud over the phone in front of Signalmen Balwant Singh, Kabul Singh and Girja Singh and,

> ... in a few hours the contents of the leaflets were known to just about all the men of "A" Coy and general discussion[s] started on the following points mentioned in the leaflets:
>
> – [The] INA had been formed in East Asia.
> – Capt. Mohan Singh was its Commander.
> – That [the] INA was formed for the Independence of India and that all Indians should join it.[46]

Yet, as far as Hardial was concerned, that alone did not explain the actions of 8 Platoon. He instead wove a tale in which he and others had been anointed as envoys of Subhas Chandra Bose in September 1939:

> At Alipore [Calcutta], B1205 [Hardial Singh] read in the newspapers of the powerful leadership of S. C. Bose, President of the Indian National Congress, and in a gurdwara which he often used to visit, B1205 found an opportunity of coming into contact with men of Congress sympathies. Sep. Gajjan Singh, "A" Coy 1/15 Punjab, who belonged to the same village as B1205, was already in contact with a Congress agitator called Mulla Singh, a Sikh durwan[47] [sic.] in the house of the Maharaja of Nepal. Through Mulla Singh B1205 received an interview with S. C. Bose in the house of a friend of Mulla Singh somewhere between Alipore Road and Ballyganj Rly. Station. B1205 was thanked by Bose for offering his services and was advised to wait until a fully organized programme for India's independence was announced.[48]

Upon realizing that others too had met Bose, Hardial claimed that all of the men began to talk of fighting for the independence of India before the INA had even been created:

> [We] were all interested in discussions about overthrowing the British Govt. Serial 1 [Sepoy Shiv Singh] suggested starting a revolt within Fort William; Serial 5 [Lance Naik Mela Singh] suggested that they should desert and form into small armed bands and loot the rich, while Serial 7 [Havildar Major Nand Lal] rebuked them for this wild and dangerous talk. B1205 [Hardial] suggested postponing all action in connection with these revolt[s] until Congress put its programme into operation.[49]

Thus, Hardial Singh created a narrative of the interrogation chamber in which the men of the 1/15th Punjab had always been anti-British and had always looked to defect. It is unlikely that he or others in his unit ever met Bose, but his repeated assertion that he had,[50] coupled with the silences and false testimonies of his peers, ensured that the 'X' remained firmly in place whenever the 1/15th Punjabis were discussed.

Hiding in the skirts of the Rani of Jhansi: Life in the INA

There was a change in the content of the interrogations after the surrender of Japan, the death of Subhas Chandra Bose[51] and the dissolution of the *Azad Hind Fauj* in August 1945. The end of World War II enabled the CSDIC(I) to gain access to handbooks and directives intended for INA officers that only partially answered the question of how INA soldiers were treated.[52] To fill in those gaps, intelligence officers began to ask *sipahis* what life was like after they had enlisted in the INA. The answers that were received were of 'Art Sections' drawing risqué cartoons, of Comedy troupes arranging burlesque shows and of 'Dramatic Parties' performing and writing their own plays. It was the latter group of erstwhile playwrights and actors that came to receive the most inquiry because one of its leading members, Dharam Chand Bhandari, was found to have been captured by British forces in the early months of 1946.[53] As will be shown, however, he was not the most cooperative of prisoners.

Bhandari was interrogated on 26 February 1946 and seemed at first to be unafraid of fully disclosing the details of his INA service. He stated that he was originally employed as a civilian 'checker' in the RIASC, supervising the reports of military clerks, before being 'militarized' and commissioned as a Jemadar on 10 September 1940.[54] He confessed that he joined the INA in Singapore in May 1942 and was soon asked to organize 'an entertaining publicity and propaganda programme', which he interpreted as a writ to write and stage plays and dramas at Neesoon Camp (north of Singapore) for Indian PWs[55]:

> B1371 [Bhandari] started writing and staging patriotic dramas and through this and his speeches, he boasts of having inspired a great enthusiasm in the PW's and every one becoming imbued with "National Spirit." Following the example of B1371, others began to write dramas which were staged in various PW camps.[56]

Bhandari commented that the plays became so popular and effective at winning new recruits for the INA that at least 43 amateur playwrights and actors were organized into a separate unit under his command.⁵⁷ Unfortunately for him, his command of the 'Drama Party' ended in December 1943 when Bose wandered into one of his performances, 'found the plays vulgar and did not greatly like them,' and immediately ordered the unit to 'cease operations'.⁵⁸

When Bhandari was asked about the precise details of his plays, he suddenly fell into an awkward silence. After much prompting, he admitted the names of some of the plays that he had written, such as *Ekhi Rasta* (The Only Way), *Milap* (Unity) and *Balidan* (Sacrifice).⁵⁹ But, he would say nothing of the content of these plays, which 'actors' had performed them, or how they had been staged. Bhandari's interrogators learnt from other sources about some of the secular and radical nationalist themes conveyed through the performances, such as showing 'how Indians were treated with torture and brutality under the British yoke through the Indian Police' in *Ekhi Rasta*,⁶⁰ encouraging 'unity between Hindus and Muslims' in *Milap*,⁶¹ and documenting how the anti-British struggle would spread when the INA reached Indian soil in *Balidan*.⁶² Even when confronted with these accounts, Bhandari refused to say anything further. The only thing he did do was push a worn and tattered booklet across the table towards his interrogators with the words *The Rani of Zanshi: A Play in Three Acts* stamped across the front.

Outdoor Theatre of the Indian Porter Corps, Cut-al-Amara [sic.]. Q24574. Photograph Courtesy of the Imperial War Museum.

According to its preface, the play was written by a P. N. Oak and was produced to commemorate the first anniversary of the founding of the Rani of Jhansi Regiment (the Women's Regiment) of the INA in July 1943 – 'a feat unique and unparalleled in world history'.[63] There were few women protagonists in the play, however, and even fewer appearances by Rani Lakshmibai herself.[64] Instead, the drama focused upon Indian soldiers and cantonment workers who mutinied and took up arms against their officers in Meerut in 1857. Act One, Scene One portrayed a weaver being arrested by *sipahis* after their *sahibs* took objection to him selling Indian rather than British-made cloth:

> Weaver: Shameless scoundrel! You came as petty hawkers and now you pose yourself to be a Government? What kind of Government? Which Government? An impertinent vagabond called Clive came here a hundred years ago to work on a job of two hundred rupees a month, and he treacherously ruined Sirajuddaula. Warren Hastings forged a document himself and hanged Nandkumar a wealthy citizen of Bengal for it. He starved the Begums of Oudh in a locked room and extorted all their wealth from them. Wellesley cheated many Rajas and now Dalhousie has begun annexing kingdom after kingdom. Is this what you call your Government? Speak out... speak out![65]

It was in order to 'speak out' that the soldiers witnessing the weaver's arrest began to circulate chapattis to symbolically incite rebellion and to link his unjust treatment to the way in which they were being treated by their officers:

> Sepoy: Anyway these chapattis have come in time, for in the name of "Discipline" that white fellow made us march for miles with hungry stomachs.[66]

Later scenes in the *Rani of Zanshi* tried to demonstrate how undeserving British officers were of *sipahis'* loyalty. In Act One, Scene Two, for instance, a 'Major General' stumbles into a malapropism after demanding to know from his *dhobi* why his clothes were not being carried in pride of place upon the back of his donkey:

> Major General: Capt. sab bhi gadha, Major sab bhi gadha, ham kion nahi gadha? [Captain Sahib is an ass, Major Sahib is also an ass, so why am I alone being deprived of that honour?] ... Kalsay ham bhi gadha!' [From tomorrow I must also be an ass!]
>
> Dhobi: Accha sarkar, ap jarur gadha. Phir kalsay kion? Ajhi say ap gadha. [Right, Sir, you are definitely an ass. But why wait until tomorrow? Today you are already an ass.][67]

There is also an instance of crass mistreatment of Indian soldiers by their superiors that leads to mutiny in Act 2 and a pledge by soldiers to fight for the Rani of Jhansi in Act 3:

> Instructor: Shut up! Now I will tell you something about "Discipline". In this British Army of ours we have got to observe "Discipline" in every little thing. From tomorrow morning onwards all persons will "Fall in" to go to W. C. which will be known as the "W. C. Parade": Later on you will all "Fall in" to go to the bathroom, then for physical training; then for parade and meals. For all these you will have to keep time, with the men in front.
>
> The Men: But in the W. C. and in the dining-room how can we keep time with the men in front?
>
> Instructor: It is a Govt. order and regulation!
>
> [The Men Mutiny]
>
> The Men: We are not ready to obey the orders of these white tyrants! Say "Bharat Mata Ki Jai"![68]

But why, if the play was so unashamedly anti-British, did Bhandari hand over a copy to his interrogators? The reason was possibly to do with the author of the play: P. N. Oak. Purushottam Nagesh Oak enlisted in the INA, served in 'propaganda sections', but was never captured by the British after the end of hostilities. According to his own account,[69] he skillfully evaded capture as he journeyed from Singapore to Calcutta in 1945 and 1946. It is possible that Bhandari knew this and that there was consequently little risk in divulging material written by Oak. It may also have been the case that Bhandari was more willing for Oak to face prosecution, in the event that he was found, than others in the 'Dramatic Party'. P. N. Oak later became (in)famous in certain circles for writing *hindutva* histories after India attained independence and equally notorious for the dubious claims made within them that Christianity was really 'Krishna-ity' and that the Taj Mahal and the Red Fort in Agra were actually 'Hindu buildings'.[70] If Oak's beliefs were similar at an earlier stage of his life, it is likely to have conflicted with the secular mores of the INA.

Yet, Bhandari's motives cannot wholly have been to implicate a man who had evaded custody or someone who he personally disliked. After all, it was presumably Bhandari's decision to have *The Rani of Zanshi* published as a booklet, to have it translated into English, and to privilege it by secreting it away on his person when other INA files and publications were being destroyed or seized by British forces. Moreover, Bhandari held on to his copy of the play for the weeks and months in which he was interned in Singapore, shuttled back to India, released and then recaptured when his interrogators realized how important he had been. And he only parted with it when confronted with summaries of plays that his interrogators had gleaned from other detainees. It was, I would argue, the dually transgressive and tractable quality of the *The Rani of Zanshi* that led Bhandari to having it among his few possessions when interrogated and to pushing it across the table when prompted to do so. The play could be read as an unvarnished version of why *sipahis* had joined the INA – because of their officers' ineptitude and the mistreatment of other Indians – and what the simple message of the INA was for its soldiers: 'We are not ready to obey the orders of these white tyrants! Say "Bharat Mata Ki Jai"!'[71] By the same token it was removed from the historical immediacy of *Ekhi Rasta*, *Milap* or *Balidan*, and could be passed off as a historical drama with the uncontroversial message that the *sipahis* of 1857 were given to intrigue and rebellion. *The Rani of Zanshi* could, therefore, defiantly communicate what Bhandari thought and wished to say even as he sat pliantly in the interrogation room.

Resisting the INA: Hong Kong and Punjabi Muslim detainees

There was one last theme to the interrogations conducted by the CSDIC(I): the detailed questioning of *sipahis who* came into contact with the INA but never joined it. Particular attention was given to *sipahis* who were captured outwith Malaya or Singapore, such as the 3300 men stationed at Hong Kong at its surrender on 25 December 1941. It was these soldiers, often classed as 'Whites', who were viewed as the most promising material for reintegration into the British Indian Army. And yet, even among these *sipahis*, very few, if any, were ever returned to their old regiments or expressed a desire to do so. Their reasons for not joining the INA or for actively resisting the *Azad Hind Fauj* were more complicated than their interrogators assumed. In Hong Kong, men were divided over the INA. Atttitudes towards the INA mirrored communal divisions – between those who advocated, and were willing to listen to, a pseudo-Congress message and those who felt alienated by it. And, just as significantly, it mirrored a divide between those who were willing to bear arms and those who no longer wished to do so.

At the fall of Hong Kong on 25 December 1941, *sipahis* from five Indian units were captured, the largest proportion of whom were classed as 'PMs' or Punjabi Muslims from the HKSRA, the 2/14th Punjab, and the 5/7th Rajputs.[72] Four *sipahis*[73] from Hong Kong were involved in ratifying the creation of the (first) INA as delegates to the Bangkok Conference between 15 and 23 June 1942. When they returned, at least 500 Sikh and Hindu PWs volunteered for the INA, and various organizations were established 'to carry out [INA] propaganda and look after the welfare of volunteers', including the 'Indian Welfare Committee', the 'Congress Committee' and the 'Azad School'.[74] But, a notable lack of enthusiasm was expressed by Punjabi Muslim detainees for the INA and the nationalist organizations associated with it. When, for instance, 'Indian Independence Day' was celebrated on 9 August 1942 at the King's Theatre, Hong Kong, 'all the PW were invited to attend' and 'all Sikhs and Hindu PW in Mautau Chung' camp accepted the offer.[75] Yet, only four Punjabi Muslims joined them. And, even when at the end of the event a procession toured around the city, only a handful more Muslim soldiers were persuaded to march along.[76]

It was not for want of trying. Immediately after the surrender of Hong Kong, the Japanese believed that Punjabi Muslims were more likely to join the INA than other *sipahis* were. A total of 561 Muslim PWs were separated from other detainees in the first week of January 1942, housed in the Gun Club Hill Barracks in King's Park, Kowloon,[77] and offered better rations than their peers elsewhere. They were joined by another 800 Punjabi Muslim PWs on 14 May 1942 and were encouraged to mix and have 'free intercourse'.[78] Only 100 of that number, however, agreed to bear arms under the Japanese and were sent as guard pickets to Guangzhou in mainland China.[79] Moreover, some of those who did volunteer had very specific reasons for doing so. Lance Naik Mohamed Shaffi, for instance, of the 5th Anti-Aircraft Regiment, HKSRA, volunteered in order to revenge himself upon superiors he accused of sexual assault and rape:

> HK/141 [L/Nk Mohd. Shaffi] alleges that the behaviour of HK/140 [BHM Jahan Dad] with the men, especially those who hailed from districts east of Gujrat, was very bad. HK/141 accuses HK/140 of forcibly committing sodomy with him. Hav. Sher Baz also committed the same act with him on the instigation of HK/140. HK/141 requested HK/142 [Nk Gheba Khan] and Nk. Jamal Khan not to indulge in such unnatural and inhumane acts. While HK/141 was talking to these NCOs, HK/140 with Hav. Sher Baz, appeared in the barrack [room] and HK/140

threatened these NCOs and told them not to have anything to do with HK/141. Both HK/142 and Nk. Jamal Din confirm this and say that they declined to say anything to HK/140 about this matter.[80]

Shaffi, once he had joined the INA, confessed that he used his position to have,

> ... many NCOs punished by the Japanese, he forced them to salute him and his relations with the Japanese were very intimate. He is also held responsible for the imprisonment of HK/140 and indirectly responsible for the death of Jemadar Ghulam Nabi.[81]

The other *sipahis* in the group of 100 may have felt a keener attachment to the INA than Shaffi may have done. The vast majority of Punjabi Muslim prisoners certainly did not, and, from what can be deduced from the interrogation reports, only four others joined.[82]

Those non-volunteers who remained at Gun Club Hill began to actively resist joining the INA. At the barracks, Subedar Hakim Khan of 2/14th Punjab assumed command and became 'a favourite with the Japanese and the Indian quisling'.[83] Hakim Khan sought to remove from the barracks Viceroy's Commission (VCOs) and NCOs who were seen as being pro-British, to drill the soldiers as if they were still on active duty, and separate the men in accordance with their views on the Indian nationalist movement.[84] Each stage of Hakim Khan's programme, however, met with protest. According to Sultan Ahmed, when the Japanese attempted to remove the Subedars and Jemadars of his detachment, the men,

> ... protested, and the remainder of the PW joined the VCOs and asked to be taken as well. After threatening them with death, the Japanese went away.[85]

Gunner Nazar Mohamed and Havildar Khuda Baksh recounted what occurred when the men were asked to bear arms[86]:

> The Japanese asked the PW of HKSRA whether they were able to handle rifles. They all feigned ignorance. The Japanese said they would teach them rifle drill with staves, but the PW protested. The Japanese Officer asked for one man to step forward and explain to him why the PW would not parade with rifles. All the PW stepped forward but they were told again that only one man should step forward. Hav. Mohd. Akbar who was standing at the side of B1398 [Havildar Khuda But] in the front rank right flank, attempted to step forward, but was stopped by B1398. The Japanese Officer who was standing on the left flank saw the move and asked who the individual was who had stepped forward, but no one informed him.[87]

And, when the 'men began talking derogatively of Sub. Hakim Khan' and the Japanese tried to separate the original group of 561 PWs from the 800 that arrived later, further trouble ensued:

> When the party of "500" was ordered to march, those who were being left behind (ie. party of "800" and 60 men of the 561 party) rushed the gate with the hope of joining the others. This compelled the Japanese forces who were outside the Camp to open overhead fire. During the incident Sub. Hakim Khan had apparently hidden in his room. The Japanese finally managed to quell the disturbance. The water supply was cut off, and no rations issued that day. There was no sign of Sub. Hakim Khan.[88]

The events at Gun Club Hill would have been classified as a mutiny had the men still been on active service. As it was, the barracks were closed, little attempt was made to recruit Punjabi Muslims into the INA, and the soldiers themselves were organized into prisoner fatigues and sent to work in Guangdong Province in China.

The reasons why Punjabi Muslims in Hong Kong were reluctant to join the INA had little to do with any lingering attachment the soldiers had to the British Indian Army. The CSDIC(I) did not even make that claim.[89] Instead, it reached the conclusion that it was the soldiers' attachment to 'their own VCOs and NCOs' that enabled 'the PMs' to 'gird their loins and resist the attentions of the INA'.[90] It is true that the soldiers at Gun Club Hill refused to be parted from their Indian superiors. That explanation, however, cannot account for the reluctance of Punjabi Muslim soldiers to follow Subedar Hakim Khan into the INA. Hakim Khan was also Muslim, was a VCO in 2/14th Punjab, styled himself as a colonel and informed the men on several occasions that he had been hand-picked by the Japanese as the personal successor to General Mohan Singh when the first INA was dissolved on 21 December 1942.[91]

Thus, additional motives need to be searched for. The interrogations reveal that the reasons were partly communal, largely a reluctance to accept the form of nationalism that was circulated in Hong Kong, and an almost universal reluctance by captured soldiers to bear arms again in any capacity. Hong Kong was the scene of protests by Sikh *sipahis* of the HKSRA and 2/14th Punjab in December 1940 after soldiers were ordered to wear steel helmets[92] over or instead of their *pagris*.[93] The willingness of the same soldiers to then join the INA appears to have coloured the *Azad Hind Fauj* as a non-Muslim institution for Punjabi Muslim *sipahis*. Noor Mohamed disliked the Sikhs who joined the INA because they 'did not pay proper respect to their officers and in some cases disobeyed their orders'.⁹⁴ Mohamed Ali claimed that the Sikhs had been using Japanese words of command even before they had surrendered and that 'Muhammedan PW had no relations or contacts with any of the Sikh PW, and their mutual relations were rather strained'.⁹⁵ The unwillingness to countenance non-Congress nationalisms in the propaganda of the INA in Hong Kong helped to further this sense of alienation. No *sipahis* mentioned any particular sympathy for the Muslim League, but they certainly disapproved of the hanging of 'framed pictures of Mahatma Gandhi' in PW camps⁹⁶ or having to hear Hindu and Sikh *sipahis* chant pro-Congress slogans.⁹⁷ Finally, there was the incident at Gun Club Hill in which PWs refused to bear arms. In the interrogation reports, the soldiers involved described the protest as a 'refusal',⁹⁸ a 'reluctance'⁹⁹ and a 'feigning of ignorance' that they had ever been 'proper soldiers before'.¹⁰⁰ The inference was that the *sipahis* would never be 'proper soldiers' again. That was the conclusion the CSDIC(I) ultimately reached. No Punjabi Muslim soldier captured in Hong Kong was invited back into the British Indian Army, and the HKSRA was unceremoniously disbanded.

Conclusion: Negating military identities

There is a perceptible silence in accounts of the INA. It is not because there is any shortage of narratives from an Indian perspective. As a result of the clamour made during and after the INA trial of Gurbaksh Singh Dhillon, Shahnawaz Khan and Prem Kumar Sahgal in November and December 1945, not only have the accounts of INA officers been published (and embellished) but also its court proceedings can still be found sitting in certain bookshops.¹⁰¹ But, all of these narratives are from the perspective of officers and none from the overwhelming majority of *sipahis* who staffed the institution. More often than not, the idea that ordinary soldiers had voices and opinions is not even present in these narratives. In an interview with the late Colonel Pritam Singh, former aide-de-camp to Subhas Chandra Bose, the question of how and why the men of the Kapurthala Light Infantry agreed to join the INA was met with a smile and a laugh:

> It was simple. I told the men under my command that I was going to join the INA and that they must join too.¹⁰²

Hopefully, this chapter will have gone some way to filling that lacuna. 'Other ranks' of the Indian Army who came in touch with the INA did have their own reasons and methods of joining it, of resisting it, and their own accounts of what life was like in the institution.

This chapter, however, was not intended to just give a voice to the voiceless. As Jacques Derrida remarked, any 'reversal' of a 'metaphysical edifice' is 'at once contained within it and transgresses it' and what is needed is to deconstruct,

> ... through a meditation of writing which would merge as it must, with the undoing [solicitation] of onto-theology, faithfully repeating it in its totality and making it insecure in its most assured evidences.[103]

This book has sought to shed some light on the strings that pulled *sipahis'* testimony in certain directions: various censoring authorities and the individual or collective body of the soldier. In the interrogation of INA personnel, who and what acted as a censor is easy to explain: it manifested itself in the CSDIC(I), the interrogation room and the angry voice that penned an accompaniment to each report. The physical presence of the *sipahi* in this testimony is harder to summarize in a single sentence because it was everywhere. The interrogations of 'X' Battalion are marked not by a refusal to cooperate but by a failure to respect the whole process and the relaying of alternate and fanciful tales. The grilling of Dharm Chand Bhandari resulted in a narrative being woven through a fictional play. And the questioning of Punjabi Muslim detainees in Hong Kong resulted in tales of mutiny, dissent and the inferred message that they were no longer willing to bear arms for the Raj. In each type of testimony, the *sipahi* – whether real or imagined – was paramount, and the physical presence of the interrogator was of lesser importance and at times completely ignored.

It is unsurprising that no INA personnel were invited back into the Indian Army in either its colonial or post-colonial guise.[104] Regiments such as the HKSRA were quietly disbanded in 1946[105] and most others divorced from British military planning. Part of the reason may have been the enduring hostility of Jawaharlal Nehru or Mountbatten to the INA, but that does not explain the failure to reintegrate men who only had a tangential connection to the rebel army. It was ultimately a decision taken by *sipahis* themselves. Few of those interrogated expressed a desire to serve as soldiers once more, but rather did quite the opposite: they negated or rejected their military identities. As Claude Auchinleck, the last Commander-in-Chief of the colonial Indian Army, admitted in 1946, the elements of fantasy that underpinned the colonial

Indian Army had been dispelled. And its officers had some hard truths to face:

> It is quite wrong to adopt the attitude that because these men had been in service in a British controlled Indian Army that therefore their loyalty must be the same as British soldiers. As I have tried to explain, they had no real loyalty towards Britain as Britain, not as we understand loyalty.[106]

Conclusion: Reading Rebels, Writing Ghosts

In 1922, Kazi Nazrul Islam, the Bengali poet, published *Bidrohi* or *The Rebel Warrior*[1]:

> Hail, my brave rebel eternal!
> Say: I outtop the great Himalayas
> in titanic majesty,
> Abashed and humbled, the snow-capped mountain
> bows its head before me.
>
> Sublime, I tower
> far above the infinite space of the universe,
> above the sun, moon, planets and stars,
> above the seat of heaven itself.
> I am an ever-lasting wonder.
> On my foreheard flames
> the mask of victory.
>
> Hail, brave hero!
> Upright forever is my head!
>
> I am tempestuous, unbound, brutal
> I am the tempest, the cyclone, I spell ruin
> I'm the great fear, the curse of the Universe.
>
> I trample on bonds,
> I obey no laws,
> I draw down loaded ferries,
> I'm a torpedo, a huge
> cataclysmic minc,
> I'm dissonance, I'm the turbulent locks,
> Of summer's furies.
> I am the wild wind:
> I crush and sweep away all in my path.[2]

It is significant that the work was immortalized in print only 2 years after Nazrul left the Indian Army as a Quartermaster-Havildar in the 49th Bengalis.[3] The 'loaded ferries', the 'torpedoes' and the 'mines' were something he saw as his battalion was shipped to fight in Mesopotamia. And the ode he wrote to that joint ideal of both 'Rebel' and 'Warrior' was an act of self-realization: a desire to be the Rebel now that the War was over; to become the logical product of his military service.

Nazrul offers a way to make sense of the testimony-ies of all *sipahis* during the two World Wars. It can be seen as an echo of Nazrul's poem: a journey towards a clear, distinct goal of rebellion. But, that has not been my intent, and to impose such a metanarrative upon the material discussed in this book is intensely problematic. Rather than concluding that *sipahis* were both Rebels and Warriors, I will conclude by arguing that they were neither one nor (quite) the other.

Failing to be that rebel

There is no shortage of studies of rebellion or resistance in the tricontinental, or 'Third', World.[4] But, with the emergence in recent years of what may be broadly categorized as 'postcolonial histories', they have taken one of two forms. The first, still identifiable as a Subalternist approach, has abandoned studies of events as resistance in favour of studying the identity of the rebel. Its mirror can be found in the pioneering works of James C. Scott, in which discourses of rebellion in the colony and post-colony subsume any individual actors. This work and its subjects fit poorly into either category. *Sipahis* fail the test of being sufficiently subaltern, and their testimony is not as 'hidden' as it ought to be.

It has been three decades since the publication of the first volume of *Subaltern Studies*[5]: time enough, perhaps, to write of the Subaltern Collective and its edited volumes as a thing that happened rather than something that is happening. To write a narrative history of *Subaltern Studies* would require an exposition of how the volumes embodied the hopes and desires of a generation of anti-colonial historians, even though the numbers of those involved in its production were small and they were writing (almost exclusively) about colonial India. It would describe how its contributors sought to retrieve a subaltern history that would challenge the received wisdoms of colonizing academics and (contemporary) ruling elites. It was to be a history of the voiceless, the excluded, of those who had been denied subjectivity under the yoke of essentializing knowledges and fantasies. Ranajit Guha's 'The Prose of Counter-Insurgency' provided the first detailed explanation of how this was to be done[6]:

> Historiography has been content to deal with the peasant rebel merely as an empirical person or member of a class, but not as an entity whose will and reason constituted the praxis called rebellion. The omission is indeed dyed into most narratives by metaphors assimilating peasant revolts to natural phenomena: they break out like thunder storms, heave like earthquakes, spread like wildfires, infect like epidemics. In other words, when the proverbial clod of earth turns, this is a matter to be explained in terms of natural history. Even when this historiography is pushed to the point of producing an explanation in rather more human terms it will do so by assuming an identity of nature and culture, a hall-mark presumably, of a very low state of civilization and exemplified in "those periodical outbursts of crime and lawlessness to which all wild tribes are subject", as the first historian of the Chuar rebellion put it. Alternatively, an explanation will be sought in an enumeration of causes – of, say, factors of economic and political deprivation which do not relate at all to the peasant's consciousness or do so negatively – triggering off rebellion as a sort of reflex action, that is, as an instinctive and almost mindless response to physical suffering of one kind or another (e.g. hunger, torture, forced labour, etc.) or as a passive reaction to some initiative of his superordinate enemy. Either way insurgency is regarded as external to the peasant's consciousness and Cause is made to stand in as a phantom surrogate for Reason, the logic of that consciousness.[7]

For the Subaltern Collective, colonial archives became active sites of colonialism: preserving/discarding knowledges in accordance with colonial paradigms even after colonialism had ceased to be a political reality. History stood complicit of substituting metaphor for analysis whenever rural Indians were to be studied (usually during acts of rebellion). Even 'radical' histories – from the overtly Nationalist to the overtly Marxian – which made peasant-rebels their subjects, were guilty of analysing their rebellions through abstractions of the ideal worker, peasant or rebel[8] and ignoring instances when their 'small voices' were recorded.[9] The common failing in history writing before *Subaltern Studies* was the denial of subaltern 'Reason'; of 'the rebel as the *conscious* subject of his own history'.[10] And, it was the study of subaltern Reason that would set *Subaltern Studies* apart. It was, partly, a political goal.[11] The 'rehabilitation' of the subaltern/*subalterno* would expose the 'unhistorical monism'[12] of contemporary narratives of Indian nationalism and the Indian nation.[13] It also inspired a particular methodological approach. Reading against the grain of the colonial/nationalist archive would expose the gaps in which this Reason operated and allow historians to write a history of the silenced subaltern:

> Thanks to such a process of narrowing down it is possible for the historian to use this impoverished and almost technical language as a clue to the antonymies which speak for a rival consciousness – that of the rebel.[14]

Under the weight of critiques from both within and outwith the Subaltern Collective, the aims and language of early Subalternists were tempered. They were accused of inverting the process that absented their subjects from history, so that the subaltern became a new hegemony (not forgotten but forcing a forgetting). Instead of trying to recover a holistic peasant consciousness, the 'new' Subalternists made more nuanced efforts to find those who occupied the margins, focus upon her/his fragmentary appearances in the archive (or outside it), and so avoid the perils of creating new delimiting subjects in place of the old. The histories that were to be written were no longer of post-colonial Reason but of partial presences and lived experiences.

James C. Scott found himself grappling with a similar problem to that identified by early Subalternists and shared in the desire to recover marginalized voices. Scott's early work focused on the class relations in a single Malay village in *The Moral Economy of the Peasant* and *Weapons of the Weak*. His anthropological fieldwork led him to pose the question why 'the poor sang one tune when they were in the presence of the rich and another tune when they were among the poor'.[15] The conclusion reached was that there was an alternative peasant consciousness at play that informed acts of surreptitious resistance:

> The argument for false-consciousness, after all, depends on the symbolic alignment of elite and subordinate class values – that is, on the assumption that the peasantry (proletariat) actually accepts most of the elite versions of the social order.... [But] any groups social outlook will contain a number of diverse and even contradictory currents. It is not the mere existence of deviant subcultural themes that is notable, for they are well-nigh universal, but rather the forms they may take, the values they embody, and the emotional attachment they inspire.[16]

Scott's later reappraisal of his own work, however, sent it veering in the opposite direction to that of Subaltern Studies. In *Domination and the Arts of Resistance: Hidden Transcripts*, the subject and intended audience widened in scope. Scott's village became the archetype for a multitude of other 'forms of domination': 'the master and the slave, the landlord and the serf, the high-caste Hindu and untouchable'.[17] The link between them was the presence of the 'hidden transcript' that was articulated both by the dominant – 'representing the practices and claims of their rule that cannot be openly avowed' – and by the dominated – 'a critique of power spoken behind the[ir] back'.[18] They further shared the potential to evolve into what is more easily recognizable as 'resistance':

> Many, perhaps most, hidden transcripts remain just that: hidden from public view and never "enacted". And we are not able to tell easily under what precise circumstance the hidden transcript will storm the stage. But if we wish to move beyond apparent consent and to grasp potential acts, intentions as yet blocked, and possible futures that a shift in the balance of power or a crisis might bring into view, we have little choice but to explore the realms of the hidden transcript.[19]

To focus on the 'hidden' is to sidestep around the problem of archivization, authorial intent and the scholarly violence of entexting the unspoken. Scott offers a curative to the dilemmas that faced the Subaltern collective by allowing for the (post)colonial peasant, the marginalized, the rebel to be written about freely as long as their voices are, or were once, sufficiently masked.

It would be easy to conclude that there are elements of both approaches in this book and leave it at that. Unfortunately, it is not so simple. I am indebted to the writings of Subalternists and Scott, but hampered by the failure of *sipahis* and their testimonies to live up to all that they ought to be. There was nothing marginal about the existence of *sipahis* under the British Raj. They were at the heart of the colonial stage in India as constant objects of a split diachronic/synchronic vision of martial narratives and military law. *Sipahis*' voices were not to be repressed or ignored, but censored; privileged in the sense that they were to be recorded, listened to, and stored for posterity. But, their testimonies are also incomplete. *Sipahis*' voices are fragmentary and their testimonies have aching holes in them that cannot be fully filled. The possibilities of other testimonies existing in German, Italian or Japanese archives remain unrealized here, in this work, because of my own linguistic failures.[20] And even if I were to find other material in other languages, it too would be subject to the perils of archivization. *Sipahis*' voices have been institutionalized, in a Derridean sense, made unhidden by that very process even before I (or others) gain access to it:

> It is thus, in this *domiciliation*, in this house arrest, that archives take place. The dwelling, this place where they dwell permanently, marks this institutional passage from the private to the public. . . .[21]

In other words, *sipahis* fail to be sufficiently subaltern. To adopt a study of the marginal for those who were at the heart of colonialism is the reverse of what

Subalternists, particularly early Subalternists, would propose. At the same time, there is no comforting veil of 'hidden-ness' to *sipahis*' testimony, and the ease of composing a single, unbroken chain where dissent morphs into rebellion is not available to this or any other historian.

So, what is available and what can the historian achieve? An alternative way of writing has to start by being mindful of one's own limitations and the limitations of history-writing as a mode of analysis. One must write, as Gayatri Chakravorty Spivak remarks, not in expectation that one day those limits will be overcome but in the realization that 'systematic research cannot capture what the everyday sense of self shores up'.[22] The *sipahi's* complete self is unavailable and unreachable to the historian. And, any transferential relationship, whereby the historian lives through his/her subject and the soldier of the past becomes a model for what those in the present can do, is closed. What remains open is that sense of haunting, of incompleteness:

> I pray instead to be haunted by her slight ghost, bypassing the arrogance of the cure. . . . To be haunted is also to lay to rest any hope of "detecting the traces of [an] uninterrupted narrative, in restoring to the surface of the text the replaced and barred reality of [a] fundamental history, [in which] the doctrine of a political unconscious finds its function and necessity," . . . . If for us the assurance of transference gives away to the possibility of haunting, it is also true that for us the only figure of the unconscious is that of a radical series of discontinuous interruptions. In a mere miming of that figure, one might say that the epistemic story of imperialism is the story of a series of interruptions, a repeated tearing of time that cannot be sutured.[23]

Towards a ghost story

To allow oneself to be haunted, in the Spivakian sense, is not an admission of defeat. I started this book by expressing my intention to write a history that would emplot the witness and treat testimony as a process, praxis or act rather than static text. To do so allows one to study representations of agency more complex than what is made permissible by searching for signs of the perfect rebel. It brings the post-colonialism of Subalternism or Scott closer to the 'post' of post-structuralist thought, but in a way that helps to broaden what is realizable in history-writing. It opens possibilities of how one reads the subject of history and writes that subject into history.

First, rather than subaltern 'Reason' or Scott's 'peasant consciousness' being defined as a fixed or essential characteristic of any one group, it becomes relational: defined by and against patriarchy, caste or religious representations. This can be seen in the more recent volumes of Subaltern Studies, which, influenced by Spivak's critique, have historicized the gendered, Muslim and Dalit body in its studies of colonial and post-colonial South Asia. It has allowed for histories to be written of peoples whom early Subalternists and Scott had ignored or only briefly touched upon. These histories have been produced by utilizing the unarchived, unarchivable or partially archived source – the political pamphlet or poster; folksong and poetry; unpublished family memoirs and letters. But, taking this step towards understanding subalternity as relational allows another of conceptualizing it as the contestatory element within dominant discourses. This makes possible the productive re-reading of the heavily conditioned source and body (in which indigenous voices are conditioned at the site of their production, translated and cropped) and an engagement with others who were liminal to colonialism. It redeems the voice of the colonial soldier.

Secondly, it encourages an awareness of the limits of historical writing, particularly the problems of writing the unhistoricized (or partly historicized) voice into history. History writing contains both demonology and exorcism: a sense of mourning or desire for the lost and inability/unwillingness to ever reclaim the lost as it was:

> None of this, however, constitutes a reconstruction. Something has been lost that will never return. Historiography is a contemporary form of mourning. Its writing is based on an absence and produces nothing but simulacra, however scientific. It offers representation in the place of bereavement. . . . A mirrorlike structure: like Narcissus, the historian-actor observes his reflection which the movement of another element makes it impossible for him to grasp. He seeks one who has vanished, who in turn sought one who has vanished, and so on.[24]

The problems of representation in history cannot be resolved because history cannot be divorced from story or testimony. The best that one can do, as Ajay Skaria – first in an article in *Subaltern Studies IX*[25] and then in *Hybrid Histories: Forests, Frontiers and Wildness in Western India* – argues, is to write mindful of this fact. As well as giving the reader the option of approaching his text 'in the normal sequential fashion',[26] Skaria offers supplementary ways of reading his various chapters: '3-10-11-9-16-6-17-7-12-4-13-14-15-5-18-8-19-20'.[27] Read this way, Skaria hopes his work would at least touch upon the contours of what is made absent by producing history:

> ... more is lost in the sequential narrative here than would be lost in Dangi accounts. When most Dangis discuss an aspect of moglai [a particular Dangi way of framing the past], they simultaneously always already know something of how it is inflected by mandini, and vice versa. This does not only mean that they can make multiple connections between narratives, that there is a deep cross referentiality made possible by simultaneous knowledge of many goth [stories], or that the transition from moglai to mandini consists of several narratives tracking back and forth rather than being one single narrative. . . . Most of all, their simultaneous knowledge of goth makes narrators sensitive to the excess of moglai. In contrast, a sequential narrative such as the one attempted here runs the risk of missing out on this excess, on the sense in which moglai is extra-colonial rather than only pre-colonial.[28]

The problems of representation still remain present in Skaria's counter-narrative of lost excess (the reliance upon the archived text; the loss of meaning through translation; the cropping of the surviving voice to allow it to sit succinctly upon the page). And, that problem is compounded by how he attempts to acknowledge the limits of historical representation. Skaria's counter-narrative is foregrounded by the main – the emplotment of Dangi histories into the expected narratives of time (sequentially moving from one event to another in the order that they happened) and space (the occasional juxtaposition of events in accordance with methodological or theoretical approaches). *Hybrid Histories* is, therefore, only a partial success – a hybrid of the old and new subaltern that is unwilling to eschew the orthodox narratives of the 'historian and sociologist'.[29] But, it does make possible histories in which the counter-narrative would be the main. Instead of a conventional arrangement of a narrative through time or space, the counter-as-main would solely emplot through the witness (towards a narrative or poetics of lost excess).

I have attempted to move towards such a poetics in this work. It has involved the analysis of the twin, competing visions the Indian Army had for its colonial soldiers and how *sipahis* lived through this contradictory gaze. And it has treated soldiers' testimonies as spaces of possibility in re-ordering colonial norms.

The Handbook programme, discussed in Chapter 1, lacked the enduring clarity it ought to have had in its pursuit for ethnological truth. The fantastical language and stereotypes created for various *sipahis* borrowed from drama and fiction and slipped seamlessly back into it during and after the end of the

British Raj. The imagined frontiersman, of Fenimore Cooper and Scott, found his way into descriptions of Pathans; Kipling's Brahmins reflected (and perhaps pre-empted) martial race ethnologies of his time; and the makers of Star Trek could not help but invoke the spectre of the martial Sikh when creating their genetically engineered, superman, Khan Noonien Singh. The published volumes of the Handbooks were often swiftly discarded or replaced, but the negatives that helped to create them lingered on, to be referred to when new martial races had to be found or discarded ones resurrected.

Chapter 2 surveyed the weight of military-legal jurisprudence and the other part to how colonial soldiers were to be defined. Under Indian military law, *sipahis* were to be indistinct from their white, metropolitan counterparts. It was a synchronic vision of the colonial soldier that acted as a contrasting counterpart to the diachrony of martial race narratives. Or rather it did in theory. In practice, the synchronic evolution of these legal tracts – the slow process of accretion that added another layer of language in the search for legal certitude – fused colonial Indian particularity with authorial intent. Discourses of colonial paternalism and the Indian Penal Code crept into the language and enactment of Indian military law. It resulted in another contradiction: of *sipahis* being rewarded more generously and being disciplined far more harshly than their white peers.

The porous impermanency of what and who was a soldier under the British Raj allowed, and in some ways mandated, a return of *sipahis* into these racial fictions. But it was by, what Homi Bhabha would term, a 'metonymy of presence' instead of a simple reversal of that 'gaze of otherness'.[30] Chapter 3 showed that *sipahis* constantly added adjuncts to their terms of service in their letters. From sexual encounters in Brighton to malingering in Flanders to fabricating means to return home in World War II, *sipahis* demanded the fulfilment of, or additions to, soldiering 'contracts'. With a few exceptions (Jagu Godbole), this occurred without soldiers perceiving their own activity as being particularly disloyal. Instead, petitions were arranged and means of leave falsely secured in the expectation that individuals would remain soldiers or would soon return to being so. Those who permanently left made it clear that they had fulfilled, or at the very least conformed to the letter of, the oaths of fealty they had made when enlisting.

The return of the soldier and his presence was not just felt in discussions of terms of service. Chapter 4 charted at least some of the re-appropriations that took place among Muslim *sipahis* during the life of the Snowball letter. A pre-existing chiliastic missive became a vehicle to offer rejoinders to Ahmadi missionaries. Its language then slipped into the everyday prose of *sipahis*' letters; both internalized as a call for soldiers to reform their own behaviour and externalized to reflect the course of World War I. Something similar, as demonstrated by Chapter 5, could occur in the colonial courtroom. The linguistic and physical space of the proceedings of the court martial was re-appropriated by *sipahis* of the 5th Light Infantry to save their own lives or those of friends and family. It was often achieved by incriminating other *sipahis* or even their own selves. The reasons, whether out of spite, self-sacrifice or peer pressure, are only hinted at. What can be deduced is that alongside the selective use of the physical and linguistic space of the courtroom came the re-appropriation of what it meant to be a soldier in the 5th Light Infantry. The strategies used by the four *sipahis* mentioned in the chapter – of unrepentant mutineer, approver, victim or outsider – conformed, in part, to the expectations colonial authorities had of its colonial soldiers in order to thwart military justice.

Finally, in the interrogations discussed throughout Chapter 6, many colonial *sipahis* refused to be soldiers. The expectations of what the CSDIC(I) had of captured INA personnel were clear: to interrogate, discover how involved they were in the rebel army, and prescribe a course of reconditioning so that they could be reinducted into the Indian Army proper. Instead of the interrogations being a chance to explain what actually happened or for individuals to redeem themselves in the eyes of their former *sahibs*, they allowed *sipahis* to create their own histories of the INA that avoided the language of wholesome praise or wholesale condemnation. So, the names of battalions remained effaced with glaring 'Xs'. Individuals avoided answering any questions of note except through profoundly anti-British plays. And even those who had engaged in protests against the INA during World War II eschewed declarations of loyalty for the quiet inference that they no longer wished to serve again in any capacity.

To write a history or poetics of haunting presences requires an embracing of life-writing; that particular form of historical narrative that exposes and analyses historical events by focusing upon an individual or a small group of individuals. It requires an emplotting of the witness that takes into account failings of memory and everyday myth-making. A history that focuses not just upon speech, but what it means to want to speak and to want to have your voice recorded and read and re-read. It is an approach that has been underused in South Asian history-writing. David Mandelbaum, some 40 years ago, sought to write such a life-history that would emphasize the 'experiences and requirements of the individual – how the person copes with society rather than how society copes with the stream of individuals.'[31] But, Mandelbaum chose to construct a narrative of the life of Mahatma Gandhi as the ideal illustration of how a life history could be written; a choice of subject that reinforces the assumption that outside certain subject areas – the lives of elites or those who were completely subjugated (dalits and women) – a 'person-centred' approach has no place in the histories of South Asia. I too am guilty of blurring identities and reducing individuals in, what David Arnold and Stuart Blackburn have termed is, a 'paradigm of "collectivity"'[32]: the belief that colonial/post-colonial studies can only ever be understood through studies of collective groups. But, those moments where I do focus upon individual soldiers – Jagu Godbole or the four soldiers of the 5th Light Infantry – are attempts to impress upon the reader that Indian *sipahis* were as complex and sophisticated as their metropolitan peers, and their prose as worthy of study as the poetry of Owen or Sassoon:

> My heart is not at ease for I can see no way of saving my life, because I am tied up in the Sircar's string and moreover cannot go outside and get the sort of medicine that I should like. . . . This is the state of affairs that whoever goes into the firing line is burned with German gas, and if he stays behind he is blown to bits by German guns. Those who go to hospital are killed by the hospital people. Now what can I do and what can I say? Oh God what can I say?[33]

To embrace a poetical approach, and to embrace life-writing, requires an acceptance of silence. It involves an acknowledgement of the inarticulate and unarticulable, whether it was because of illiteracy, trauma, or because their testimonies were never preserved. Only a fragment of collective or personal experience is ever available to historians. Very little is available of soldiers' lives outside the Army; of their families or of their careers once their military service was over. But to be aware of silences in testimony also requires an appreciation of the strategic use of silence: the unwillingness to convey information in a manner that can be deciphered by anyone other than its intended recipient and to punctuate a statement with a pregnant pause that itself conveys meaning. To read silence allows a re-engagement with the deposition of Dost Mohamed of the 5th Light Infantry, which is significant precisely because of his clear desire to present himself as unimportant and insignificant. And it enables an analysis of the double rejection of both the British Indian and Indian National Armies, in the testimonies of the Punjabi Musalman *sipahis* in the HKSRA: 'As I have tried to explain, they had no real loyalty.... not as we understand loyalty.'[34]

Finally, the testimonies that remain accessible are marked by performance: the process or praxis that leads to letters, depositions and interrogations being constantly manipulated by censor, interlocutor and witness. To perform is at once to adhere to a set script but also to inject that script with forms of emotion and re-interpretation which can significantly alter the end product from the playwright's intent. Letters, depositions and transcripts of interrogations are remarkable for how much they allowed the ghostly return of soldiers despite the constant effacement of the censor's pen. Performance permits for a wider array of potential agency, and to read more, and more subtly, into the actions and words of individuals than many historians have been accustomed to accept. *Sipahis* added words to their scripts as adjuncts were added to the terms of their military service. They also re-drafted their own stage directions as they occupied courtrooms or discussed Islam in ways that threatened the maintenance of colonial military order.

The move towards a poetics involves a move away from established certainties. A poetical approach resists the temptation of demonology and exorcism: the historian's double desire to efface 'the line of death' and trace 'it anew'.[35] And, the sudden mutability of historical source reduces the possibility of prosopopoeia. The result is an insubstantial and unresolved work; a narrative of ghosts and a ghostly story that is not able to definitively convey what preceded or followed a moment of testimony-writing, nor what definitively linked one form of testimony to another. In addition, this work of history has mirrored some of the strategies of both censor and soldier in deciding what is worthy of comment and what is not, emphasizing certain characteristics above others, and grouping forms of testimony into chapters. But, allowing those flaws to remain unhidden has allowed for the book to be more honest and more truthful to *sipahis'* voices. Constructing a definitive narrative has been an impossibility, but that very impossibility reveals how colonialism operated for those who were neither colonizer nor quite colonized; and representations of agency that were more complex than the nihilism of despair or the narrative of progress:

> I have often thought before I joined the Army how true were the words of the poet, "Oh bee, how often have I warned you against sipping the honey of flowers, because one day or other you will get caught and yield up your life writhing in agony". This is the situation in which we find ourselves.[36]

Notes

Introduction

1 The museum has been closed since 2008, and, although the collection remains *in situ*, its fate remains undecided.
2 *India: Parachinar Durbar, 1929, (Reel 57)*; Dalyell Collection, Film Archive, Empire and Commonwealth Museum, Bristol, BECMV446/1998/005/028.
3 I will use the term 'sipahi' throughout this book to refer to Indian soldiers below the rank of a commissioned officer. The use of that word instead of the anglicized 'sepoy' or the current word 'jawan' is simply because it is the word that soldiers themselves at that time would have used. The anglicized 'sipahis' will be used as a plural, due to the inability to fit the correct plural, 'sipahiyon', into possessive phrases.
4 Samuel P. Huntington, *The Soldier and the State: The Theory and Politics of Civil-Military Relations*, (Cambridge, MA: Harvard University Press, 1964), p. 61.
5 Ibid., p. 84.
6 Ibid.
7 Samuel E. Finer, *The Man on Horseback: The Role of the Military in Politics*, (Harmondsworth, Middlesex: Penguin, 1976 rpt.), p. 21.
8 Amos Perlmutter, *The Military and Politics in Modern Times: On Professionals, Praetorians, and Revolutionary Soldiers*, (New Haven: Yale University Press, 1977), p. 92.
9 Leon Trotsky, *Military Writings*, (New York; Merit, 1969), pp. 96 7.
10 Leon Trotsky, *The History of the Russian Revolution, Volume 1*; translated by Max Eastman, (London: Sphere Books, 1967), p. 242.
11 Ibid., p. 122.
12 Bernard S. Cohn, 'Cloth, Clothes and Colonialism: India in the Nineteenth Century'; idem, *Colonialism and its Forms of Knowledge: The British in India*, (New Delhi: Oxford University Press, 2002), p. 129.
13 Or in other words a desire 'for a reformed recognizable Other; as a subject of a difference that is almost the same, but not quite'. Homi Bhabha, *The Location of Culture*, (Abingdon, Oxford: Routledge, 2004), p. 122.
14 Bernard Cohn, *Colonialism and its Forms of Knowledge*, pp. 106–51.

15 Or, to borrow a further phrase from Albert Memmi, 'those who are neither the colonizers nor colonized'. Albert Memmi, *The Colonizer and the Colonized: A Destructive Relationship*, (Penang, Malaysia: Citizens International, 2005), p. 13.
16 Stanley Kubrick, *Full Metal Jacket*, (1987).
17 Despite what some scholars have recently asserted: '. . . most Indian soldiers hailed from the poor peasantry and were largely illiterate. . . . As a result, Sikh and Gurkha soldiers seldom were able to keep written records of their thoughts and experiences and their voices were rarely directly preserved.' Heather Streets, *Martial Races: The Military, Race and Masculinity in British Imperial Culture, 1857–1914*, (Manchester: Manchester University Press, 2004), p. 199.
18 Jacques Derrida, *Archive Fever: A Freudian Impression*; translated by Eric Prenowitz, (Chicago, IL: Chicago University Press, 1996).
19 Michel de Certeau, 'History is Never Sure', *The Possession at Loudon*; translated by Michael B. Smith, (Chicago, IL: Chicago University Press, 2000); Jacques Rancière, *The Names of History*; translated by Hassan Melehy, (Minneapolis: University of Minnesota Press, 1994).
20 Gayatri Chakravorty Spivak, *A Critique of Postcolonial Reason: Toward a History of the Vanishing Present*, (Cambridge, MA: Harvard University Press, 2003).
21 Jacques Derrida, *Of Grammatology*; translated by Gayatri Chakravorty Spivak, (Baltimore, MD: John Hopkins University Press, 1997 rpt.), p. 23.
22 Ranajit Guha, 'On Some Aspects of the Historiography of Colonial India'; *idem.*, *Subaltern Studies I: Writings on South Asian History and Society*, (New Delhi: Oxford University Press, 2005a rpt.), pp. 1–7.
23 Gyanendra Pandey, *Remembering Partition: Violence, Nationalism and History in India*, (New Delhi: Cambridge University Press, 2003 rpt.), p. 67.
24 Ibid., p. 68.
25 M. M. Bakhtin, 'Discourse in the Novel'; *The Dialogic Imagination: Four Essays*; edited by Michael Holquist, translated by Caryl Emerson and Michael Holquist, (Austin, TX: Texas University Press, 1992), pp. 304–5.
26 A methodology shared by Leonard Smith. Although his use of the French *témoignage* to refer to that quality that is absent from the word 'testimony' is not something I will adopt. Leonard V. Smith, *The Embattled Self: French Soldiers' Testimony of the Great War*, (Ithaca, NY: Cornell University Press, 2007), pp. 12–19.

Chapter 1

1 The articles were subsequently compiled and published in 1940.
2 Donovan Jackson, *India's Army*, (London: Sampson, Low, Marston & Co., c.1940), Author's Foreward.

3   Ibid.
4   Ann Laura Stoler, 'Developing Historical Negatives: Race and the (Modernist) Visions of a Colonial State'; Brian Keith Axel (ed.), *From the Margins: Historical Anthropology and Its Futures*, (Durham, NC: Duke University Press, 2002), pp. 180–1.
5   Major George Fletcher MacMunn, *The Martial Races of India*; illustrations by Major A. C. Lovatt; with foreword by Field-Marshal Earl Roberts, (Somerton, Somerset: Crécy, 1988 rpt.), p. 129.
6   Lieutenant General Sir George Fletcher MacMunn, *The Martial Races of India*, (London: Sampson Low, Marston and Co., 1933), p. 2.
7   Ibid.
8   Ibid., throughout Chapter 13.
9   Stephen P. Cohen, *The Indian Army: Its Contribution to the Development of a Nation*, (Berkeley, CA: California University Press, 1971), especially Chapter 2.
10 Frederick Sleigh Roberts, *Forty-One Years in India: From Subaltern to Commander-in-Chief, Vol. II*, (London: Richard Bentley & Son, 1897), p. 383; also quoted and paraphrased by S. P. Cohen, *The Indian Army*, pp. 46–8.
11 Frederick Sleigh Roberts, Correspondence with England while Commander-in-Chief in Madras, 1881–1885, Vol. 2, (Simla: Govt. Central Printing Office, 1890), pp. 25–6.
12 Roberts, *Forty-One Years*, p. 493.
13 Byron Farwell, *Armies of the Raj, From the Great Indian Mutiny to Independence: 1858–1947*, (London: W.W. Norton and Co., 1989), p. 217.
14 Cohen, *The Indian Army*, p. 48.
15 'The character of the Sikhs, or rather Singhs, which is the name by which the followers of Gúrú Góvind, who are all devoted to arms, are distinguished, is very marked. They have, in general, the Hindú cast of countenance, somewhat altered by their long beards, and are to the full as active as the Mahrátas; and much more robust, from their living fuller, and enjoying a better and colder climate. Their courage is equal, at all times, to that of any natives of India; and when wrought upon by prejudice or religion, is quite desperate. They are all horsemen, and have no infantry in their own country, except for the defence of their forts and villages, though they generally serve as infantry in foreign armies. They are bold, and rather rough, in their address; which appears more to a stranger from their invariably speaking in a loud tone of voice; but this is quite a habit, and is alike used by them to express the sentiments of regard and hatred. The Sikhs have been reputed deceitful and cruel; but I know no grounds upon which they can be considered more so than the other tribes of India. They seemed to me, from all the intercourse I had with them, to be more open and sincere than the Mahrátas, and less rude and savage than the Afgháns. They have, indeed, become, from national

success, too proud of their own strength, and too irritable in their tempers, to have patience for the wiles of the former; and they retain, in spite of their change of manners and religion, too much of the original character of their Hindú ancestors, (for the great majority are of the Hindú race,) to have the constitutional ferocity of the latter. The Sikh soldier, is, generally speaking, brave, active, and cheerful, without polish, but neither destitute of sincerity nor attachment; and if he often appears wanting of humanity, it is not so much to be attributed to his national character, as to the habits of a life, which, from the condition of the society in which he is born, is generally passed in scenes of violence and rapine.' John Malcolm, *Sketch of the Sikhs; A Singular Nation, Who Inhabit the Provinces of Penjab, Situated Between the Rivers Jumna and Indus*, (London: John Murray, Albemarle Street, 1812), pp. 129–31.

16 Anon., 'The Indian Army. No. 3', *United Service Journal* (1836); Douglas M. Peers, '"Those Noble Exemplars of the True Military Tradition": Constructions of the Indian Army in the Mid-Victorian Press'; *Modern Asian Studies*, Vol. 31, No. 1, (February 1997), p. 132.

17 Ibid., p. 132.

18 Channa Wickremesekera, '*Best Black Troops in the World*': *British Perceptions and the Making of the Sepoy, 1746 1805*, (New Delhi: Manohar, 2002), p. 183.

19 There are two pamphlets that I have found from 1918, each of which relays the same story – *How Gul Mahomed Joined the King's Army* (for Punjabi Mussalmans) and *Teja Singh Khalsa Joins the Army* (for Sikh Jats). It is quite possible that other pamphlets were written for the edification of other 'martial classes'.

20 C. M. Enriques, 21st Punjabis, *The Pathan Borderland: A Consecutive Account of the Country and People on and Beyond the Indian Frontier from Chitral to Dera Ismail Khan*, (Calcutta and Simla: Thacker, Spink and Co., 1910), pp. 52–3.

21 MacMunn, *The Martial Races*, pp. 13–14.

22 *Notes for Officers Wishing to Join the Indian Army*, (London: Military Department, India Office, 1942).

23 The principles upon which land in the canal colonies was to be apportioned was made clear by the Revenue Secretary of the Punjab Government, on 22 July 1891: 'It seemed essential to preserve the tradition of the Punjab as a country of peasant farmers. No other general frame of society is at present possible or desirable in the Province. The bulk of the available lands has therefore been appropriated to peasant settlers while the size of the individual grants has been fixed on a scale which will, it is hoped, attract the sturdy, the well-to-do, and the enterprising classes.' *Gazetteer of the Chenab Colony, Vol. 31A, 1904*, (Lahore: Civil and Military Press, 1907), p. 29.

24 Ibid., p. 50.

25 It was present in Alexander Dow's *History of Hindostan* and early nineteenth-century medical opinion. See Alexander Dow, *The History of Hindostan; Translated from the Persian. To Which Are Prefixed Two Dissertations; The First Concerning the Hindoos and the Second on the Origin and Nature of Despotism in India*. (London: J. Walker; White and Cochrane; Lackington, Allen and Co.; Black, Parry and Kingsbury; J. Nunn; J. Cuthell; R. Lea; Longman, Hurst, Rees, Orme and Brown; and J. Faulder, 1812 rpt.); and E. M. Collingham, *Imperial Bodies: The Physical Experiences of the Raj, c.1800–1947*, (Molden, MA: Polity, 2002), Chapter 2.

26 Robert J. C. Young, *Colonial Desire: Hybridity in Theory, Culture and Race*, (London and New York: Routledge, 1995), p. 98.

27 Thomas de Quincey, *Confessions of an English Opium-Eater, and Other Writings*; in Young, *Colonial Desire*, p. 98.

28 *Manual of Physical Training for the Indian Army, 1911*, (Calcutta: Office of the Superintendent, Government Printing, India, 1911), pp. 2–5.

29 A. H. Bingley; revised by A. B. Longden, *Class Handbooks for the Indian Army: Dogras*, (Calcutta: Office of the Superintendent Government Printing, India; 1910), pp. 71–2.

30 *Our Sowars and Sepoys: Official Text-Book for the Lower Standard Examination in Urdu (English)*, (New Delhi: Government of India Press, 1941), Preface.

31 Take, for instance, the Memorandum issued by the Shiromani Gurdwara Parbandhak Committee to the French Government over the issue of religious accoutrements being prohibited in the French education system: 'Your Excellency, it may also be not out of place to mention that the Sikhs have age old ties with the French people. The sovereign Khalsa State of Punjab had senior French officers. The Sikhs fought against the dictatorial and despotic regimes and for the forces of liberty, freedom and democracy along with the French people & State. Thousands of Sikhs were killed in action & your esteemed country has graves of such brave Sikh soldiers who sacrificed their lives to protect the dignity and freedom of every human being. They were all Sikhs having unshorn hair and wearing turban in accordance with the Sikh religious discipline. Your Excellency, we seek your personal intervention to undo this injustice and allow the Sikhs to practice and manifest their religion by restoring their right to wear the turban.' Shiromani Parbandhak Committee, Amritsar, to Dominque de Villepin, Ministère des Affaires étrangères et européennes 13 February, 2004. http://www.sgpc.net/dastar/index.asp.

32 'Space Seed'; *Star Trek, The Original Series*, Series 1, Episode 2, (1967).

33 Punjab Administration Report, 1849–1851; Rajit K. Mazumdar, *The Indian Army and the Making of Punjab*, (Delhi: Permanent Black, 2003), p. 9.

34 Mazumdar, *Making of Punjab*, p. 8.

35 Engels did stumble upon some truth in making this comment. Older versions of *Raj karega Khalsa*, the popular *ardas* (prayer) among Sikhs, did make specific mention of sitting upon the throne of Delhi:

> 'Dilli takht par bahegi aap Guru ki fauj
> Chatter phirega sis paar barhi karegi mauj
> Raj karega Khalsa aaki rahe na koe
> Khwar hoe sab milenge bache saran jo hoye'.

Or:

> 'The Guru's army will sit upon the throne of Delhi
> Over their heads will revolve a *chatter* (a parasol that is a sign of royalty) and they will enjoy themselves immensely
> The Khalsa will rule unchallenged
> They will unite after overcoming evil and will be saved after entering the refuge of the Guru'.

36 Friedrich Engels, 'The Revolt in India'; New York Daily Tribune, 17 September 1858; Karl Marx and Friedrich Engels, *The First Indian War of Independence, 1857–1859*, (Moscow: Progress Publishers, 1988), pp. 152–3.

37 A. H. Bingley, *Handbooks for the Indian Army: Sikhs*, (Simla: Government Central Printing Office, 1899), p. 37.

38 Ibid., p. 39.

39 Ibid., p. 49.

40 Lepel Griffin; ibid., p. 93.

41 A total of 88,925 out of a total of 739,938 combatants were recruited. That ignores, of course, the Sikhs in the 'regular' Indian Army as well as those in the State Forces. It also does not count the numbers of Sikhs in other colonial regiments, such as the Malay States Guides or HKSRA. The total proportion may have been as high as 20%. *India's Contribution to the Great War, published by Authority of the Government of India*, (Calcutta: Superintendent Government Printing, India, 1923), Appendix C.

42 The total Sikh population in Punjab was about 3,238,803 according to the Census of 1921.

43 Bingley, *Handbooks: Sikhs*, pp. 29–30.

44 Such as between Doaba Sikhs nearer the Majha area, areas bordering the Himalayas, etc., ibid., Chapter 5.

45 *Punjab District Gazetteers: Vol. XXA, Amritsar District, 1914*, (Lahore: Civil and Military Gazette Press, 1914), p. 84.

46 Ibid., pp. 33–4.

47 Ibid.

48 *Gazetteer of the Chenab Colony, Vol. 31A, 1904*, (Lahore: Civil and Military Gazette Press, 1904), p. 158.
49 Frederick Yeats-Brown, *Martial India*, (London: Eyre and Spottiswoode, 1945), p. 31.
50 It is also interesting to note that an attack on a minister's house is deemed more important than the arson of government buildings; *Punjab District Gazetteers: Vol. XXXIVA, Gujranwala District, 1935*, (Lahore: Office of the Superintendent, Government Printing, Punjab, 1936), p. 36.
51 B. H. Dobson, *Final Report on the Chenab Colony Settlement*, (Lahore: Office of the Superintendent, Government Printing, Punjab, 1915), p. 37.
52 *East India (Sedition Committee, 1918), Report of Committee Appointed to Investigate Revolutionary Conspiracies in India*, Parliamentary Papers, 1918, p. 68.
53 A. E. Barstow, 11th Sikhs, *The Sikhs: Revised at the Request of the Government of India* (re-titled *The Sikhs: An Ethnology*), (Delhi: Low Price Publications, 2004 rpt.), pp. 19–20.
54 Ibid., p. 25.
55 Ibid., pp. 54–5.
56 'Subversive Attempts on the Loyalty of the Indian Army', 3 April 1943; *Indian Army Morale and Possible Reduction, 1943–1945*, War Staff Papers, Asia and Africa Collections, British Library L/WS/1/707, p. 378.
57 Winston Churchill; ibid., p. 408.
58 *Class Composition of the Army in India*, Asia and Africa Collections, British Library, (L/WS/1/456), p. 23.
59 Ibid.
60 Ibid., p. 24.
61 Ibid., p. 31.
62 Lit. 'There is One Revered, Timeless Truth'.
63 Interrogation of Lt. Col. J. D. Wray; *General Court Martial, Royal Artillery, Hong Kong, 20 January 1941*: War Office Records, National Archives, Kew, Surrey, WO 71/1057.
64 James Fenimore Cooper, *The Last of the Mohicans*; Introduction and Notes by David Blair, (Ware, Hertfordshire: Wordsworth, 2002 rpt.), p. 8.
65 As, for instance, in the *Annual Caste Return of the Native Army in India, on the 1 January 1893*, Asia and Africa Collections, British Library, (L/MIL/7/7081).
66 Denzil Ibbetson, *'Panjab Castes': Being a Reprint of the Chapter on 'The Races, Castes and Tribes of the People' in the Report on the Census of the Punjab published in 1883 by the late Sir Denzil Ibbetson, K.C.S.I.*, (Lahore: Office of the Superintendent, Government Printing, Punjab, 1916), p. 58.
67 *A Dictionary of the Pathan Tribes on the North-West Frontier in India, compiled Under the Orders of the Quartermaster General in India, in the Intelligence Branch*, (Calcutta: Office of the Superintendent, Government Printing, India, 1899), Preface.

68 Enriquez, *Pathan Borderland,* pp. 52–3.
69 R.T.I. Ridgway, 40th Pathans, *Handbooks for the Indian Army: Pathans*, (Calcutta: Office of the Superintendent, Government Printing, India, 1910), p. 19.
70 Enriquez, *The Pathan Borderland*, p. 89.
71 *Annual Return Showing the Class Composition of the Armed Forces of India, on the 1 January 1908*, Asia and Africa Collections, British Library, (L/MIL/7/7084).
72 W. Fitz and G. Bourne, *Handbooks for the Indian Army: Hindustani Musalmans and Musalmans of the Eastern Punjab*, (Calcutta: Office of the Superintendent, Government Printing, India, 1914), pp. 47 and 83.
73 Ibid., pp. 47–8.
74 Ridgway, *Handbooks: Pathans*, p. 15.
75 Ibid., pp. 50–1.
76 Ibid., p. 94.
77 Ibid., p. 56.
78 'Their defects as soldiers are that their tribal customs are so democratic that they can be disciplined only by a leader they know; they tend to lose cohesion if their officers become casualties . . . .' Yeats-Brown, *Martial India*, p. 38.
79 'The border tribes were naturally excited by the entry of Turkey into the war; they were encouraged by the preaching of a few prominent mullahs to look towards Kabul and prepare for Jihad; [and] they heard the wildest rumours about the military situation in India and abroad. . . . [This fomented] a general rising.' The General Staff, Army Headquarters, *Operations in Waziristan, 1919–1920*, (Delhi: Government Central Press, 1923 2nd edn), pp. 11 and 30.
80 Ibid., p. 4.
81 8 from a total of 152; 'Statements Showing "Class Composition" of Newly Raised Indian Infantry Battalions, on 1 January 1917'; *Class Composition*.
82 18 from a total of 120; 'Appendix II: Composition of Indian Regiments Serving in France, 1914–1915'; *Indian Voices of the Great War: Soldier's Letters, 1914–1918*; selected and introduced by David Omissi, (Basingstoke: MacMillan, 1999), pp. 363–4.
83 Paul Jackson, *One of the Boys: Homosexuality in the Military during World War II*, (Montreal and Kingston: McGill-Queens University Press, 2004), pp. 79–80.
84 Several letters do contain deeply homoerotic poems. It is difficult to say if this accurately reflects authorial intent, as the particular soldiers may have just been using pre-existing and well-established registers, and the censor may have failed to communicate precise nuances in his translation. *Viz.*:

> 'Since the day you went to the field, Oh heart
>   of my heart,
> From that day I know no ease,

> ...
>   My soul languishes for communion with you
>   And my body is like water...'

Kot Dafadar Kutubuddin Khan, 3rd Corps Remount, Lahore, to Gulab Khan, 11 Lancers attached 19 Lancers, France, 7 March 1917; *Reports of the Censor of Indian Mails in France, 1917–1918*, Asia and Africa Collections, British Library, L/MIL/5/827, Part 2.

And a letter recounting the 'hospitality' of two French gentlemen;

'Since the 21st March I have been separated from the [French] gentlemen in whose house I lived; but I have exchanged letters with them and have written and told them what you say. I have also given them that if they want anything from India and I am not present, they should without fail write to you .... They are kind and hospitable people and as long as I live I will serve them in whatever way I can ....'

Risaldar Nadir Ali, 11 Lancers attached 9 Hodson's Horse, France, to Mahomed Amir, Peshawar, NWFP; ibid.

85 Maurice Willoughby, *Echo of a Distant Drum: The Last Generation of Empire*, (Lewes, East Sussex: Book Guild, 2001), p. 21.
86 Ibid.
87 MacMunn, *The Martial Races of India*, p. 244.
88 Extrapolated from figures on the Indian Army, 1/1/41, and later. *Class Composition*.
89 There are those who have argued that the narrative is genuine, but I severely doubt it. No original manuscript, in Avadhi, has ever been found, and Sita Ram must have served in several regiments at the same time in order to have been present at all the events recounted in the tale. For a fuller analysis of the narrative's authenticity, see Alison Safadi, 'From *Sepoy to Subedar*/*Khvab-o-Khayal* and Douglas Craven Phillott', *The Annual of Urdu Studies*, Vol. 25, (2010).
90 Foreword by 'Sita Ram'; *From Sepoy to Subedar: Being the Life and Adventures of Subedar Sita Ram, a Native Officer of the Bengal Army written and Related by Himself*; edited by James Lunt, translated and first published by Lieutenant Colonel James Norgate, Bengal Staff Corps at Lahore, 1873, (London: Routledge and Kegan Paul, 1970), p. xxix.
91 Ibid., p. 164.
92 As it is for Douglas M. Peers, '"The Habitual Nobility of Being": British Officers and the Social Construction of the Bengal Army in the Early Nineteenth Century'; *Modern Asian Studies*, Vol. 25, No. 3, (1991); and Wickremesekera, '*Best Black Troops*'.
93 Rudyard Kipling, *Kim*, (Oxford: Oxford University Press, 1998), p. 161.

94 A. H. Bingley, and A. Nicholls, *Caste Handbooks for the Indian Army: Brahmans*, (Simla: Government Central Printing Office, 1897), p. 42.
95 Ibid.
96 As with the village Brahmin encountered in Chapter 3. Kipling, *Kim*.
97 As apparently among the Kanoujiya Gaur Brahmins of UP. Bingley and Nichols, *Brahmans*, p. 18.
98 Ibid., p. 42.
99 Ibid., p. 51.
100 In Kipling's work, the same village Brahmin referred to above tries to steal the purse of a Tibetan lama after slipping an opiate into his drink. Kipling, *Kim*, p. 50.
101 When apparently they refused to adhere to a 'group system of messing.' At least that is the conclusion drawn by the presiding officers at the courts martial. The testimony of the soldiers had more prosaic concerns over pay and leave. *Native Regiments – Insubordination, Misconduct etc.: Conduct of the 3rd Brahman Regiment in Mesopotamia,* Military Department Papers, Asia and Africa Collection, British Library, L/MIL/7/7277.
102 Bingley and Nicholls, *Brahmans*, p. 10.
103 Ibid., pp. 7–9.
104 Ibid., p. 20.
105 Ibid.
106 Ibid., pp. 13–20.
107 *Typewritten minute marked 'Strictly Personal and Secret' from General Auchinleck,* p. 4.
108 'It is in Kangra, and perhaps in Kangra alone, that we find caste existing nearly in the same state as that which the Musulman invaders found it when they entered the Punjab. It is certainly here that the Brahman and the Kshatriya occupy positions most nearly resembling those originally assigned them by Manu.' A. H. Bingley; revised by A. B. Longden, *Class Handbooks for the Indian Army: Dogras*, (Calcutta: Superintendent Government Printing, India; 1910), pp. 11–12.
109 Ibid., p. 25.
110 Ibid., p. 24.
111 Ibid., p. 26.
112 'Annual Return Showing the Class Composition of the Indian Army etc., on 1 January 1941'; *Class Composition.*
113 Bingley; revised by Longden, *Handbooks: Dogras*, p. 71.
114 Claude J. Auchinleck, 'A Note on the Size and Composition of the Indian Army, August 1943'; *Indian Army Morale and Possible Reduction, 1943–1945,* War Staff Papers, Asia and Africa Collection, British Library L/WS/1/707, p. 416.
115 Auchinleck, 'Note on the Size and Composition of the Indian Army'.
116 *Our Sowars and Sepoys: Official Text-Book for the Lower Standard Examination in Urdu (English),* (New Delhi: Government of India Press, 1941), Preface.

117 Substitute the word 'Taliban' with 'Pathan' and the language of *New York Times* editorials is remarkably similar:

> 'Lt. Gen. Stanley McChrystal, President Obama's choice to be the next military commander in Afghanistan, has defined America's essential goals there in a way that represents an overdue change in military strategy. He told senators last week that "the measure of effectiveness will not be the number of enemy killed. It will be the number of Afghans shielded from violence."
>
> If General McChrystal can carry it off, he will have a far better chance of turning around a war America has not been winning — but must.
>
> ... Afghanistan's people have few illusions about the Taliban. They have felt the lash of its medieval punishments, witnessed its brutal attacks on women's rights and girls' education and noted its cynical and sinister ties with major drug traffickers. But they have little enthusiasm for a war in which foreign troops and Taliban fanatics shoot at each other with seeming indifference to the civilians caught in the cross-fire. Last year, some 2,000 Afghan civilians were killed, according to the United Nations and private aid agencies.'
>
> Editorial, *The New York Times*, (7 June 2009).

Chapter 2

1. *Armed Forces Act, 2006*, (London: The Stationery Office, 2006), Part 17, Section 359 (Pardons for Servicemen Executed for Disciplinary Offences: Recognition as Victims of the First World War).
2. Des Browne (Secretary of State for Defence), *House of Commons Hansard Ministerial Statements*, 18 September 2006, Column 135WS.
3. Particularly for the Shot at Dawn Pardons Campaign: www.shotatdawn.info.
4. Including: Private Fatoma, West African Regiment (executed 19 July 1915); Private A Frafra, Gold Coast, 1st East African Rifles (18 September 1916); Lance Corporal A Mamprusi, Gold Coast, HANForce, (28 April 1917); Private H Morris, 6th British West Indies, (20 September 1917). Julian Putkowski and Julian Sykes, *Shot at Dawn*, (Barnsley, South Yorkshire: Wharncliffe, 1989).
5. No records were kept of the numbers or names of men executed under Indian military law.
6. Des Browne 18 September 2006, *Hansard*.
7. 'The War Office "Manual of Military Law" has furnished the model on which the present work has been compiled, and the rulings contained in that manual have been largely drawn upon in its preparation. When the works of legal writers, other than the authors of the abovementioned [sic.] manual, have been quoted, the

source of the information in the text has been indicated in a footnote.' *Manual of Indian Military Law, 1911*, (Calcutta: Superintendent Government Printing, India, 1922, 2nd edn.), Preface to the First Edition by Malcolm Henry Stanley Grover, Major-General, Secretary to the Govt. of India, Army Department.

8 *How Gul Mahomed Joined the King's Army*, (Simla: G.M. Press, 1918), p. 5.
9 The oath of affirmation for Muslim and Hindu recruits was: 'Main . . . Hakk Taála Khudá ko házir aur názir jan ke (Parmeshwar Bhagwán ko ján mán ke) imán (dharm) se ikrár (bachan) kartá hún ki main Sháh Álam-panáh aur uske wárison aur ja-nishinon ká wafádár aur sachchá farmánbardár rahúngá aur jaisá ki merá farz hai, main imándári aur wafádári se Sháh-Álam-panáh ki Hindústáni fauj men naukari karúngá aur jahán mujhe hukm hogá, tari yá khushi ke ráste jáúnga, aur har ek afsar jo ki mere upar mukarrar hogá us ke tamám hukman ká khiyál rahúngá, aur mánúngá kháh ján ká bhi dar ho.' Sikhs began with: 'Main . . . Shri Gurú Granth Sáhib ji ki sugand khátá hún ki main. . .'. And, a Pushtu version was included for Pathans. *Manual of Indian Military Law, 1911*, (Calcutta: Superintendent Government Printing, India, 1922 2nd edn.), p. 184.
10 *Army Regulations, India; Vol. II: Regulations and Orders for the Army* (Calcutta: Office of the Superintendent, Government Printing, India, 1918), Article 581.
11 *Manual of Indian Military Law*, Chapter 1 – Indian Military Law – Its Origin and Extent'.
12 Ibid., pp. 1–4.
13 An Act for the 'punishing Mutiny and Desertion of officers and soldiers in the service of the United Company of Merchants of England trading to the East Indies, and of the punishment of offences committed in the East Indies, or at the Island of Saint Helena' passed in 1754. Ibid., p. 1.
14 Ibid.
15 Ibid., p. 2.
16 Ibid., p. 3.
17 Ibid.
18 *The Indian Articles of War: As Modified up to the 1st January 1895*, (Calcutta: Office of the Superintendent, Government Printing, India, 1895).
19 *The Army Act, 1881*; 'Scots Statutes Revised, 1881–1885', Advocates Library, National Library of Scotland, Edinburgh, 44 and 45 v.c.58.
20 *The Indian Army Act, 1911, (Act No. VIII of 1911): As Modified up to the 15th October, 1937*; Military Department Papers, Asia and Africa Collection, British Library, L/MIL/17/5/1817.
21 Ibid., Paragraph 126.
22 *Manual of Indian Military Law*, Preface to the First Edition by Malcolm Henry Stanley Grover, Major-General, Secretary to the Govt. of India, Army Department.

23 As a military punishment, cashiering was the legacy of an era when officers bought their commissions, and so, by being cashiered, they would thus suffer financial loss.
24 Indian Commissioned Officers suffering these punishments would also be cashiered.
25 *Indian Hemp Drugs Commission, Supplementary Volume: Answers Received to Selected Questions for the Native Army*, (Calcutta: Office of the Superintendent of Government Printing, India, 1895). Answer to question 53: 'Does excessive indulgence in any of these drugs incite to unpremeditated crime, violent or otherwise? Do you know of any case in which it has led to temporary homicidal frenzy?', p. 110.
26 Ibid., Answer to question 53: 'Does excessive indulgence in any of these drugs incite to unpremeditated crime, violent or otherwise? Do you know of any case in which it has led to temporary homicidal frenzy?', p. 136.
27 Ibid., Answer to question 54: 'Are these drugs used by persons to fortify themselves to commit a premeditated act of violence or other crime?', p. 142.
28 Ibid., Answer to question 53: 'Does excessive indulgence in any of these drugs incite to unpremeditated crime, violent or otherwise? Do you know of any case in which it has led to temporary homicidal frenzy?', p. 81.
29 Ibid., Answers to question 53: 'Does excessive indulgence in any of these drugs incite to unpremeditated crime, violent or otherwise? Do you know of any case in which it has led to temporary homicidal frenzy?' and 54: 'Are these drugs used by persons to fortify themselves to commit a premeditated act of violence or other crime?', p. 130.
30 Ibid., Answer to question 53: 'Does excessive indulgence in any of these drugs incite to unpremeditated crime, violent or otherwise? Do you know of any case in which it has led to temporary homicidal frenzy?', p. 30.
31 *How Gul Mahomed Joined the King's Army*, (Simla: G.M. Press, 1918), pp. 2–3.
32 Particularly Volume II.
33 Thomas Babington Macaulay, *Indian Law: A Copy of the Penal Code Prepared by the Indian Law Commissioners, and Published by Command of the Governor-General in India in Council*, 30 July 1838. Parliamentary Papers, 1838, p. 72.
34 Captain E. B. Howell, 23 January 1915; *Reports of the Censor of Indian Mails in France, 1914–1915*, [hereafter *CIM 1914–1915*]; Military Department Papers, Asia and Africa Collection, British Library, L/MIL/5/825, Part 1.
35 'Interview: Pat Mills'; http://charleyswar.sevenpennynightmare.co.uk/?page_id=54.
36 Ibid.
37 General Robert Napier, 22 September 1873; Roy, *Brown Warriors*, p. 152.
38 In 1893, for instance, the 23rd Pioneers were granted warm clothing and free rations as part of their batta while being posted to Gilgit and Chitral in the Hindu Kush.

39 *Gazetteer of the Chenab Colony, Vol. 314, 1904*, p. 50.
40 *Army Regulations, India, Volume II*, p. 25.
41 For a full description of the work of DSBs in colonial Punjab, see Tan Tai-Yong, *The Garrison State: The Military, Government and Society in Colonial Punjab, 1849–1947*, (New Delhi: Sage, 2005).
42 Secretary of the Indian Soldiers' Board, Autumn 1919; *India's Contribution to the Great War; Published by Authority of the Government of India*, (Calcutta: Superintendent Government Printing, India, 1923), p. 248.
43 Sowar Jawan Singh, 19th Lancers, France, to Nur Din, Chowkidar, Sialkot dist., Punjab, India, 4 March 1917; *CIM 1917–1918*, Part 2.
44 Peter Leese, 'Problems Returning Home: The British Psychological Casualties of the Great War'; *The Historical Journal*, 40, 4, (1997), p. 1056.
45 A total of 58% of all men out of work in the United Kingdom in 1929 were World War I veterans. Ibid., p. 1058.
46 Such as the amputees retrained by the Local War Pensions Committee in Leeds: 'Of course, after spending a full year learning the trade, I was given a bag of tools and £10, so I was very upset when I went for job interviews that there was no work for hand tailors anymore as the work was out of date and firms needed machine tailors.' Testimony of Bill Thompson; Ena Elsey, 'Disabled Ex-Servicemen's Experiences of Rehabilitation and Employment after the First World War'; *Oral History*, 25, 2, Autumn 1997, p. 56.
47 *East India (Army in India Committee, 1919–1920). Report of the Committee Apppointed by the Secretary of State for India to Enquire into the Administration and Organisation of the Army in India*. Parliamentary Papers, 1920, p. 78.
48 Ibid., p. 82.
49 Analysed in greater detail in Ben Shephard's excellent book, *A War of Nerves*. Ben Shephard, *A War of Nerves*, (London: Jonathan Cape, 2000).
50 Emile Durkheim, *Suicide: A Study in Sociology*; translated by John A. Spalding and George Simpson; edited and with an introduction by George Simpson, (London: Routledge, 2002 rpt.).
51 Shephard, *War of Nerves*, p. 11.
52 Zohreh T. Sullivan, 'Race, Gender and Imperial Ideology in the Nineteenth Century'; *Nineteenth Century Contexts*, 13, 1, (1989), p. 25.
53 Testimony of J. I. C. Dunn, Esq., D.S.O., M.C., D.S.M., M.D., D.P.H.; *Report of the War Office Committee of Enquiry into 'Shell-Shock'*, Parliamentary Papers, 1922, p. 59.
54 'What the politicians said no longer matters, as far as these memoirs of mine are concerned, though I would give a lot for a few gramaphone records of my talks with Rivers. All that matters is my remembrance of the great and good man who gave me his friendship and guidance. I can visualize him, sitting at his table in the late summer twilight, with his spectacles pushed up on his forehead and his

hands clasped in front of one knee; always communicating his integrity of mind; never revealing that he was weary, as he must often have been after long days of exceptionally tiring work on those war neuroses which demanded such an exercise of sympathy and detachment combined. . . . He liked me and he believed in me.' Siegfried Sassoon, *Sherston's Progress*, (London: Faber and Faber, 1936), pp. 20–1.

55 W. H. R. Rivers, 'War Neurosis and Military Training', (First published in *Mental Hygiene*, 2, 4, (1918); Id., Instinct and the Unconscious: A Contribution to a Biological Theory of the Psycho-Neuroses, (Cambridge: Cambridge University Press, 1924 rpt.), p. 209.

56 Ibid., pp. 206–7.

57 '. . . there is little doubt that the average private enters upon his military training with less aversion from the expression of fear than the average officer, and that his simpler mental training makes him more easily content than the officer with the crude solution of the conflict between instinctive and acquired motives which is provided by some bodily disability'. Ibid., p. 210.

58 Ibid., p. 217.

59 Ibid., p. 220.

60 Ibid., p. 209.

61 Particularly Montague Eder who was working among shell shock victims in Cyprus, M. D. Eder, *War-Shock: The Psycho-Neuroses in War Psychology and Treatment*, (London: William Heinemann, 1917).

62 Shephard, *War of Nerves*, p. 159.

63 *Report of the War Office Committee of Enquiry into 'Shell-Shock'*, p. 92.

64 Ibid., p. 96.

65 'The establishment of an atmosphere of cure is the basis of all successful treatment, the personality of the physician is, therefore, of the greatest importance. While recognising that each individual case of war neurosis must be treated on its merits, the Committee are of [the] opinion that good results will be obtained in the majority by the simplest form of psycho-therapy, i.e., explanation, persuasion and suggestion, aided by such physical methods as baths, electricity and massage. Rest of mind and body is essential in all cases.' Ibid., p. 192.

66 Capt. E. B. Howell, 23 January 1915; *CIM 1914–1915*, Part 1.

67 Behari Lal, (Punjabi Hindu), Supply and Transport Corps, Secunderabad Cavalry Brigade, France, to Kosho Sheran [sic?], Assistant Commissioner's Office, Rajputana, India, 29 October 1916; *CIM, 1915–1916*, Part 9.

68 Sikh Soldier [name censored], Milford-on-Sea, England, to his father, Punjab, India, 22 January 1915; *CIM, 1914–1915*, Part 1.

69 Jemadar Abdul Rahim Khan, (Decanni Musalman), 36th Jacob's Horse, France, to Mir Hussein Khan, Hyderabad, India, 7 February 1917; *CIM, 1917–1918*, Part 1.

70 Rifleman Gokul Singh Rawat, (Garhwali), 1/39th or 2/39th Garhwali Rifles, France, to Subedar Ram Kishan Rawat, Nadar Syang, Upper Burma, India, 17th October 1915; *CIM, 1914–1915*, Part 7.

71 Nur Mohamed Khan, (Punjabi Musalman), Signal Troop, Secunderabad Brigade, France, to Armourer Sher Mohamed Khan, Jhelum, Punjab, India, 25 October 1916; *CIM, 1915–1916*, Part 8.

72 From Asst. Director Med. Service to Surg. Gen., 28 Jan. 1918; James Mills, 'The History of Modern Psychiatry in India, 1858–1947', *History of Psychiatry*, 12, (2001), p. 445.

73 *Indian Army Act, 1911; As Modified to 1937.*

74 Ibid.

75 From Government of Bombay to the office of the Surgeon General in India, 8 February 1918; Mills, 'History of Modern Psychiatry in India', p. 446.

76 Ibid., p. 449.

77 Eder, *War-Shock,* Introduction.

78 Mulk Raj Anand, *The Sword and the Sickle,* (London: Jonathan Cape, 1942), p. 25.

79 *The Army in India: Acts of Violence by Soldiers, 1887–94 – Withdrawal of ball ammunition and Comparative Returns of Murders and Suicides*; Military Department Papers, Asia and Africa Collection, British Library, L/MIL/7/13230.

80 Major-General Sir T. D. Baker, Adjutant-General in India, to Secretary to the Government of India, Military Department, Simla, 11 October 1886. *Acts of Violence by Soldiers.*

81 Ibid.

82 According to Kipling, Roberts was referred to as 'Bobs' by his (British) soldiers.

> 'Then 'ere's to Bobs Bahadur –
>   Little Bobs, Bobs, Bobs!
> 'E's or pukka Kandaharder –
>   Fightin' Bobs, Bobs, Bobs!
> 'E's the Dook of *Aggy Chel*;
> 'E's the man that done us well,
> An' we'll follow 'im to 'ell
>   Won't we Bobs?'

Rudyard Kipling, 'Bobs'; idem, *The Complete Barrak-Room Ballads*; edited by Charles Carrington, (London: Methuen & Co., 1973), p. 92.

83 Government of Bombay, Military Department, 19 July 1887. *Acts of Violence by Soldiers.*

84 C. B. Pritchard, Acting Commissioner in Sind, to Lord Reay, Governor and President of Bombay, Karachi, 17 June 1887. *Acts of Violence by Soldiers.*

85 William Marsden, 'A Dictionary of Malayan and English'; idem, *A Dictionary of the Malayan Language; To which Is Prefixed a Grammar with an Introduction and Praxis*, (London: Cox and Baylis, 1812), p. 15.
86 'I mean to say, that a very trifling offence at one period may be punished with two or three hundred lashes, whilst, at another time, a gross or severe offence would scarcely get fifty or a hundred lashes.' Testimony of Joseph Hume, MP, *Report from His Majesty's Commissioners for Inquiring into the System of Military Punishments in the Army* [hereafter *Military Punishments*], Parliamentary Papers, 1836, p. 56.
87 The instrument used was similar to a cat o'nine tails in that it was a multiple whip consisting of nine knotted cords. But, in the Army, the handle was made from a drumstick (and the punishment was ordinarily administered by a drummer).
88 Henry S. Spry (a military surgeon who spent his career among European soldiers in India); Douglas M. Peers, 'Sepoys, Soldiers and the Lash: Race, Caste and Army Discipline in India, 1820–1850'; *Journal of Imperial and Commonwealth History*, Vol. 23, No. 2, p. 213.
89 Testimony of Lord William Bentinck, 'Military Punishments', p. 285.
90 Ibid., p. 284.
91 Thomas R. Metcalf, *The Aftermath of Revolt: India, 1857–1970*; C. A. Bayly, *Indian Society and the Making of the British Empire, Rulers, Townsmen and Bazaars & Empire and Information: Intelligence Gathering and Social Communication in India, 1780–1870*; Nicholas B. Dirks, *Castes of Mind: Colonialism and the Making of Modern India*.
92 Kaushik Roy, *Brown Warriors of the Raj: Recruitment and the Mechanics of Command in the Sepoy Army, 1859–1913*, (New Delhi: Manohar, 2008).
93 *A Copy of the Penal Code Prepared by the Indian Law Commissioners, and Published by Command of the Governor-General in India in Council* [hereafter *Draft of the Indian Penal Code*]. Parliamentary Papers, 1837–1838, p. 3.
94 'Definitions in the Indian Penal Code', *The Indian Articles of War*, Appendix 1.
95 Ibid.
96 Clare Anderson, *Convicts in the Indian Ocean: Transportation from South Asia to Mauritius, 1815–53*, (Basingstoke, Hampshire: Macmillan, 2000), pp. 12, 17.
97 'Note (A): On the Chapter of Punishments'; *Draft of the Indian Penal Code*.
98 *Draft of the Indian Penal Code*, p. 10.
99 Satadru Sen, *Disciplining Punishment: Colonialism and Convict Society in the Andaman Islands*, (New Delhi: Oxford University Press, 2000), p. 63.
100 *Indian Army Act, 1911*.
101 *Report of the Indian Jails Committee, 1919–1920*. Parliamentary Papers, 1921, p. 282.
102 Ibid., p. 296.

103 Lance Dafadar Mahmud Khan, (PM), 15th Lancers, Banadar Abbas, Persia, to Dafadar Mohamed Khan, 18th Lancers, France, 11 May 1916; *Reports of the Censor of Indian Mails in France, 1915–1916*, [hereafter *CIM 1915–1916*]; Military Department Papers, Asia and Africa Collection, British Library, L/MIL/5/827, Part 5.
104 Roy, *Brown Warriors*, p. 267.
105 Peers, 'Sepoys, Soldiers and the Lash', p. 240.
106 *Indian Articles of War, 1895.*
107 Indian Army Act, 1911.
108 *Indian Articles of War, 1895.*
109 Lord George Hamilton, Secretary of State for India, House of Commons Debate, 13 March 1896, *Hansard*, HC Deb 13 March 1896 vol. 38 c.876.
110 'Private' Din Iman was sentenced to 30 lashes on 4 April 1916. The incident is an exception in that it was listed in the British registry of military punishments. Gerard Oram, *Worthless Men: Race, Eugenics and the Death Penalty in the British Army During the First World War*, (London: Francis Boutle, 1998), p. 106.
111 Richard Smith, for instance, recounts the illegal flogging of Private Jim Riley of the West India Regiment, in his study of Jamaican soldiers in World War I. Richard Smith, *Jamaican Volunteers in the First World War: Race, Masculinity and the Development of National Consciousness*, (Manchester: Manchester University Press, 2004), p. 127.
112 Henry Marshall, Deputy Inspector General of Army Hospitals, *Military Miscellany; Comprehending a History of the Recruiting of the Army, Military Punishments, &c, &c*, (London: John Murray, Albemarle Street, 1846), pp. 254–6.
113 Testimony of Private William Nelson, 14th Durham Light Infantry; Julian Putkowski, 'Private Nelson', http://www.shotatdawn.info/page22.html.
114 James Macpherson MP, Parliamentary Under-Secretary of State, 19 December 1916; *Hansard*, HC Deb 19 December 1916, Vol. 88, CC 1282–5.
115 Tan Tai-Yong, *The Garrison State*; Rajit K. Mazumdar, *The Indian Army and the Making of Punjab*, (New Delhi: Permanent Black, 2003).
116 Henry Cubbit-Smith, *Yadgari or Memories of the Raj*, (Saxlingham, Norfolk: Anchor Press, 1987), p. 12.
117 'Under stress of necessity many Indian soldiers during their stay in Europe have learned to read and write their own languages, and primers and spelling books come in large quantities from India to [soldiers in] the Army.'
Captain E. B. Howell, 11 December 1915, *CIM 1914–1915*, Part 8.
118 Abdul Jaffar Khan, (Hindustani Muslim), Signal Troop, Sialkot Cavalry Brigade, France, to Dafadar Inayat Khan, Rohtak, Punjab, India, 20 August 1916, Part 7. The expression 'ca ne fait rien' also entered the everyday speech of British, Dominion and American soldiers (as 'san fairy ann', 'san ferry ann', 'sanfarian'

etc.). W. H. Downing, *Digger Dialects*; J. M. Arthur and W. S. Ramson (eds), (Melbourne: Oxford University Press, 1990), p. 183. Hugh Kimber, *San Fairy Ann*, (London: Robert Holden & Co., 1927).
119 'The Experiences of Ram Singh, Daffadar of Horse: An Echo of 1914' (unpublished manuscript); Captain Roly Grimshaw, Indian Cavalry Officer, 1914–1915, (Tunbridge Wells, Kent: Costello, 1986), p. 147.

Chapter 3

1 Brian Friel, *Translations*, (London: Faber and Faber, 2000 rpt.), p. 53.
2 'Towards the end of September 1914 the Lahore and Meerut Divisions of the Indian Army, with the normal complement of British troops included, began to arrive in France. The Force was disembarked at Marseilles and after a few days' rest there was conveyed by train to Orleans. The route chosen for the troop trains was a circuitous one leading through Toulouse and other places in south-western France. While the force was in transit a member of the Indian Revolutionary Party [*Ghadar* Party], if it may be so called, was arrested in Toulouse, and upon examination his pockets were found to be stuffed with seditious literature intended for dissemination among Indian soldiery.

 The authorities, thus set upon their guard, decided that, at least during the stay of the Indian troops in Europe, their correspondence must be subjected to systematic examination, and cast about as [sic.] a suitable person to appoint as Indian Mail Censor. It was not easy to find anyone possessing anything like the requisite qualifications, but eventually Second Lieutenant E. B. Howell, a member of the Political Department of the Indian Civil Service, who chanced to be serving in France as an interpreter attached to a regiment of Indian cavalry, was chosen and directed to undertake this duty.'

 Captain E. B. Howell, 'Report on Twelve Months' Writing of the Indian Mail Censorship', 7 November 1915; *Reports of the Censor of Indian Mails in France, 1914–1918*, [hereafter *CIM 1914–1918*]; Military Department Papers, Asia and Africa Collection, British Library, L/MIL/5/828, Part 1.
3 Howell, 23 January 1915; *CIM 1914–1915*, Part 1.
4 Some of the original staff assigned to the Chief Censor's office at Boulogne never appeared, and Howell had particular difficulty translating Gurumukhi.
5 It took until 14 November 1917 before absolutely every letter was redirected to the Censor's office. *CIM 1917–1918*, Part 5.
6 Howell, 4 February 1915; *CIM 1914–1915*, Part 1.
7 'It was felt that it would be quite unfair to withhold the whole of a long letter containing as often as not what the writer believed to be his last will and

testament, simply because here and there through the letter advice was given to younger relatives to stay at home or not to leave the village, or to be guided by the direction of so and so, or not to join the army.' Howell, 28 August 1915; *CIM 1914–1915*, Part 5.

8   Howell, 15 February 1915; *CIM 1914–1915*, Part 1.
9   Howell, 'Report on Twelve Months' Writing'.
10 The fictional letters were serialized in the *American Saturday Evening Post* between May and June 1917, and then later published in the 'Sussex Edition' and then as 'Eyes of Asia'.
11 The surviving reports are incomplete, and not ordered, but each began with instructions on how it ought to be properly destroyed: 'This Summary should be kept under lock and key in suitable custody or destroyed by fire if not required for record.' *Middle East Military Censorship: Fortnightly Summaries Covering Indian Troops, September 1942 – April 1943* [hereafter *MEMC September 1942 – April 1943*]; Public and Judicial Papers, Asia and Africa Collection, British Library, L/PJ/12/655, File 2336/42.
12 Friel, *Translations*, pp. 36–7.
13 Ibid., p. 54.
14 Ibid., p. 53.
15 Anon. (Sikh), Military Hospital, England, to Brother, India, 14 February 1915, *CIM 1914–1915*, Part 1.
16 See Lous E. Fenech for a discussion of martyrdom in the Sikh and wider Punjabi tradition. Louis E. Fenech, *Martyrdom in the Sikh Tradition: Playing the 'Game of Love'*, (New Delhi: Oxford University Press, 2000).
17 Malik Mohamed Khan, (Punjabi Musalman), Punjab Canal Colonies, India, to Tikka Khan, 38th Central India Horse, France, 13 July 1917; *CIM 1917–1918*, Part 4.
18 *MEMC September 1942 – April 1943*.
19 James C. Scott, *Domination and the Arts of Resistance: Hidden Transcripts*, (New Haven, CT: Yale University Press, 1990), Preface.
20 'Many, perhaps most, hidden transcripts remain just that: hidden from public view and never "enacted". And we are not able to tell easily under what precise circumstance the hidden transcript will storm the stage. But if we wish to move beyond apparent consent and to grasp potential acts, intentions as yet blocked, and possible futures that a shift in the balance of power or a crisis might bring into view, we have little choice but to explore the realms of the hidden transcript.' Ibid., p. 16.
21 Anurag Jain, 'The Eyes of Asia: Introduction'; http://www.kipling.org.uk/rg_asia_intro.htm#4.
22 'As to the Censor's reports (Indian letters) I'd be immensely grateful for more of them. They are a complete revelation. If in my floods of work I can manage ever

to do what I want and compile some sort of article out of them – not, of course, giving the source of my information – may I send it you to be checked?' To Sir J. R. Dunlop Smith, 19 June 1916; Thomas Pinney (ed.), *The Letters of Rudyard Kipling, Vol, 4, 1911–19*, (London: Macmillan, 1999), pp. 374–5.

23   Rudyard Kipling, *The Eyes of Asia*, (Gloucester: Dodo Press, 2011 rpt.), p. 1.
24   Ibid., pp. 4–5.
25   Ibid., p. 6.
26   Ibid.
27   Ibid., p. 8.
28   To Sir J. R. Dunlop Smith, 19 June 1916; *The Letters of Rudyard Kipling, Vol. 4, 1911–19*, pp. 374–5.
29   To Lord Sydenham, 5 May 1916; *The Letters of Rudyard Kipling, Vol. 4, 1911–19*, p. 493.
30   Howell, 15 February 1915; *CIM 1914–1915*, Part 1.
31   Howell, 26 December 1914; *CIM 1914–1915*, Part 1.
32   Jemadar Hasan Shah, (Punjabi Musalman), 9th Hodson's Horse, France, to a lady addressed as "Dearer than life", c/o Bheja Mul, Shopkeeper, Adowal, Jhelum dist., Punjab, India, 19 September 1916; *Reports of the Censor of Indian Mails in France, 1915–1916*, [hereafter *CIM, 1915–1916*]; Military Department Papers, Asia and Africa Collection, British Library, L/MIL/5/826, Part 7.
33   Gurdit Singh, (Sikh), France, to India, 19 November 1915; *CIM, 1914–1915*, Part 8.
34   Amir Khan, (Punjabi Musalman), 129th Baluchis, France, to brother, Lance Naik Zaman Khan, 34th Regiment, Rawalpindi, Punjab, India, 18 March 1915; *CIM, 1914–1915*, Part 2.
35   Ibid.
36   *Military Operations on the North-West Frontiers of India, Vol. 1: Papers Regarding British Relations with the Neighbouring Tribes on the North-West Frontier of India, and the Military Operations Undertaken Against them During the Year 1897–1898*, Parliamentary Papers, 1898, pp. 295–6.
37   One of the many plaques erected in the complex by the British and by the post-colonial Indian Army.
38   Indian Soldier, Back Areas, Egypt, to India, October 1942; *Middle East Military Censorship: Fortnightly Summaries Covering Indian Troops, September 1942 – April 1943* [hereafter *MEMC September 1942 – April 1943*]; Public and Judicial Papers, Asia and Africa Collection, British Library, L/PJ/12/654, File 2336/42.
39   [Name Unclear or Censored], (Sikh), French Post Office 13, France, to Mahant Partab Das, Patiala, Patiala State, Punjab, India, 18 October 1915, *CIM 1914–1915*, Part 7.
40   Khillullah, (Punjabi Mussalman), 8th Cavalry attached 2nd Lancers, France, to Dilawar Ali, Head Clerk, Forest Office, Dharamsala, Punjab, India, 4 July 1917, *CIM 1917–1918*, Part 4.

41 Nur Zaman Khan, (Baluchi), 36th Jacob's Horse, France, to Syed Mahmud Khan, Mianwali dist., Punjab, India, 8 November 1917; *CIM 1917–1918*, Part 5.
42 The author's own paternal grandfather briefly enlisted in the Indian Parachute Brigade during World War II after the height requirement was relaxed. Or at least he did until *his* father found out.
43 From Malabar Coast, South India, to Soldier, Middle East, October 1943; *Middle East Military Censorship: Fortnightly Summaries Covering Indian Troops, September 1942 – April 1943* [hereafter *MEMC September 1942 – April 1943*]; Public and Judicial Papers, Asia and Africa Collection, British Library, L/PJ/12/655, File 2336/42.
44 Atta Mohamed, (Punjabi Musalman), Patiala State, Punjab, to Abdul Majid Khan, 34th Poona Horse, France, 23 May 1917; *CIM, 1917–1918*, Part 4. And Fakir Mohamed, (Pathan), Shankargarh, Peshawar dist., NWFP, India, to his son, Mahsud, 38th Central India Horse, France, 14 July 1916; *CIM, 1915–1916*, Part 6.
45 Rahman, (Pathan), 57th Wilde's Rifles (Frontier Force), Hospital, England, to an unknown soldier, 8 April 1915; *CIM, 1914–1915*, Part 2.
46 Draughtsman, Forward Survey Company, Egypt, to India, June 1943; *MEMC April 1943 – Sept. 1943*.
47 Gurbaksh Singh Dhillon, *From My Bones: Memoirs of Col. Gurbaksh Singh Dhillon of the Indian National Army*, (New Delhi: Aryan Books, 1999), pp. 29–30.
48 Ibid., p. 33.
49 'The fact has come to notice in this World Wide War namely that those who go on field service suffer in the matter of promotion while those who remain in India benefit. For instance Jemadar Gholam Mohamed Khan of 27th Light Cavalry who is attached to the 34th Poona Horse in France, is senior to the two Jemadars of his Squadron who have been made Risaldars. The same thing has happens in the case of the rank and file. Before the war it was the practice to give promotion to the senior [man], and, if he happened to be absent from the Regiment on field service, a second promotion was given in the Regiment in the place of a seconded senior. You should now represent the matter to your CO and press him to send it to the Commander-in-Chief.' Ali Gaur Khan, (PM), Jhelum dist., Punjab, India, to Hussain Baksh Khan, 34th Poona Horse, France, 12 May 1917; *CIM 1917–1918*, Part. 4.
50 Taj Mohamed Khan, (Muslim Rajput), Bareilly Cant., UP, India, to Nur Mohamed Khan, 3rd Skinner's Horse, France, 9 June 1916; *CIM, 1915–1916*, Part 5.
51 *Army Regulations, India, Volume II*, p. 4.
52 See Chapter 2.
53 Mulk Raj Anand, *Across the Black Waters*, (Delhi: Orient Paperbacks, 2000 rpt.), pp. 72–3.

54 Although, of course, the term does predate both English public schools and cricket.
55 VCO, 98th GPT Company, RIASC, Italy, to India, January 1944; *Middle East Military Censorship: Fortnightly Summaries Covering Indian Troops, November 1943 – March 1944* [hereafter *MEMC November 1943 – March 1944*]; Public and Judicial Papers, Asia and Africa Collection, British Library, [misfiled as 'Indian Chief Censor's Fortnightly Reports, 1943–1944'], L/PJ/12/578, File 471 (XN/37).
56 Havildar Clerk, 98th GPT Company, RIASC, Italy, to India, January 1944, *MEMC November 1943 – March 1944*.
57 Lance Naik, 98th GPT Company, RIASC, Italy, to India, January1944, *MEMC November 1943 – March 1944*.
58 'Sir,

   When we were summoned as reservists from 35th Scinde Horse at Dera Ismail Khan and sent to join 36th Jacob's Horse, your honour informed us that all reservists on joining would be paid as sowars. But we have been paid at the same rate as syces [grooms], and we respectfully claim to receive pay as sowars from the date that we were ordered to the 36th Jacob's Horse.' Natha Singh, Mal Singh, Hari Singh, and Fauju Khan, Reservists, 35th Scinde Horse attached 36th Jacob's Horse, France, to Officer Commanding, 35th Scinde Horse, Jabalpur, India, (not dated, 1916); *CIM 1914–1915*, Part 4.

   'I tell you frankly without fear of opposition that the military authorities in charge of our hospital are not treating us as they ought to have done. The public of England is quite ignorant about it and so the matter is not brought to light. We have drawn up an application [sic., petition] and we intend submitting it in a day or two laying out our chief troubles and wait for the result patiently . . . .' Ram Jawan Singh, (Hindustani Hindu), Storekeeper, Kitchener Indian Hospital, Brighton, England, to his father, Lucknow, UP, India, 30 September 1915; *CIM 1914–1915*, Part 6.
59 Wazir Chand Chopra, (Punjabi Hindu), Office of the Field Controller of Military Accounts, Indian Cavalry Corps, Rouen, France, to Lal Har Kishan Das, Branch Postmaster, Ghota, Fatehgarh, Sialkot dist., Punjab, India, 8 December 1915; *CIM 1914–1915*, Part 8.
60 KCIO and ICO are abbreviated forms of King's Commissioned Indian Officer and Indian Commissioned Officer, respectively. The history of Indians with a full commission and with a full officer's rank, outwith favours bestowed on Indian royalty, begins as early as 1905, but the history of Indians permitted to actually command soldiers only begins in July 1920. For this purpose, Indians were selected as 'gentleman cadets', trained at Sandhurst, and given the same type of King's Commission as any of their British counterparts (hence the abbreviation KCIO). In July 1932, however, with the creation of the Indian Military Academy

(IMA) at Dehra Dun, and the closure of Sandhurst to Indians, one had the creation of a new type of fully commissioned officer. Much like the KCIOs that had preceded them, these ICOs would serve a probationary year in a British regiment before being drafted to an Indian one, but unlike KCIOs who had a King's Commission, ICOs were commissioned by the Viceroy into 'His Majesty's Indian Land Forces' giving them complete authority over Indian *sipahis* anywhere in the world but only over British troops in India. See Apurba Kundu, *Militarism in India: The Army and Civil Society in Consensus*, (London: Taurus Academic Studies, 1998), for a more detailed exposition of the changing status of the Indian Officer.

61 *Army Regulations, India, Volume II*, (1904), p. 73.
62 Naik Buland Khan, (Punjabi Musalman), 69th Punjabis, to Mohamed Ashraf Khan, son of Subedar Gul Mohamed Khan, Peshawar, NWFP, India, 5 October 1915; *CIM 1914–1915*, Part 7.
63 Bihari Lal, (Punjabi Hindu), Supply and Transport Corps, Secunderabad Cavalry Brigade, France, to Pandit Mathura Prasad Bhargava, Quetta, Baluchistan, India, November 1917; *CIM 1917–1918*, Part 5.
64 Sher Khan, (Pathan), Signalling Troop, 19th Lancers, Sialkot Cavalry Brigade, France, to Fateh Khan, Pensioned Dafadar, Mianwali, Punjab, India, 5 July 1916; *CIM 1915–1916*, Part 6.
65 Rifleman Gokul Singh Rawat, (Garhwali), 1/39th or 2/39th Garhwali Rifles, France, to Subedar Ram Kishan Rawat, Nadar Syang, Upper Burma, India, 17 October 1915; *CIM 1914–1915*, Part 7.
66 Nur Mohamed Khan, (Punjabi Musalman), Signal Troop, Secunderabad Brigade, France, to Armourer Sher Mohamed Khan, Jhelum, Punjab, India, 25 October 1916; *CIM 1915–1916*, Part 8.
67 Name Censored, (Sikh), 47th Sikhs, France, to a Clerk, 47th Sikhs, Regimental Depot, Punjab, India, 9 December 1915; *CIM 1914–1915*, Part 8.
68 Gunga Ram, (Hindu Jat), 3rd Company, [regiment censored], Kitchener General Hospital, Brighton, England, to Lance Naik Suji Ram, 5th Company, 113th Infantry, Dabarugad, Assam, India, May 1915; *CIM 1914–1915*, Part 3.
69 '[If] there remains a considerable number of young men not engaged in [exempted] pursuits who could perfectly be spared for military service they should be compelled to serve. On the other hand, if the number should prove to be, as I hope it will, a rather negligible minority, there would be no question of legislation.' Lord Derby, 19 November 1915; Roy Douglas, 'Voluntary Enlistment in the First World War and the Work of the Parliamentary Recruiting Committee'; *The Journal of Modern History*, Vol. 42, No. 4, (Dec. 1970), p. 580.
70 Yusuf Khan, (Pathan), Kitchener Indian Hospital, Brighton, England, to Abdull Jan, 40th Pathans, France, 6 October 1915; *CIM 1914–1915*, Part 6.

71 In addition to the Kitchener Indian Hospital in Brighton, six other Indian military hospitals were established in Britain in World War I. They were at the Brighton Pavilion, Milford-on-Sea, New Milton, Bournemouth, Brockenhurst, and Netley (the last was a temporary hospital that was closed in February 1915).

72 Bruce Seton was the father of the somewhat successful actor of the same name.

73 *Report on the Kitchener Indian Hospital, Brighton,* Colonel Sir Bruce Seton Papers, European Manuscripts, Asia and Africa Collection, British Library, MSS Eur/F143/66.

74 Ann Laura Stoler, 'Sexual Affronts and Racial Frontiers: European Identities and the Cultural Politics of Exclusion in Colonialist Southeast Asia'; *Comparative Studies in Society and History*, Vol. 34, (1992), p. 515.

75 The first 'bantam battalions' of men who failed to exceed the minimum height requirement of 5'3" were established in Britain as early as 1914.

76 Captain J. C. Dunn, 2nd Royal Welsh Fusiliers; Richard Smith, *Jamaican Volunteers*, p. 14.

77 *New Haven Chronicle*, 14 October 1915; Ibid., p. 104.

78 Graham Smith, *When Jim Crow Met John Bull: Black American Soldiers in World War II Britain*, (London: I.B. Taurus, 1987), p. 199.

79 Anon. (Katherine Lourd), *Diary of a Nursing Sister on the Western Front, 1914–1915*, (Edinburgh and London: William Blackwood and Sons, 1915), pp. 97–8.

80 Smith, *Jamaican Volunteers*, pp. 113–7.

81 As part of its intriguingly named 'Mixed Race Season' in October 2011.

82 'The state of affairs here is this. Ten annas are equal to one franc. So by paying 6, 7 or 8 francs the [French] women get men to have carnal intercourse with them. So that for little money sexual pleasure is sold, especially by Drabis [men of the Transport Corps] and Sikhs [who] have got a lot of money from this.' V. S. Pranje, (Maratha), I.S.M.D., Lahore Indian General Hospital, France, to Pirdan Singh, Ward Orderly, Depot, 54th Poona Horse, Ambala, Punjab, India, April 1915; *CIM 1914–1915*, Part 3.

83 Kot Dafadar Wazir Khan, (Punjabi Musalman), Meerut Cavalry Brigade, France, to Mother, Shahpur dist., Punjab, India, 23 May 1916; *CIM 1915–1916*, Part 5.

84 'I am off to Paris which has been hitherto "out of bounds" to everyone but officers. Now we (up to Dafadars) can go. Paris is a city of fairyland and God will give us an opportunity of seeing it. I will write [to] you all about it. Whatever happens do not let anyone know about this. I intend to enjoy whatever pleasures there are. Don't let anyone know that Jai Singh is spending Rs. 250 in 4 days. If father heard of it he would be very angry. I should like to marry in France but I am afraid the family would be ashamed. You can marry very fine girls if you like.' Jai Singh,

(Hindu Jat), 6th Cavalry or 19th Lancers, France, to Sirdar Singh, Lahore, Punjab, India, 6 November 1917; *CIM 1917-1918*, Part 5.

85 Nabi Buksh, (HM), [unknown regiment], Kitchener Indian General Hospital, Brighton, England, to Frarijie Esq., Head Clerk, Cantonment Magistrate's Office, Neemuch, NWFP, India, 12 June 1915; *CIM 1914-1915*, Part 4.

86 'Just tell me, if I were to bring them out what would be the difficulties in the way? Do you think that I should bring them with me? Would there be any harm? Of course people would laugh, but "can en fait rien". Your mouth will water when you see them but you won't be able to see. You will do your best no doubt to peep around the corner. Well write me at length what the drawbacks may be, as compared with the advantages. Both of them are quite willing to come.' Abdul Jaffar Khan, (Hindustani Muslim), Signal Troop, Sialkot Cavalry Brigade, France, to Dafadar Inayat Khan, Rohtak, Punjab, India, 20 August 1916; *CIM 1915-1916*, Part 7.

87 Dad Gul Khan, (Pathan – Mahsud), 129th Baluchis, Hospital, England, to friend, Waziristan, NWFP, India, 18 March 1915; *CIM 1914-1915*, Part 2.

88 J. H. Godbole, (Maratha Brahmin), Sub Assistant Surgeon, Indian General Hospital (Kitchener), Brighton, England, to H. Godbole, Dapoli, Rutnagari dist., Bombay Presidency, 16 November 1915; *CIM 1914-1915*, Part 8.

89 Ibid.

90 'Alas, we are not free to go about at will. In fact we Indians are treated as prisoners. On all sides there is barbed wire and a sentry stands at each door, who prevents us from going out. In cases of urgent necessity, when the C.O. is satisfied that urgency exists, leave of absence for three hours is obtained with great difficulty. . . . If I had known that such a state of affairs would exist, I would never have come. In India we were assured that once our work for the day was finished, we would be free to go where we pleased. . . . If you ask me the truth, I can say that I have never experienced such hardship in all my life. True, we are well fed, and are given plenty of clothing; but the essential thing – freedom – is denied. Convicts in India are sent to the Andaman Islands; but we have found our convict station here in England. Tell me, how are they treated?' Mithan Lal, (Hindustani Hindu), Storekeeper, Indian Convalescent Home, New Milton, England, to Maulvi Abdul Jabar Sahib, Ballygunj, Calcutta, Bengal, India, 2 December 1915; *CIM 1914-1915*, Part 8.

91 Ram Jawan Singh, (Hindustani Hindu), Kitchener Indian Hospital, Brighton, England, to Mr Jacques Derel, 5th Avenue Victor Hugo, Vernon, France, 26 September 1915; *CIM 1914-1915*, Part 6.

92 'Out of the blackest part of my soul, across the zebra striping of my mind, surges this desire to be suddenly *white*.

   I wish to be acknowledged not as *black* but as *white*.

Now – and this is a form of recognition that Hegel had not envisaged – who but a white woman can do this for me? By loving me she proves that I am worthy of white love. I am loved like a white man.

I am a white man.

Her love takes me onto the noble road that leads to total realization....

I marry white culture, white beauty, white whiteness.

When my restless hands caress those white breasts, they grasp white civilization and dignity and make them mine.'

Frantz Fanon, Black Skins, White Masks, (London: Pluto Press, 1987 rpt.), p. 63.

93 Howell, 19 June 1915; *CIM, 1914–1915*, Part 4.
94 *Report on the Kitchener Indian Hospital.*
95 Ibid.
96 Both the *Report on the Kitchener Indian Hospital* and soldiers' correspondence made mention of this. For example: 'Formerly we used to go into town, but the men began to misbehave badly and we were stopped from going. Now only the sick go to the town. If anyone climbs the wall and stays out he gets a dozen lashes. We are let out into the town once a month – and then only two or three men with two or three white soldiers. For this we have only ourselves to thank, for had those rascals not misbehaved we should still be allowed to go out every day. In the days when there was no restriction two or three men used to spend a couple of nights or more in this town. They were given a dozen lashes, but this did not prevent them from behaving as before.' Assistant Shopkeeper Tulsi Ram, (Punjabi Hindu), Kitchener Indian Hospital, Brighton, England, to a friend, Peshawar, NWFP, India, 12 August 1915; *CIM 1914–1915*, Part 4.
97 'The Pavilion Hospital is in the middle of town and to go too and fro is forbidden, for the patients are not allowed to go between hospitals which are in the town.' Muhabbat Khan, (Pathan), [unknown regiment], Hospital in Brighton, England, to Abdullah Khan, Peshawar, NWFP, India, 2 July 1915; *CIM 1914–1915*, Part 4.
98 Sepoy Hoshanki [sic], (Dogra), 37th Dogras, attached 41st Dogras, Kitchener Indian Hospital, Brighton, England, to Lance Naik Hira Singh, 74th Infantry, attached 59th FFR, France, c. September 1915; *CIM 1914–1915*, Part 5.
99 'England is a dog's country. India is a very fine country. Our people are very angry. They do not allow us out to the bazaars etc. They do not let the French or English talk to us nor do they let us talk to them. The English [Officers] have now become very bad. They have become dogs. Our Indian soldiers are very much oppressed, but they can do nothing. Now they have sent us across the river [English Channel]. There is an abundance of everything but there is not honour. No black man has any 'izzatt'. Men wounded 4 or 5 times are sent back to the trenches. Men who have lost their arms or legs are sent back to India.' Sepoy Pirzada, (Pathan), [unknown regiment] Kitchener Indian Hospital, Brighton, England, to Zaman

Khan and Hasan Shah, 40th Pathans, Depot, Fategarh, [UP?], India, 3 June 1915; *CIM 1914–1915*, Part 4.

100 Or even back to the Front on rare occasions: 'I am very much annoyed because the officers here are very bad. The work which they give us here to do, if I were to do it, could not be accomplished [if I worked] day and night. I came here to serve as a soldier, but they threaten me with severe punishment. I have written to the officer commanding the 47th Sikhs to say that I want to come away from my present task. I do not care for death. . . . But I will not be spoken to by Babus in a way that pierces a soldier's heart. It is worse than bullets.' Ward Orderly Diwan Singh, (Sikh), 'at one of the hospitals in England', to Bir Singh, 47th Sikhs, France, 24 July 1915; *CIM 1914–1915*, Part 4.

101 For example: 'I am left here still, as there was a case in which I was concerned. A sub assistant surgeon threatened the surgeon of my hospital (who is a Colonel but who expects to be promoted to General) with a revolver. By the Grace of God the revolver missed fire [sic. misfired], and I immediately caught hold of the man.' Nahar Singh, (Hindu Jat), Kitchener Indian Hospital, Brighton, England, to Lance Dafadar M. Bashir Khan, 30th Lancers, France, 27 November 1915; *CIM 1914–1915*, Part 8.

102 Jagu Godbole, (Maratha Brahmin), Sub Assistant Surgeon, Kitchener Indian Hospital, Brighton, England, to India, 14 December 1915; *CIM 1914–1918*, Part 3.

103 Ibid.

104 Ibid.

105 Jagu Godbole, (Maratha Brahmin), Sub Assistant Surgeon, Kitchener Indian Hospital, Brighton, England, to India, 19 December 1915; *CIM 1914–1918*, Part 3.

106 Ibid.

107 Ram Jawan Singh, (Hindustani Hindu), Storekeeper, Kitchener Indian Hospital, Brighton, England, to his father, Lucknow, UP, India, 30 September 1915; *CIM 1914–1915*, Part 6.

108 Letter addressed to the King-Emperor, from Milford-on-Sea, 24 April 1915; *CIM 1914–1915*, Part 3.

109 Ram Jawan Singh, (Hindustani Hindu), Storekeeper, Kitchener Indian Hospital, Brighton, England, to his father, Lucknow, UP, India, 30 September 1915; *CIM 1914–1915*, Part 6.

110 Jaroslav Hašek, *The Good Soldier Schweik*; illustrated by Joseph Lada, translated by Paul Sewer, (Harmondsworth, Middlesex: Penguin, 1941), pp. 42–3.

111 Senchi Khan, (Pathan), Peshawar, NWFP, India, to Dafadar Yakub Khan, 38th CIH, France, 4 May 1917; *CIM 1917–1918*, Part 3.

112 Azizuddin, (Hindustani Musalman), 6th Cavalry, France, to Mohamed Nazirul Zaman, Farrukhabad, UP, 29 June 1917; *CIM 1917–1918*, Part 3.

113 Kaka Singh, (Sikh), 38th CIH, France, to Narinjan Singh, Ludhiana dist., Punjab, India, 30 July 1917; *CIM 1917–1918*, Part 4.
114 Kallu Khan, (Muslim Rajput), Jodhpur Lancers, France, to Kasim Khan, Jaipur, Rajputana, 3 March 1917; *CIM 1917–1918*, Part 2.
115 Abdul Wahab Khan, (Hindustani Muslim), 6th Prince of Wales' Cavalry, France, to Atta Khan, Pertabgarh, UP, India, 27 March 1917; *CIM 1917–1918*, Part 2.
116 Ranging from the downing of tools for 7 days by the 50th North West Frontier Labour Company to threats by Nagas that they would 'burn their camp down or do anything that occurs to them as suitable to the occasion'. *Correspondence and Memorandum on the Indian Labour Corps in France and Flanders, July 1917 – June 1919*, Military Department Papers, Asia and Africa Collection, British Library, L/MIL/5/738.
117 Man Singh, (Sikh), 6th Prince of Wales' Cavalry, France, to Sirdar Gurdatt Singh, Risaldar Major, 6th Prince of Wales' Cavalry, Depot, Sialkot, Punjab, India, 9 June 1917; *CIM 1917–1918*, Part 3.
118 [Name Censored], (Afridi Pathan), 58th Vaughan's Rifles (Frontier Force), hospital, England, to friend, 58th Vaughan's Rifles, France, February 1915; *CIM 1914–1915*, Part 1.
119 Byron Farwell, *Armies of the Raj*, p. 251.
120 Gordon Corrigan, *Sepoys in the Trenches: The Indian Corps on the Western Front, 1914–1915*, (Staplehurst, Kent: Spellmount, 1999), p. 182.
121 [Name Censored], (Garhwali), Hospital, England, to his Guru in India, 17 February 1915; *CIM 1914–1915*, Part 1.
122 Colour Havildar Mir Haider Jan, (Pathan), Hospital, England, to Subedar Shah Nawaz Khan, 82nd Regiment [82nd Punjabis], Attached to another regiment, France, 20 March 1915; *CIM 1914–1915*, Part 2.
123 Uttam Singh, 57th Rifles [57th Wilde's Rifles, Frontier Force], France, to Shib Singh, 28th Punjabis, Colombo, Ceylon, 1 September 1915; *CIM 1914–1915*, Part 5.
124 [Name Censored], (Sikh), 107th Pioneers, France, to Indian Officer, 128th Pioneers, India, 23 March 1915; *CIM 1914–1915*, Part 2.
125 Abdul Karim, (Hindustani Muslim), 3rd Company, 1st Sappers and Miners, Meerut Division, France, to Risaldar Shahzad Khan, Saharanpur dist., UP, India, 19 December 1915; *CIM 1914–1915*, Part 6.
126 Kot Dafadar Talib Mohamed Khan, (Punjabi Muslim), 34th Poona Horse, France, to Kharim Khan, Reservist, 1st Lancers (Skinner's Horse), Risalpur, NWFP, India, 9 November 1916; *CIM 1915–1916*, Part 8.
127 A Royal Commission was busily documenting the prevalence of sexually transmitted diseases in Britain from 1914 to 1916. The earliest official report into venereal disease in the military was as early as 1868. The established practice was to look for sores or other abnormalities on or near the genitals. *Report of the*

Committee Appointed to Enquire into the Pathology and Treatment of Venereal Disease, with the View to Diminish its Injurious Effects on the Men of the Army and Navy, with Appendices, and the Evidence Taken before the Committee, Parliamentary Papers, 1868; *Royal Commission on Venereal Diseases: Final Report of the Commissioners,* Parliamentary Papers, 1916.

128 *Bhailawa* is also referred to as 'teliya' by one Garhwali *sipahi*.

129 Mohamed Qaki Khan, (Hindustani Muslim), Shahjehanpur, UP, Sowar Mohamed Rafiq Khan, 30th Lancers (Gordon's Horse), France, 6 June 1915; *CIM 1914–1915*, Part 4.

130 Ibid.

131 Sepoy Diwana, (Dogra), 37th Dogras, Kitchener Indian Hospital, Brighton, England, to Sepoy Ramdatta, 37th Dogras, attached 41st Dogras, Marseilles, France, 17 July 1915; *CIM 1914–1915*, Part 4.

132 'Dhobi Ram Lal', 40th Pathans, France, to Dhobi Siraj-ud-Din, Depot, 40th Pathans, Fatehgarh, Punjab, India, 19 September 1915; *CIM 1914–1915*, Part 6.

133 Niamat Ullah, (Pathan), 9th Hodson's Horse, France, to Ali Mohamed Khan, Farrier, 10th Lancers, Loralai, Baluchistan, India, 4 July 1916; *CIM 1915–1916*, Part 6.

134 Sadar Singh, (Dogra), Lady Harding Hospital, Brockenhurst, England, to Katoch Ragbir Singh, Palompra tahsil, Kangra dist., Thural P. O., Punjab, May 1915; *CIM 1914–1915*, Part 3.

135 Lieutenant Colonel M. G. M. Mair, Chief Field Censor, Summary No. 163, 15 December to 28 December 1943; *MEMC November 1943 – March 1944.*

136 Or at least it did according to *sipahis'* correspondence: 'Nowadays it is very hard to make both ends meet with your Rs. 65/- per month. Everything has become dearer. Perhaps you see the rates in Fauji Akhbar, but there is a great difference between them and the actual rates.' Father of a soldier, India, to a Naik, IBT Company, Middle East, August 1943; *Middle East Military Censorship: Fortnightly Summaries Covering Indian Troops, April 1943 – September 1943* [hereafter *MEMC April 1943 – September 1943*], Public and Judicial Papers, Asia and Africa Collection, British Library, L/PJ/12/655, File 2336/42.

137 Lieutenant Colonel M. G. M. Mair, Chief Field Censor, Summary No. 133, 21 October to 4 November 1942; *MEMC September 1942 – April 1943.*

138 Sepoy, Egypt, to India, January 1943; *MEMC September 1942 – April 1943.*

139 Draughtsman, Indian Draughtsman Unit, Egypt, Tripolitania, Cyrenaica, to India, February 1944; *MEMC November 1943 – March 1944.*

140 From Dacca, Bengal, India, to Soldier, Middle East, December 1942; *MEMC Sept. 1942 – April 1943.*

141 From Bengal, India, to Subedar, IMD, Palestine, Syria and Transjordan, June 1943; *MEMC April 1943 – Sept. 1943.*

142 From Bengal, India, to Havildar Clerk, Middle East, August 1943; *MEMC April 1943 – Sept. 1943*.
143 Ibid.
144 From a Soldier, India, to a Soldier, Middle East, September 1943; *MEMC April 1943 – Sept. 1943*.
145 Havildar, Tunisia, Tripolitania, and Cyrenacia, to Garhwal, India, June 1943, *MEMC April 1943 – September 1943*.
146 Madrasi Sepoy, 9th Army Area, Italy, to India, November 1943, *MEMC November 1943 – March 1944*.
147 Soldier, Middle East, to Sialkot, Punjab, India, February 1944, *MEMC November 1943 – March 1944*.
148 'Please let me know if you are receiving my allotment of Rs. 22/- monthly. It is to feed the family that I joined the service in distant foreign lands. If what I earn can't feed them properly, what will be the use of such service?' Sepoy, Indian Division Headquarters, Palestine, Syria and Transjordan, to India, June 1943, *MEMC April 1943 – September 1943*.
149 Sipahi, Indian Infantry Brigade, Transport Company, 10th Indian Division, Italy, to India, November 1943, *MEMC November 1943 – March 1944*.
150 'I asked my officer commanding to write to the authorities in India to give you a permit so that you may buy sugar and kerosene oil. Have you received the permit? If not go to the officer and ask about it, and write to me about your position. It seems that in India no one listens to our grievances.' VCO, North Africa, to India, January 1944, *MEMC November 1943 – March 1944*.
151 'It simply tortures me to learn that my children undergo such hardships and waste so much time in buying a small quantity of sugar and kerosene oil. It is really shocking that the Government do[es] nothing to help the families of soldiers serving overseas although they claim a lot is being done for them. I have written to the Deputy Commissioner but doubt if he will do anything. We can bear any hardship on our person, but cannot tolerate the sufferings of our families.' Sikh Subedar-Major, IAMC, Middle East, to India, 28 August 1943, *MEMC April 1943 – September 1943*.
152 'My heart burns when I hear about the conditions at home, but I am helpless, because I cannot get leave. I [have] approached the OC many times for leave, but I was not successful in get[ting] it. These people are so stony-hearted that in spite of my genuine requests for leave, made under very pressing circumstances, I get a heart-breaking response from them. I am feeling so much dejected over home affairs that I often pray God to take me away from this cruel, tyrannical and unjust world, and if the circumstances remain as they are, [it will be] no wonder if I may succeed in leaving this world. I am so much worried that my brain does not work and I feel as if I am becoming mad.' Draughtsman, Forward Survey Company,

Tunisia, Tripolitania, and Cyrenaica, to India, June 1943, *MEMC April 1943 – September 1943*.

153 Havildar Clerk, HQ, 10th Indian Division, Italy, to India, November 1943, *MEMC November 1943 – March 1944*.

154 Havildar, 4/11th Sikhs, Egypt, to father, Kaim Karan Dist., Punjab, 1 August 1942, *MEMC September 1942 – April 1943*.

155 Sipahi, Back Areas, Egypt, to India, November 1942, *MEMC September 1942 – April 1943*.

156 Lance-Naik, Palestine, Syria and Transjordan, to father, India, April 1943, *MEMC April 1943 – September 1943*.

157 Naik, 5/5th Royal Maratha Light Infantry, Palestine, Syria and Transjordan, to India, 5 September 1943, *MEMC April 1943 – September 1943*.

158 'The official letter about my marriage, sent by you has not arrived here so far, and I will know about it as soon as it reaches here . . . this is the only means of getting leave from here.' Sipahi, Pioneer Regiment, Egypt, to India, 9 September 1943, *MEMC April 1943 – September 1943*.

159 'I have submitted a petition for leave. I have stated in it the deplorable condition of my family affairs. As, for instance, my parents are old and my brother is POW. They [my parents] have lost heart and keep wailing for him. Therefore I want to go home to console my old parents and to make some proper arrangements for them and the property. This application has been sent to India for verification. [Make sure] You explain these difficulties to the man who comes to you for verification.' Sepoy, Indian Field Ambulance, 8 Indian Division, Central Mediterranean Force, Italy, to India, January 1944, *MEMC November 1943 – March 1944*.

160 'In my opinion you should apply to my C.O. for my leave through the C.O., I.G.S.C. Depot Aurangabad, attaching a certificate of your illness. . . . Get this petition recommended by the Magistrate of the High Court.' Sipahi, Egypt, to India, [not dated], *MEMC, April 1943 – September 1943*.

161 Sapper, Madras Sappers and Miners, Palestine, Syria, Transjordan or Lebanon, to India, [not dated], *MEMC September 1942 – April 1943*.

162 British Commanding Officer, Indian Pioneer Company, 8th Indian Division, Central Mediterranean Force, Italy, to Britain, February 1944, *MEMC November 1943 – March 1944*.

163 The other two parts of the trilogy are *The Village* and *The Sword and the Sickle*.

164 Upon reaching Orleans, Anand's soldiers head for the comforts of the brothel. Their fun is frustrated only by a lack of money. Mulk Raj Anand, *Across the Black Waters*, pp. 42–9.

165 As when Hanumant Singh is shot for malingering. Ibid., pp. 145–6.

166 Ibid., pp. 84–5.

167 Anand, somewhat unimaginatively, chose to translate *madarchod* as 'rape-mother'.
168 Or more accurately the words of the Berlin Committee, viz. Maulvi Barkatullah, Champakaraman Pillai, and Virendranath Chattopdhyaya.
169 Mulk Raj Anand, *The Sword and the Sickle*, (London: Jonathan Cape, 1942), pp. 25–6.
170 'On the 3/3/16 five men of the police were killed and 4 were wounded. Robbery is very prevalent, and unprincipled men have spoilt the country. Especially the "American Ones" have done much mischief [sic], and many men are under observation as suspicious characters.' Ganga Singh, (Sikh), 45th Sikhs attached 15th Sikhs, Peshawar, NWFP, India, to Jemadar Sahib Singh, 30th Lancers, France, 6 March 1916; *CIM 1915–1916, Part 4.*
171 Pay Havildar Mir Dast, (Pathan), 28th Punjabis, Bannu, NWFP, India, to Subedar Arala Khan, 57th Wilde's Rifles (Frontier Force), France, 11 June 1915; *CIM 1914–1915*, Part 4.

Chapter 4

1 As transcribed by *Sipahi* Gasthip Khan, (Punjabi Mussalman), France, to Pir Sahib Akhbar Khan Badshah, Jhelum, Punjab, India, 4 July 1916; *CIM 1915–1916*, Part 6.
2 The term is used as early as August 1915, when the Censor at the time (E. B. Howell) makes mention of a chain letter from Medina circulating among the troops. Howell doses not see fit, however, to include the text of the letter in his fortnightly reports.
3 An excerpt from the third of the letters Katz studies. It was written in Maghribi script (so presumably originated from North Africa) in 1779. Jonathan G. Katz, 'Shaykh Ahmad's Dream: A 19th-Century Eschatological Vision'; *Studia Islamica*, No. 79 (1994), pp. 163, 167–8.
4 Katz, 'Shaykh Ahmad's Dream', pp. 157–8.
5 A full discussion of this German propaganda can be found in Heike Leibau, 'The German Foreign Office, Indian Emigrants and Propaganda Efforts Among the "Sepoys"'; Franziska Roy, Heike Leibau and Ravi Ahuja (eds), *'When the War Began We Heard of Several Kings': South Asian Prisoners in World War I Germany*, (New Delhi: Social Science Press, 2011).
6 Professor Salenka, '*Ihr tapferen Kreiger von Indien!*' (Ye Brave warriors of India!), 16 October 1914; ibid, pp. 111–12.
7 The testimony of approvers during the 'Hindu-German Conspiracy Case' of 1917–18 (also referred to as the 'San Francisco Conspiracy Case') reveals that the German Consular attaché, Lt. William Von Brincken, purchased a large bundle

of a particular *Ghadar* leaflet, printed on broadsheet and entitled *Don't Fight with the Germans, Because They Are Our Friends*, 'at the end of 1914 or beginning of 1915'. Von Brincken is said to have claimed that 'these leaflets were to be sent to Germany to be dropped from aeroplanes to the Indian forces in France'. 'Notes on the Accused'; *RG 118, Records of the Office of the U.S. Attorney, Northern District of California, Neutrality Case Files, 1913–1920;* [US] National Archives at San Francisco, San Bruno, California, NRHSA Accession #'s 118 72-001, 118-73-001, Box 4, Folder 6.

8   'A letter came from you once before, which I answered. So now I am writing to you a second time. I am now all well by the Grace of God. I am a German prisoner. I hope you will send me an answer quickly on receipt of this, though I know that you have not much leisure.' Jemadar Id Mohamed Khan, Zossen, Germany, to Jemadar Adjudant Abdulla Khan, 129th Baluchis, France, 17 August 1915; *CIM 1914–1915*, Part 6.

9   Also called Mir Dast and also a Jemadar. Mir Dast VC, however, served in 55th Coke's Rifles.

10 It is possible that he may have received the Iron Cross. E. B. Howell was unsure whether he had or not, and the records were destroyed during World War II so, it's impossible to know for certain.

11 Afridi Pathan Havildar, 40th Pathans, France, to father in Peshawar, 26 February 1915; *CIM 1914–1915*, Part 1.

12 Ajrud Din, (Pathan – Afridi), Tirah, NWFP, India, to Havildar Gul Badshah, 58th Rifles, France, 19 October 1915; *CIM 1914–1915*, Part 8.

13 See K. H. Ansari, 'Pan-Islam and the Making of the Early Indian Muslim Socialists'; *Modern Asian Studies*, Vol. 20, No. 3 (1986). And, Maia Ramnath, *Haj to Utopia: How the Ghadar Movement Charted Global Radicalism and Attempted to Overthrow the British Empire*, (Berkeley, CA: University of California Press, 2011).

14 *The Review of Religions*, Vol. II, No. 3 and 4 (March & April 1903), (Qadian, Gurdaspur, Punjab: Published by the Anjuman-i-Isha'at Islam, 1903).

15 *The Review of Religions*, Vol. II, No. 1 (January 1903), (Qadian, Gurdaspur, Punjab: Published by the Anjuman-i-Isha'at Islam, 1903).

16 Iqbal Singh Sevea, 'The Ahmadiyya Print Jihad in South and Southeast Asia'; R. Michael Feener and Terenjit Sevea (eds), *Islamic Connections: Muslim Societies in South and Southeast Asia*, (Singapore: Institute of South East Asian Studies, 2009).

17 Ghulam Ahmad, *The Review of Religions*; Sevea, 'The Ahmadiyya Print Jihad', p. 141.

18 'Over half a century has passed since the advent if the British in the Punjab and from this long experience we can say that the British Government is an invaluable blessing to the people of this country in general, and to the Muhammadans in

particular. Under its peaceful rule the Muhammadans have made a great advance in learning. Their honour, property and lives are safe under its protection, and peace has been established under the country in such a manner that we can hardly conceive any improvement upon it.'

'A Proposal for the Utter Extinction of Jehad,' *Review of Religions*, Vol. II, No. 1 (January 1903), p. 21.

19 'Bombay Advocate,' 31 August 1915; H. A. Walter, *The Religious Life of India: The Ahmadiya Movement*, (Calcutta: Association Press, 1918), p. 120.

20 H. A. Walter, the Literary Secretary of the National Council of the YMCA of India and Ceylon, investigated the matter on behalf of the YMCA. The work was only published in 1918, however, after Walter died while writing the last chapter of the volume. Walter, *Ahmadiya Movement*, p. 136.

21 Soldiers' correspondence refers to visits by Frederick Sleigh Roberts, Field Marshal and Earl of Kandahar, a former Lieutenant Governor of the Central Provinces (probably Reginald Craddock), and two of the children of Maharaja Dalip Singh.

22 Nur Ahmed, (Punjabi Mussalman), Abbotabad, NWFP, India, to Raffi-ud-din Khan, Assistant Surgeon, Sialkot Field Ambulance, France, 28 May 1917; *CIM 1915–1916*, Part 4.

23 Ghulam Haidar Khan, (Punjabi Mussalman), Police Pensioner, Shahpur, Punjab, India, to Haqq Nawaz Khan, 18th Lancers, France, 21 September 1917; *CIM 1917–1918*, Part 5.

24 'I am going to repeat the orders that His Highness the Khalifa gave me when I left for Europe. He was emphatic that nothing could be eaten which had been strangled or which had been killed by a blow to the back of the neck. He added that we could eat meat killed by Christians or Jews provided that they cut the throat in front. It does not matter whether the Bismillah is said or not. The Jews are most careful and certainly we can eat meet killed by them in confidence but we have to be very careful about the Christians as they generally knock down or strangle their cattle. . . . I am a real Mohamedan and act up to my faith. The Sirdar when he spoke to you must have been thinking of the Mohamedans who do not trouble themselves about these things and think all meat is lawful. They have not had proper light vouchsafed to them by which to regard God [sic]. I feel confident about my enlightenment and that it is impossible for me to do anything against His commands. He who breaks God's obediences never thinks of Him.' Kazi Abdullah Quadiyani, (Punjabi Mussalman), Honorary Secretary of the Muslim Mission Society, 41 Great Russell Street, London, to Dafadar Haqq Nawas, 18th Lancers, France, 21 November 1916; *CIM 1915–1916*, Part 9.

25 Ibid.
26 Ibid.

27 Dafadar Haq Nawaz, (Punjabi Mussalman), 18th Lancers, France, to Moulvi Mohamed Sadiq, Sadar Bazaar, Meerut, UP, India, 13 August 1917; *CIM 1917–1918*, Part 5.

28 Abdul Sultan Khan, (Punjabi Mussalman), 36th Jacob's Horse, France, to Abdurrazaq Khan, Deolali, Punjab, India, 15 March 1917; *CIM 1917–1918*, Part 2.

29 Jemadar Hussein Shah, (Pathan), 9th Hodson's Horse, France, to Pir Badshah, Kohat, NWFP, India, 26 June 1917; *CIM 1917–1918*, Part 3.

30 Jemadar Abdul Rahim Khan, (DM), 36th Jacob's Horse, France, to Mir Hussein Khan, Hyderabad, India, 7 February 1917; *CIM 1917–1918*, Part 1.

31 Lance Dafadar Sher Mohamed, (Punjabi Mussalman), 38th CIH, France, to Editor of the 'Khabit', Delhi, 26 October 1917; *CIM 1917–1918*, Part 5.

32 'Please send me the weekly edition of your paper. I want to see all the proceedings of the All-India Muslim League which no doubt will be recorded in your paper. I am particularly interested in this matter.' Clerk Mohamed Yusuf, (Punjabi Mussalman), Deputy Adjudant General's office, 3rd Echelon, France, to the Manager of Paisa Akhbar, Lahore, Punjab, India, 3 December 1917; *CIM 1917–1918*, Part 5.

33 'The Secretary of State for India has come to India and is taking the views of everyone about Self-Government and will make his decision after hearing these opinions. Hindus will get the best of this because, through their education, they have a larger representation. Mohamedans are poorly represented because of their lack of education. Differences of opinion therefore seem likely. The Hindus and about half [of] the Mohamedans want Self-Government while the other half of the Mohamedans don't want it. I believe that Montague Sahib will give a just decision.' Ali Alam Khan, (Punjabi Mussalman), War Hospital, Khendwa, (India?), to Malik Khan Mohamed Khan, 36th Jacob's Horse, France, 15 December 1917; *CIM 1917–1918*, Part 6.

And: 'The Secretary of State for India, Montague Sahib, has come to India and is staying at Delhi. Formerly he had declared his intention of visiting the principal towns in India so as to meet the people; but when the Hindus started rioting he said he would not leave Delhi. He gave a whole day to the Mussalmans, conversing with them, and made a favourable impression on them. They feel honoured. The Hindus are agitating for Home Rule, but the Mussalmans are against it and wish the Government to remain as at present as they do not wish for Home Rule. This is the reason for the trouble between the Hindus and Mussalmans. The Hindus have rebelled in various places and in Bengal seditious letters have been found in which it is urged that the unclean races should be driven out of the country or slain. This is what they did in Arrah. Many disturbances are taking place.' Mohamed Yusuf Ali Khan,

(Hindustani Mussalman), Amethi, UP, India, to Sowar Ali Khan, Acting Lance Dafadar, 2nd Lancers, France, 28 November 1917; *CIM 1917–1918*, Part 6.
34. Heike Leibau, 'The German Foreign Office, Indian Emigrants and Propaganda Efforts Among the "Sepoys"'; *'When the War Began We Heard of Several Kings'*.
35. Nile Green, Islam and the Army in Colonial India: Sepoy Religion in the Service of Empire, (Cambridge: Cambridge University Press, 2009).
36. Ibid., pp. 71–85.
37. Such as the post-colonial and transnational cult of Zindapir studied by Pnina Werbner. Pnina Werbner, 'Murids of the Saint: Migration, Diaspora and Redemptive Sociality in Sufi Regional and Global Cults'; Ian Talbot and Shinder Thindi (eds), *People on the Move: Punjabi Colonial and Post-Colonial Migration*, (Oxford: Oxford University Press, 2004).
38. *India's Contribution to the Great War*. Published by Authority of the Government of India. (Calcutta: Office of the Superintendent. Government Printing, India, 1923).
39. For the pre-colonial and early colonial history of *munazaras*, see Avil A. Powell, *Muslims and Missionaries in Pre-Colonial India*, (Richmond: Curzon, 1993).
40. Justin Jones, 'The Local Experiences of Reformist Islam in a "Muslim" Town in Colonial India: The Case of Amroha'; *Modern Asian Studies*, Vol. 43, No. 4, 2009.
41. 'A certain calamity is coming which will involve both the open country and also large cities. It will so assail the servants of God as to render them helpless. It will cause destruction to men, to mountains, to trees and to rivers. At the first stroke of this calamity the earth will be turned upside down, and rivers of blood will flow in a swift current. Those who were wont to sleep in linen white as the jessamine flower will in the morning find themselves sprinkled with blood like the plane tree. They will be robbed of understanding, and even the birds of the air will be distraught, and the nightingales will forget their song. That time will be a terrible one for travellers. They will lose their way in their distraction. The blood of men will flow in streams, like torrents issuing from the mountains. Spirits and human beings will disappear. The Tzar himself will be reduced to a spirit of lamentation. It will be [a] sign from God like the Day of Judgement, and even the heavens will wage war. Do not hastily throw doubt on my prophesy, oh people, without understanding. Events will prove its truth. It comes from me from God, and will certainly come to pass, watch with patience and see. Do not think that there is any escape. The tyranny that has ruled the world must pay the price.' Transcribed Pamphlet by Maulvi Mohamed Ali Khan. Nur Ahmed, (Punjabi Mussalman), Abbotabad, NWFP, India, to Raffi-ud-din Khan, Assistant Surgeon, Sialkot Field Ambulance, France, 28 May 1917; *CIM 1915–1916*, Part 4.
42. Snowball letter; Sipahi Gasthip Khan, (Punjabi Mussalman), France, to Pir Sahib Akhbar Khan.
43. Ibid.
44. Ibid.

45 Ibid.
46 *India's Contribution to the Great War.* Published by Authority of the Government of India. (Calcutta: Office of the Superintendent. Government Printing, India, 1923).
47 Havildar Umr-al-Din Khan, (Pathan – Orakzai), [unit not stated], France, to Subedar Niamat Ullah Khan, Co. No. 4, 1st Sappers and Miners, France, 23 August 1915; *CIM 1914–1915*, Part 5.
48 Abdul Alim, (Hindustani Mussalman), Signal Troop, Sialkot Cavalry Brigade, France, to Risaldar Farzand Ali Khan, 6th Cavalry Depot, Sialkot, India, (May 1916); *CIM 1915–1916,* Part 5.
49 Fyazuddin, Printer, (Muslim Rajput), Aber Lali Steam Press, Agra, UP, India, to Mirza Hasain Beg, 38th Central India Horse, France, 7 October 1916; *CIM 1915–1916,* Part 8.
50 Havildar Umr-al-Din Khan, (to Subedar Niamat Ullah Khan, 23 August 1915.
51 Ibid.
52 Sowar Rahmat Khan, (Punjabi Mussalman), 15 Lancers, Pavilion Hospital, Brighton, England, to Hazrat Sahib Pir Faqir Shah, Peshawar, NWFP, India, 6 December 1915*; CIM 1914–1915*, Part 8.
53 'Pir' Dil Khan, (Pathan – Mahsud), 129 Baluchis, France, to Naik Mir Gul Khan, Secunderabad Brigade Hospital, France, 2 September 1915; *CIM 1914–1915*, Part 5.
54 Abdul Ghani, (Punjabi Mussalman), Murree Hills, Punjab, India, to Mohamed Ismail Khan, private servant to the Officer of Lahore Indian Stationary Hospital, Marseilles, France, 16 November 1915; *CIM 1914–1915*, Part 8.
55 Mohamed Ghans, (Dekhani Muslim), Signal Troop, Secunderabad Cavalry Brigade, to Abdul Ghafur, 26 Light Cavalry, Bangalore, India, 3 July 1916; *CIM 1915–1916*, Part 6.
56 Nur Mohamed, (Pathan), 38 Central India Horse, France, to Sultan Mohamed Khan, Turangazai, Peshawar, NWFP, India, 26 July 1916; *CIM 1915–1916*, Part 6.
57 [Honorary?] Captain Malik Muhammad Mumtaz, (Pathan), Staff, Secunderabad Brigade, France, to Khan Niaz-ud-din Khan Sahib, Jalandhar, Punjab, India, 10 September 1916; *CIM 1915–1916*, Part 7.
58 According to several letters, it was the appeals of French women and the French government that finally caused the Indian Army to relax its stance on interracial sex and marriage.
59 See Chapter 2.
60 Balwant Singh, (Sikh), French Post Office 39, France, to Pandit Chet Ram, Kang, Amritsar dist., Punjab, India, 29 October 1915; *CIM 1914–1915*, Part 7.
61 V. S. Pranje, (Maratha), I.S.M.D., Lahore Indian General Hospital, France, to Pirdan Singh, Ward Orderly, Depot, 54th Poona Horse, Ambala, Punjab, India, April 1915; *CIM 1914–1915*, Part 3.

62 Abdul Jaffar Khan, (Hindustani Muslim), Signal Troop, Sialkot Cavalry Brigade, France, to Dafadar Inayat Khan, Rohtak, Punjab, India, 20 August 1916; *CIM 1915–1916*, Part 7.

63 Jai Singh was one of those who had sworn to his family that he would not indulge in 'carnal pleasures'. A letter to a fellow soldier reveals how insincere this promise was: 'I am off to Paris which has been hitherto "out of bounds" to everyone but officers. Now we (up to Dafadars) can go. Paris is a city of fairyland and God will give us an opportunity of seeing it. I will write [to] you all about it. Whatever happens do not let anyone know about this. I intend to enjoy whatever pleasures there are. Don't let anyone know that Jai Singh is spending Rs. 250 in four days. If father heard of it he would be very angry. I should like to marry in France but I am afraid the family would be ashamed. You can marry very fine girls if you like.' Jai Singh, (Hindu Jat), 6th Cavalry or 19th Lancers, France, to Sirdar Singh, Lahore, 6 November 1917; *CIM 1917–1918*, Part 5.

64 Nazir Ullah, (Hindustani Muslim), c/o Rev N. G. Leather, St. Stephen's College, Delhi, to Risaldar Satter Shah, 34th Poona Horse, France, 11 April 1917; *CIM 1917–1918*, Part 3.

65 Inayat Ali Khan, (Hindustani Muslim), Depot, 6 Cavalry, Sialkot, Punjab, to Abdul Jabbar Khan, 6th Cavalry, France, 2 February 1917; *CIM 1917–1918*, Part 2.

66 Naubet Rai (father), (Punjabi Hindu), Rawalpindi, Punjab, India, to Mehta Deoki Nandan, Supply and Transport Agent, Marseilles, France, 18 June 1917; *CIM 1917–1918*, Part 4.

67 Anwar Shah, (Punjabi Mussalman), Camel Corps, Suez, Egypt, to Aurangzeb Shah, Signal Troop, Lucknow Cavalry Brigade, France, 18 August 1916; *CIM 1915–1916*, Part 7.

68 'Is this the effect of the climate of France, that it washes all love out of the heart and makes it hard like a stone? Have you become a perfect "gentleman"? Turn aside any thought of becoming a "Gentleman"!' Anon. wife, (Punjabi Mussalman), Ludhiana, Punjab, India, to Jemadar Khan Shirin Khan, No. 1 Base Remount, Rouen, France, 4 April 1917; *CIM 1917–1918*, Part 3.

69 Ahmed Ali, (Punjabi Mussalman), 5th Cavalry, Risalpur, NWFP, India, to Yakub Khan, Mhow Cavalry Brigade, France, 28 September 1916; *CIM 1915–1916*, Part 8.

70 'I swear to you that although I have been in France for two and a half years, I have not even taken so much as a cup of tea in a "hotel". I swear also that up till this moment I have committed no evil deed in France and nor am I a Christian. I am your true son, and your advice is plainly written on my heart.' Mohamed Feroz Khan, Ward Orderly, (Punjabi Mussalman), Ambala Cavalry Field Ambulance, France, to father, Chaudhuri Ghulam Ahmad, Sialkot dist., Punjab, India, 7 December 1917; *CIM 1917–1918*, Part 5.

71 Ajab Khan, (Pathan), 38th CIH, France, to Amir-ud-Din, Peshawar, NWFP, India, 14 October 1917; *CIM 1917–1918*, Part 5.
72 Mohamed Khan, (Hindustani Mussalman), 6th Cavalry, France, to Ahmed Khan, 12th Infantry, Calcutta, India, 28 May 1917; *CIM 1917–1918*, Part 3.
73 Mohamed Khan, (Hindustani Mussalman), 6th Cavalry, France, to Dafadar Ghans Mohamed Khan, Rohtak, Punjab, India, 18 June 1917; *CIM 1917–1918*, Part 3.
74 Mohamed Khan, (Hindustani Mussalman), 6th Cavalry, France, to Dafadar Manvah Khan, 5th Cavalry, Risalpur, NWFP, India, 20 August 1917; *CIM 1917–1918*, Part 4.
75 Anwar Shah, (Punjabi Mussalman), Camel Corps, Suez, Egypt, to Aurangzeb Shah, Signal Troop, Lucknow Cavalry Brigade, France, 18 August 1916; *CIM 1915–1916*, Part 7.
76 The Turkish ships were actually led by German battleships operating under a Turkish flag, but it was intended to be a declaration of war from the Ottoman Empire.
77 Few *sipahis* distinguished between 'Turkey' and the wider 'Ottoman Empire'. I will use the two terms interchangeably for that reason.
78 Although it was an infantry division, 15th Lancers were attached to it as 'Divisional Reconnaissance'.
79 X. Y. [name censored], a Mohammedan Native Officer in France, to brother in India, 1914; *CIM 1914–1915*, Part 1.
80 The earliest instance was from February 1915, but it was from a soldier in India rather than France. 'Remember this one thing, that the Sultan Badshah is one of us. We hear that the German Badshah has become a Mussulman. You are a wise man, understand and think over this. Then draw your own conclusion. Islam is a good thing. You are out of our reach nor can we help you. But we pray much.' Pathan Sepoy, 55th Rifles, Kohat, NWFP, India, to a friend, 58th Rifles, France, 15 February 1915; *CIM 1914–1915*, Part 1.
81 Risaldar Zabida Khan, (Pathan), 1st Lancers, attached 19th Lancers, France, to Risaldar Major Munshi Akram Khan, 1st Lancers, Risalpur, India, 17 April 1915; *CIM 1914–1915*, Part 3.
82 Abbas Ali Khan, (Punjabi Mussalman), 38 CIH, France, to Karam Ali Khan, Abdullapur, Sultanpur PO, Mirpur dist., Kashmir State, 8 January 1917; *CIM 1917–1918*, Part 1.
83 Sowar Gul Mohamed Khan, (Pathan), Baghdad, Mesopotamia, to Mohamed Nur Khan, 38th CIH, France, 18 October 1917; *CIM 1917–1918*, Part 5.
84 'Muhamedan of Punjab' serving in France to his brother in India, 6 February 1915; *CIM 1914–1915*, Part 1.
85 Sowar Ajab Gul, (Pathan), 38th CIH, France, to Bhai Ahmed Pul, Peshawar, NWFP, India, 22 December 1916; *CIM 1917–1918*, Part 1.

86 There was another letter written by the same author which was not quite as ambiguous. Although it began with a standard pledge of loyalty towards the King-Emperor – 'It is necessary to point out also that our religion does not permit us to perform any bad habits. Further our religion teaches us to be in accord with our King.' – the verses within the letter conveyed a different message:

> '"In the garden of this world what grievances can be urged against the hunter
> When the flowers themselves place thorns on my resting place?"

This is my condition. What more can I say? The evils of this world have entered into my soul. I ask why this should be and tell you the simple truth:

> "Those on whom I relied have turned their face away from me.
> What grievances can I urge against an enemy when friendship is such!
> None whatever! It is the fashion of the times!"'

Hamidullah Khan, (Hindustani Mussalman), Contractor, Inderkot, Meerut City, UP, India, to Kot Dafadar Mohamed Wazir Khan, 18th Lancers, France, 5 May 1916; *CIM 1915–1916*, Part 5.

87 Hamidullah Khan, (Hindustani Mussalman), Contractor, Inderkot, Meerut City, UP, India, to Kot Dafadar Mohamed Wazir Khan, 18th Lancers, France, 18 May 1916; *CIM 1915–1916*, Part 5.

88 Dada Amir Haider Khan, *Chains to Lose: The Life and Struggle of a Revolutionary, Vol. 1*; edited by Hasan N. Gardezi; preface by V. D. Chopra, (New Delhi: Patriot Publishers, 1989), p. 80.

89 Another account records that the Korans were placed 'upon the heads' of the *sipahis* taking the oath, but that, while possibly true, is written by a soldier from another regiment reporting what he had been told.

90 Maulvi Ghulam Sarvar, (Punjabi Mussalman), 15th Lancers, attached 27 Lancers, Remount Depot, Sagar, UP, India, to Talib Hussain Khan, 18th Lancers, France, 26 September 1917; *CIM 1917–1918*, Part 5.

91 Ibid.

92 Ashrafali Khan, (Hindustani Mussalman), 6th Cavalry, Sialkot, Punjab, India, to Dafadar Fateh Mohamed Khan, Signalling Instructor, 6th Cavalry, France, 24 March 1916; *CIM 1915–1916*, Part 4.

93 Ghulam Sarvar to Talib Hussain Khan, 26 September 1917.

94 Safdar Ali Khan, (Punjabi Mussalman), 15th Lancers, attached 27th Lancers, Sagar, UP, India, to Signaller Jalib Hussain Khan, 18th Lancers, France, 17 July 1917; *CIM 1917–1918*, Part 4.

95 Ashrafali Khan, (Hindustani Mussalman), 6th Cavalry, Sialkot, Punjab, India, to Dafadar Fateh Mohamed Khan, Signalling Instructor, 6th Cavalry, France, 24 March 1916; *CIM 1915–1916*, Part 4.

96 Fateh Khan, (Punjabi Mussalman), Lyallpur, Punjab, India, to Fateh Ahmed, Supply and Transport No.5 Base Supply Depot, France, 30 June 1916; *CIM 1915–1916*, Part 6.

97 Lance Dafadar Mahmud Khan, (Punjabi Mussalman), Banadar Abbas, Persia, to Dafadar Mohamed Khan, 18th Lancers, France, 11 May 1916; *CIM 1915–1916*, Part 5.

98 'I asked concerning Haq Ghulam because I had sent 3 or 4 petitions about the 15th Lancers and had received no reply. I knew all about the matter from the first, but I did not wish to distress you with it. I hear now that they will all be released, please God, before I return. If not, then, as soon as I return to India, I will again agitate about their release. Nothing can be done from here at the present time, but do not be anxious everything possible is being done on their behalf. A certain man here has received a letter in which it is stated that Sultan Hussein of Hangu and his fellows have been released as the result of an appeal made on their behalf by Risaldar Sahib Dost Mohamed Khan of the 37th Lancers. Don't be anxious God will certainly be merciful. It is not as though only one man was involved. There are many men involved and some of them are important personages.' Lance Dafadar Sabaz Ali Khan, (Pathan), Signal Troop, Lucknow Cavalry Brigade, France, to Alim Hussein, Ustarzai, Kohat, NWFP, India, 3 October 1916; *CIM 1915–1916*, Part 8.

99 Niazi being one of the largest Muslim castes in Mianwali district.

100 'I am in the Remount Depot here and you must have heard how our regiment was imprisoned and I was among the prisoners. Now Government has released us and broken up our regiments into parts. Some of us have been sent to Hissar, Sagar and Sihore and the men who were not imprisoned were made into a separate wing and another wing has been made of Sikhs and Jats. There is great excitement there about recruiting. The Deputy Commissioner of Mianwali had a meeting to which all the lumberdars of the district came. The Deputy Commissioner told them to supply recruits and the lumberdars of the Nayazi refused. The Deputy Commissioner then dismissed 3 of them, the lumberdars of Datke, Ukri, and Shahbag Khel. 107 recruits were collected at the meeting.' Sowar Kunda Buksh Khan, (Pathan), 15th Lancers, Sihore, UP, India, to Ghulam Hasan Khan, 36th Jacob's Horse, France, 14 September 1917; *CIM 1917–1918*, Part 5.

101 'At the time there were a few companies of Pathan infantrymen who were notorious for their dirty tactics and even sabotage at the Front – the story was that there were only a few companies in a mixed infantry battalion and therefore could not openly defy the authorities. . . . the Pathan units were put in the middle or rear of the line so they could not desert. But whenever they were ordered to maintain firing, the Pathan units instead of shooting at the enemy would take aim at the British units in front of them. While this could not be

proved definitively, some soldiers had been wounded in the back by bullets fired from the rear. The Pathans were suspected of this mischief and immediately removed from the Front and brought back to Basra where they were assigned to various guard duties such as watching over prisoners of war, supplies, etc.' Khan, *Chains to Lose*, p. 81.
102 With thanks to Syed Hussain Shaheed Soherwordi for forwarding the email to me.
103 From the song 'Javeda Zindagi' and the (Bollywood) film 'Anwar'.
104 Nur Mohamed, (Pathan), 38 Central India Horse, France, to Sultan Mohamed Khan, Turangazai, Peshawar, NWFP, India, 26 July 1916; *CIM 1915–1916*, Part 6.
105 Snowball letter; Sipahi Gasthip Khan, (Punjabi Mussalman), France, to Pir Sahib Akhbar Khan.
106 Ram Jawan Singh, (Hindustani Hindu), Kitchener Indian Hospital, Brighton, England, to Mr Jacques Derel, 5th Avenue Victor Hugo, Vernon, France, 26 September 1915; *CIM 1914–1915*, Part 6.
107 Clerk Mohamed Yusuf to the Manager of Paisa Akhbar, Lahore, 3 December 1917; Ali Alam Khan to Malik Khan Mohamed Khan, 36th Jacob's Horse, France, 15 December 1917; Mohamed Yusuf Ali Khan, Amethi, UP, India, to Sowar Ali Khan, 2nd Lancers, France, 28 November 1917.
108 Balwant Singh, (Sikh), French Post Office 39, France, to Pandit Chet Ram, Kang, Amritsar dist., Punjab, India, 29 October 1915; *CIM 1914–1915*, Part 7.
109 Faqir Khan, (Swati Pathan), 33rd Punjabis, attached 40th Pathans, France, to Lal Khan, Machand, NWFP, India, 24 August 1915; *CIM 1914–1915*, Part 5.

Chapter 5

1 The right wing of the 5th Light Infantry was officially described as being filled with Ranghars, a Muslim Rajput 'clan' found primarily in Punjab. As with a lot of regiments that recruited Musulmans, however, many of the soldiers were not Ranghars and some in their testimony even admitted to being Jats or Lohias (blacksmiths). I will use the phrase Muslim Rajput rather than Ranghar when referring to the men of the right half of the 5th Light. The left half of the battalion was staffed by Hindustani Pathans, a term that is even more troubling than that of Ranghar. So, I will avoid the term altogether except in those (rare) cases that soldiers expressly stated they were Pathan.
2 A total of 12 British Officers and 14 European civilians were killed.
3 A further two Indian Officers were also executed. All of the men were shot, except for one *sipahi* who was hung. It is possible that this was an extrajudicial punishment that the Court of Inquiry was keen to gloss over, since all military executions at the time ought to have used firing squads as a matter of law.

4 *Report in Connection with the Mutiny of the 5th Light Infantry at Singapore (1915)*, [hereafter *Singapore Mutiny Report* or *SMR*] Military Department Papers, Asia and Africa Collection, British Library, L/MIL/17/19/48. Also reproduced in T. R. Sareen (ed.), *Secret Documents on Singapore Mutiny, Volumes 1 and 2*, (New Delhi: Mounto Publishing, 1995).

5 The others being Nicholas Tarling, 'The Singapore Mutiny, 1915', *Journal of the Malaysian Branch of the Royal Asiatic Society*, Vol. LV, Part 2, 1982; Sho Kuwajima, *The Mutiny in Singapore: War, Anti-War and the War for India's Independence*, (New Delhi: Rainbow Publishers, 2006).

6 R. W. E. Harper and H. Miller, *Singapore Mutiny*, (Singapore: Oxford University Press, 1984), 'Dramatis Personae', pp. xi–xiii.

7 'Forwarding Letter by Brigadier-General F. A. Hoghton, President of the Court of Inquiry, to Chief of the General Staff, Army Headquarters, India, 20 May 1915'; *SMR*.

8 Testimony of No.2637, Lance Naik Feroze, 'C' Company, 5th Light Infantry; *SMR*; Section 3A: Evidence on Events at Alexandra.

9 Testimony of No.2523, Lance Naik Fazal Azim, 'D' Company, 5th Light Infantry; ibid.

10 Testimony of No.1878, Naik Sazawar Khan, 'C' Company, 5th Light Infantry; ibid.; Section 3: Evidence on Events at Alexandra.

11 Testimony of No.3179, Sipahi Dost Mohamed, 'B' Company, 5th Light Infantry; ibid.; Section 3A: Evidence on Events at Alexandra.

12 Michel de Certeau, 'History is Never Sure', *The Possession at Loudon*; translated by Michael B. Smith, (Chicago, IL: Chicago University Press, 2000), p. 8.

13 *SMR*; Section 2: Proceedings of the Court of Inquiry.

14 That was the experience of Laxmi Sahgal, née Swaminathan, and many others who later came to join the INA. Peter Ward Fay, *The Forgotten Army: India's Armed Struggle for Independence, 1942–1945*, (Ann Arbor, MI: Michigan University Press, 1993), p. 47.

15 'Report from Brigadier-General Dudley Ridout, General Officer Commanding, Singapore, with remarks on proceedings of the Court of Inquiry'; *SMR*.

16 *SMR*; Section 2: Proceedings of the Court of Inquiry.

17 Testimony of Subedar-Major Khan Mohamed Khan, 5th Light Infantry; *SMR*; Section VII: Evidence of the Indian Officers.

18 *SMR*; Section 2: Proceedings of the Court of Inquiry.

19 Martin explained his actions away by stating, 'I decided to remain at the house as I thought if there were any loyal men they would come [to me]'. The Court remained unconvinced. Testimony of Lieutenant Colonel E. V. Martin, Commanding Officer, 5th Light Infantry; *SMR*; Section VIII: Evidence of the British Officers.

20 *SMR*; Section 2: Proceedings of the Court of Inquiry.

21 Testimony of No.1811, ½ Colour Havildar Jamaluddin Khan, 'F' Company, 5th Light Infantry; *SMR*, Section 3: Evidence on Events at Alexandra Barracks.
22 *SMR*; Section 2: Proceedings of the Court of Inquiry.
23 Ibid.
24 Subedar Dunde Khan and Jemadar Chiste Khan were shot on 21 February 1915. The firing party was commanded by a Lieutenant Malcolm Bond Shelley, who was an officer in the Malay States Volunteers – a hastily drawn up and primarily European militia. During the account he gives of the execution, he mentions that he was unsure of what was required of a firing party, that two of the ten men on the firing party were unable to load their clips into their rifles, and when they did fire, many of them missed their targets. Malcolm Bond Shelley, 'Brief Account of the Happenings in Singapore', (1927); Sareen (ed.), *Secret Documents*.
25 'We have evidence of his [Jemadar Chiste Khan] at Pulo Brani in a strain deprecatory of British prestige, and calculated to foster ideas of German ascendancy. We are also told of his enlarging upon the benefits eventually to be derived from supporting the German cause against the British. From another quarter we hear of meetings of non-commissioned officers and others of the right wing Companies under Jemadar Chiste Khan at which soldiers would smoke and at which subjects of a doubtful nature appear to have been discussed . . . .'

And: 'What is more likely than these disaffected officers, having played on the feelings of Colour Havildar Imtiaz Ali, now probably thoroughly discontented and ready to give trouble, utilized him as the instrument to bring about the outbreak that ensued?' *SMR*; Section 2: Proceedings of the Court of Inquiry.
26 *SMR*; Section 2: Proceedings of the Court of Inquiry.
27 Such as 'Revolt in India Hatched in America: Sacramento Meeting Planned a Revolution, Witnesses Testify at Lahore Trial'; *New York Times*, 15 May 1915.
28 Ridout Report; *SMR*.
29 Liaquat Hyat Khan (later Nawab Sir Liaquat Hyat Khan), the Deputy Superintendent of Police in Lahore, brother of Sir Sikander Hyat Khan and later Prime Minister of Patiala State, employed a spy, Kirpal Singh, to infiltrate the Ghadar Conspiracy in January and February 1915. *Lahore Conspiracy Case: Judgement. In re King Emperor Versus Anand Kishore and Others. Charges under Sections, 121, 123, 396 and others*; Public and Judicial Papers, Asia and Africa Collection, British Library, London; L/PJ/6/1405.
30 'A Special Telegram has arrived from Philippine [sic.], Manila, on the 2 March, which says that the *Ghadr* is still going on at Singapore, that the flames are burning with great intensity, that the condition of the English is weakening very much and that the entire Indian troops [sic.] have been taking part in the *Ghadr*.' 'Now Is the Time for Fighting Against the English in India' (Pamphlet; Gurumukhi); *RG 118, Records of the Office of the U.S. Attorney, Northern District*

of California, Neutrality Case Files, 1913–1920*; National Archives at San Francisco, NRHSA Accession #'s 118 72-001, 118-73-001; Box 1, Folder 2.
31 Ibid.
32 Lowell Thomas, *Lauterbach of the China Sea: The Escapes and Adventures of a Sea-Going Falstaff*, (London: Hutchinson & Co., 1931), pp. 109–10.
33 Ibid., p. 113.
34 The German sailors were from the SMS Emden, a light cruiser that was sunk at the Cocos Islands on 9 November 1914 by HMAS Sydney.
35 Nigel Barley, *Rogue Raider: The Tale of Captain Lauterbach and the Singapore Mutiny*, (Singapore: Monsoon, 2006), p. 152.
36 Some German prisoners were praised for their 'correct behaviour' in assisting the officers and soldiers of the guard posted at the internment camp and at a hospital nearby in combating the mutineers. *SMR*; Section 2: Proceedings of the Court of Inquiry.
37 Kuwajima, *Mutiny in Singapore*, Chapter III.
38 *SMR*.
39 Ibid.
40 Testimony of No.1795, Havildar Major Ghafur Khan, 'E' Company, 5th Light Infantry; *SMR*; Section 3: Evidence on Events at Alexandra.
41 Testimony of Colour Havildar Mahboob, 'C' Company, 5th Light Infantry; *SMR*; Section 3: Evidence on Events at Alexandra.
42 Testimony of No.2612, Lance Naik Maksud, 'D' Company, 5th Light Infantry; *SMR*; Section 3: Evidence on Events at Alexandra.
43 Milliarium Zero and Winterfilm, in association with Vietnam Veterans Against the War, *Winter Soldier*, (1971).
44 Testimony of Feroze Khan.
45 Ibid.
46 Ibid.
47 Ibid.
48 Ibid.
49 Ibid.
50 Testimony of Captain L. P. Ball, 5th Light Infantry; *SMR*; Section VIII: Evidence of the British Officers.
51 Testimony of Fazal Azim.
52 Testimony of No.1840, Gulam Mohamed, 'H' Company, 5th Light Infantry; ibid.; Testimony of No.2716, Sepoy Maksud, 5th Light Infantry; ibid.
53 Testimony of No.3067, Sepoy Fateh Mohamed Khan, 'C' Company, 5th Light Infantry; ibid.
54 For instance, Sepoy Udmi of 'E' Company was also in the hospital and was adamant that he could not tell if Feroze Khan was among the party that attacked

it, and Naik Khuda Baksh stated that he ran into the jungle with Feroze Khan after they had been attacked by the mutineers. Testimony of No.2512, Sepoy Udmi, 'E' Company, 5th Light Infantry; Ibid.; Testimony of No.1809, Naik Khuda Baksh, 'C' Company, 5th Light Infantry; ibid.
55 Captain Ball, for instance, appears to have singled out Feroze Khan for condemnation because of the reprimand he had been given after the aforementioned incident in which sick and feverish *sipahis* were given irregular fatigues as summary punishments.
56 The whole of the 5th Light Infantry was interned in the months after the mutiny, many aboard a 'prison ship'. At the time *sipahis* were giving evidence, however, there were moved to within earshot of the firing squads that executed 47 *sipahis* and VCOs. According to one account, as the shots were fired: '[the crowd seemed] to utter some kind of gasp. From within the prison, however, came an anguished wail, the voices of comrades of the dead men. . . . Such, with one exception, was the pattern of each group of executions that I witnessed.' Cadet Dickinson, Straits Settlements Police; R. W. E. Harper and H. Miller, *Singapore Mutiny*, (Singapore: Oxford University Press, 1984).
57 Testimony of Feroze Khan.
58 Ibid.
59 Ibid.
60 Ibid.
61 Testimony of Fazal Azim.
62 Ibid.
63 Fazal Azim's testimony was used to incriminate *sipahis* far more often than the testimonies of his fellow approvers were. For instance, it was largely Fazal Azim's testimony that resulted in Feroze Khan being implicated in the mutiny, even though there were others who cast aspersions on the Lance Naik.
64 Ibid.
65 Testimony of Fazal Azim.
66 Ibid.
67 Ibid.
68 Fazal Azim claimed that Sepoy Shamsuddin Khan admitted to shooting Lieutenant Elliot – an officer from the 5th Light Infantry – and that Sepoy Basharat saw the man who shot Captain Maclean – an officer from the Malay States Volunteers; ibid.
69 Ibid.
70 Testimony of Sepoy Maksud.
71 Testimony of Gulam Mohamed.
72 Testimony of Subedar Wahid Ali, Commander of 'D' Company, 5th Light Infantry; *SMR*; Section VII: Evidence of the Indian Officers.

73 Sipahi Maksud was asked to pick out any mutineers he recognized from a line-up, and he identified both Fazal Azim and Feroze Khan. Only his identification of Feroze, however, received any attention. My best guess is that this was because Gulam Mohamed was asked to undertake the same task at (roughly) the same time and because he failed to successfully identify Fazal. Testimony of Sepoy Maksud; Testimony of Gulam Mohamed.
74 Subedar Wahid Ali was one of the VCOs for whom the President of the Court of Inquiry reserved special condemnation.
75 The Court did call Dost Mohamed to give evidence but not, as I show later, to cast aspersions on Fazal Azim's testimony.
76 *Viz.*, Naik Ruk Nurdin, Havildar Murad Ali Khan and Sipahis Maizar, Fulkhan and Ismail. Testimony of Fazal Azim.
77 *Viz.*, Abdul Ghani and Nur Mohamed. Ibid.
78 The exception to this is Dost Mohamed. The reason for this will be examined later.
79 Testimony of Fazal Azim.
80 Testimony of Sazawar Khan.
81 The term *khalasi* was used by the British in colonial India to specifically refer to servants or labourers serving as seamen. Among many North Indians, however, it was a colloquial term applied to any unskilled labourer. Thus, for instance, a stoker aboard a railway engine was commonly referred to as a *khalasi*. In the case of Mahbub Khan, the term was used to describe his employment as a man who would carry heavy loads to and from in the cantonment.
82 A Quarter Guard was ostensibly a selection of men from a battalion who were given live rounds in order to protect a camp or cantonment from external threats. In practice, however, they acted as a form of security against any internal problems. Only the handful of men selected for Quarter Guard duty would have live rounds, and any man found to have committed a minor offence could expect to be imprisoned within the building housing the Quarter Guard.
83 Testimony of Sazawar Khan.
84 Ibid.
85 Ibid.
86 Ibid.
87 Testimony of No.1663, Havildar Mahomed Yar Khan, 'H' Company, 5th Light Infantry; ibid.
88 Testimony of Mahboob Khan, Khallassi or Storeman; ibid.
89 Testimony of Sambhudutt, Brahmin grocer; ibid.
90 Testimony of No.2210, Sepoy Mahbub Khan, 'C' Company, 5th Light Infantry; ibid.
91 Testimony of Sazawar Khan.
92 Jamaluddin describes himself as '½ Colour Havildar'. He may have used that term to imply that he was an Acting Colour Havildar who had been promised a full

promotion to that position. This, however, is not certain, and it is possible that I am in error by describing him simply as an 'Acting Colour Havildar'.

93 'Everyone was present in the Guardroom including the Havildar [Jamaluddin] when the first shot was fired. The Havildar at once gave the order – Guard turn out – and they fell in on the veranda.' Testimony of No.2612, Lance Naik Maksud, 'D' Company, 5th Light Infantry; *SMR*; Section 3.

94 'Colour Havildar Jamaluddin came to the Armourer's shop about 6 o'clock on 15 February and told the Armourer to come and open the Treasure chest. The Armourer went to the quarterguard and tapped the Treasure chest and said he could not open it. He came back and told me to take a hammer and chisel and [to] try to open the Treasure chest. There were 20 or 30 men [a]round the chest when I was trying to open it amongst whom I recognized Havildar Jamaluddin. I said, after attempting [to open it] for some time, "I cannot open the chest" and then I went back to the Armourer's shop where I remained.' Testimony of Sepoy Karim Baksh, (one of several regimental carpenters), 'F' Company, 5th Light Infantry; ibid.

95 Jamaluddin's own alibi was that he was defecating in the lavatory at the time, so he can't have been involved. Of course, no one actually saw him there, but that did not prevent the Havildar from sticking to his guns (metaphorically speaking).

96 Testimony of Dost Mohamed.
97 Ibid.
98 Ibid.
99 Ibid.
100 Ibid.
101 Ibid.
102 Ibid.
103 Ibid.
104 Testimony of Fazal Azim.
105 Testimony of Dost Mohamed.
106 Ibid.
107 Stanley Kubrick (dir.), Paths of Glory, (1957).
108 Ibid.
109 Ibid.
110 Two Indian officers were also executed.

The official breakdown of the sentences given are as follows:

'Death: 2 Indian Officers; 6 Havildars; 39 Rank and File
Transportation for Life: 2 Havildars; 62 Rank and File
Transportation for 20 years: 1 Havildar; 7 Rank and File
Transportation for 15 years: 26 Rank and File
Transportation for 10 years: 30 Rank and File

Transportation for 7 years: 9 Rank and File
Rigorous Imprisonment for 5 years: 3 Rank and File
Rigorous Imprisonment for 3 years: 1 Rank and File
Rigorous Imprisonment for 2 years: 7 Rank and File
Rigorous Imprisonment for 1 years: 1 Rank and File
Simple Imprisonment without Solitary Confinement for 2 years: 1 Rank and File
Simple Imprisonment without Solitary Confinement for 11 months: 1 Rank and File (member of the Malay States Guides)
Simple Imprisonment without Solitary Confinement for 9 months: 6 Rank and File (members of the Malay States Guides)
Simple Imprisonment without Solitary Confinement for 1 month: 4 Rank and File
Simple Imprisonment without Hard Labour for 2 years: 1 Rank and File (member of the Malay States Guides)
Simple Imprisonment without Hard Labour for 1½ years: 3 Rank and File (member of the Malay States Guides)'
SMR; Section 2: Proceedings of the Court of Inquiry.

Chapter 6

1. Ketan Mehta (dir.), *Mangal Pandey: The Rising* (2005), provides an example of a popular narrative of 1857 collapsing the causes of the rebellion into a narrative of a single, heavily mythologized soldier. See Rudrangshu Mukherjee, *Mangal Pandey: Brave Martyr or Accidental Hero?*, (New Delhi: Penguin, 2005) for more.
2. From the groups of 'young Indians' jeering and taunting at columns of Europeans about to be interned in Singapore in Farrell's work to Kishen Singh, a batman in 1/1 Jats, troubling his officer by asking if he was a mercenary in *The Glass Palace*. Sadly, the 'Other Ranks' presented in Ghosh's work appear as individuals lacking self-knowledge and individuality, 'no vocabulary with which to shape their self-awareness' as one character puts it. J. G. Farrell, *Singapore Grip*, (London: Wiedenfeld and Nicolson, 1978), Chapter 74; Amitav Ghosh, *The Glass Palace*, (London: HarperCollins, 2001 rpt.), pp. 346–7.
3. Strictly speaking, the term 'Indian National Army' ought to only be used for the first phase of its existence between 1941 and 1942, since it was reformed and renamed the *Azad Hind Fauj* (the Free Indian Army or Army of Free India), after Netaji Subhas Chandra Bose arrived in Singapore in 1943. For the purposes of this chapter, however, I will use 'Indian National Army', 'INA' or 'Azad Hind Fauj' interchangeably. Many *sipahis* were unaware that the first 'INA' was ever disbanded and failed to draw any distinction between the two armies in their interrogations.

4 General Mohan Singh, *Soldiers' Contribution to Indian Independence*, (New Delhi: Army Educational Stores, 1974), pp. 108–9.
5 It is unclear quite how many joined the INA. The final tally reached by (British) military intelligence was 23,266. That does not include the number of men who may have joined the INA and left again without British knowledge, or those who evaded capture altogether. 'Indian National Army', 28 January 1947; *Indian National Army and Free Burma Army, Vol. 3*; War Staff Papers, Asia and Africa Collection, British Library, L/WS/1/1578.
6 For example: '. . . in reality the INA's brief moment on the stage was over [by October 1944]. Some units fought resolute and brave battles as they retreated south into Burma. Some melted away or gave themselves up. At any rate, the INA was to become a much more powerful enemy of the British Empire in defeat than it had been during its ill-fated triumphal march on Delhi.' Christopher Bayly and Tim Harper, *Forgotten Armies: The Fall of British Asia, 1941–1945*, (London: Allen Lane, 2004), p. 402.
7 A large number of works have reduced the INA into a chapter in the life of Subhas Chandra Bose. *Viz.* Hugh Toye, *Subhash Chandra Bose: The Springing Tiger*, (Bombay: Jaico, c.1959); Leonard A. Gordon, *Brothers Against the Raj: A Biography of Indian Nationalists Sarat and Subhas Chandra Bose*, (New York, Oxford: Columbia University Press, 1990); Sugata Bose, *His Majesty's Opponent: Subhas Chandra Bose and India's Struggle Against Empire*, (Cambridge, MA: Harvard University Press, 2011). Part of the enduring fascination with the circumstances of Bose's death has been the various commissions launched after Independence to investigate the matter (the Shah Nawaz Commission of 1956; Khosla Commission from 1970–1974; and the Mukherjee Commission from 1999 to 2005). The last has thrown doubt on whether Bose actually died in August 1945. But, for the sake of simplicity, I am assuming that he did.
8 The memoirs of Fujiwara Iwaichi (the Japanese intelligence liaison with Indian nationalists and then the INA in South-east Asia) offer a fascinating defence of Japanese motives and Japanese Imperialism. Fujiwara Iwaichi, *F. Kikan: Japanese Army Intelligence Operations in Southeast Asia during World War II*; translated by Akashi Yoji, (Hong Kong: Heinemann, 1983).
9 Numerous memoirs of the INA have been written by its leading officers who were involved. They tend to be either from its progenitors (Mohan Singh) or from those who obtained notoriety/fame through the Red Fort Trials which began in November 1945 (Colonel Shah Nawaz Khan, Colonel Gurbaksh Singh Dhillon, Colonel Prem Kumar Sahgal. Gurbaksh Singh Dhillon, *From My Bones: Memoirs of Col. Gurbaksh Singh Dhillon of the Indian National Army*, (New Delhi: Aryan Books, 1999); Shahnawaz Khan, *My Memories of INA & Its Netaji*, (Delhi: Rajkumal, 1946); Peter Ward Fay, *The Forgotten Army: India's Armed Struggle for*

Independence, 1942–1945, (Ann Arbor, MI: Michigan University Press, 1993) [based on conversations with Prem Kumar Sahgal and Lakshmi Sahgal]; Mohan Singh, *Soldiers' Contribution to Indian Independence*.

10 Peter Ward Fay, *The Forgotten Army*, p. 10.

11 'Mr Banerjee' was how Gurbaksh Singh Dhillon's interrogator introduced himself when he was interned alongside Loganathan in the Red Fort. It is likely that he was one of the men whom Loganadan termed a 'Biff'. Gurbaksh Singh Dhillon, *From My Bones*, p. 403.

12 The charges laid against INA men fell under civil rather than military law. 'Waging War Against the King', contrary to Section 121 of the Indian Penal Code, was a charge used for all those who were found to have joined the INA voluntarily. Additional charges of 'Murder' and 'Abetment of murder' were also laid in the INA trials.

13 Interrogation of Lt. Col./Major General Arcot Doraisamy Loganadan [sic.]; *CSDIC (India), No.2 Section Information Reports* [hereafter *CSDIC(I) Reports*]; INA Papers, National Archives of India, New Delhi, 379/INA; Parts 17–22. Italics added.

14 All save 176 of that number were *sipahis* or VCOs in the Indian Army before being captured. The remaining 176 were commissioned officers of the rank of 2nd Lieutenant or higher.

15 'Indian National Army', 28 January 1947; *Indian National Army and Free Burma Army, Vol. 3*.

16 Claude Auchinleck, C-in-C, Indian Army, Typewritten minute marked 'Strictly Personal and Secret' from General Auchinleck, concerning the effect on the Indian Army as a whole of the first trial of members of the Indian National Army, 12 February 1946; Major-General Thomas Wynford Rees Papers, Asia and Africa Collection, British Library, MSS Eur/F274/95.

17 This is particularly so for interrogations that took place after the Red Fort Trial of (INA) Colonel Gurbaksh Singh Dhillon, Colonel Prem Kumar Sahgal and Major General Shah Nawaz Khan. After Claude Auchinleck (as C-in-C) commuted their sentences in January 1946 and made it clear that there would be no future prosecutions, the interrogators adopted the practice of interrogating *sipahis* in large groups (some as big as 30). The questions asked were also rarely more than inquiries into their date of birth, date of enlistment, standard of education and date of joining the INA. Only officers or men deemed to have played a 'big part' in the rebel Army were interrogated individually and in depth from that time on. And even they, such as Colonel Pritam Singh who was the aide-de-camp to Subhas Chandra Bose at his death, were often questioned quickly and then released.

18 Numerous works are available with the INA as its subject in Britain, but none have actually been published in the country. The sole exception is Christopher

Bayly and Tim Harper's *Forgotten Armies*, but the sections relating to the INA compare poorly to the discussions of nationalist movements in South-East Asia and Burma.

19 Paul Scott, *The Day of the Scorpion*, (London: Heinemann, 1975 rpt.), pp. 373–4.
20 British Intelligence had heard of the INA but did not wish to disclose the matter to the United States. So, when Viscount Halifax, the British Ambassador in Washington, was asked about the matter on 6 September 1942, he was ordered to respond in a curt manner:

> 'We suggest that any answer sent to America should be couched in general terms only. There is, indeed, every argument for not giving publicity in cases of disloyalty among Indian Prisoners of War. The Japanese are undoubtedly pressing forward with plans for encouraging subversive activity in INDIA, and with the formation of the Indian National Army from Indian malcontents. Equally undoubtedly they have had some success in enlisting the support of disaffected elements, both Prisoners of War and civilian.' MI2 Report, to the War Office, London, c.30 September 1943; *Indian Prisoners of War held by Japanese, Sep.-Dec. 1942*; Public and Judicial Papers, Asia and Africa Collection, British Library, L/PJ/12/641, File 2213/40.

21 General Staff Branch (MI Directorate), 'The Problem of the Indian National Army and of Indian Military Personnel Rejoining from Japanese-Occupied Territory', 12 November 1942, *Indian National Army and Free Burma Army, Vol. 1*; War Staff Papers, Asia and Africa Collection, British Library, L/WS/1/1576.
22 Ibid.
23 Ibid.
24 Ibid.
25 Ibid.
26 It only managed to produce 18 reports in the 3 years between September 1939 and November 1942.
27 There was good reason for this. Individuals involved in the Quit India Movement, such as Jayaprakash Narayan, took inspiration from, and tried to contact, the INA. The information was, admittedly, extracted through torture and may not have been the whole truth. But it still makes for fascinating reading:

> 'I tried to contact the Subhas Bose but could not find a suitable person to arrange that contact. I wanted to consult him to chalk out a plan for coordinating our efforts for the liberation of the country. I wanted that he should continue his activities from outside while I should carry on my work from inside the country.
>
>   . . .

> As far as [the] military was concerned we never asked them to desert. We had pledges of loyalty to the Indian Republic printed which were required to be signed by military men offering to join us. We were contacting them with a view to make them disloyal to the British Government and to get arms through them. This was also the work and an item in the programme of the Azad Senas. We knew that [the] military never revolted unless their masters were in a crippled state. We did not feel that the present international situation was such that the Government was weak and a military revolt could have been successful. We only wanted them to be ready for action when the Government was about to collapse. The Indian military is generally dissatisfied and we were able to win over 80 per cent of the men in [the] Air service, 50 per cent of Garhwalis, 50 per cent of Sikhs and we also succeeded in the formation of cells in all technical units stationed in Bihar and Assam.'

Extracts from Reports on Talks with Jai Prakash Narain, Recorded up to the 25 November 1943; General Staff Branch to GOC Indian Army, 'Comments on the Subversive Activities in the Indian Army from Abroad and its Linkage with the Indian Nationalists Inside the Country: Issues Directions to Deal with the Situation'; T. R. Sareen (ed.), *Indian National Army: A Documentary Study, Vol. 1 (1941–1942)*, (New Delhi: Gyan, 2004a), pp. 265–8.

28 'Appendix "A" to CSDIC (I) No.2 Section Report, No.19, 6 November 1942', *Indian National Army and Free Burma Army, Vol. 1*, italics added.
29 General HQ, India, to General Staff Branch, New Delhi, 'Subversive Activities Directed Against the Military,' 18 March 1943, *Indian National Army and Free Burma Army, Vol. 1*.
30 'Subversive Activities Directed Against the Indian Army,' 29 April 1943, *Indian National Army and Free Burma Army*, Vol. 1.
31 General HQ, India, to General Staff Branch, New Delhi, 3 May 1943, *Indian National Army and Free Burma Army, Vol. 1*.
32 General Headquarters (INDIA), New Delhi, to: – All Commanding Officers of Indian Army Units, May 1944, 'Instructions on Josh work and Josh group organization within units', *Indian National Army and Free Burma Army, Vol. 1*.
33 Ibid.
34 Interrogation of Sepoy Fakir Singh, 8 Platoon, A Coy, 1/15th Punjabis, 24 April 1944; *Arakan INA*; INA Papers, National Archives of India, New Delhi, 379/INA.
35 'F' Kikan was the Japanese unit that helped to create the first INA and was led by Fujiwara Iwaichi. His own book documents the origins of that organization and the Indian Independence League and their activity in winning over Indian soldiers as the Japanese advanced into Malaya. Fujiwara, *F. Kikan*.
36 'Extracts from "Security" History of "X" Battalion', March 1943, *Indian National Army and Free Burma Army, Vol. 1*.

37 Ibid.
38 Interrogation of Sepoy Fakir Singh.
39 Ibid.
40 Some conflicting accounts are given before that date that suggest that Fakir was not being wholly truthful. But, it does not seem to have challenged the prevailing notion that some or all of the men were duped into defecting.
41 Interrogation of Havildar Surat Singh, 1/15th Punjabis, 18 January 1946; 'Reports on Defections to the INA'.
42 'Extracts from "V" Section CSDIC Report No. F/298 dated 14 December 45 on civilian JAGAT SINGH DHILLON @ DOST MOHD. who worked under HATTORI and TADAKURO in Arakan in 1943 as Chief Indian agent for the Akyab branch of Hikari Kikan'; ibid.
43 Interrogation of Havildar Surat Singh.
44 Extract from supplementary statement by Havildar Hardial Singh, 1/15th Punjabis; *Arakan INA*.
45 Ibid.
46 Ibid.
47 It is uncertain whether Mulla Singh, who is described as a 'durwan', was a *diwan* or minister in Nepal, or whether he was a *durban* or courtier.
48 2 Section Report, 'Previous Congress Connections of Hav. Hardial Singh, CQMH, "A" Coy., 1/15 Punjab'; 'Reports on Defections to the INA'.
49 Ibid.
50 Hardial Singh appears to have been interrogated on three separate occasions.
51 Or rather the reported death since there was a great deal of uncertainty whether the news was accurate or some elaborate ruse on the part of Bose.
52 *Discourse of Cultural and National Subjects for the Indian National Army*, (Syonan: Indo Sinbun Shan, c.1943).
53 It appears that Bhandari was being prepared for release without an in-depth interrogation before being hauled back into the interrogation chamber.
54 Interrogation of Subedar Dharam Chand Bhandari, Unit 203 Supply Pers. Section, RIASC; 'Reports on Defections to the INA'; *CSDIC(I) Reports*; Parts 43–47.
55 Ibid.
56 Ibid.
57 Ibid.
58 Ibid.
59 Ibid.
60 Appendix A, Interrogation of Subedar Dharam Chand Bhandari.
61 Ibid.
62 Ibid.
63 P. N. Oak, 'Rani of Zanshi: A Play in Three Acts'; *Magazines and Pamphlets*; INA Papers, National Archives of India, New Delhi, 291/INA.

64 Rani Lakshmibai, the Rani of Jhansi, was the queen of the princely state of Jhansi, and involved in the Uprisings of 1857. She died (reputedly) battling the 8th Hussars at Gwalior on 18 June 1858.
65 'Rani of Zanshi'.
66 Ibid.
67 Ibid.
68 Ibid.
69 Or rather that of a crude website that was commissioned by him before his death in 2007. The website relates to one his last publications: 'Taj Mahal: A Hindu Temple Vandalised.' http://home.freeuk.net/tajmahal/index.htm.
70 Ibid.
71 P. N. Oak, *Rani of Zanshi*.
72 The estimated number of Indian prisoners taken was HKSRA – 1500; 2/14 Punjabis – 900; 5/7 Rajputs – 630; Hong Kong Mule Corps – 250; RIASC Supply Section – 20. 'A General Report on Indian PW in Hong Kong with Particular Reference to HKSRA', 10 June 1946; *CSDIC (I) Reports*; Parts 8–12.
73 Subedar Hakim Khan, 2/14 Punjab; Jemadar Aya Singh, HKSRA; Lance Naik Tara Singh, HKSRA; and Lance Naik Mohamed Iqbal (regiment unknown). Interrogation of Subedar Major Mohamed Ali, 30/8 Coast Regt., HKSRA, 14 May 1946; *CSDIC(I) Reports*; Parts 61–70.
74 'General Report on Indian PW in Hong Kong'.
75 Interrogation of Subedar Major Mohamed Ali.
76 Leading to a total of 'around 25'. Lance Naik (Clerk) Raghbir Singh, 36th Coast Battery, 8th Coast Regt., HKSRA, 25 May 1946; *CSDIC(I) Reports*, Parts 71–80.
77 The barracks are, interestingly enough, still in use today by the Jiefangjun (People's Liberation Army).
78 Joint interrogations of Gunner Nazar Mohamed, 4th Medium Battery, 1st Hong Kong Regiment, HKSRA; Havildar Sagar Khan, 25th Medium Battery, 1st Hong Kong Regiment, HKSRA; Havildar Rehmat Khan, 18th Battery, 5th AA Regiment, HKSRA; and Havildar Ahmed Din, 36th Battery, Coast Regiment, HKSRA, 7 May 1946; CSDIC(I) Reports; Parts 55–60.
79 Ibid.
80 Interrogation of Lance Naik Mohamed Shaffi, 17th AA Battery, 5th AA Regiment, HKSRA, 13 May 1946; *CSDIC(I) Reports*; Parts 61–70.
81 Ibid.
82 In all the interrogations, only four other Punjabi Muslim *sipahis* (excluding VCOs) are said to have joined. It is possible, however, that others did do so. The men in question were listed as Havildar Jamroz Khan, 2/14th Punjab; Lance Naik Yar Khan, 2/14th Punjab; Lance Naik Barkat Ali, HKSRA; and Gunner Israel Khan, HKSRA. Interrogation of Subedar Major Mohamed Ali.

83 Joint interrogations of Gunner Nazar Mohamed et al.
84 Ibid.
85 Interrogation of Subedar Sultan Ahmed, (Battery and Regiment not listed), HKSRA, 10 May 1946; *CSDIC(I) Reports*; Parts 61–70.
86 Nazar Mohamed's account differed from Khuda Baksh's account in one respect. According to Nazar Mohamed, after the men refused, they were imprisoned and deprived of food and water for 24 hours, after which they agreed to bear arms. Joint interrogations of Gunner Nazar Mohamed et al.
87 Interrogation of Havildar Khuda But, (Battery and Regiment not listed), HKSRA, 10 May 1946; *CSDIC(I) Reports*, Parts 61–70.
88 Ibid.
89 It did, however, do so regarding the HKSRA in Singapore. 'A General Report on HKSRA, Singapore', 3 June 1946; *CSDIC (I) Reports*, Parts 8–12.
90 'A General Report on Indian PW in Hong Kong'.
91 It is difficult to know how serious Hakim Khan was in making the last of these claims. The report detailing his interrogation is not very lengthy and mostly consists of him being labelled as 'the blackest of the black'. Interrogation of Subedar Hakim Khan, 2/14th Punjab, 29 May 1946; *CSDIC(I) Reports*, Parts 71–80.
92 As per Indian Army Ordinance 994, of 6 September 1940.
93 The official charges were: 'When on active service joining in a mutiny in His Majesty's military forces in that they at Hong Kong on or about the 20th day of December, 1940, when No. 2607, Havildar Gujjan Singh, 12th Heavy Regiment, Royal Artillery, was marched in custody to the Guard Room of the 20th Heavy Battery (12th Heavy Regiment, Royal Artillery), [the 82 accused] joined in a mutiny by moving in a body to the said Guard Room, entering the same and remaining inside, without having been ordered to do so.' And: 'When on active service joining in a mutiny in His Majesty's military forces in that they at Hong Kong between [the] 20th day of December, 1940 and the 24th day of December, 1940, joined in a mutiny by collectively refusing to take food.' *General Court Martial, Royal Artillery, Hong Kong, 20 January 1941*; (British) National Archives, Kew, Richmond, Surrey; WO 71/1057.
94 Interrogation of Subedar Noor Mohammed, 36 Coast Battery, 8 Coast Regt., HKSRA, 2 April 1946; *CSDIC(I) Reports*, Parts 48–54.
95 Interrogation of Subedar Major Mohamed Ali.
96 'He was carrying framed photos of Mahatma Gandhi, Capt. Mohan Singh, Lt. Col. Gill and a booklet, containing many other photos to show to the PWs. He told them about the Bangkok conference which was then in progress.' Ibid.
97 'Messrs D. M. Khan and Parwani, visited Mautau Chung Camp and gave anti-British propaganda lectures and advised the PW to co-operate with the Japanese. This was the real beginning of subversive activities. At the end of the lecture large

number[s] of Sikhs and Hindus shouted "Inquilab Zindabad!". S. M. Karnail Singh's attitude from this day was changed – he was the first one to cheer the lecturers.' Ibid.
98 Joint interrogations of Gunner Nazar Mohamed et al.
99 Ibid.
100 Interrogation of Havildar Khuda But.
101 Particularly the Defence Address by Bhulabhai Desai. V. S. Kulkarni and K. S. N. Murty (eds), *First Indian National Army Trial*, (Poona: Mangal Sahitya Prakashan, 1946).
102 Pritam Singh, interview held at Doiwala, Dehradun dist., Uttarakhand, March 2006.
103 Jacques Derrida, *Of Grammatology*; translated by Gayatri Chakravorty Spivak, (Baltimore, MD: John Hopkins University Press, 1997 rpt.), pp. 65–73.
104 The exception is the Pakistan Army which did invite (at least some) officers to re-enlist. The invite was not extended to the rank and file.
105 15 October 1946 to be precise.
106 Claude Auchinleck, *Typewritten minute marked 'Strictly Personal and Secret'*.

Conclusion

1 This is the translation employed by Asian Dub Foundation in the track 'Rebel Warrior'; Asian Dub Foundation, *Facts and Fictions*, (Nation Records, 1995). It could also be translated as 'Rebel' or 'The Rebel'.
2 Kazi Nasrul Islam, 'Bidrohi'; translated by Syed Sajjad Husain, amended by Santanu Das; Rafiqul Islam (ed.), *Kazi Nazrul Islam: A New Anthology*, (Dhaka: Bangla Academy, 1990), p. 20.
3 During the latter half of 1920 when the regiment was being disbanded (it was not fully disbanded until 24 February 1921).
4 A term used, but not coined, by Robert Young. In his words, it 'avoids the problems of the "Third World", the bland homogenization of "the South", and the negative definition of "the non-west" which also implies a complete dichotomy between the west and the rest which two or more centuries of imperialism have hardly allowed.' Robert J. C. Young, *Postcolonialism: An Historical Introduction*, (Oxford: Blackwell, 2009 rpt.), p. 5.
5 The first volume was published in 1982.
6 It is, however, not quite the first article outlining the aims of the Collective (which can be found in Ranajit Guha, 'On Some Aspects of the Historiography of Colonial India'; idem. (ed.), *Subaltern Studies I: Writings on South Asian History and Society*). And, there are lengthy articles by Guha before the creation of the Collective which expound ideas that would later be classified as subalternist

(e.g. 'Neel Darpan: The Image of a Peasant Revolt in a Liberal Mirror'; Journal of Peasant Studies, 2, 1, (October 1974), pp. 1–46 and reprinted in Ranajit Guha (ed.), *The Small Voice of History: Collected Essays*; edited and with an introduction by Patha Chatterjee, (New Delhi: Permanent Black, 2009).

7   Ranajit Guha, 'The Prose of Counter-Insurgency'; idem (ed.), *Subaltern Studies II: Writings on South Asian History and Society*, (New Delhi: Oxford University Press, 2005b rpt.), pp. 18–19.

8   'In this ahistorical view of the history of insurgency all moments of consciousness are assimilated to the ultimate and highest moment of the series – indeed to an Ideal Consciousness. A historiography devoted to its pursuit (even when that is done, regrettably, in the name of Marxism) is ill-equipped to cope with contradictions which are indeed the stuff history is made of. Since the Ideal is supposed to be one hundred per cent secular in character, the devotee tends to look away when confronted with the evidence of religiosity, as if the latter did not exist, or explain it away as a clever but well-intentioned fraud perpetrated by enlightened leaders on their moronic followers – all done, of course, "in the interest of the people"! Hence, the rich material of myths, rituals, rumours, hopes for a Golden Age, and fears of an imminent End of the World, all of which speaks of the self-alienation of the rebel, is wasted on this abstract and sterile discourse.' Ranajit Guha, 'Prose of Counter-Insurgency', p. 83.

9   Ranajit Guha, 'The Small Voice of History'; idem (ed.), *The Small Voice of History*, p. 307.

10 Ibid., p. 33.

11 Influenced by the introduction of Antonio Gramsci into Bengali intellectual life by Susobhan Chandra Sarkar in 1968 (who had earlier been something of a mentor to Ranajit Guha) and the publications of Gramsci's *Prison Notebooks* into English.

12 Ranajit Guha, 'On Some Aspects of the Historiography of Colonial India'; idem, *Subaltern Studies I: Writings on South Asian History and Society*, (New Delhi: Oxford University Press, 2005a rpt.), p. 7.

13 'A child of experience educated in theory, it was emphatically political, something that shocked the academic establishment which had been the custodian of South Asian Studies both in England and India since the nineteenth century.' Ranajit Guha, 'Gramsci in India: Homage to a Teacher'; idem (ed.), *The Small Voice of History*, p. 364.

14 Ranajit Guha, *Elementary Aspects of Peasant Insurgency in Colonial India*, (Delhi: Oxford University Press, 1992 rpt.), p. 17.

15 James C. Scott, *Domination and the Arts of Resistance: Hidden Transcripts*, (New Haven, CT: Yale University Press, 1990), Preface.

16 James C. Scott, *Weapons of the Weak: Everyday Forms of Peasant Resistance*, (New Haven, CT: Yale University Press, 1985), p. 40.

17 Scott, *Domination and the Arts of Resistance*, Preface.
18 Ibid.
19 Ibid., p. 16.
20 Phillip Scheffner's film *The Halfmoon Files* indicates what can be done when working with the sound recordings of Indian POW in Germany during World War I. Phillip Scheffner (dir.), *The Halfmoon Files: A Ghost Story* (2007). And Nobuko Nagasaki has painstakingly collated the testimonies of Japanese working alongside the INA during World War II, but has, unfortunately for myself, only published in Japanese. Nobuko Nagasaki et al. (eds), *Shiryoshu Indo Kokumingun Kankeisha Shogen*, (Tokyo: Kenbunshuppan, 2008).
21 Derrida, *Archive Fever*, p. 2.
22 Spivak, *Critique of Postcolonial Reason*, p. 239.
23 Ibid., pp. 207–8.
24 Michel de Certeau, *The Mystic Fable, Volume One: The Sixteenth and Seventeenth Centuries*; translated by Michael B. Smith, (Chicago, IL: Chicago University Press, 1995), pp. 10–11.
25 Ajay Skaria, 'Writing, Orality and Power in the Dangs, Western India, 1800s–1920s'; Shahid Amin and Dipesh Chakrabarty (eds), *Subaltern Studies IX: Writings on South Asian History and Society*, (New Delhi: Oxford University Press, 1996).
26 Ajay Skaria, *Hybrid Histories: Forests, Frontiers and Wildness in Western India*, (Delhi: Oxford University Press, 1999), p. 16.
27 Ibid., p. 17.
28 Ibid.
29 Ibid.
30 Bhabha, *Location of Culture*, pp. 126–7.
31 David G. Mendelbaum, 'The Study of Life History: Gandhi'; *Current Anthropology*, Vol. 14, No. 3, (June 1973), p. 177.
32 David Arnold and Stuart Blackburn, 'Introduction: Life Histories in India'; Id. (ed.), *Telling Lives in India: Biography, Autobiography and Life History*, (Bloomington and Indianapolis: Indiana University Press, 2004), p. 2.
33 Man Singh Rawat, (Garhwali), 1/39th Garhwali Rifles, France, to Partab Singh, Ringwari, Garhwal, India, 22 September 1915; *CIM 1914–1915*, Part 6.
34 Claude Auchinleck, *Typewritten Minute Marked 'Strictly Personal and Secret'*.
35 Jacques Rancière, *The Names of History*; translated by Hassan Melehy, (Minneapolis: University of Minnesota Press, 1994), pp. 74–5.
36 Sobha Ram, (Hindu Jat), 2nd Lancers, France, to Kalu Ram, Hissar, Punjab, India, 24 January 1917; *CIM 1917–1918*, Part 1.

Appendix I: Recruitment, Military Service and Casualties in the Indian Army during World War I

Recruitment by province, August 1914 – November 1918

Province	Combatants	Non-combatants	Total
Punjab	349,688	97,288	446,976
UP	163,578	117,565	281,143
Madras	51,233	41,117	92,340
Bombay	41,272	30,211	71,483
Bengal	7,117	51,935	59,052
NWFP	32,181	13,050	45,231
Bihar and Orissa	8,576	32,976	41,552
Burma	14,094	4,579	18,673
Assam	942	14,182	15,124
CP	5,376	9,631	15,007
Ajmer-Merwara	7,341	1,632	8,973
Baluchistan	1,761	327	2,088
Total	683,149	414,493	1,097,642

Recruitment by class, August 1914–November 1918
(20 most recruited classes, supplying 90% of combatant enlistments.)

Class	Number
Punjabi Muslims	136,126
Sikhs	88,925
Gurkhas	55,589
Rajputs	49,086
Jats	40,272
Other Hindus	38,586
Hindustani Muslims	36,353
Pathans	27,857
Dogras	23,491
Brahmans	20,382
Ahirs	19,544
Gujars	18,296
Tamils	16,390

(*Continued*)

Class	Number
Rajputana Jats	14,967
Rajputana and Central India Muslims	14,224
Rajputana Rajputs	13,104
Dekhani Mahrattas	12,266
Burmans	12,163
Konkani Mahrattas	12,038
Dekhani Muslims	8,118
Total	657,739

Recruitment by year, 1914–1919

Year	Recruits
1914 (1 August – 31 December)	24,666
1915	84,353
1916	93,388
1917	179,364
1918 (to 30 November)	290,687
1919 (to 31 December)	50,200
Total (Indian Army combatants)	722,658
Total combatants (including Imperial Service Troops from the Princely States and Indians enlisted in the British Army)	877,068
Total Non-combatants	563,369
Grand total	1,440,437

Theatres in which *Sipahis* from India Served, by 31 December 1919
(Figures do not take into account Indian troops already overseas at the start of the War, or transfers of troops from one theatre to another.)

Theatre	Combatants	Non-combatants
France	87,412	49,273
East Africa	33,835	13,021
Mesopotamia	317,142	348,735
Egypt and Palestine	107,743	34,075
Total	546,132	445,104

Total casualties, up to 30 April 1920

	Dead	Wounded	Missing or prisoners
France:			
Combatants	6,094	15,893	
Non-combatants	2,227	144	
Mesopotamia:			
Combatants	19,186	12,261	
Non-combatants	12,261	450	
Total	61,041	67,771	1,262

Sources: India's Contribution to the Great War, (Calcutta: Government of India, 1923); *Indian Voices of the Great War: Soldier's Letters, 1914–1918*; selected and introduced by David Omissi, (Basingstoke: MacMillan, 1999).

Appendix II: Recruitment into the Indian Army during World War II

Size of the Indian Army during World War II

	Total	Indian other ranks	Annual cost
1 September 1939	210,656	157,330	Rs. 22 crores
1 January 1941(combatants only)	418,531		
1 February 1942 (combatants only)	690,000		
29 May 1944	2,668,470		
1 April 1945	2,285,936	1,611,050	Rs. 387 crores

Class composition of the Indian Army (Combatants only), 1941–1942

Class	Numbers, 1 January 1941	Numbers, 1 February 1942
Mussalmans	155,237	239,000
Sikhs	51,006	72,000
Dogras	28,071	
Garhwalis	9,932	
Rajputs	26,928	
Jats	23,778	
Marathas	18,450	
Gurkhas	46,185	
Madrassis	15,464	
Other Hindus	36,171	
Christians	7,149	14,000
Hindus (including Rajputs, Dogras, etc., but not Gurkhas)		284,000
Others (excluding Christians)		41,000
Total	418,531	690,000

Appendix II

Composition of the Indian Army by Province (Combatants only), 1 January 1941

Province	Muslims	Hindus and other religions	Total	Percentage of total
NWFP	35,253	0	35,253	8.5%
Punjab	96,826	104,919	201,745	48%
UP and Bihar	5,245	33,587	38,432	9.5%
Rajputana and Central India	6,559	21,689	28,248	7%
Bombay	5,339	18,703	24,102	6%
Madras	2,603	19,320	21,923	5%
Nepal	0	46,185	46,185	11%
CP	0	267	267	0.06%
Other	3,352	18,624	21,976	5%
Grand Total	155,237	263,494	418,531	

Detailed class composition of the Indian Army, 1 January 1941

Province	Class (Muslim)	Numbers	Class (Hindus and others)	Numbers
NWFP	*Pathan*	28,785		
	Hazarawal	5,021		
	Baluchi	1,447		
Punjab	*Punjabi Mussalmans*	92,897	*Sikhs*	51,005
	Muslim Rajputs	3,360	*Dogras*	28,071
	Meos	569	*Rajputs*	3,546
			Hindu Jats	14,487
			Brahmans	1,992
			Ahirs	3,852
			Christians	825
			Gujars	1,140
UP and Bihar	*Hindustani Mussalmans*	4,858	*Garhwalis*	9,932
	Muslim Rajputs	387	*Kumaonis*	8,094
			Rajputs	7,381
			Hindu Jats	3,334
			Brahmans	2,948
			Ahirs	1,170
			Gujars	728
Rajputana and Central India	*Rajputana and Central Indian Mussalmans*	6,336	*Rajputs*	13,563
			Hindu Jats	5,886
	Meos	223	*Ahirs*	501
			Gujars	1,739
Bombay	*Dekhani Mussalmans*	5,399	*Brahmans*	253
			Marathas	18,450

(*Continued*)

Province	Class (Muslim)	Numbers	Class (Hindus and others)	Numbers
Madras	*Madrasi Mussalmans*	2,603	*Madrasis*	19,320
Nepal			*Gurkhas*	46,185
CP			*Rajputs*	60
			Brahmans	207
Other	*Meos*	536	*Rajputs*	2,378
	Other Mussalmans	2,816	*Hindu Jats*	71
			Brahmans	2,082
			Ahirs	236
			Gujars	33
			'*Other Hindus*'	13,824
Total		155,237		263,494

Sources: *Class Composition of the Army in India*, Asia and Africa Collections, British Library, (L/WS/1/456); *Indian Army Morale and Possible Reduction, 1943–1945*, Asia and Africa Collections, British Library, (L/WS/1/707).

Appendix III

Enumeration of Suicide, Attempted Suicide, Murder and Attempted Murder in the Indian Army, 1887–1893

Military areas	1/10/1886 – 30/9/1887				1/10/1887 – 30/9/1888				1/10/1888 – 30/9/1889				1/10/1889 – 30/9/1890				1/10/1890 – 30/9/1891				1/10/1891 – 30/9/1892				1/10/1892 – 30/9/1893			
	S.	A.S.	M.	A.M.	S.	A.S.	M.	A.M.	S.	A.S.	M.	A.M.	S.	A.S.	M.	A.M.	S.	A.S.	M.	A.M.	S.	A.S.	M.	A.M.	S.	A.S.	M.	A.M.
Allahabad	1											1																
Bundelkhand															1													
Lahore								1	2						1													
Meerut		2			1										1	1												
Oudh					1				2				2		1													
Peshawar	1						1	1	1						3													
Presidency																												
Quetta	3				2				2		2		1		1	1												
Rawalpindi	1	1																										
Rohilkhand		1			2		1	1																				
Nerbudda							1	1	2																			
Sirhind		1																										
Punjab Frontier Force	2	1			1				1						1													
Upper Burma Force	3	1	1		3																							
Sikkim Expeditionary Force																												
Assam	1				1				1																			
Military and civil totals																												
Bengal Presidency	12	1	7	1	8	1	2	2	8	0	4	1	9	2	5	3	3	2	2	2	5	4	6	3		3	4	2
Madras Presidency	5	2	1		2		2		4		1		3		7		7		6	1	2	2	3	1		1	1	1
Bombay Presidency	6	1	13	1	7		6	4	2		1	2	3		2	3	1		1		2	5	4	3				
Total																												
Indian troops	23	2	22	3	15	1	10	6	14	0	6	3	15	2	7	6	11	3	9	0	7	11	6	12	4	5	3
(British comparison)	27	17	5	11	18	8	1	4	11	3	1	0	10	1	1	2	6	3	3	0	19	3	2	1	17	1	0	1

Glossary

alam al-Jabarut	Lit. 'The World of Omnipotence'.
al-Dhajjal/al-Dajjal	The Muslim False Messiah/Antichrist, whose appearance is to precede the Day of Judgement.
Angrezi	The English language (as a noun), or the English (as an adjective).
anna	One sixteenth of a rupee or 4 *paise*.
ata	Flour.
Azad Hind Fauj	Lit. 'The Army of Free India'. The official name of the INA after its reformation under Subhas Chandra Bose.
babu	A term of respect used to address men in pre-colonial India (especially in Bengal). The term evolved into a generic term for an Indian clerk or minor official under the British Raj, and a derogatory British term for an anglicized or learned Indian.
batta	System of extraordinary payments for enlisted men in the Indian Army
battalion	A body of soldiers, composed of 8 companies, and numbering 750 Indian officers and men.
bhailawa	(Reputedly) a plant, the seeds of which were used by washermen to mark clothes.
bhang	Beverage made from cannabis.
Bharat Mata Ki Jai!	Long Live Mother India!
bidi/beedi	Thin, often flavoured, Indian cigarette.
bigha	Unit used to measure an area of land. It varied in size throughout colonial India, but was generally less than an acre.
brigade	A body of soldiers, composed of regiments/battalions, and forming part of a division.
bulbul	A type of South Asian songbird.
charas	Hashish.
chatak	A small unit of weight measurement roughly equivalent to an ounce. There are 16 *chataks* in 1 *seer*.
company	A unit of infantry, composed of platoons, and forming one eighth of a battalion or regiment.
crore	Ten million.
dafadar	An Indian cavalry NCO, corresponding to a sergeant.
dal	Split pulses.

dharm/dharma	Religious term common in Hinduism and Sikhism, delineating broad codes of behaviour necessary to preserve and maintain the natural order.
dhikr	Islamic devotional recitation of the name of God.
dhobi	Washerman.
dhoti	Rectangular piece of unstitched cloth, usually around 7 yards long, wrapped around the waist and legs and knotted at the waist. Traditionally worn by Hindus in northern India.
division	A body of soldiers, composed of brigades, and forming part of a corps.
Doaba	Lit. 'Two Rivers' or 'Land of the Two Rivers'. Refers to the area of Punjab between the Ravi and Sutlej rivers.
durbar	A state reception given by Indian princes for a British sovereign or by an Indian prince for his subjects; the court of an Indian prince.
faqir	Term applied to both Muslim and (incorrectly) Hindu religious itinerants.
Faujdar	Military.
F Kikan	Japanese military intelligence operation established during World War II. It was tasked to contact members of the Indian Independence Movement and played a pivotal role in the formation of the INA. Led, initially, by Fujiwara Iwaichi.
ganja	Cannabis.
Ghadar/Ghadr	Lit. 'mutiny' or 'struggle'.
ghee	Clarified butter used in cooking.
gol/gotra	A lineage or sub-caste that divides broader South Asian castes or *varnas*.
gora/gori	Lit. 'White'. Term colloquially used to refer to Europeans.
Granth/Guru Granth Sahib	Sikh scriptures.
hadith	Islamic oral traditions relating to the words and deeds of Mohammed.
hajji	A Muslim individual who has completed the pilgrimage to Mecca.
havildar	An Indian infantry NCO, corresponding to a sergeant.
hindutva	Lit. Hindu-ness. Coined by Vinayak Damodar Savarkar. Cornerstone of contemporary Hindu nationalism.
huzoor	Equivalent to 'My Lord'. Used as a form of address by soldiers to refer to a (British) officer.
ICO	'Indian Commissioned Officer'. Refers to the 4411 Indian Officers educated at the IMA, Dehradun between 1932 and 1946. They were granted full authority over British troops but only within the geographical boundaries of the subcontinent.

izzat	Honour.
Jazirat-al-Arab	Lit. 'The Island of the Arabs' (i.e. Arabia).
jemadar	Junior Indian VCO of infantry or cavalry. Equivalent to a Naib-Subedar in the contemporary armies of India and Pakistan.
Jif	'Japanese Influenced Forces'. British euphemism for members of the INA.
kafir	An 'unbeliever' (non-Muslim).
Kala Pani	Lit. 'Black Water'. Can refer to the taboo of the sea in Indian culture, or the Penal Colonies established in the Andaman Islands.
kazi/qazi/qadi	Islamic judge of *sharia* law.
KCIO	'King's Commissioned Indian Officer'. Refers to the 95 Indian Officers trained at RMC, Sandhurst between 1921 and 1933. They held full authority over British troops unlike VCOs or ICOs.
khadim	Custodian or caretaker (usually of a mosque or Islamic shrine).
khalasi	Labourer.
Khalsa	The community of Sikhs.
khatib	The person delivering the Friday prayers in a mosque.
khel	Kinship groups dividing a Pathan *ttabar* (tribe).
kot/kote	Various meanings depending on the context: village; fort/fortress; house; armoury.
lakh	One hundred thousand.
lambadar	Registered village headman, responsible for the collection of local tax revenue.
lance-dafadar	An Indian cavalry NCO, corresponding to a corporal.
lance-naik	An Indian infantry NCO, corresponding to a lance-corporal.
lascar	Sailor.
lungi	Long garment worn around the waist.
ma-bap	Lit. 'mother and father'.
madarchod	Lit. 'Mother-fucker'.
Malwa	Area of Punjab (and parts of modern-day Haryana) lying between the Sutlej and Yamuna rivers.
Majha	Historical region of the Punjab comprising the modern Indian districts of Amritsar, Gurdaspur and Tarn Taran, and the Pakistani districts of Lahore and Kasur.
majum	sweet cake containing *charas*, *bhang* or *ganja*.
maulvi/moulvi	Honorific used to refer to any Muslim religious cleric or teacher.
maund	Unit to measure weight, equivalent to 82.28 lbs.
mem/memsahib	Term of address used for a European woman.
mihrab	Niche in the wall of a mosque indicating the direction of Mecca.
mufti	Islamic scholar and interpreter of *sharia* law.

mujtahid	Lit. an Islamic scholar able to interpret *sharia* independently of any school of law or established jurisprudence.
munazara	Public religious debates in South Asia. Esp. in Islam.
Musalman	Muslim.
naik	An Indian infantry NCO, corresponding to a corporal.
Netaji	Lit. 'Revered Leader'. Term of respect given to Subhas Chandra Bose.
pagri	Turban.
paisa	Smallest unit of denomination in South Asia, roughly equivalent to a penny.
Paltan	Regiment.
pir	Title used by and to refer to a Sufi teacher.
Pushtunwali/ Pakhtunwali	The honour or 'tribal' code of Pathans/Pushtuns.
Ramzan/Ramadan	Muslim month of fasting.
regiment	The basic unit of the Indian Army comprising four squadrons of cavalry or eight companies (one battalion) of infantry. Each regiment would (usually) have several battalions.
risala/risallah	A troop or regiment of Indian horse.
risaldar/ressaidar	The senior Indian VCO of a cavalry squadron; the head of a risala.
risaldar-major	The senior Indian VCO of a cavalry regiment.
roti	Unleavened flatbread, slightly thicker than a *chapatti*.
sahib	Term used to address an Englishman or European; used in the Army to refer to an officer.
sardar	Lit. 'Headholder' (Persian). Used to refer to the leaders of various Pathan tribes, and as a term of respect for any male follower of the Sikh faith; used in the army to refer to VCOs.
sarkar	Government or Presiding Authority; used as term of respect for someone in a position of authority.
Sat Sri Akal	Lit. 'There is One Revered, Timeless Truth'. Sikh salutation.
seer	Unit of measure weight. 40 *seers* are in 1 *maund*.
shaheed/shahadat	Martyr/martyrdom. Originally of Arabic and Muslim origin, but has become a trans-religious honorific bestowed on individuals after death in South Asia. Especially prevalent in Punjab.
sipahi	Soldier; infantrymen. Anglicized by the British into 'sepoy'.
sowar	Cavalry trooper. From Urdu *sawar* ('horseman')
squadron	A unit of cavalry, composed of troops, and forming one quarter of a regiment.
subedar	The chief Indian VCO of an infantry company, ranking immediately superior to a Jemadar.

tahsil	Sub-division of a district.
thana	Police station.
ttabar	Lit. 'Family' (Pushtu).
ulama/ulema	A scholar versed in Islam, who has (usually) completed at least 7 years of study.
VCO	Viceroy Commissioned Officer. Refers to 'native' officers (Jemadar, Subedar, Subeda-Major, Risaldar and Risaldar-Major) who had a Viceregal rather than a King's Commission, and were thus of a lower rank than a full officer. Equivalent to a JCO in the contemporary armies of India and Pakistan.
wakil	Lawyer/trustee (Arabic).
Zakat	Obligatory Muslim tithe to charity.

Bibliography

Unpublished primary sources

British Library, London

European Manuscripts, Asia and Africa Collection:

INA. Indian Police Collection. MSS Eur F 161/162.

Report on the Kitchener Indian Hospital, Brighton. Colonel Sir Bruce Seton Papers. MSS Eur/F143/66.

Typewritten Minute Marked "Strictly Personal and Secret" from General Auchinleck, Concerning the Effect on the Indian Army as a Whole of the First Trial of Members of the Indian National Army. Major-General Thomas Wynford Rees Papers. MSS Eur/F274/95.

Military Department Papers, Asia and Africa Collection:

Annual Caste Return of the Native Army in India, on the 1 January 1893. L/MIL/7/7081.

Annual Return Showing the Class Composition of the Armed Forces of India, on the 1 January 1908. L/MIL/7/7084.

The Army in India: Acts of Violence by Soldiers, 1887–94 – Withdrawal of Ball Ammunition and Comparative Returns of Murders and Suicides. L/MIL/7/13230.

Attempts by Turks to Tamper with the Loyalty of Indian Mohammedan Troops in Constantinople. L/MIL/5/747.

Confidential Reports, Regiments etc.: Review Reports on Indian Army Units, 1914–1915. L/MIL/7/17024.

Confidential Reports, Regiments etc.: Confidential Reports and Review Reports for 1915–1916 on Indian Army Units and Depots. L/MIL/7/17026.

Confidential Reports, Regiments etc.: Confidential Reports 1917 – Officers Employed Under War Office. L/MIL/7/17027.

Confidential Reports, Regiments etc.: Confidential Reports on Indian Army Units and Officers in India, 1916–1917. L/MIL/7/17028.

Confidential Reports, Regiments etc.: Confidential Reports and Review Reports for 1917–18 on Units, Depots, and British Service Officers of the Indian Army. L/MIL/7/17029.

Correspondence and Memorandum on the Indian Labour Corps in France and Flanders, July 1917 – June 1919. L/MIL/5/738.

Correspondence on Unsolicited Copies of 'Islamic News' Addressed to Indian Muslim Cadets at Sandhurst, Jan. 1921. L/MIL/5/859.

Demobilisation 1918: Progress of Demobilisation. L/MIL/7/19205.

Guide to Summary General Courts Martial under the Indian Army Act. L/MIL/17/5/1820.

The Indian Army Act, 1911, (Act No. VIII of 1911): As Modified up to the 15th October, 1937. L/MIL/17/5/1817.

Indian Regiments – Insubordination: 4/2nd Punjab Regiment – Report on the Shooting Outrage at Nowshera [in] 1938 & Disbandment of the 4/2nd Punjab Regiment. L/MIL/7/7284.

Insubordination, Mutiny, etc.: Mutiny of the 2/18th Garhwal Rifles. L/MIL/7/7282.

Memorandum on Summary General Courts Martial. L/MIL/17/5/1821.

Native Regiments – Insubordination, Misconduct etc.: Treachery of a Native Officer and Misconduct of 20 Men of 29th Punjab Infantry at Peiwar Kotal, Dec. 1978. L/MIL/7/7266.

Native Regiments – Insubordination, Misconduct etc.: Insubordination of Certain Men of the 3rd Goorkha Regt. at Almorah in April 1886. L/MIL/7/7267.

Native Regiments – Insubordination, Misconduct etc.: Disturbances between the 17th Bombay Infantry and Local Police in Bombay in Sept. 12 1887. L/MIL/7/7269.

Native Regiments – Insubordination, Misconduct etc.: Court Martial of Certain Rangur Sepoys of 17th Bengal Infantry for Insubordination. L/MIL/7/7271.

Native Regiments – Insubordination, Misconduct etc.: Insubordination of the Hindu Companies of 25th Madras Inf. at Shwebo, Burma, October 1894. L/MIL/7/7273.

Native Regiments – Insubordination, Misconduct etc.: Mutinous Behaviour of Certain Men of the 14th Bombay Infantry at Bareilly in September 1897. L/MIL/7/7274.

Native Regiments – Insubordination, Misconduct etc.: Insubordinate Conduct of Certain Konkani Mahrattas of the 17th Bombay Infy. at Bhuj, Nov. 1897. L/MIL/7/7275.

Native Regiments – Insubordination, Misconduct etc.: Insubordinate Behaviour of Certain Men of the 27 Madras Infantry, 1897. L/MIL/7/7276.

Native Regiments – Insubordination, Misconduct etc.: Conduct of the 3rd Brahman Regiment in Mesopotamia. L/MIL/7/7277.

Native Regiments – Insubordination, Misconduct etc.: 18 Infantry in China – Offence Reported to Have Been Committed by 20 Sepoys. L/MIL/7/7278.

Native Regiments – Insubordination, Misconduct etc.: 49th Bengalis – Report of Shooting Affray in which 3 Indian Officers were Attacked and Shot. L/MIL/7/7279.

Native Regiments – Insubordination, Misconduct etc.: Insubordination amongst Hill Brahmans Attached to the Depot of the 38th Dogras. L/MIL/7/7280.

Native Regiments – Insubordination, Misconduct etc.: Treasonable Literature Emanating from [the] USA Landed to Native Troops at Hong Kong. L/MIL/7/7281.

Native Regiments – Insubordination, Misconduct etc.: Mutiny of the 2/18th Garhwal Rifles. L/MIL/7/7282.

Proceedings of a Court of Inquiry Held at Abottabad and Peshawar, 7th May 1930: To Investigate the Circumstances in which Certain Incidents Occurred in the

2nd Battalion, 18th Royal Garhwal Rifles, at Peshawar, on the 23rd and 24th April, 1930. L/MIL/5/861.
Report in Connection with the Mutiny of the 5th Light Infantry at Singapore (1915). L/MIL/17/19/48.
Reports of the Censor of Indian Mails in France, 1914–1915. L/MIL/5/825.
Reports of the Censor of Indian Mails in France, 1915–1916. L/MIL/5/826.
Reports of the Censor of Indian Mails in France, 1917–1918. L/MIL/5/827.
Reports of the Censor of Indian Mails in France, 1917–1918. L/MIL/5/828.

Public and Judicial Papers, Asia and Africa Collection:

DIB Reports and Proposals on the Treatment of Members of the Indian National Army, October – December 1945. L/PJ/12/771, File 2188/45.
Indian Civilians and Prisoners of War Suspected of Collaboration with Nazis, January 1944 – April 1945. L/PJ/12/659, File 1519/43.
Indian Prisoners of War held by Japanese, September – December 1942. L/PJ/12/641, File 2213/40.
Lahore Conspiracy Case: Judgement. In re King Emperor Versus Anand Kishore and Others. Charges Under Sections, 121, 123, 396 and Others. L/PJ/6/1405.
Middle East Military Censorship: Fortnightly Summaries Covering Indian Troops, September 1942 – April 1943. L/PJ/12/654, File 2336/42.
Middle East Military Censorship: Fortnightly Summaries Covering Indian Troops, April 1943 – September 1943. L/PJ/12/655, File 2336/42.
Middle East Military Censorship: Fortnightly Summaries Covering Indian Troops, November 1943 – March 1944, [misfiled as 'Indian Chief Censor's Fortnightly Reports, 1943–1944']. L/PJ/12/578, File 471 (XN/37).
Middle East Military Censorship: Fortnightly Summaries Covering Indian Troops, June 1944 – March 1945. L/PJ/12/656, File 2336/42.
Subhas Chandra Bose: Activities in UK, Germany, Burma, Thailand and Japan, 1937–1947. L/PJ/12/217, File 1115A/24.
Unrest Among Sikhs in Hong Kong, October 1940 – October 1941, L/PJ/12/641, File 2213/40.

War Staff Papers, Asia and Africa Collection:

Class Composition of the Army in India. L/WS/1/456.
Disaffection of Sikh Troops. L/WS/1/303.
Disaffection of Nepalese Troops. L/WS/1/506.
Discipline of Indian Troops in Singapore. L/WS/1/391.
Indian Army Morale and Possible Reduction, 1943–1945. L/WS/1/707.
Indian National Army. L/WS./1/1711.
Indian National Army and Free Burma Army, Vol. 1. L/WS/1/1576.
Indian National Army and Free Burma Army, Vol. 2. L/WS/1/1577.
Indian National Army and Free Burma Army, Vol. 3. L/WS/1/1578.

Indian National Army and Free Burma Army: Press Cuttings and Debates. L/WS/1/1579.
Intelligence: India Monthly Intelligence Summary. L/WS/1/317.
Plan 288: War Organization – Army in India. L/WS/1/1068.
Note on Sikhs. L/WS/2/44.
Situation in India. L/WS/1/1504.
Anderson, G. D., CSDIC (I). *A Brief Chronological and Factual Account of the INA.* L/WS/2/45.

National Archives of India, New Delhi

Private Papers:

1. *Japanese Reports on INA. 2. Reactions of the INA to the Surrenders of its Personnel. 3. Mutiny in INA Units. 4. IK (iv) (Deserters to INA). 5. Malaya General.* INA Records. 263/INA.
1. *Burma Campaign. 2. Early Organisation of 'Jiffery' in Burma. 3. Ramsarup Early Contact Parties.* INA Records. 261/INA.
Arakan INA. INA Records. 144/INA.
Copies of "Onto Delhi". INA Records. 288/INA.
CSDIC (India), Red Fort, Delhi. No. 2 Section Information Reports. INA Records. 379/INA.
Discourses of Cultural and National Subjects for the Indian National Army. Syonan [Singapore]: Indo Sinbun Shan, c.1943. INA Records. 335/INA.
Do's and Don'ts for the Officers and Men of the Indian National Army, Syonan [Singapore]: Headquarters Director of Military Bureau, Indian Independence League, East Asia, c.1942.
Durga Mal's Party. INA Records. 143/INA.
INA Gazette, 1943–1945. INA Record. 12/INA
Interrogation Report, Bose Brigade or 1 Guerrilla Rgt. INA Records. 198/INA.
Interrogation Report (Reinforcement Gp.). INA Records. 11/INA.
Interrogation Report ("X" Regiment). INA Records. 78/INA.
Magazines and Pamphlets. INA Records. 291/INA.
Platoon Lectures, Nos. 1–10, 1943. INA Records. 294/INA.
Venereal Disease in Singapore and How to Avoid It – 1941. INA Records. 331/INA.

Empire and Commonwealth Museum, Bristol (since closed)

Film Archive:

India, Mysore Residency, 1929, (Reel 54). Dalyell Collection. BECMV446/1998/005/025.
India: Parachinar Durbar, 1929, (Reel 57). Dalyell Collection. BECMV446/1998/005/028.
Scenes in the Life of the Bengal Sappers, c.1930. Duke Collection, BECMV129/2001/029/001.
The Khyber Pass and the Kajuri Plain, 1931, Kendal Collection, BECMV357/1997/153/036.

National Archives, Kew, Richmond, Surrey

General Court Martial, R.A., Hong Kong, 20th January 1941. WO 71/1057.
Hong Kong and Singapore Royal Artillery – Disbandment, 1949–1950. WO 32/10912.

National Library of Scotland, Edinburgh

The Army Act, 1881; 'Scots Statutes Revised, 1881–1885'. Advocates Library, 44 and 45 v.c.58.

National Archives at San Francisco, San Bruno, California

RG 118, *Records of the Office of the U.S. Attorney, Northern District of California, Neutrality Case Files, 1913–1920*. NRHSA Accession #'s 118 72-001, 118-73-001.

House of Commons Parliamentary Paper (http://parlipapers.chadwyck.co.uk/home.do)

A Copy of the Penal Code Prepared by the Indian Law Commissioners, and Published by Command of the Governor-General in India in Council. 1837–1838.
East India (Army in India Committee, 1919–1920). Report of the Committee Appointed by the Secretary of State for India to Enquire into the Administration and Organisation of the Army in India. 1920.
East India (Sedition Committee, 1918). Report of Committee Appointed to Investigate Revolutionary Conspiracies in India. 1918.
Report from His Majesty's Commissioners for Inquiring into the System of Military Punishments in the Army. 1836.
Report of the Committee Appointed to Enquire into the Pathology and Treatment of Venereal Disease, with the View to Diminish its Injurious Effects on the Men of the Army and Navy, with Appendices, and the Evidence Taken before the Committee. 1868.
Report of the Indian Jails Committee, 1919–1920. 1921.
Report of the War Office Committee of Enquiry into "Shell-Shock". 1922.
Royal Commission on Venereal Diseases: Final Report of the Commissioners. 1916.

Hansard (House of Commons Daily Debates).

Hansard, 1803–2005. (http://hansard.millbanksystems.com)
Hansard, 2005 – To Present. (http://www.parliament.uk/business/publications/hansard)

Interviews

Colonel Pritam Singh (INA). Doiwala, Dehradun (dist.), Uttarakhand, India. March 2006.

Published primary sources

Annual Reports for the Chenab, Jhelum, Chunian and Sohang Para Colonies, for the Year Ending 30 September 1902. Lahore: Civil and Military Gazette Press, 1903.

Annual Report on the Punjab Colonies, 1915–1928. Lahore: Office of the Superintendent, Government Printing, Punjab. 1916–1929 [Several volumes].

Armed Forces Act, 2006. London: The Stationery Office, 2006.

Army Regulations, India; Vol. II: Regulations and Orders for the Army. Calcutta: Office of the Superintendent, Government Printing, India, 1904, 1918, 1923. [Different editions of the same volume].

A Dictionary of the Pathan Tribes on the North-West Frontier of India. Compiled Under the Order of the Quarter Master General in India, in the Intelligence Branch. Calcutta: Office of the Superintendent, Government Printing, India, 1899.

From Sepoy to Subedar: Being the Life and Adventures of Subedar Sita Ram, a Native Officer of the Bengal Army Written and Related by Himself; edited by James Lunt, translated and first published by Lieutenant Colonel James Norgate. London: Routledge and Kegan Paul, 1970 rpt.

Gazetteer of the Chenab Colony, Vol. 31A, 1904. Lahore; Civil and Military Gazette Press, 1904.

Handbook for the Use of Postal Censors (India), 1939. Simla: Government of India Press, 1939.

How Gul Mahomed Joined the King's Army. Simla: G.M. Press, 1918.

Indian Army List. Government of India, 1931–1936.

The Indian Articles of War: As Modified up to the 1st January 1895. Calcutta: Office of the Superintendent, Government Printing, India, 1895.

Indian Hemp Drugs Commission, Supplementary Volume: Answers Received to Selected Questions for the Native Army. Calcutta: Office of the Superintendent of Government Printing, India, 1895.

Indian Voices of the Great War: Soldier's Letters, 1914–1918; selected and introduced by D. Omissi. Basingstoke: MacMillan, 1999.

India's Contribution to the Great War. Published by Authority of the Government of India. Calcutta: Office of the Superintendent. Government Printing, India, 1923.

Manual of Indian Military Law, 1911. Calcutta: Superintendent Government Printing, India, 1922, 2nd edn.

Manual of Physical Training for the Indian Army, 1911. Calcutta: Office of the Superintendent, Government Printing, India, 1911.

Memorandum on the Moral and Material Progress in the Punjab During the Years 1901–02 to 1911–12. Lahore: Office of the Superintendent, Government Printing, Punjab, 1914.

Notes for Officers Wishing to Join the Indian Army. 31st July 1942. Military Department, India Office.

Operations in Waziristan, 1919–1920. Compiled by the General Staff, Army Headquarters. Delhi: Govt. Central Press, 1923 rpt.

Our Sowars and Sepoys: Official Text-Book for the Lower Standard Examination in Urdu. New Delhi: Government of India Press, 1941.

Punjab District Gazetteers: Vol. XXA, Amritsar District, 1914. Lahore: Civil and Military Gazette Press, 1914.

Punjab District Gazetteers: Vol. XXXIVA, Gujranwala District, 1935. Lahore: Office of the Superintendent, Government Printing, Punjab, 1936.

Report on the Administration of the Criminal Tribes in Punjab, for the Year Ending December 1918. Lahore: Office of the Superintendent, Government Printing, Punjab, 1919.

The Review of Religions, Vol. II, No. 3 and 4 (March and April 1903). Qadian, Gurdaspur, Punjab: Published by the Anjuman-i-Isha'at Islam, 1903.

The Review of Religions, Vol. II, No. 1 (January 1903). Qadian, Gurdaspur, Punjab: Published by the Anjuman-i-Isha'at Islam, 1903.

Rules of Procedure, 1907. London: HM Stationery Office, 1907.

Selected Speeches of Subhas Chandra Bose. New Delhi: Publications Division, Ministry of Information and Broadcasting, Govt. of India, 1983 rpt.

Teja Singh Khalsa Joins the Army. Simla: G.M. Press, 1918.

Anon. (Katherine Lourd). *Diary of a Nursing Sister on the Western Front, 1914–1915.* Edinburgh and London: William Blackwood and Sons. 1915.

Barstow, A. E. *The Sikhs: An Ethnology.* Revised at the Request of the Government of India. Delhi: Low Price Publications, 2004 rpt.

Bentham, R. M. *Handbooks for the Indian Army: Marathas and Dekhani Musalmans.* New Delhi: Asian Educational Services, 1996 rpt.

Bingley, A. H. *Handbooks for the Indian Army: Sikhs.* Simla: Government Central Printing Office, 1899.

—. *Class Handbooks for the Indian Army: Dogras.* Revised by A. B. Longden. Calcutta: Office of the Superintendent Government Printing, India, 1910.

Bingley, A. H. and A. Nicholls. *Caste Handbooks for the Indian Army: Brahmans.* Simla: Government Central Printing Office, 1897.

Bristow, R. C. B. *Memories of the British Raj: A Soldier in India.* London; Johnson, 1974.

Cole, B. L. *Handbooks for the Indian Army: Rajputana Classes.* Simla: Government Monotype Press, 1922.

Cubbitt-Smith, H. *Yadgari or Memories of the Raj.* Saxlington, Norfolk: Anchor Press, 1987.

Dhillon, G. S. *From My Bones: Memoirs of Col. Gurbaksh Singh Dhillon of the Indian National Army.* New Delhi: Aryan Books, 1999.

Dobson, B. H. *Final Report on the Chenab Colony Settlement.* Lahore: Office of the Superintendent, Government Printing, Punjab, 1915.

Dow, A. *The History of Hindostan; Translated from the Persian. To Which Are Prefixed Two Dissertations; The First Concerning the Hindoos and the Second on the Origin and Nature of Despotism in India*. London: J. Walker; White and Cochrane; Lackington, Allen and Co.; Black, Parry and Kingsbury; J. Nunn; J. Cuthell; R. Lea; Longman, Hurst, Rees, Orme and Brown; and J. Faulder, 1812 rpt.

Enriquez, C. M. *The Pathan Borderland: A Consecutive Account of the Country and People on and Beyond the Indian Frontier from Chitral to Dera Ismail Khan*. Calcutta and Simla: Thacker, Spink and Co., 1910.

Evatt, J. *Handbooks for the Indian Army: Garhwalis*. Revised by Henderson, K. Calcutta: Office of the Superintendent, Government Printing, India, 1924.

Fitz, W. and Bourne G. *Handbooks for the Indian Army: Hindustani Musalmans and Musalmans of the Eastern Punjab*. Calcutta: Superintendent Government Printing, India, 1914.

Fujiwara I. *F. Kikan: Japanese Army Intelligence Operations in Southeast Asia during World War II*; translated by Akashi Yoji. Hong Kong; Heinemann, 1983.

The General Staff, Army Headquarters. *Operations in Waziristan, 1919-1920*. Delhi: Government Central Press, 1923 2nd edn.

Grimshaw, R. *Indian Cavalry Officer, 1914-1915*. Tunbridge Wells, Kent: Costello, 1986.

Hookway, J. D. (ed.). *M&R: A Regimental History of the Sikh Light Infantry, 1941-1947*. Oxford: Oxford University Computing Services, 1999.

Ibbetson, D. *'Panjab Castes': Being a Reprint of the Chapter on 'The Races, Castes and Tribes of the People' in the Report on the Census of the Punjab Published in 1883 By the Late Sir Denzil Ibbetson, K.C.S.I.* Lahore: Office of the Superintendent, Government Printing, Punjab, 1916.

Jackson, D. *India's Army*. London: Sampson Low, Marston & Co., Ltd., c.1940.

Kasliwal, R. M. *Netaji, Azad Hind Fauj and After*. New Delhi: Today and Tomorrow Printers and Publishers, 1983.

Khan, D. A. H. *Chains to Lose: The Life and Struggle of a Revolutionary, Vol. 1*. Edited by Hasan N. Gardezi. Preface by V. D. Chopra. New Delhi: Patriot Publishers, 1989.

Khan, S. *My Memories of INA & Its Netaji*. Delhi: Rajkumal, 1946.

Kulkarni, V. S. and Murty, K. S. N. (eds). *First Indian National Army Trial*. Poona: Mangal Sahitya Prakashan, 1946.

Lever, J. C. G. *The Sowar and the Jawan: The Soldiers of the Former Indian Army and their Homelands*. Elms Court, Devon: Arthur H. Stockwell Ltd., 1981.

MacMunn, G. *The Armies of India*. Illustrated by A. C. Lovett. Somerton, Somerset: Crécy, 1988 rpt.

—. *The Martial Races of India*. London: Sampson Low, Marston and Co., 1933.

Malcolm, J. *Sketch of the Sikhs; A Singular Nation, Who Inhabit the Provinces of Penjab, Situated Between the Rivers Jumna and Indus*. London: John Murray, Albemarle Street, 1812.

Marsden, W. *A Dictionary of the Malayan Language; To Which Is Prefixed a Grammar with an Introduction and Praxis*. London: Cox and Baylis, 1812.

Marshall, H. *Military Miscellany; Comprehending a History of the Recruiting of the Army, Military Punishments, &c, &c*. London: John Murray, Albemarle Street, 1846.

Menon, K. A. K. *From the Diary of a Freedom Fighter*. Madras: Kavungal Anat, 1989.

Mereweather, J. W. B. and Smith, F. *The Indian Corps in France*. London: John Murray, 1919, 2nd edn.

Movat, G. E. T. *Handbooks for the Indian Army: Madras Classes*. Calcutta: Government of India, Central Publication Branch, 1927.

O'Dwyer, Michael. *India as I Knew It*. London: Cornstable and Co., 1925.

Pauw, C. S. *Report on the Tenth Settlement of the Garhwal District*. Allahabad: North-Western Provinces and Oudh Government Press, 1896.

Pinney, T. (ed.), *The Letters of Rudyard Kipling, Vol, 4, 1911–19*. London: Macmillan, 1999.

Prasad, B. (ed.), *Official History of the Indian Armed Forces in the Second World War, 1939–1945*. Kanpur and Calcutta: Orient Longmans, 1958–1963. [Numerous Volumes].

Ridgway, R. T. I. *Handbooks for the Indian Army: Pathans*. Calcutta: Office of the Superintendent, Government Printing, India, 1910.

Roberts, F. S. *Forty-One Years in India: From Subaltern to Commander-in-Chief, Vols. I and II*. London: Richard Bentley & Son, 1897.

Sareen, T. R. (ed.). *Indian National Army: A Documentary Study, Vols. 1 (1941–1942)*. New Delhi: Gyan, 2004a.

—. *Indian National Army: A Documentary Study, Vol. 2 (1943–1944)*. New Delhi: Gyan, 2004b.

—. *Indian National Army: A Documentary Study, Vol. 3 (1943–1944)*. New Delhi: Gyan, 2004c.

—. *Secret Documents on Singapore Mutiny, 1915. Vols. 1 and 2*. New Delhi: Mounto, 1995.

Sharma, G. *Valour and Sacrifice: Famous Regiments of the Indian Army*. New Delhi: Allied, 1990.

Singh, B. N. and Kirpal Singh, B. *Struggle for Free Hindustan: Ghadr Movement, Vol. 1, 1905–1916*. New Delhi: Atlantic Publishers & Distributors, 1986.

Singh, J. *In the Battle for Liberation*. New Delhi: National Book Centre, 1990.

Singh, M. *Soldiers' Contribution to Indian Independence*. New Delhi: Army Educational Stores, 1974.

Singh, R. *History of the Indian Army*. New Delhi: Sardar Attar Singh Army Educational Stores, 1963.

Vansittart, E. *Handbooks for the Indian Army: Gurkhas*. Revised by Nicolay, B. V. Calcutta: Office of the Superintendent, Government Printing, India, 1915.

Wikeley, J. M. *Handbooks for the Indian Army: Punjabi Musalmans*. Calcutta: Office of the Superintendent, Government Printing, India, 1915.

Willoughby, Maurice. *Echo of a Distant Drum: The Last Generation of Empire*. Lewes, East Sussex: Book Guild, 2001.

Wilson, W. Arthur. *Mutiny Musings and Volunteer Sketches*. With a Preface by B.-G. Dudley H. Ridout, CMG, GOC Troops, Straits Settlements. Singapore: Kally and Walsh, 1916.

Yadav, K. *British Lions and the Indian Tigers: Triumph of the Sepoy against the British Sword*. New Delhi: Manas Publications, 2004.

Yeats-Brown, F. *Martial India*. London: Eyre and Spottiswoode, 1945.

Younghusband, G. *Forty Years a Soldier*. London: Herbert Jenkins, 1923?.

Secondary sources

Articles and Chapters

Aldrich, R. J. 'Britain's Secret Intelligence Service in Asia during the Second World War'. *Modern Asian Studies*, Vol. 32, No. 1, February, 1998, pp. 179–217.

Ansari, K. H. 'Pan-Islam and the Making of the Early Indian Muslim Socialists'. *Modern Asian Studies*, Vol. 20, No. 3, 1986, pp. 509–37.

Arnold, D. 'The Armed Police and Colonial Rule in South India, 1914–1947'. *Modern Asian Studies*, Vol. 11, No. 1, 1977, pp. 101–25.

Bailey, V. 'The Fabrication of Deviance: "Dangerous Classes" and "Criminal Classes" in Victorian England'. In J. Rule and R. Malcolmson (eds). *Protest and Survival: The Historical Experience; Essays for E.P. Thompson*. London: Merlin Press, 1993.

Bates, C. 'Race, Caste and Tribe in Central India: the Early Origins of Indian Anthropometry'. In P. Robb (ed.). *The Concept of Race in South Asia*. Delhi: Oxford University Press, 1995.

Bhabha, H. K. 'In a Spirit of Calm Violence'. In G. Prakash (ed.). *After Colonialism: Imperial Histories and Postcolonial Displacement*. Princeton, NJ: Princeton University Press, 1995.

Caplan, L. '"Bravest of the Brave": Representations of 'The Gurkha' in British Military Writings'. *Modern Asian Studies*, Vol. 25, No. 3, July 1991, pp. 571–97.

Cohen, S. P. 'Subhas Chandra Bose and the Indian National Army'. *Pacific Affairs*, Vol. 36, No. 4, Winter, 1963–1964, pp. 411–29.

—. 'The Untouchable Soldier: Caste, Politics and the Indian Army'. *Journal of Asian Studies*, Vol. 28, No. 3, May 1969, pp. 453–68.

Constable, P. 'The Marginalization of a *Dalit* Martial Race in Late Nineteenth and Early Twentieth Century Western India'. *Journal of Asian Studies*, Vol. 60, No. 2, May 2001, pp. 439–78.

Cronier, E. *Les Poilus*. In M.-F. Auzépy and J. Cornette (eds). *Histoire du Poil*. Paris: Belin, 2011.

Douglas, R. 'Voluntary Enlistment in the First World War and the Work of the Parliamentary Recruiting Committee'. *The Journal of Modern History*, Vol. 42, No. 4. December 1970, pp. 564–85.

Ellinwood, D. C. 'Ethnicity in a Colonial Asian Army: British Policy, War, and the Indian Army, 1914–1918'. In D. C. Ellinwood and C. H. Enloe (eds). *Ethnicity and the Military in Asia*. New Brunswick, NJ: Transaction, 1981.

Elsey, E. 'Disabled Ex-Servicemen's Experiences of Rehabilitation and Employment after the First World War'. *Oral History*, Vol. 25, No. 2, Autumn 1997, pp. 49–58.

Greenhut, J. 'The Imperial Reserve: The Indian Corps on the Western Front, 1914–15'. *The Journal of Imperial and Commonwealth History*, Vol. 12, No. 1, pp. 54–73.

—. 'Sahib and Sepoy: An Inquiry into the Relationship between the British Officers and Native Soldiers of the British Indian Army'. *Military Affairs*, Vol. 48, No. 1, January 1984, pp. 15–18.

Gupta, A. K. 'The Garhwali Mutiny, Peshawar, 22–4 April 1930'. In R. Dayal (ed.). *We Fought Together For Freedom: Chapters from the Indian National Movement*. Delhi: Oxford University Press, 1995.

Haron, N. 'Colonial Defence and British Approach to the Problems in Malaya, 1874–1918'. *Modern Asian Studies*, Vol. 24, No. 2, May 1990, pp. 275–95.

Hyam, R. 'Empire and Sexual Opportunity'. *The Journal of Imperial and Commonwealth History*, Vol. XIV, No. 2, January 1986, pp. 34–90.

Jones, J. 'The Local Experiences of Reformist Islam in a 'Muslim' Town in Colonial India: The Case of Amroha'. *Modern Asian Studies*, Vol. 43, No. 4, 2009, pp. 871–908.

Katz, J. G. 'Shaykh Ahmad's Dream: A 19th Century Eschatological Vision'. *Studia Islamica*, No. 79, 1994, pp. 157–80.

Ketalaar, E. 'Archival Temples, Archival Prisons: Modes of Power and Protection'. Archival Science, Vol. 2, 2002, pp. 221–38.

Kirk-Greene, A. H. M. '"Damnosa Hereditas": Ethnic Ranking and the Martial Races Imperative in Africa'. *Ethnic and Racial Studies*, Vol. 3, 1980, pp. 393–414.

Leese, P. 'Problems Returning Home: The British Psychological Casualties of the Great War'. *The Historical Journal*, Vol. 40, No. 4, 1997, pp. 1055–67.

Levine, Philippa. 'Battle Colors: Race, Sex, and Colonial Soldiery in World War I'. *Journal of Women's History*, Vol. 9. No. 4, 1998, pp. 104–30.

Mandelbaum, D. G. 'The Study of Life History: Gandhi'. *Current Anthropology*, Vol. 14, No. 3, June 1973, pp. 177–206.

Menezes, S. L. 'Race, Caste, Mutiny and Discipline in the Indian Army, from its Origins to 1947'. In A. J. Guy and P. B. Bowden (eds). *Soldiers of the Raj: The Indian Army 1600–1947*. Coventry: Clifford Press, 1997.

Mills, J. 'The History of Modern Psychiatry in India, 1858–1947'. *History of Psychiatry*, Vol. 12, 2001, pp. 431–58.

Peers, D. M. '"The Habitual Nobility of Being": British Officers and the Social Construction of the Bengal Army in the Early Nineteenth Century'. *Modern Asian Studies*, Vol. 25, No. 3, 1991, pp. 545–69.

—. '"Those Noble Exemplars of the True Military Tradition": Constructions of the Indian Army in the Mid-Victorian Press'. *Modern Asian Studies*, Vol. 31, No. 1, February 1997, pp. 109–42.

—. 'Sepoys, Soldiers and the Lash: Race, Caste and Army Discipline in India, 1820–1850'. *Journal of Imperial and Commonwealth History*, Vol. 23, No. 2, May 1995, pp. 211–47.

Prakash, G. 'Writing Post-Orientalist Histories of the Third World: Perspectives from Indian Historiography'. *Comparative Studies in Society and History*, Vol. 32, No. 2, April 1990, pp. 383–408.

Raheja, G. G. 'Caste, Colonialism and the Speech of the Colonized: Entextualization and Disciplinary Control in India'. *American Ethnologist*, Vol. 23, No. 3, August 1996, pp. 494–513.

Safadi, A. 'From *Sepoy to Subedar/Khvab-o-Khayal* and Douglas Craven Phillott'. *The Annual of Urdu Studies*, Vol. 25, 2010.

Sevea, I. S. 'The Ahmadiyya Print Jihad in South and Southeast Asia'. In R. Michael Feener and T. Sevea (eds). *Islamic Connections: Muslim Societies in South and Southeast Asia*. Singapore: Institute of South East Asian Studies, 2009.

Smith, L. V. 'Narrative and Identity at the Front: "Theory and the Poor Bloody Infantry"'. In J. Winter, G. Parker and M. R. Habek (eds). *The Great War and the Twentieth Century*. New Haven, CT: Yale University Press, 2000.

Spivak, G. C. 'Can the Subaltern Speak'. In C. Nelson and L. Grossberg (eds), *Marxism and the Interpretation of Culture*. Macmillan: Basingstoke, 1988.

—. 'Rani of Sirmur: An Essay in Reading the Archives'. *History and Theory*, Vol. 24, No. 3, October 1985, pp. 247–72.

Stoler, A. L. 'Sexual Affronts and Racial Frontiers: European Identities and the Cultural Politics of Exclusion in Colonialist Southeast Asia'. *Comparative Studies in Society and History*, Vol. 34, 1992, pp. 514–51.

—. 'Developing Historical Negatives: Race and the (Modernist) Visions of a Colonial State'. In B. K. Axel (ed.). *From the Margins: Historical Anthropology and Its Futures*. Durham, North Carolina: Duke University Press, 2002.

Stoler, A. L. and Cooper, F. 'Between Metropole and Colony: Rethinking a Research Agenda'. In F. Cooper and A. L. Stoler (eds). *Tensions of Empire: Colonial Cultures in a Bourgeois World*. Berkeley, CA: California University Press, 1997.

Sullivan, Z. T. 'Race, Gender and Imperial Ideology in the Nineteenth Century'. *Nineteenth Century Contexts*, Vol. 13, No. 1, 1989, pp. 19–32.

Tan, T.-Y. 'An Imperial Home-Front: Punjab and the First World War'. *Journal of Military History*, Vol. 64, No. 2, April 2000, pp. 371–410.

—. 'Assuaging the Sikhs: Government Responses to the Akali Movement, 1920–1925'. *Modern Asian Studies*, Vol. 29, No. 3, July 1995, pp. 655–703.

—. 'Maintaining the Military Districts: Civil-Military Integration and District Soldiers' Boards in the Punjab, 1919–1939'. *Modern Asian Studies*, Vol. 28, No. 4, October 1994, pp. 833–74.

Tarling, N. 'The Singapore Mutiny, 1915'. *Journal of the Malaysian Branch of the Royal Asiatic Society*, Vol. LV, Part 2, 1982.

Werbner, P. 'Murids of the Saint: Migration, Diaspora and Redemptive Sociality in Sufi Regional and Global Cults'. In I. Talbot and S. Thindi (eds). *People on the Move: Punjabi Colonial and Post-Colonial Migration*. Oxford: Oxford University Press, 2004.

Books

Alavi, S. *The Sepoys and the Company: Transition and Change in Northern India, 1770-1830*. Delhi: Oxford University Press, 1995.

Aldrich, R. J. *Intelligence and the War against Japan: Britain, America and the Politics of Secret Service*. Cambridge: Cambridge University Press, 2000.

Allen, R. L. *The Port Chicago Mutiny*. New York: Warner Books, 1989.

Amin, S. *Event, Metaphor, Memory: Chauri Chaura, 1922-1992*. Berkeley, CA: California University Press, 1995.

Amin, S. and Chakrabarty, D. (eds). *Subaltern Studies IX: Writings on South Asian History and Society*. New Delhi: Oxford University Press, 1996.

Anand, M. R. *Across the Black Waters*. New Delhi: Orient Paperbacks, 2000 rpt.

—. *The Sword and the Sickle*. London: Jonathan Cape, 1942.

Anderson, C. *Convicts in the Indian Ocean: Transportation from South Asia to Mauritius, 1815-53*. Basingstoke, Hampshire: Macmillan, 2000.

Arnold, D. and Hardiman, D. (eds). *Subaltern Studies VIII: Essays in Honour of Ranajit Guha*. Delhi: Oxford University Press, 2005 rpt.

Arnold, D. and Blackburn, S. (eds), *Telling Lives in India: Biography, Autobiography, and Life History*. Indianapolis: Indiana University Press, 2004.

Bakhtin, M. M. *The Dialogic Imagination: Four Essays*. Edited by Michael Holquist; translated by Caryl Emerson and Michael Holquist. Austin, TX: Texas University Press, 2006 rpt.

Barley, N. *Rogue Raider: The Tale of Captain Lauterbach and the Singapore Mutiny*. Singapore: Monsoon, 2006.

Ballhatchet, K. *Race, Sex and Class under the Raj: Imperial Attitudes and Policies and their Critics, 1793-1905*. London: Weidenfeld and Nicolson, 1980.

Bayly, C. A. and Harper, T. *Forgotten Armies: The Fall of British Asia, 1941-1945*. London: Allen Lane, 2004.

—. *Forgotten Wars: The End of Britain's Asian Empire*. London: Penguin, 2008 rpt.

Bayly, C. A. *Indian Society and the Making of the British Empire*. Cambridge: Cambridge University Press, 1988.

—. *Rulers, Townsmen and Bazaars: North Indian Society in the Age of British Expansion, 1770-1870*. Cambridge: Cambridge University Press, 1983.

—. *Empire and Information: Intelligence Gathering and Social Communication in India, 1780-1870*. Cambridge: Cambridge University Press, 1996.

Beaumont, R. A. *The Hidden Truth: A Tribute to the Indian Independence Movement in Thailand*. Based on the recollections of Darshan Singh Bajaj. London: Minerva Press, 1999.

Bhabha, H. K. *The Location of Culture*. Abingdon, Oxford: Routledge, 2004 rpt.

—. *The Location of Culture*. London: Routledge Classics, 2006 rpt.

Bose, M. *The Lost Hero: A Biography of Subhas Bose*. London: Quartet, 1982.

Bose, S. *His Majesty's Opponent: Subhas Chandra Bose and India's Struggle Against Empire*. Cambridge, MA: Harvard University Press, 2011.

Buchanon, A. R. *Black Americans in World War II*. Santa Barbara, CA: Clio, 1997.
Burton, A. (ed.). *Archive Stories: Facts, Fictions and the Writing of History*. Durham and London: Duke University Press, 2005.
Caplain, L. *Warrior Gentlemen: "Gurkhas" in the Western Imagination*. Providence, Rhode Island: Berghahn Books, 1995.
Certeau, M. de. *Heterologies: Discourse on the Other*. Translated by Brian Massumi; foreword by Wlad Godzich. Minneapolis, MN: Minnesota University Press, 1986.
—. *The Mystic Fable, Volume One: The Sixteenth and Seventeenth Centuries*; translated by Michael B. Smith. Chicago, IL: Chicago University Press, 1995.
—. *The Possession at Loudon*. Translated by Michael. B. Smith; foreword by Stephen Greenblatt. Chicago and London: Chicago University Press, 2000.
—. *The Practice of Everyday Life*. Translated by Steven Randall. Berkeley, Los Angeles and London: California University Press, 1988.
Chakrabarty, D. *Habitations of Modernity: Essays in the Wake of Subaltern Studies*. Delhi: Permanent Black, 2002.
—. *Provincializing Europe: Postcolonial Thought and Historical Difference*. New Delhi: Oxford University Press, 2001.
Chatterjee, P. and Pandey, G. (eds). *Subaltern Studies VII: Writings on South Asian History and Society*. Delhi: Oxford University Press, 2005 rpt.
Chaturvedi, V. (ed.). *Mapping Subaltern Studies and the Postcolonial*. London: Verso, 2000.
Cohen, S. P. *The Indian Army: Its Contribution to the Development of a Nation*. Berkeley, CA: California University Press, 1971.
Cohn, B. S. *Colonialism and its Forms of Knowledge: The British in India*. New Delhi: Oxford University Press, 2002.
Collingham, E. M. *Imperial Bodies: The Physical Experience of the Raj, c.1800-1947*. Molden, MA: Polity, 2002.
Collins, J. *Dr Brighton's Indian Patients: December 1914 - January 1916*. Brighton: Brighton Books, 1997.
Corrigan, G. *Sepoys in the Trenches: The Indian Corps on the Western Front, 1914-1915*. Staplehurst, Kent: Spellmount, 1999.
Cortright, D. *Soldiers in Revolt: GI Resistance During the Vietnam War*. Introduction by Howard Zinn. Chicago: Haymarket Books, 2005 rpt.
Das, S. T. *Indian Military: Its History and Development*. New Delhi; Sagar Publications, 1969.
Das, S. *Touch and Intimacy in First World War Literature*. Cambridge: Cambridge University Press, 2008 rpt.
—. (ed.). *Race, Empire and First World War Writing*. Cambridge: Cambridge University Press, 2011.
Derrida, J. *Archive Fever: A Freudian Impression*. Translated by Eric Prenowitz. Chicago: Chicago UP, 1996.
—. *A Derrida Reader: Between the Blinds*. Edited by Peggy Kamuf. New York: Columbia University Press, 1991.

—. *Of Grammatology*. Translated by Gayatri Chakravorty Spivak. Baltimore, Maryland: John Hopkins University Press, 1997 rpt.

Deshpande, A. *British Military Policy in India, 1900–1945: Colonial Constraints and Declining Power*. New Delhi: Manohar, 2005.

Dirks, N. B. *Castes of Mind: Colonialism and the Making of Modern India*. Princeton, NJ: Princeton University Press, 2001.

Downing, W. H. *Digger Dialects*; J. M. Arthur and W. S. Ramson (eds). Melbourne: Oxford University Press, 1990.

Durkheim, E. *Suicide: A Study in Sociology*. Translated by John A. Spalding and George Simpson. Edited and with an introduction by George Simpson. London: Routledge, 2002 rpt.

Echenberg, M. *Colonial Conscripts: The Tirailleurs Senegalais in French West Africa, 1857–1960*. Portsmouth, New Hampshire: Heinemann, 1991.

Eder, M. D. *War-Shock: The Psycho-Neuroses in War Psychology and Treatment*. London: William Heinemann, 1917.

Fanon, F. *Black Skins. White Masks*; translated by C. L. Markmann. London: Pluto, 1986.

Farrell, J. G. *Singapore Grip*. London: Wiedenfeld and Nicolson, 1978.

Farwell, B. *Armies of the Raj: From the Mutiny to Independence, 1858–1960*. London: Viking, 1989.

Fay, P. W. *The Forgotten Army: India's Armed Struggle for Independence, 1942–1945*. Ann Arbor, MI: Michigan University Press, 1993.

Fenech, L. E. *Martyrdom in the Sikh Tradition: Playing the 'Game of Love'*. New Delhi: Oxford University Press, 2000.

Fenimore Cooper, J. *The Last of the Mohicans*. Introduction and Notes by David Blair. Ware, Hertfordshire: Wordsworth, 2002 rpt.

Finer, S. E. *The Man on Horseback: The Role of the Military in Politics*. Harmonsworth, Middlesex: Penguin, 1976 rpt.

Forrest, A. *Conscripts and Deserters: The Army and French Society During the Revolution and Empire*. New York: Oxford University Press, 1988.

Foucault, M. *Discipline & Punish: The Birth of the Prison*. Translated by Alan Sheriden. New York: Vintage Books, 1979.

—. *Power/Knowledge: Selected Interviews & Other Writings, 1972–1977*. Edited by Colin Gordon. Translated by Colin Gordon, Leo Marshall, John Mepham and Kate Sopher. New York: Pantheon Books, 1980 rpt.

Friel, B. *Translations*. London: Faber and Faber, 2000 rpt.

Fuller, J. G. *Troop Morale and Popular Culture in the British and Dominion Armies, 1914–1918*. Oxford: Clarendon Press, 1991.

Gawankar, R. *The Women's Regiment and Captain Lakshmi of the INA: An Untold Episode of NRI Women's Contribution to India's Freedom Struggle*. New Delhi: Devika Publishers, 2003.

Getz, M. J. *Subhas Chandra Bose: A Biography*. Jefferson, NC: McFarland & Co., 2002.

Ghosh, A. *The Glass Palace*. London: HarperCollins, 2001 rpt.

Ginzburg, C. *The Cheese and the Worms: The Cosmos of a Sixteenth-Century Miller*; translated by John and Anne Tedeschi. London: Penguin, 1992.

Gooch, J. *A History of Brighton General Hospital*. London: Phillimore, 1980.

Gordon, L. A. *Brothers Against the Raj*. New York: Columbia University Press, 1990.

Green, N. *Islam and the Army in Colonial India: Sepoy Religion in the Service of Empire*. New Delhi: Cambridge University Press, 2009.

Guha, R. *Elementary Aspects of Peasant Insurgency in Colonial India*. Delhi: Oxford University Press, 1992 rpt.

—. (ed.), *The Small Voice of History: Collected Essays*; edited and with an introduction by Patha Chatterjee. New Delhi: Permanent Black, 2009.

—. *A Subaltern Studies Reader, 1986–1995*. Minneapolis: Minnesota University Press, 1995.

—. *Subaltern Studies I: Writings on South Asian History and Society*. Delhi: Oxford University Press, 2005a rpt.

—. *Subaltern Studies II: Writings on South Asian History and Society*. Delhi: Oxford University Press, 2005b rpt.

—. *Subaltern Studies III: Writings on South Asian History and Society*. Delhi: Oxford University Press, 2005c rpt.

—. *Subaltern Studies IV: Writings on South Asian History and Society*. Delhi: Oxford University Press, 2005d rpt.

—. *Subaltern Studies V: Writings on South Asian History and Society*. Delhi: Oxford University Press, 2005e rpt.

—. *Subaltern Studies VI: Writings on South Asian History and Society*. Delhi: Oxford University Press, 2005f rpt.

Guha, R. and Spivak, G. C. *Selected Subaltern Studies*. Oxford: Oxford University Press, 1988.

Gupta, P. S. and Deshpande, A. (eds). *British Raj and its Indian Armed Forces, 1857–1939*. New Delhi: Oxford University Press, 2002.

Harfield, A. *British and Indian Armies in the East Indies, 1685–1935*. Chippenham, Wiltshire: Picton, 1984.

Harper, R. W. E. and H. Miller. *Singapore Mutiny*. Singapore. Oxford University Press, 1984.

Hašek, J. *The Good Soldier Schweik*. Illustrated by Joseph Lada; translated by Paul Selver. Harmondsworth, Middlesex: Penguin, 1941.

Haynes, D. E. and Prakash, G. *Contesting Power: Resistance and Everyday Social Relations in South Asia*. Delhi: Oxford University Press, 1991.

Heathcote, T. A. *The Military in British India: The Development of British Land Forces in South Asia, 1600–1947*. Manchester: Manchester University Press, 1995.

Huntington, S. P. *The Soldier and the State: The Theory and Politics of Civil-Military Relations*. Cambridge, MA: Harvard University Press, 1964.

Islam, R. (ed.), *Kazi Nazrul Islam: A New Anthology*. Dhaka: Bangla Academy, 1990.

Jackson, P. *One of the Boys: Homosexuality in the Military during World War II*. Montreal and Kingston: McGill-Queens University Press, 2004.

James, L. *Mutiny in the British and Commonwealth Forces, 1797–1956*. London: Buchan and Enright, 1987.

Johnson, J. J. (ed.). *The Role of the Military in Underdeveloped Countries*. Princeton, NJ: Princeton University Press, 1967 rpt.

Kaushik, S. N. *Amadiya Community in Pakistan: Discrimination, Travail and Alienation*. New Delhi: South Asian Publishers, 1996.

Kilfeather, T. P. *The Connaught Rangers*. Tralee, County Kerry: Anvil, 1969.

Kimber, H. *San Fairy Ann*. London: Robert Holden & Co., 1927.

Kipling, R. *The Complete Barrack-Room Ballads*. Edited by Charles Carrington. London: Methuen & Co., 1973.

—. *The Eyes of Asia*. Gloucester: Dodo Press: 2011 rpt.

—. *Kim*. Oxford: Oxford University Press, 1998.

Kundu, A. *Militarism in India: The Army and Civil Society in Consensus*. London: Taurus Academic Studies, 1998.

Kuwajima, S. *The Mutiny in Singapore: War, Anti-War and the War for India's Independence*. New Delhi: Rainbow Publishers, 2006.

Lebra, J. C. *Japanese-Trained Armies in Southeast Asia: Independence and Volunteer Forces in World War II*. Hong Kong: Heinemann, 1977.

Leibau, H., Bromber, K., Lange, K., Hamzah, D. and Ahuja, R. (eds.). *The World in World Wars*. Leiden & Boston: Brill, 2010.

Marx, K. and Engels, F. *The First Indian War of Independence, 1857–1859*. Moscow: Progress Publishers, 1988 rpt.

Mason, P. *A Matter of Honour: An Account of the Indian Army, Its Officers and Men*. London: Jonathan Cape, 1974.

Mathur, L. P. *Indian Revolutionary Movement in the United States of America*. Delhi: S. Chand and Co., 1970.

Mayaram, S., Pandian, M. S. S., and Skaria, A. (eds). *Subaltern Studies XII: Muslims, Dalits and the Fabrications of History*. Delhi: Oxford University Press, 2005.

Mazumdar, R. K. *The Indian Army and the Making of Punjab*. Delhi: Permanent Black, 2003.

Memmi, A. *The Colonizer and the Colonized: A Destructive Relationship*. Penang, Malaysia: Citizens International, 2005 rpt.

Menezes, S. L. *Fidelity and Honour: The Indian Army from the Seventeenth to the Twenty-First Century*. New Delhi: Oxford University Press, 1999.

Metcalf, T. R. *The Aftermath of Revolt: India, 1857–1970*. Princeton, NJ: Princeton University Press, 1964.

Mills, P. and Colquhoun, J. *Charley's War, 1 August 1916 – 17 October 1916*. London: Titan Books, 2005.

Mitchell, T. (ed.). *Questions of Modernity*. Minneapolis: University of Minnesota Press, 2000.

Moore-Gilbert, B. *Postcolonial Theory: Contexts, Practices, Politics*. London: Verso, 1997.

Moranweiser, K. *British Empire Civil Censorship Devices in World War II, Section 4: British Asia*. Civil Censorship Study Group, 1997.

Mukherjee, R. *Mangal Pandey: Brave Martyr or Accidental Hero?* New Delhi: Penguin, 2005.

Myers, C. S. *Shell Shock in France, 1914–1918: Based on a War Diary Kept by Charles S. Myers, CBE, FRS, Temporary Lieutenant-Colonel, Royal Army Medical Corps, Sometimes Consulting Psychologist to British Armies in France*. Cambridge: Cambridge University Press, 1940.

Nandy, A. *Exiled at Home: Comprising at the Edge of Psychology, The Intimate Enemy and Creating a Nationality*. Delhi: Oxford University Press, 1998.

Omissi, D. *The Sepoy and the Raj: The Indian Army, 1860–1940*. London: Macmillan, 1994.

Oram, G. *Worthless Men: Race, Eugenics and the Death Penalty in the British Army During the First World War*. London: Francis Boutle, 1998.

Pandey, G. *Remembering Partition: Violence, Nationalism and History in India*. New Delhi: Cambridge University Press, 2003 rpt.

—. *Routine Violence: Nations, Fragments, Histories*. New Delhi: Permanent Black, 2006.

Parsons, T. H. *The African Rank-and-File: Social Implications of Colonial Military Service in the King's African Rifles, 1902–1964*. Portsmouth, New Hampshire: Heinemann, 1999.

—. *The 1964 Army Mutinies and the Making of Modern East Africa*. Westport, CT: Praeger, 2003.

Pasha, M. K. *Colonial Political Economy: Recruitment and Underdevelopment in the Punjab*. Karachi: Oxford University Press, 1998.

Peers, D. M. *Between Mars and Mammon: Colonial Armies and the Garrison State in India, 1819–1835*. London: Tauris, 1995.

Perlmutter, A. *The Military and Politics in Modern Times: On Professionals, Praetorians, and Revolutionary Soldiers*. New Haven: Yale University Press, 1977.

Pollock, S. *Mutiny for the Cause*. London: Sphere, 1971.

Powell, A. A. *Muslims and Missionaries in Pre-Colonial India*. Richmond: Curzon, 1993.

Prakash, G. (ed.). *After Colonialism: Imperial Histories and Postcolonial Displacements*. Princeton, NJ: Princeton University Press, 1995.

Putkowski, J. and Sykes, J. *Shot at Dawn*. Barnsley, South Yorkshire: Wharncliffe, 1989.

Ramnath, M. *Haj to Utopia: How the Ghadar Movement Charted Global Radicalism and Attempted to Overthrow the British Empire*. Berkeley: University of California Press, 2011.

Rancière, J. *The Names of History*; translated by Hassan Melehy. Minneapolis: University of Minnesota Press, 1994.

Rivers, W. H. R. *Instinct and the Unconscious: A Contribution to a Biological Theory of the Psycho-Neuroses*. Cambridge: Cambridge University Press, 1924 rpt.

Rosen, S. P. *Society & Military Power: India and Its Armies*. Ithaca, NY: Cornell University Press, 1996.

Roy, F., Leibau, H. and Ahuja, R. (eds). *'When the War Began We Heard of Several Kings': South Asian Prisoners in World War I Germany*. New Delhi: Social Science Press, 2011.

Roy, K. *Brown Warriors of the Raj: Recruitment and the Mechanics of Command in the Sepoy Army, 1859-1913*. New Delhi: Manohar, 2008.

—. (ed.). *The Indian Army in the Two World Wars*. Leiden and Boston: Brill, 2012.

Rubin, G. R. *Murder, Mutiny and the Military: British Court Martial Cases, 1940-1966*. London: Francis Boutle, 2005.

Said, E. W. *Orientalism: Western Conceptions of the Orient*. London: Penguin, 1995.

Sassoon, S. *Sherston's Progress*. London: Faber and Faber, 1936.

Scott, J. C. *The Art of Not Being Governed: An Anarchist History of Upland Southeast Asia*. New Haven, CT: Yale University Press, 2009.

—. *Domination and the Arts of Resistance: Hidden Transcripts*. New Haven, CT: Yale University Press, 1990.

—. *The Moral Economy of the Peasant: Rebellion and Subsistence in Southeast Asia*. New Haven, CT: Yale University Press, 1979.

—. *Weapons of the Weak: Everyday Forms of Peasant Resistance*. New Haven, CT: Yale University Press, 1985.

Scott, P. *The Day of the Scorpion*. London: Heinemann, 1975 rpt.

Scott, W. *Waverley*. London: Dent, 1905.

Sen, S. *Disciplining Punishment: Colonialism and Convict Society in the Andaman Islands*. New Delhi: Oxford University Press, 2000.

Shephard, B. *A War of Nerves*. London: Jonathan Cape, 2000.

Singh, I. *History of Malay States Guides: 1873-1919*. Penang: Cathay Printers Limited, 1965.

Skaria, A. *Hybrid Histories: Forests, Frontiers and Wildness in Western India*. Delhi: Oxford University Press, 1999.

Smith, G. *When Jim Crow Met John Bull: Black American Soldiers in World War II Britain*. London: I.B. Taurus & Co., 1987.

Smith, L. V. *Between Mutiny and Obedience: The Case of the French Fifth Infantry Division during World War 1*. Princeton, NJ: Princeton University Press, 1994.

—. *The Embattled Self: French Soldiers' Testimony of the Great War*. Ithaca, NY: Cornell University Press, 2007.

Smith, R. *Jamaican Volunteers in the First World War: Race, Masculinity and the Development of National Consciousness*. Manchester: Manchester University Press, 2004.

Spivak, G. C. *A Critique of Postcolonial Reason: Toward a History of the Vanishing Present*. Cambridge, MA: Harvard University Press, 2003 rpt.

—. *Other Asias*. Malden, MA: Blackwell, 2008.

—. *The Post-Colonial Critic: Interviews, Strategies, Dialogues*; edited by Sarah Harasym. London: Routledge, 1990.

Stoler, A. L. *Along the Archival Grain: Epistemic Anxieties and Colonial Common Sense*. Princeton, NJ: Princeton University Press, 2009.

—. *Carnal Knowledge and Imperial Power: Race and the Intimate in Colonial Rule*. Berkeley, Los Angeles and London: California University Press, 2002.

—. (ed.). *Haunted by Empire: Geographies of Intimacy in North American History*. Durham and London: Duke University Press, 2006.

Streets, H. *Martial Races: The Military, Race and Masculinity in British Imperial Culture, 1857–1914*. Manchester: Manchester University Press, 2004.

Sue-White, B. *Turbans and Traders: Hong Kong's Indian Communities*. Hong Kong: Oxford University Press, 1994.

Tan, T.-Y. *The Garrison State: The Military, Government and Society in Colonial Punjab, 1849–1947*. New Delhi: Sage, 2005.

Thomas, L. *Lauterbach of the China Sea: The Escapes and Adventures of a Sea-Going Falstaff*. London: Hutchinson & Co., 1931.

Thomas, R. C. W. *The Soldier's Pocket Book*. London: Montague House, 1955.

Toye, H. *The Springing Tiger: Subhash Chandra Bose*. Bombay: Jaico, 1991 rpt.

Trench, C. C. *The Indian Army and the King's Enemies, 1900–1947*. London: Thames and Hudson, 1988.

Trotsky, L. *The History of the Russian Revolution*. Vols 1–3. Translated by Max Eastman. London: Sphere Books, 1967 rpt.

—. *Military Writings*. New York: Merit, 1969.

Walter, H. A. *The Religious Life of India: The Ahmadiya Movement*. Calcutta: Association Press, 1918.

Wickremesekera, C. *"Best Black Troops in the World": British Perceptions and the Making of the Sepoy, 1746–1805*. New Delhi: Manohar, 2002.

Wisram, R. *Indians in Britain*. London: B.T. Batsford Ltd., 1987.

Woddis, J. *Armies and Politics*. London: Lawrence and Wishart, 1977.

Wolpin, M. D. *Militarism and Social Revolution in the Third World*. Totowa, NJ: Allanheld, Osmun & Co., 1981.

Young, R. J. C. *Colonial Desire: Hybridity in Theory, Culture and Race*. London and New York: Routledge, 1995.

—. *Postcolonialism: An Historical Introduction*. Oxford: Blackwell, 2009 rpt.

—. *White Mythologies: Writing History and the West*. London and New York: Routledge, 1990.

Film

Kubrick, S. (dir.). *Full Metal Jacket*. 1987.

—. *Paths of Glory*. 1957.

Mehta, K. (dir.). *Mangal Pandey: The Rising*. 2005.

Milliarium Z. and Winterfilm, in association with Vietnam Veterans Against the War. *Winter Soldier*. 1971.
Scheffner, P. (dir.). *The Halfmoon Files: A Ghost Story.* 2007.
'Space Seed'; *Star Trek, The Original Series.* Series 1, Episode 2. 1967.

Unpublished

Jain, A. 'The Eyes of Asia: Introduction'. http://www.kipling.org.uk/rg_asia_intro.htm#4.
Putkowski, J. 'Private Nelson'. http://www.shotatdawn.info/page22.html.

Index

A Dictionary to the Pathan Tribes   25
Ahmadiyya movement   104–9
Alam Shah, Pir Nur   133
Anand, Mulk Raj
   Across the Black Waters   97–8
Army Regulations, India   42, 45–6, 77
Arnold, David   191
Auchinleck, Claude   178
Azad, Maulana Abul Kalam   107
Azad Hind Fauj   158–9, 169, 173, 176, 242n. 3
Azad School   174

Baden-Powell, Robert   48
Bakhtin, Mikhail Mikhailovich
   The Dialogic Imagination   194n. 25
   'Discourse in the Novel'   7
Balidan (play)   170, 173
Barley, Nigel
   Rogue Raider   134
Barstow, A. E.   21–2
Bayly, Christopher
   Forgotten Armies: The Fall of British Asia, 1941–1945   158
Bhabha, Homi
   The Location of Culture   193n. 13
Bhandari, Dharam Chand   169–70, 172–3, 247nn. 53–4
   'Dramatic Party' of the INA   160, 170, 172
Bhojki caste   32
Bingley, Alfred Horsford
   Caste Handbooks for the Indian Army: Brahmans   30
   Handbooks for the Indian Army: Sikhs   19–21, 30–1, 33
Blackburn, Stuart   191
Bose, Subhas Chandra   158, 168–70, 177, 242n. 3, 243n. 7, 244n. 17
Brahmins (soldiers)   29–32
British Army Act (1881)   36, 38

British Intelligence in India   162, 165, 245n. 20 *see also* Combined Services Detailed Interrogation Centre (India); Directorate of Military Intelligence
British Mutiny Act   38
British Raj   3, 9, 11, 21, 23, 45, 105, 157, 185, 189 *see also* colonial fantasies/neuroses; Indian Army; martial races; paternalism; punishments; sex
Brooke, Rupert   48
Browne, Desmond Henry   48–9

6th Cavalry   89, 117–18, 123
38th Central India Horse (CIH)   89, 107, 111, 116, 120
Certeau, Michel de
   Possession at Loudon   194n. 19, 236n. 12
   The Mystic Fable   252n. 24
chain emails   125–6
Charley's War   43–4
Chief Censor of Indian military correspondence in France   50, 63, 66, 68, 99, 118, 126 *see also* Evelyn Berkeley Howell; Tweedy, G.
Churchill, Winston   23
civil and military legal systems   57
climactic theories of race in India   13–15
Cockerill, George   66
Cohen, Stephen   13
Cohn, Bernard S.   4
   Colonialism and its Forms of Knowledge   193nn. 12, 14
colonial fantasies/neuroses   13–18, 33–4, 57–8, 61–4, 69–71, 73, 82, 114, 130–5, 160–3, 178–9, 182–3
colonial film   1
colonial Indian military penal code   36
   see also Indian military law

colonial soldiers 11, 36, 82, 102, 126
see also *sipahis*
definition 2–5
pardon of 35
professionalism 3
testimonies (*see* soldiers' testimonies)
Colquhoun, Joe 43
Combined Services Detailed Interrogation Centre (India) (CSDIC(I)) 162, 164, 169, 173, 176–8, 190
Commander-in-Chief, India 14, 19, 54, 178
'Congress Committee' 174
contracts, soldiers 88–9, 189
Cooper, James Fenimore 24
corporal punishment 59–60
Corrigan, Gordon 90
Court of Inquiry (mutiny of the 5th Light Infantry) 130–2, 136–7, 139–40, 144, 146–9, 151–3, 235n. 3
German collusion 134
Ghadaris 133–4
Creagh, Garrett O'Moore 14
crucifixion (field punishment) 60–1

20th Deccan Horse 92
Dekhani Muslims 110
department of the Judge Advocate General in India 37, 40
depositions 6–9, 63, 129–55, 191–2
see also 5th Light Infantry, Singapore; testimonies
of Dost Mohamed 240nn. 75, 78, 241n. 96
of E.V. Martin 236n. 19
of Fateh Mohamed Khan 238n. 53
of Fazal Azim 236n. 9
of Feroze Khan 238n. 44, 239nn. 54, 55, 57, 63, 240n. 73
of Ghafur Khan 238n. 40
of Gulam Mohamed 238n. 52, 239n. 71
of Jamaluddin Khan 237n. 21
of Karim Baksh 241n. 94
of Khan Mohamed Khan 236n. 17
of Khuda Baksh 239n. 54
of L.P. Ball 238n. 50
of Mahboob 238n. 41
of Mahboob Khan 240n. 88
of Maksud 238nn. 42, 52, 239n. 70, 240n. 73, 241n. 93
of Mohamed Yar Khan 240n. 87
of Sambhudutt 240n. 89
of Sazawar Khan 236n. 10, 240nn. 80, 83, 91
of Udmi 239n. 54
of Wahid Ali 239n. 72
Derrida, Jacques 6, 178
Of Grammatology 194n. 21, 250n. 103
Archive Fever 194n. 18, 252n. 21
desertion 92–9
dharm 68, 72, 74, 80
Directorate of Military Intelligence (DMI) 161
District Soldiers' Boards (DSBs) 46, 95
Dogras 31–2, 116–18
Dogra Brahmin 31–2
Duff, Beauchamp 133
Dunn, J. I. C. 48
Durkheim, David Emile 48
Suicide: A Study in Sociology 206n. 50

Eder, Montague
War-Shock: The Psycho-Neuroses in War Psychology and Treatment 53
Ekhi Rasta (play) 170, 173
Engels, Friedrich 18, 198n. 36
Enriques, C. M.
The Pathan Borderland 25
Erb, Willhelm Heinrich 48

Fanon, Frantz
Black Skins, White Masks 218–19n. 92
Farrell, J. G.
The Singapore Grip 157
Fay, Peter Ward
The Forgotten Army: India's Armed Struggle for Independence, 1942–1945 158
Fenimore Cooper, James
The Last of the Mohicans 199n. 64
field punishments 60
Finer, Samuel E.
The Man on Horseback 193n. 7
flogging 55–6, 59–62

Friel, Brian
   Translations 65, 67
Full Metal Jacket (film) 5

Garhwalis 94
Ghadar Party 20, 22, 98, 103, 127, 133–4
Ghosh, Amitav
   The Glass Palace 157
Ghulam Ahmad, Mirza 104–5
Green, Nile 108
Guha, Ranajit
   'The Prose of Counter-Insurgency' 183
   The Small Voice of History 251nn. 6, 9, 13
Gun Club Hill (Hong Kong)
   events 174–7
Gurbaksh Singh Dhillon 76

Handbooks for the Indian Army 32–4
   colonial fantasies 17
   martial races (*see* martial races)
Harper, Tim
   Forgotten Armies: The Fall of British Asia, 1941–1945 158
Harper, W. E.
   Singapore Mutiny 129
Hindustani Muslims 110 *see also* 'Rajputana and Central India Muslims'
9th Hodson's Horse 92
Hoghton, Frederick Aubrey 130–3, 153
Hong Kong and Singapore Royal Artillery (HKSRA) 23, 160, 174, 176–8, 192
Howell, Evelyn Berkeley 50, 66, 71
Huntington, Samuel P.
   The Soldier and the State 2–3

Indian Army 4, 41, 44, 46, 52–3, 55, 59, 61–2, 178–9, 182, 190, 198n. 41, 230n. 58, 244n. 14, 246n. 27
   casualties 255
   colonial fantasies and neuroses 13–18, 33–4, 57–8, 61–4, 69–71, 73, 82, 114, 130–5, 160–3, 178–9, 182–3
   depositions 130, 139, 192
   interrogations 157, 160–1, 163, 176–8
   martial races 11, 17, 22–3, 26, 28, 31–3
   murder and suicide 260

   mutiny 131, 155
   problem of soldiers' correspondence' 68, 74–6, 78, 80, 88–9, 97
   recruitment 253–4, 256–8
   soldiers' letters 68, 74–6, 78, 80, 88–9, 97
Indian Army Act (1911) 36–9, 59
   amendments 42, 52
Indian Articles of War 37–8, 54, 58–9
Indian Commissioned Officers 16, 40, 165, 215n. 60
Indian Labour Corps 88–9
Indian Military Academy, Dehradun 76
Indian military law 36–7, 52, 59, 61–2, 74, 189
Indian National Army (INA) 76, 157–60, 190 *see also* Combined Services Detailed Interrogation Centre (India); *Lal Qila*/Red Fort Trials
   colonial fantasies and neuroses 160–2
   1/15th Punjabis, defection of 165
   existence of 161
   playwrights and actors 169–73
   Punjabi Muslim detainees, Hong Kong 174–7
   Sikh *sipahis* 176
   Wavell's assessment 162–3
   'X' Battalion 165
Indian Penal Code, 1860 56–7
Indian Prisoners of War (PWs) 157–9, 162, 169, 174, 176–7, 249nn. 96–7
Indian Welfare Committee 174
Information Centre for the Orient (Nachrichtenstelle für den Orient) 102, 107
interrogations 7–9, 63, 158–78, 190–2 *see also* CSDIC(I); Indian National Army; testimonies
   of Ahmed Din 248n. 78
   of Arcot Doraisamy Loganathan 244n. 11
   of Dharam Chand Bhandari 247nn. 54, 60
   of Fakir Singh 246n. 34
   of Hakim Khan 249n. 91
   of Khuda But 249n. 87
   of Mohamed Ali 248–50n. 95
   of Nazar Mohamed 248n. 78, 249nn. 83, 86, 250n. 98

of Noor Mohamed 249n. 94
of Raghbir Singh 248n. 76
of Rehmat Khan 248–50n. 78
of Sagar Khan 248n. 78
of Sultan Ahmed 249n. 85
of Surat Singh 247nn. 41, 43
intoxication 41
izzat 68, 72, 74, 80

Jackson, Donovan 11
Jats (Hindu) 118, 165
Josh Groups 163–4

Kala Pani 57
Kanoujiya (Kanyakubja) Brahmins 31
Katz, Jonathan G. 101
King's Commissioned Indian Officer (KCIO) 215n. 60
Kipling, Rudyard 48, 66
  The Eyes of Asia 69, 81
  Kim 30
Kitchener Indian Hospital 81, 84, 86
Kubrick, Stanley
  Full Metal Jacket 5
  Paths of Glory 152–3
Kuwajima, Sho 135

Lal Qila/Red Fort Trials 158, 243n. 9, 244nn. 11, 17
15th Lancers 119, 122–4, 234n. 98
18th Lancers 106
Lauterbach, Julius 134
letters *see* military letters
5th Light Infantry, Singapore 190, 235n. 1
  Court of Inquiry 131, 133, 135, 147
  courtroom, linguistic and physical space of 190
  executions 154
  Muslim Rajput soldiers 129
  mutiny 137
  World War I 134
Loganathan, Doraisamy 158–9

Macaulay, Thomas Babington 56–7
MacMunn, George Fletcher
  The Armies of India 13
  The Martial Races of India 195nn. 5, 6, 201n. 87

Madrassi *sipahis* 14
Mahmud Khan, Lance Dafadar 58
Mair, M. G. M. 92–3
Malcolm, John 15
malingering 88, 90, 98, 137, 189
Mandelbaum, David 190–1
Mansur, Kasim Ismail 133
Manual of Indian Military Law, 1911 37, 40, 42
Manual of Physical Training for the Indian Army 17
5th Maratha Light Infantry 96
Marsden, William
  A Dictionary of the Malayan Language 55
martial races
  Brahmins 29–32
  climactic theories 13–15
  colonial paternalism 62–3, 70, 76, 189
  infantalization 15–16
  Pathans 24–9
  physical aptitude 13
  proto-Britons 16
  sexual desire 17
  Sikhs 18–23
Marx, Karl 198n. 36
Memmi, Albert
  The Colonizer and the Colonized 194n. 15
Milap (play) 170, 173
military punishments 40, 42, 89–90, 123, 137
  corporal punishment 59
  crucifixion 60–1
  death 58
  field punishments 60
  Indian Penal Code 57–8
  provost-marshal 59
  transportation 56–8, 60
Miller, H.
  Singapore Mutiny 129
Mills, James 52
Mills, Pat 43
Montague, Edwin 107
Multani Pathans 119
Muslim Rajputs (Ranghar)
  mutiny 129, 132, 134, 235n. 1
  Snowball letter 111
Muslim *sipahis* 15, 100, 102–4, 107–12

and French women 113–18
Punjabi Muslims 174–8
Snowball letters 126–7
Mutiny
 1857 4, 18, 29, 53, 55–6, 61, 119, 157, 171, 173
 of the 5th Light Infantry, Singapore *see* separate entry
 of the 15th Lancers, Basra 118–19, 122–4
 of the Hong Kong and Singapore Royal Artillery, Hong Kong 249nn. 89, 93
 in the INA 157–63
 in the *Rani of Zanshi* 172
 of the Royal Indian Army Service Corps, Egypt 165
 of the 38th Central India Horse, Bombay 165
Myers, Charles Samuel 49

Nazrul Islam, Kazi
 Bidrohi 181
neurasthenia 48
Nicholls, Arthur
 Caste Handbooks for the Indian Army: Brahmans 30
non-commissioned officers (NCOs) 30, 63, 67, 75–6, 123, 129, 132, 145, 147, 153, 166, 175–6
North West Frontier Province (NWFP) 1, 24–5, 29, 75, 88

Oak, Purushottam Nagesh
 Rani of Zanshi 171–2
Offences in Respect of Military Service 39–40 *see also* Army Act (1881) and Indian Army Act (1911)
Opponheim, Max Freiherr von 102
oriental correspondence *see* military letters

pagris 1, 23, 165, 176 *see also* 'steel helmets'
 Mutiny of the Hong Kong and Singapore Royal Artillery 23–4, 176
Pandey, Gyanendra
 Remembering Partition 194n. 23
Pathan soldiers

defined against Afghans 25
desertion 27, 33
homosexuality 28
recruitment 27
tribalness 26–7
40th Pathans 25, 92
Paths of Glory (film) 152
Peers, Douglas 15, 59
pensions 45, 47, 75
Perlmutter, Amos
 The Military and Politics in Modern Times 193n. 8
Pritam Singh 177
Provost-Marshal 59
punishments 89–90 *see also* military punishments
Punjabi Muslims 99, 108, 110–11, 174–6, 192
1/15th Punjabis 160, 164–9
14th Punjabis 76

Qadianis/Qadiyanis *see also* Ahmadiyya Movement 104
Quit India movement 162

Rajputana and Central India Muslims 110 *see also* Hindustani Muslims
Rajputs 15, 31–2, 110, 116–18, 129, 134, 235n. 1 *see also* Muslim Rajputs
The Rani of Zanshi: A Play in Three Acts 170–3
Report of the Esher Committee, 1920 47
Report of the Indian Hemp Drugs Commission 41
Report of the War Office Committee of Enquiry into "Shell-Shock" 48, 50
Reports of the Censor of Indian Mails in France (CIM) 201
Ridgway, R. T. I. 25
Ridout, Dudley 131–3
Rivers, William Halse Rivers 48–9
 Instinct and the Unconscious 207n. 55
Roberts, Frederick Sleigh 13–14, 19, 45–7
Roehle, Reinhard
 Als Fluechtling um den halben Erdball 134
Roosevelt, Theodore 48
Royal Army Medical Corps 48

Royal Army Temperance
    Association   47
Royal Indian Army Service Corp
    (RIASC)   31, 78, 165, 169
Roy, Kaushik   59

Said, Edward
    Orientalism   15
Saragarhi Day   72
Sassoon, Siegfried
    Sherston's Progress   49
Sat Sri Akal, insubordinate nature of   23
Scott, James C.   182
    *Domination and the Arts of Resistance:
        Hidden Transcripts*   184
    *The Moral Economy of the
        Peasant*   184
    Weapons of the Weak   184
Scott, Paul
    The Day of the Scorpion   160
Scott, Walter   24
self-mutilation   87–92 *see also*
    malingering Seton, Bruce   81,
    85–6
Sevea, Iqbal Singh   104
sex   81–7, 113–18
shaheedi   68, 72, 74, 80
shell-shock   35, 43, 48–9
Sikhs   18–23
    Jat soldiers   19–21, 23, 33, 116–18
sipahis
    'acts of violence'   54–5
    batta system   45
    disciplinary management   56
    flogging   55–6, 58–62
    heteroglot voice   8
    INA (*see* INA)
    Indian military law   189
    interrogations (*see* interrogations)
    letters (*see* military letters)
    military punishments   40, 42, 56, 58,
        89–90, 123, 137
    neurasthenia   48
    payments   43–5
    pensions   45, 47, 75
    psychiatry   52–3
    racial degeneration   81–2
    'running amok'   53, 55
    subaltern   185–6

welfare system   45–7, 53
war trauma, letters of   50–1
Skaria, Ajay
    *Hybrid Histories: Forests, Frontiers
        and Wildness in Western
        India*   187–8
Smiles, Samuel   48
Smith, Graham
    When Jim Crow Met John Bull   82
Smith, Richard   81
Snowball letter
    Ahmadi message   105–6
    Ahmadiyya message   109
    chain letter   111–12
    German propaganda   103–4
    impermanency   126
    interracial sex   116–18
    munazara   108–9
    Muslim *sipahis*   108, 126–7
    Punjabi Muslims   108–10
    sentiments   112
    Sheikh Ahmad's dream   101, 109, 111,
        124, 124–7
soldiers' letters *see also* testimonies and
    Snowball   6–9, 50–1, 55,
    58, 60, 63, 65–99, 100–27, 135,
    189–92
    analysis of   66
    censorship   61–4, 66–9
    censorship, subverting of   71–81
    collective memories and spaces   67
    colonial paternalism   61–4, 75–81
    consensual relationships   83–4
    desertion   92–9
    falling houses, incidents of   95–6
    famine and starvation   93–5
    literacy   42, 62–3, 105, 191
    loyalty   68, 71–2
    malingering   98
    monetary reward   74
    promotion   74–6
    racial essentializations and
        differences   70
    reasons for enlisting   72–81
    record keeping   67
    regimental censorship   68
    self-mutilation   87–92
    sex   81–7, 113–18
    soldierly adjuncts   76–81

war trauma   50–1
by 'Dhobi Ram Lal' 222n. 132
by 'Maulvi' Ghulam Sarvar   122–3
by 'Pir' Dil Khan   111–12
by Abbas Ali Khan   120
by Abdul Alim   110
by Abdul Ghani   112
by Abdul Jaffar Khan   83
by Abdul Karim   221n. 125
by Abdul Rahim Khan   207n. 69, 228n. 30
by Abdul Wahab Khan   89
by Ahmed Ali   231n. 69
by Ajab Gul   120–1
by Ajab Khan   116–17
by Ajrud Din (civilian)   226n. 12
by Ali Alam Khan   228n. 33
by Ali Gaur Khan (civilian)   214n. 49
by Ali Khan (civilian)   228–9n. 33
by Amir Khan   72
by Anwar Shah   231n. 67, 232n. 75
by Ashrafali Khan   233n. 92
by Atta Mohamed   75
by Azizuddin   89
by Balwant Singh   230n. 60, 235n. 108
by Behari Lal   79
by Bihari Lal   216n. 63
by Buland Khan   216n. 62
by Dad Gul Khan   218n. 87
by Diwan Singh   220n. 100
by Diwana   222n. 131
by Fakir Mohamed   75
by Faqir Khan   235n. 109
by Fateh Khan (civilian)   124
by Fyazuddin (civilian)   111
by Ganga Singh   225n. 170
by Gasthip Khan   108–11
by Ghulam Haidar Khan (civilian)   227n. 23
by Gokul Singh Rawat   79
by Gul Mohamed Khan   120
by Gunga Ram   216n. 68
by Gurdit Singh   71–2
by Hamidullah Khan   233n. 86
by Haq Nawaz   106–7
by Hasan Shah   71
by Hoshanki [sic.]   219n. 98
by Hussein Shah   228n. 29
by Id Mohamed Khan   226n. 8
by Inayat Ali Khan   115
by Jagu Godbole   85–6
by Jai Singh   83, 231n. 63
by Jawan Singh   206n. 43
by Kaka Singh   89
by Kallu Khan   89
by Kazi Abdullah Quadiyani (civilian)   227n. 24
by Khilullah   213n. 40
by Kunda Buksh Khan   234n. 100
by Kutubuddin Khan   201n. 84
by Mahmud Khan   58
by Malik Mohamed Khan (civilian)   212n. 17
by Malik Muhammad Mumtaz   230n. 57
by Man Singh   89–90
by Man Singh Rawat   252n. 33
by Maulvi Mohamed Ali Khan (civilian)   229n. 41
by Mir Dast   225n. 171
by Mir Haider Jan   221n. 122
by Mithan Lal   84
by Mohamed Feroz Khan   231n. 70
by Mohamed Ghans   230n. 55
by Mohamed Khan   117–18
by Mohamed Qaki Khan (civilian)   222n. 129
by Mohamed Yusuf   228n. 32, 235n. 107
by Muhabbat Khan   219n. 97
by Nabi Buksh   218n. 85
by Nadir Ali   201n. 84
by Nahar Singh   220n. 101
by Naubet Rai (civilian)   231n. 66
by Nazir Ullah   115
by Niamat Ullah   222n. 133
by Nur Ahmed (civilian)   227n. 22
by Nur Mohamed   230n. 56, 235n. 104
by Nur Mohamed Khan   79–80
by Nur Zaman Khan   74
by Pirzada   219n. 99
by Rahman   75, 214n. 45
by Rahmat Khan   111
by Ram Jawan Singh   215n. 58, 218n. 91, 220nn. 107, 109, 235n. 106
by Sabaz Ali Khan   234n. 98
by Sadar Singh   222n. 134

by Safdar Ali Khan 233n. 94
by Senchi Khan 220n. 111
by Sher Khan 79
by Sher Mohamed 107
by Sobha Ram 252n. 36
by Taj Mohamed Khan
 (civilian) 214n. 50
by Talib Mohamed Khan 91
by Tulsi Ram 219n. 96
by Umr-al-Din Khan 110–11
by unknown civilians
 (from Bengal) 93–4,
 (wife of soldier) 231n. 68
by unknown soldiers
 Bengalis 93
 in Egypt, Middle East &
  North Africa 73, 214n. 43,
  222n. 138, 223n. 150
 Garhwalis 94, 221n. 121
 in Italy 78, 223n. 146
 Marathas 96
 Pathans 90, 103
 petitions 86–7
 Punjabi Muslims 95, 120
 Sikhs 96, 207n. 68, 212n. 15,
  221n. 124
 Tamils 95
by Uttam Singh 221n. 123
by V.S. Pranje 217n. 82, 230n. 61
by Wazir Chand Chopra 215n. 59
by Wazir Khan 217n. 83
by Yusuf Khan 80
by Zabida Khan 119
Spivak, Gayatri Chakravorty 186
 Critique of Postcolonial Reason 194n. 20,
  252n. 22
Star Trek 18, 189, 197n. 32
Stoler, Ann Laura 81
 'colonial negatives' 12
 'Developing Historical
  Negatives' 195n. 4
 'Sexual Affronts and Racial Frontiers'
  217n. 74
Subaltern Studies 182–4, 187
Sullivan, Zohreh T. 206n. 52

Tamils *sipahi* 95
testimonies *see also* soldiers' letters,
 depositions, interrogations

identity 4–5, 185–6
 as performance 192
 poetics 188, 190–2
 as praxis 8, 186, 192
 reading of 5–9, 65–9, 124–7, 152–5,
  177–9, 181–92
 silence 136–9, 167, 170–1,
  191–2
Thomas, Lowell
 Lauterbach of the China Sea 134
transportation see Kala Pani and
 military punishments 55–8, 60,
  129, 153
Trotsky, Leon
 *The History of the Russian
  Revolution* 2, 4
 Military Writings 193n. 9
Tweedy, G. 99–100

United Provinces of Agra and Oudh
 (UP) 29, 31
Uprisings (Mutiny) of 1857 4, 18, 29,
 53, 55, 61, 119, 157, 171, 173,
 242n. 1, 248n. 64

Viceroy's Commission officers
 (VCOs) 75–6, 78–9, 85,
 131–3, 175–6

war trauma 53, 62
 anxiety-neurosis 49
 emotional shock 50
 hysteria 49
 mental breakdowns, Bombay
  asylums 51–2
 nervous and mental exhaustion 50
 neurasthenia 48
 sipahis' letters 50–1
Wavell, Archibald 162–3
Wickremesekera, Channa 15
Wilde, Oscar 48
Willoughby, Maurice 28
Winter Soldier Investigation 136
Wolfe, Virginia 48
World War I 4–5, 8, 35–7, 43, 46–8,
 51–2, 58–60, 62–3, 190, 217n. 71,
 252n. 20
 Indian Army recruitment 253–4
 martial races 19–20, 26–8, 30, 33

military casualties 255
mutiny 134, 152
oriental correspondence 65, 69, 72–4, 87–8, 97
Snowball letters 100, 105, 107–10, 119, 122, 124, 126
World War II 8, 46, 52, 63, 189–90, 214n. 42, 226n. 10, 252n. 20
    Indian Army recruitment 256–8

interrogations 157, 160, 169
martial races 16, 23, 29, 31–2
oriental correspondence 66, 68, 72–4, 82, 93

Young, Robert J. C. 17
    Colonial Desire 197nn. 26–7
    Postcolonialism: An Historical Introduction 250n. 4

Lightning Source UK Ltd.
Milton Keynes UK
UKOW06f1215010715

254396UK00003B/29/P